When the Lord's House Closes

When the Lord's House Closes

Church Repurposing and Urban Community Practice

MELVIN DELGADO

OXFORD
UNIVERSITY PRESS

Oxford University Press is a department of the University of Oxford.
It furthers the University's objective of excellence in research, scholarship,
and education by publishing worldwide. Oxford is a registered trade mark of
Oxford University Press in the UK and in certain other countries.

Published in the United States of America by Oxford University Press
198 Madison Avenue, New York, NY 10016, United States of America.

© Oxford University Press 2024

All rights reserved. No part of this publication may be reproduced, stored in
a retrieval system, or transmitted, in any form or by any means, without the
prior permission in writing of Oxford University Press, or as expressly permitted
by law, by license or under terms agreed with the appropriate reprographics
rights organization. Inquiries concerning reproduction outside the scope of the
above should be sent to the Rights Department, Oxford University Press, at the
address above.

You must not circulate this work in any other
form and you must impose this same condition on any acquirer

Library of Congress Cataloging-in-Publication Data
Names: Delgado, Melvin, author.
Title: When the Lord's house closes : Church Repurposing and Urban
Community Practice / Melvin Delgado, Emeritus Professor of Social
Work, Boston University School of Social Work, 264 Bay State Road Boston, MA.
Description: New York, NY, United States of America : Oxford University Press, 2024. |
Includes bibliographical references and index.
Identifiers: LCCN 2024020114 | ISBN 9780197767887 (hardback) |
ISBN 9780197767900 (epub) | ISBN 9780197767894 | ISBN 9780197767917
Subjects: LCSH: Church closures. | Church buildings—Remodeling for other use.
Classification: LCC BV652.9 .D55 2024 | DDC 254—dc23/eng/20240628
LC record available at https://lccn.loc.gov/2024020114

DOI: 10.1093/9780197767917.001.0001

Printed by Marquis Book Printing, Canada

This book is dedicated to those on the front lines undertaking urban church repurposing by embracing social justice goals and enlisting communities supporting these undertakings, thus opening the door for further advances that will help society.

Contents

Acknowledgments   xi

SECTION 1 SETTING THE FOUNDATION

1. Overview	3
Introduction	3
Another Cautionary Note Before the Journey	6
Focus on Urban Areas, People of Color, and Youth	7
Repurposing as an Urban Concept and Strategy	8
Repurposing Church Pews and Other Items	17
Church Buildings as Sacred Structures	18
Religion and Its Affiliated Institutions	21
Cleveland and Philadelphia Church Closures: A Snapshot	40
Trauma and Houses of Worship	44
Book Goals	44
Conclusion	46
2. Urban Community Practice Realm	47
Introduction	47
Definitional Parameters of Community Practice	50
Anti-Urban Sentiments	54
Community Practice and the Urban Setting	57
Trust and Community Practice	57
Churches as Communities	59
Churches as Targets and Vehicles for Social Activism	60
Church Buildings as Community Assets	61
Repurposing, State Government, and Religious Attention	65
Key Competencies and Community Practice	66
Enhance community competencies	66
Incorporating local culture into initiatives	67
Community decision-making as central	68
Multifaceted interactive skills	68
Characteristics of Successful Community Practitioners	69
Feeling comfortable in our own skin	70
The quest for learning never stops	71
Optimism as a genuine world outlook	71

    A genuine like of people   71
    Every day has a new lesson to share   72
    Embrace the thrill of the adventure   72
    Ability to bounce back from failure (resiliency)   72
  Importance of Participatory Approaches   73
  Potential Community Practice Roles and Church Repurposing   74
  Conclusion   77

3. **Boston Case Illustration: The Blessed Sacrament Church**   78
  Introduction   78
  Brief Historical Overview   79
  Boston Demographic Profile Overview   81
  Religious Beliefs and Church Attendance   81
  Blessed Sacrament Church Closure   82
  Lessons Learned for the Field of Urban Community Practice   88
    The more ambitious the project, the more time, money, and expertise will be needed, which may not be in house   88
    Closed churches cannot be easily or cheaply repurposed into new structures   89
    Multipurpose church repurposing involves being able to negotiate with varied interest groups   89
    Repurposing based on the past   90
    Time is an enemy of repurposing   90
    Municipal support is essential   91
    All views are welcomed   91
    Expertise when needed   92
  Conclusion   93

4. **Social Forces Shaping Church Closing Trends**   94
  Introduction   94
  Statistics and Caution   96
  Demography as Destiny   97
  The Urban Church   102
  Psychology and Repurposed Structures   103
  Religious Practice Trends: A Window into the Future?   104
  Catholic Church Righting the Ship Against Prevailing Winds   110
  Land Owned by Churches   113
  Vacant Church Buildings and the Urban Landscape   116
  Predicting Church Closures   119
  COVID-19 and Church Closings: Black and Latino Churches   123
  Language Used in Church Closings and Repurposing   127
  Economics of Church Closings   127
  Organizational Efforts to Repurpose Churches   136
  A Brief Glimpse of Chicago   138
  Extent of Church Closing Challenges   142

Churches of Christ as a Case in Point	145
Church Repurposing from a Life-Cycle View	146
Catholic Schools Caught in the Closing/Repurposing Movement	147
Potential Municipal Governmental Repurposing Roles	150
State Legislatures and Repurposing	155
Megachurches: Where Do They Stand in the National Landscape?	157
Repurposing: Not an "Either/Or" Proposition	159
Land Banks and Church Properties	160
Religious Organizations as Real Estate Developers	161
New Model for Priest/Pastor Deployment: More with Less?	162
Conclusion	163

SECTION 2 BLACK AND LATINO CHURCHES

5. The Black Church	167
Introduction	167
What Is Meant by "the Black Church"?	172
Are Blacks Losing Their Religion?	177
Generational Importance of a Social Justice Agenda	178
A Black Church's Vision Beyond Ministerial Duties: A Case Illustration	181
COVID-19 and Black Church Closures	181
D.C.'s Lincoln Congressional Temple United Church of Christ	182
The Black Church and Other Urban Centers	183
Outreach as a Mission: Two Dimensions	184
The Black Church as a Living Institution	186
Black Millennials and Church Closures	188
Repurposing Black Churches as Housing	192
Initiatives to Save the Black Church	193
Conclusion	195
6. The Latino Church	197
Introduction	197
The Church and Latinos	200
What Is Meant by Latino Religious Beliefs and Practices?	202
The Growth of the Latino Church	203
Demographic Distribution and Projections	203
Age Demographics and Latino Churches	207
Latino Church: Language and Culture	208
Latino Church Attendance and COVID-19	210
Latino Church Attendance: Trends and Nuances	210
Latinos and the Catholic Church	211
Latino Church Closures	213
Conclusion	214

SECTION 3 IMPLICATIONS FOR RESEARCH, EDUCATION, AND PRACTICE

7. Implications for Research, Education, and Practice — 217
   Introduction — 217
   Section A: Research — 217
      Challenges in obtaining existing data — 219
      Research comes in many forms — 220
      Photovoice: Capturing an historical process — 220
      Community asset mapping — 222
      A charge to institutions of higher learning — 223
   Section B: Implications for Community Practice Education — 224
      Community practice principles for guiding church repurposing — 225
      Church repurposing and community service learning — 229
      Conferences and other gatherings of like-minded souls — 229
      Community fellows cadre education — 231
      Community technology education — 232
      Community practice: church closures and collective history — 232
      Capacity enhancement and community assets — 233
   Section C: Implications for Community Practice — 234
      Brokering gatherings of local faith organizations — 236
      Brokering of transfer of church property — 239
      The ability to form partnerships and collaborative undertakings — 239
      Designation as historical property — 240
      Repurposing churches into nonprofit organizations: opportunities for local contributions — 241
      Opening the door for innovation — 242
      Community practice and local talent — 243
      Sole community practitioner/activists and God's work — 245
      Desperate times call for desperate measures? — 246
      Obtaining funding for repurposing and programming — 246
   Closing Reflections — 247

References — 251
Index — 281

Acknowledgments

I want to thank Dr. Celina Miranda for her generosity of time and effort in helping me better understand her repurposing effort of a Boston church, and the anonymous external reviewers for their thoughtful suggestions in how to strengthen this book. I also want to thank Ms. Barbara Civill Montoya for helping to select the photographs used in Chapter 3 to illustrate the Blessed Sacrament Church repurposing project. Finally, I want to thank the photographers for their kind permission to use their photos: Greg Canna (Figure 3.1, Blessed Sacrament, front of church); Mark Saperstein (Figure 3.2, Blessed Sacrament Church, outdoor performance); and Joni Lohr (Figure 3.3, Blessed Sacrament, broad view of internal deterioration and Figure 3.4, Blessed Sacrament Church, focused view of internal deterioration).

SECTION 1
SETTING THE FOUNDATION

The section provides an overview of the church repurposing field, including the challenges inherent in implementing these projects, and examines the varied social, cultural, economic, and political forces creating a wave of church closings throughout the nation. These forces involve shifting demographics, major national events such as COVID-19, and changes in religious practices that de-emphasize church attendance, causing millions of former attendees to disengage and/or stop attending services. A detailed case illustration of a Boston project is provided.

Communities of color in this nation's major urban centers are spotlighted whenever possible to help us understand how church closings affect these specific communities and the repurposing that follows. Although the Black and Latino community are experiencing major changes in religious attendance trends, with consequences for their religious institutions and communities, there are differences that are significant and require attention. These trends require grounding within a broader national and international scene. This is essentially a worldwide movement and can help us understand what is happening in our backyard within a much wider context.

1
Overview

Introduction

This chapter sets the stage for the book and follows a conventional path, in the hope that readers will become engaged with the material and that it will influence community practice—which, quite frankly, is the bottom line. I do not believe in advancing knowledge for the sake of knowledge; I am much too practical! Some readers, however, may beg to differ. Books challenge readers to entertain new ways of thinking on a subject, supplying a rationale for the subject's importance. Books require major time, financial, and intellectual commitment to a subject, bringing heightened expectations and serving as a key motivator for action. Readers have a right to have lofty expectations from a book because of the time they invest, and that must be confirmed and met by an author!

It is impossible for authors to suspend their experiences and worldviews from the task of writing a 300-or-so-page document. In fact, the more authors uplift their values, motivations, biases, limitations, and experiences (both good and bad), the better grasp readers can have of why a topic is framed in a particular manner. This stance ascends in significance in this journey, and even more so when it covers religion.

Readers may ask about my personal stands on religion, religious beliefs, and houses of worship. More specifically, although raised Catholic up to my late teenage years, I am a member of a Church of Christ congregation because of the values that this church embraces. This church, too, is facing its challenges with dwindling congregations and closures. Suffice it to say that I respect people's religious/spiritual beliefs that are different from mine, although I am not a "very" religious person by nature, it is fair to say.

Finally, this book draws on a variety of sources, primary and secondary, as well as those considered unconventional, casting a wide net to paint a portrait of a salient subject that has slowly appeared and garnered much attention. Some topics will doubtless surprise readers, but all will help to reveal of the vastness of the subject of church closures and repurposing and will explain why a "narrow" view does an injustice to this topic. Cities are front and center as contextual grounding because of my personal and professional experiences.

Although this book is about the rebirth of structures, it is impossible to have this focus without due deference to the death of an institution. Being a hopeless romantic does not mean totally suspending realism! Houses of worship are integral to urban living; they always have been and are currently so, although facing turbulent winds on the horizon. These structures have the potential to continue providing a better and more harmonious life for urban residents. When repurposed, they occupy the same physical space as before but in a transformed manner—a reincarnation if you wish!

The nation's future rests on how well cities respond to demographic, ecological, economic, and political trends or challenges. These are certainly not unique to the United States but are profoundly obvious in this country, even more so in its cities. The nation must also respond to buildings that have closed, churches and otherwise. Secular forces can make church buildings redundant, as with any other buildings. Religion is declining globally due to modernization, largely fed by secularization, with growing empirical and theoretical arguments undergirding this conclusion (Kasselstrand et al., 2023). As readers will see, this is not just a national phenomenon but also an international one.

Church closures are manifested differently in cities than in rural areas, with implications for how the nation views these closures and the political will to address this trend. However, regardless of their physical location, churches have ascended in prominence within society and are viewed as important social anchors, bringing together art, faith, and culture. They enjoy a special place in society and were developed with a specific set of reasons or mission, one being to allow visitors to leave their world behind to enter a new world that provides solace, even if for a short period of time (Grinberg, 2013).

Church buildings have remained as urban artifacts with great symbolism and instrumental meaning because of their physical structure and location. Nevertheless, as discussed in Chapter 2, urban practice cannot be isolated from the historical and current-day bias against cities due to their demographic profiles and histories. This perspective makes it that much more challenging to achieve a successful repurposing.

When we talk about an ecological movement and the important role cities must play, for instance, their role increases in significance in this nation and across the world. Finding ways of undertaking "urban community development," or what I prefer to call "community capacity enhancement," without displacement must be a perennial goal. Empty churches may ascend in prominence in this movement—not because they are closing, but because their rebirth becomes more significant on the urban scene if church closures continue to outnumber plantings.

Urban community practice is an effective mechanism through which marginalized residents can gather to focus on a goal of repurposing churches in service to their community. Practitioners help achieve this goal by tapping a wide spectrum of approaches that can be tailored to meet local needs, ensuring that all major constituents are enfranchised in these undertakings.

Kilde (2022) names four approaches to the study of religious spaces with applicability to this book: (1) stylistic and liturgical (specific architectural styles); (2) phenomenological and hermeneutical; (3) social scientific; and (4) critical spatial. The social science perspective becomes more important and shapes much of the discussion on church repurposing. I would add to this list a social service stance because of its emphasis on church closing and repurposing from a practice viewpoint, bringing very practical outcomes for readers.

Case illustrations of varying lengths are interspersed throughout the book to emphasize essential points in understanding church closures and their eventual repurposing. The Boston case illustration in Chapter 3 includes a more extensive narrative and photos and ties together key book themes, helping readers appreciate a nuanced view of the range of outcomes of church repurposing projects. My stance on church closures/repurposing respects these structures due to their importance locally and nationally in the past, now, and in the future. Churches are much more than buildings, fulfilling third-place roles, as discussed later in this book; nevertheless, buildings they are, occupying significant physical public spaces.

Putscher (1980), over 40 years ago, studied closed church buildings and noted that they played valued roles in the cognitive and formal ordering of a city and its neighborhoods, connecting residents currently and historically. Repurposing these structures results in new images within the urban landscape, reconciling the "real" and the "ideal." These projects involve immense challenges and potential rewards when respecting local needs and wishes. This is a tall order, but that must not dissuade us from looking to achieve it! An easily achievable goal is never inspirational.

Another Cautionary Note Before the Journey

Finally, I need to make an editorial comment, so to speak. Religion, it is fair to say, is a key force worldwide involving the pursuit of a higher purpose in life. It stresses social justice, the good in people, and the importance of community. However, religious institutions can also be oppressive organizations that have enslaved and caused the deaths of countless people across the globe. Consider the sexual abuse scandals that have surfaced over the past several decades in the United States and worldwide; these are still being litigated as this book goes to press.

Schools serve multiple key functions in society, although their educational function is often the one that is emphasized. Schools, however, also socialize children to a set of values and belief systems, and this role often goes unrecognized. Churches, too, socialize us to explicit and implicit values about social interactions—for instance, the importance of following a set of rules, supporting a cause, and keeping a level of social control. Readers can certainly speculate on whether the absence of "civility" in our nation, particularly as expressed through our electoral politics, is in part a result of the decline of church attendance.

Religion, as with education, fulfills many important functions in a society. However, it is also a mechanism for socially controlling behavior, which the eminent sociologist Émile Durkheim pointed out over a century ago. It helps society to weave social values into a cohesive whole. Religion punishes behavior that does not conform to expectations and threatens the status quo. One does not have to be a history major to see the pain that religion has caused over the centuries, and that must not be overlooked.

The Catholic Church's role in the enslavement of Black people, for example, has well been documented (Swarns, 2016):

> At Georgetown, slavery and scholarship were inextricably linked. The college relied on Jesuit plantations in Maryland to help finance its operations, university officials say. (Slaves were often donated by prosperous parishioners.) And the 1838 sale—worth about $3.3 million in today's dollars—was organized by two of Georgetown's early presidents, both Jesuit priests.

How can enslavement be justified by the Catholic Church? Jesuits drew upon the work of Saint Paul and Bible passages that referenced the responsibility of the enslaved and that of their "masters." And the Catholic Church was not the only religion receiving economic help from institutionalized exploitation.

Church history presents practitioners with challenges in navigating local reactions to these closures. Durkheim argued over a century ago that religion promotes both division and social unity and solidarity. These two outcomes are ever present in communities, urban or otherwise, and they certainly come to a head when these institutions close. The practice of repurposing churches is not for the faint of heart, as I like to say.

Churches are considered the most racially segregated institutions in the country. Although American churches are largely segregated, there is one exception—Latinos (Contreras, 2023a, 2023b). Less than half (47%) of Latino Protestants say that their churches are composed mostly of Latinos. Readers must recognize these tensions if they are to have a productive future in urban church repurposing. Churches generally are a mirror of the society they are embedded within.

Focus on Urban Areas, People of Color, and Youth

Books like this cannot be all things to all practitioners, calling for a focus on specific population groups to maximize their impact. I gave serious thought to how to focus this book on population groups and geographical settings to develop a consistent narrative that would tie together chapters in a conceptually coherent manner and increase the book's readability and practice impact. Readers should be prepared for a focus on youth (who represent the future of any religion), people of color (Blacks and Latinos), and urban areas, although other segments will also be covered because communities, after all, consist of a myriad of groups.

Rural community practice involves many of the same elements outlined above. However, urban settings include a high percentage of people of color, which introduces a dimension not shared by rural settings. Public transportation systems and access to public services are two other dimensions where rural areas differ from urban ones. Community practice is grounded in a contextual setting that applies to the area's geography as well as the specific project, as with church repurposing.

Urban youth of color are an endangered group, occupying a highly marginalized position within their communities and society, even though they represent the future of their communities. They have incredible strengths that must be fostered and mobilized, including enlisting them in repurposing houses of worship. Developing a comprehensive and unified vision of urban communities, and their buildings, will help readers to see the relevance of this book to day-to-day practice as well as making lasting changes at the local level. The overlap between history, geography, race/ethnicity, and age group can be a powerful way to have practice enhance scholarship, serving as a recruiting mechanism for future community practitioners.

I focus on youth, people of color, and urban settings for two interrelated reasons: (1) there has been a lack of scholarly attention to these groups, and when they have been addressed, it invariably has been from a deficit perspective; and (2) it promotes a cohesive narrative introducing multifaceted community practice aspects. Readers familiar with my writings will not blink at the above; new readers, however, must understand these biases, if you wish. Of course, other groups will also be discussed in order to supply a comprehensive foundation. The beauty of urban practice is that it has an expansive and hopeful view of community, acknowledging the interrelatedness of all groups to make a community successful.

Repurposing as an Urban Concept and Strategy

For repurposing to be salient as a major national movement, we must counter the human fascination with replacing the old with the new, as if there is an inherent value in this action (Gedeo, 2023). Buildings, including churches, have a life cycle: Building are gutted or demolished every 30 years as a norm, reinforcing this human fascination and helping to feed a disastrous climatic situation. Readers may have even longer lifetime expectations of 50 to 60 years for a building in their midst (Grecchi, 2022).

Repurposing may be a concept readers are familiar with, and perhaps one integral to their daily life. Repurposing as a strategy, versus tearing down, may not be viewed as a practical choice, as in the case of Hitler's birthplace in Braunau, Austria, for example. In 2023, the "house of evil," after decades of debate, was to be repurposed into a police station, causing a negative response from those wishing to keep it as is or to have it house social service programming (Tulsa World, 2023). It is fair to say that most of us will not be confronted with this type of decision-making.

Repurposing church buildings is not a recent phenomenon. Ironically, most Catholic churches in Rome, Italy, were the result of repurposing ancient Roman buildings. What goes around comes around! Longhi (2022) discusses the process of decommissioning and reusing liturgical architectures, and its long history in Western society.

Bullen and Love (2011a, p. 32) undertook a qualitative study of 81 experts in the field (architects, developers, planners, building managers/owners, and property and construction consultants) and developed three criteria for examining repurposing: capital investment, asset condition, and regulations. They concluded:

> While financial criteria such as development and construction costs were the primary determinants influencing the decision to reuse or demolish, the physical condition of the asset juxtaposed with regulations were also considered. Additionally, issues associated with the environmental, economic and social tenets of sustainability were identified as being important but had been given less priority when considering reuse.

These three points are still relevant today. Each point, of course, has various stages or perspectives to consider, depending on the history and social purpose of the building being repurposed, as well as the environmental context.

Thomson and Pojani (2019, p. 1) comment that any serious effort at sustainability must include houses of worship: "In the planning sphere, the rhetoric surrounding sustainability rarely includes the relationship between urban development and churches—seen as a component of social sustainability." This movement has picked up steam within this past decade and has responded to the nuances of an urban built environment. The built environment is an integral factor in global temperature increases (Neidig, 2023), including extreme weather events.

Repurposing has historically been conceptualized as a regeneration strategy integral to the sustainability movement (Bullen & Love, 2009), and that stance has gathered strength over the past decade, particularly in cities. Wall (as quoted by McClung, 2019) considers repurposing as a way to honor historical buildings: "Adaptive reuse is a great opportunity to save and honor the heritage of a city and the history within. Repurposing a building from a different era creates a unique atmosphere for guests when creating a destination location." Repurposing historical buildings provides a link from one era to the next—and there is something poetic about that.

Repurposing, which goes by many different terms, is an ecological-economic concept and strategy that has found its way into the basic social fabric of society, as well as various academic and professional realms. "*Save the environment*" is a saying we are all familiar with. Cars, clothing, drugs, furniture, and countless other items are finding new life in a different shape, in the process helping the environment and saving money. One repurposing advocate (Elefante) said it well (as quoted by Anderton, 2021): "We're recycling Coke cans; we're recycling beer bottles. Why are we tearing viable buildings down in the name of progress? The greenest building is one that is already built."

Are there limits to the field of repurposing? I would venture to say "no"—and therein lies the challenge for this field! Even large structures, such as stadiums, for example, have been repurposed into homes, water parks, a Bass Pro Shop, an aquatic center, a shopping center, and even a church (Houston, Texas), for example (Newcomb, 2014). Burnham (2018) presents 40 examples of adaptive reuse in urban centers of 17 countries, illustrating innovative ways of repurposing. Our ability to envision a new purpose for a structure, church or otherwise, is only limited by our imagination and ability to transform an idea or dream into a reality by enlisting others in this quest.

It takes approximately 65 years for an energy-efficient new building to actually save the amount of energy lost through the demolition of an existing building (McClung, 2019). Further, the costs of producing and buying new building materials have more negative consequences on the environment from a financial and energy standpoint.

However, with new construction, building qualities are more predictable. Repurposed materials introduce greater complexity and require more in-depth analysis and care in handling. This special handling takes on even greater importance and corresponding costs when the materials used in the original building are toxic to humans. The presence of asbestos, for example, can cause major delays in repurposing churches, as in the case of Roanoke, Virginia (Preston, 2023). Embracing repurposing does not mean suspending reality; it means that careful deliberation is called for in the planning process.

Although this book is on repurposing churches, we should take a moment and cast these projects within the broader U.S. repurposing field. It has been estimated that almost 33% of new apartment dwellings have been built in converted former offices (Ballinger, 2023). There are approximately 122,000 apartment units in the pipeline for construction in 2023, an increase from

77,000 in 2022, or a 36.9% increase (Fabris, 2023a). Forty-five thousand are the result of office repurposing (37%); hotel conversions account for 23% and factory conversions for 14% (figures for churches were not available). Repurposing factories into housing, for example, requires special conversion permits, adding another complication. Church closures have much in common with factory closures, although on the surface they may appear to share very little; with factory closures, the emphasis is usually on the loss of jobs (Beer et al., 2019).

One-third of the office buildings in the largest cities in the United States are suitable for residential conversion (Fabris, 2023b). For example, there are plans in Boston to convert office commercial buildings (104,000 square feet) in downtown and the West End into 170 apartments, signaling an anticipated trend toward addressing the massive housing shortage in the city (Carlock, 2022). The decrease in demand for office space is largely due to the impact of the COVID-19 pandemic and the popularity of working from home.

Other major cities have a prominent role in this repurposing—Los Angeles leads with 4,566 apartments, followed by New York City with 3,987 and Chicago with 3,519. These cities are prominently covered in this book, particularly related to church conversions into housing. Of course, repurposing can also mean transforming a nonreligious building (say, a bank) into a church (Falconer, 2023). Houses of worship can be either a source or an outcome of repurposing.

Readers can now see that the repurposing field has a broad foundation from which to garner lessons learned, and it is important that we view this field through a broad lens so as not to miss critical lessons. Houses of worship, and the schools attached to them, are the latest addition to this list, which will expand in the future. U.S. religious spaces are not permanent (Kilde, 2022), with repurposing entering the picture from a practice standpoint. If we think of churches as belonging only to history, we will need to change our basic assumptions to think of them as supplying modern-day options.

Few residents will complain about having a house of worship on their street. Local churches are often very well appreciated by more than just the attendees. However, efforts to enlist local support for them after closure can be challenging (J. Graham, 2023):

> Church member Mary Overholt knocked on doors, trying to get support for the rezoning. One man told her he loved looking out from his house at a church. But he and others who liked having a church in the neighborhood

weren't motivated enough to join it. This paradox is playing out as churches close across the world. Like the man Overholt spoke to, people like the *idea* of churches; they appreciate their beauty, the community meeting space that some provide, and their charitable work and donations. Many don't want churches razed or turned into nightclubs or hotels, as is happening in some cities in Europe.

This attempt at changing the zoning was unsuccessful because of residents' concerns that what would replace the church would be unattractive. Engaging community members in these undertakings cannot be an afterthought. Rezoning, which is a topic that will be addressed in this book, will be a major obstacle in any mixed-use repurposing. Zoning regulations are often outdated and hinder development due to restrictive land-use classifications and height restrictions.

Repurposing encompasses difficult technical building dimensions and considerations and an explicit embrace of a set of values. We must not overlook the interplay of these two aspects, because site-specific approaches will increase the likelihood of success within prescribed budget constraints (Lami et al., 2023):

> Adaptive reuse has progressively become a useful approach for generating new values concerning abandoned or underused buildings, sites, and areas to the extent that the topic is no longer conceived and perceived merely as a "bricks-and-mortar" issue. Instead, it has a dual nature: (i) one that is technical, linked to the difficult balance between low costs and fostering sustainable building solutions, and (ii) one that is social, which refers to social equity, well-being, and quality of life.

Any successful repurposing project involves balancing practical, economic, technical, and values considerations, and adding a religious aspect increases the challenge. Due to their symbolism, size, and purpose in society, churches are "special" and are unlike other buildings—and that is an understatement. Ignoring this status will doom any project aiming to maximize their potential for positive community transformations.

Mian and Reinhard (2023) identified three key elements of successful conversion of houses of worship into housing: (1) zoning reform; (2) strong partnerships; and (3) creative funding of projects. These three elements are emphasized throughout this book. Each is profoundly shaped by the community undertaking the church repurposing.

Viola and Diano (2022) eloquently refer to the field of built heritage repurposing as "a privileged field of commitment." Communities can use nonrenewable resources to create a better future, relying on environmental principles balancing ecology with human needs. Repurposing shapes an environment; it is a rare privilege for residents to inherit churches and, in turn, leave them for future generations, particularly because of their holy purposes in society. Further, it shapes these buildings for one or two generations in the future.

Many of this nation's cities, and those around the world, are growing in population but running out of horizontal room, calling attention to the need to reconceptualize spaces that either are not being used ("urban voids," such as vacant lots) or are underutilized, making them attractive for rejuvenation or repurposing, particularly in city centers (Rana & Kumar, 2022). Space is always at a premium in cities, and that will only increase in the future. Lessons learned about church repurposing can help to shape repurposing in other spheres. How these spaces are used, however, will be a point of contention in many communities.

The topic of controversy is a prominent one throughout this book because social interventions bring tensions, particularly when undertaken in a nonparticipatory manner. Christman (2021) asks a provocative question about what activities should be held in a former church:

> How would you feel about someone skateboarding in a church? I imagine many of us instantly recoil at the thought. But what if it was a church that was no longer in use? It's not just a theoretical question. There is no disputing that what occurs to a closed church will have extensive ramifications across a community . . . Some places are deemed sacred because some holy event or miraculous occurrence is believed to have transpired there. Other places are considered sacred because holy objects, such as relics, are housed there. Still other places are considered sacred because some tragedy has occurred in that exact location.

In Europe, for example, closed churches have been converted into dance halls, breweries, self-storage facilities, restaurants, and hotels (Cguske, 2023). Readers and communities will ultimately have to answer this question if repurposing is to succeed. The risk that repurposing will cause community consternation cannot be ignored.

Repurposed churches take on new identities and functions, becoming restaurants, condominiums, stores, gyms, libraries, liquor establishments, exercise clubs, day care centers, dance clubs, schools, or human service organizations (Milstein, 2023):

> Once abandoned places of worship, deserted churches across the South have taken on glorious new purposes. Keeping with the canon, these beautiful churches have been resurrected. They're now gorgeous places to gather, enjoy a meal, or spend a night—and we dare say that their second comings are even more stunning. Rich with history and brimming with remarkable remnants of their past lives, these restored churches are now impressive restaurants and hotels that live up to their locale.

No two buildings have the same challenges. Some buildings lend themselves to conversion into office buildings or housing but present unique challenges because of rerouting utilities, for example. Repurposing an historical church into a restaurant or event venue might be easier if it entails minimal changes to physical aspects, while keeping visible attractive aspects of the building (Costello, 2023).

Repurposing can focus on specific age groups, such as older adults. In the Netherlands, to introduce an international example, an estimated 25% of all religious buildings have been repurposed for non-religious purposes. Independent senior housing represents 4% of these new structures, with the potential for a greater number (van Zantvliet, 2023). Senior housing in repurposed churches must take into account acoustics because of the resonance between the walls and ceilings. This can result in overstimulation, causing restlessness and fatigue.

Repurposing introduces creative thinking about urban ecology, public spaces, and the built environment, particularly in urban centers, bringing U.S. efforts in line with a worldwide movement (Morel & Dorpalen, 2023). This allows us to apply lessons learned from throughout the world to our situation. Cities, and more specifically neighborhoods occupied by low-income people of color, are also one of the most heavily polluted with toxins, and repurposing must address this environmental problem rather than compounding it.

Zijlstra (2022, p. 1) rethinks the old axiom "form follows function" in a way that has saliency for urban church repurposing:

> Buildings today are subject to change. New functions are accommodated in vacant buildings. This is a favorable development from both a sustainability point of view and a cultural-historical perspective. Originally, the volume and form of a building was dictated by its original function: form follows function. We now see that a spatial form is already present. Is it logical to conclude that the new functions adapt to the existing available form and space: function follows form?

Repurposing allows for bold imagination to enter a picture of a building's transformation in terms of its structure and purpose. It is exciting for the fields of architecture, planning, and community practice, to list three outside of religious circles.

We associate physical structures, such as buildings, with memories, both good and bad, and churches are no exception. When we talk to long-time parishioners whose church has been closed, we invariably hear stories about the major religious events they attended there—baptisms, confirmations, weddings, funerals—and how the church has shaped the lives of church members and the broader community. Attending services translates into connectedness with others, and the building is the space where this occurs. These connections can continue outside of a church gathering, strengthening a sense of community with the church as central facilitator.

As Dewanjee (2022, p. 31) wrote, "Architecture is closely related to memory; we craft spaces which remind us of things we want to remember. But what about those memories which we want to forget? How do we face the difficult questions—are we to gloss over memories, carefully hide and push the anger under the rug?"

Church closures elicit intense reactions, as in the case of Chicago's St. Adalbert (Wisniewski, 2023):

> Cerrado agrees that the building's closure hurts the character of the neighborhood, and passions are running high. "Even people who are not parishioners remember seeing the towers and knowing they were home." But he says people have to ask themselves if it is more important to practice their faith or maintain old buildings. "That's the question—is being a

Catholic about keeping the bricks together on these old buildings, is that achieving your spirituality?" Cerrado says. "We'd say, no, it's not, it doesn't do anything for the community... The church is not about the buildings, but about the parishioners who are there for the fellowship."

St. Adalbert will be discussed again in Chapter 4.

Past experiences and corresponding memories often influence our actions and views, and the same can be said for our communities and their buildings. For example, I find it impossible to think back to my elementary school education without also thinking of the building and playground of this school—and that was more decades ago than I care to admit. I had my share of pleasant and not-so-pleasant experiences there. The same be said for other structures holding profound memories in my life. Readers can relate to this perspective—institutions hold prominent places in our memory bank.

Physical structures help give shape and hold memories for both members and non-members (Wisniewski, 2023):

> "Tall, architecturally distinctive structures that soar above nearby two-flats and bungalows, they often serve as visual anchors of neighborhoods," says former Chicago Tribune architecture critic Blair Kamin. "They're also repositories of memories and identity; their lure is so strong that ethnic groups who have left behind the 'old neighborhood' for the suburbs still make pilgrimages to them."

Some in the church repurposing field argue there is a difference between "deconstructing" an old church and "demolishing" it (Cloud, 2023). Recycling, reusing, and repurposing is a specialized skill and strategy. Demolition, in contrast, entails using a wrecking ball, reducing the building to debris and transporting it to a landfill, with no regard for its history and meaning to a community and no attempt to salvage anything.

The U.S. Environmental Protection Agency (EPA) estimates that building material generates over 600 tons of waste debris annually, twice that collected from urban homes and businesses. Demolition accounts for 25% of total waste in landfills. In 2018, over 90% of all construction and demolition debris originated from demolition, causing around 145 million tons ending up in landfills. Planners and builders must consider how building projects are built and dismantled, since these are two sides of the same coin (Kilde, 2022).

Repurposing may not require any major restructuring of a building. In essence, a new purpose supplements an old purpose, without altering a space or requiring upgrades (Armstrong et al., 2023). However, repurposing often entails structural changes, and these may be minimal to major depending upon goals and circumstances. Repurposing will also incorporate recycled components, which can significantly reduce carbon emissions when compared to new construction.

Repurposing projects seek to achieve various economic goals and corresponding environmental benefits, such as reducing the community's carbon footprint and minimizing disruption around the site. According to estimates, construction and later building operations account for 41% of all primary energy use and 48% of all carbon emissions (Merlino, 2018). Repurposing projects, too, can take less time to bring to fruition, which can reduce disruption to a construction site.

Repurposing is also a sustainable tool for climate change mitigation within the built environment and can help to reduce carbon emissions, integral to sustainable planning for low-carbon cities (Aigwi et al., 2023). There is a call to action for churches to play an increasingly significant role in addressing climate change, what Antal (2023) considers "the greatest moral challenge humanity has ever faced." This factor appeals to younger generations because of their ecological concerns for the planet. Thus, churches, even after closure, can continue to contribute to this movement.

Repurposing Church Pews and Other Items

We must broaden our vision of repurposing, and I say this knowing how challenging this may be. When we think of repurposing, we usually think of the physical structure. However, that is too narrow a view of this field, missing key dimensions that can help other congregations and households, too. Jerry Gerber (2023), for example, takes a unique approach toward repurposing by emphasizing repurposing church pews, for example:

> As churches close up and pews become harder to find, repurposing church pews is becoming an increasingly popular way to give an old piece of furniture a new lease of life. Church pews are often built to last, so they are the perfect items to repurpose and make use of in our homes. Whether you decide to upcycle a church pew into a dining table, bench, or coffee table,

there are lots of creative ideas you can use to bring your vision to life . . . Repurposing a church pew is a great way to add character to your home and make use of an old piece of furniture. It's also a great green initiative, as you're giving a piece of furniture that may otherwise have ended up in a landfill a second chance at life.

Smeengee (2023) argues that religious objects, such as those found in religious buildings, are often an afterthought in repurposing or are simply overlooked, destroying the "sublimity" of the object. Other church items may be attractive for repurposing, such as stained-glass windows, for example, although due to their size and shape there may be a very limited market for them (Fletcher, 2023). Repurposing, in essence, depends on creativity in seeing possibilities for an item's new life and in an economically feasible manner.

Church Buildings as Sacred Structures

Church buildings have profound spiritual meanings for parishioners and the community. The responses of two long-time parishioners of Minnesota's Virginia Catholic Church to its demolition are quite telling and illustrative of this point (Riebemesabi, 2019):

> "I cried all day," said 94-year-old Kathleen Kishel to *Mesabi Daily News*. She had hoped, she said, that her funeral could one day be held in the church rooted in the early 1900s, known for its beautiful stained glass windows and designated as a historic place. Eighty-eight-year-old Val Bazzani, who was baptized at the church, said it was "heart-wrenching" to see it go down. He had stood at the site, taking photos as heavy machinery razed the structure, baring to the outdoors the choir loft where he had sung for years.

Clearly, a church is much more than a building to worshipers and the community, and we must never forget this if repurposing is to achieve its potential of helping transform urban communities.

Not all buildings are equal in symbolism for repurposing. Nevertheless, the ecology of built structures marches on bringing together a host of disciplines and professions, and why coalitions help solve challenges in addressing church closures and repurposing. The church has historically assumed a prominent position in the West. In Europe at first and then the United States, for example, with congregants integrating spiritual needs and social needs in churches first occurred in Europe, first and the United States. Churches even began to shape local politics.

Although this book supplies many examples of repurposing, houses of worship bring unique circumstances to this practice field (Pham, 2017):

> Among the many instances of reuse of historical buildings, there is a unique thread of conversions that pertain specifically to the transformation of religious buildings. It is perhaps undeniable that all buildings hold some inventory of memories and significant history, but a house of worship operates under a complex set of conditions, contexts and values. In the case of churches, the values are manifold: aesthetic, historical, and cultural.

I would also add an economic benefit to note their unique position more comprehensively in this emerging field.

Church opening and closing dynamics dramatically shape corresponding actions and are influenced by how society views these buildings and their symbolism (Longhi, 2022, p. 85):

> The decommissioning and transformation of underused Christian places of worship is not a recent or contingent phenomenon, caused only by a decline in religious practices or secularization in Western society; rather, it is a constitutive historical consequence of the specific nature of Christian architecture. From the earliest Christian times, in fact, community sensitivity and reactions have focused not on the sacredness of buildings, but on their "sacredness." The community is interested in the sanctity of those who gather to celebrate.

Longhi's stance on church structures eases their repurposing, but these efforts will invariably elicit strong initial and potentially long-term reactions from various segments. This can create a political climate that makes repurposing arduous.

For instance, how well will a community accept a church the is repurposed into a residential drug treatment facility? I could not find such an example to illustrate this point, but readers can imagine the range of responses. It raises the key question about the limits of repurposing, if any (Roach, 2023):

Closing churches "robs God of his glory," Clifton said. "What about a dying church says our God is great and his gospel is powerful?" The church "is not a store. It's not a restaurant. It's not a mall. It's the bride of Christ. It's worth fighting and battling to keep those churches going as a testimony to the power of the gospel."

Such strong feelings cannot be ignored and bring with them powerful ramifications for any successful repurposing undertaking, highlighting the emotional dimension.

I wonder how accepting a community would be of a repurposed church that is transformed into a microbrewery, for example (Sheridan, 2023):

Not far from Chicago, a deconsecrated Methodist church in New Buffalo, Michigan, is now known as Beer Church. The microbrewery, which opened in 2017, leans into the building's religious past, keeping iconography and serving such beers as the "Pontius Pilate" India pale ale. The growing popularity of microbreweries combined with dwindling congregation numbers has led to the opening of establishments similar to Beer Church across the United States—and in the Chicago area.

Local circumstances, as already noted, shape the acceptance or rejection of any repurposed structures.

Readers must consider church repurposing within the broader building repurposing movement, which has seen prisons turned into hotels and warehouses, factories converted into residential and retail establishments, and schools turned into community centers and housing. Closed hospitals, too, await new fates and will be part of this brave new world. Healthcare facilities are considered complex and challenging from a regeneration and reuse view (Gola et al., 2022). A former hospital complex in Florida was repurposed into luxury multifamily residential living: the Ritz-Carlton Residences in Miami Beach. This case highlights the business saying that "space equals revenue." Readers may be surprised to learn that the repurposing field has expanded into exciting new arenas; for instance, repurposed inner-city parking garages now house controlled environmental agriculture systems (Szopińska-Mularz, 2022).

Not even golf courses are exempt from repurposing. For instance, Los Angeles (Conroy & Cha, 2022) has 19 golf courses within the city limits and 65 within 20 miles. As an aside, having grown up in the South Bronx, the nation's poorest congressional district, I have always had great difficulty appreciating the game of golf. It needs countless number of acres to play, putting aside environmental questions. One does not have to be a golfer to imagine how acres of land can be repurposed to meet the needs of thousands rather than just a small group.

Repurposing is only limited by our imagination and embrace of social justice, as is community practice. Even tennis, a sport catering to those who can pay for lessons and proper clothing, equipment, and possible court time, does not require acres of land! Space is always at a premium in low-resourced urban communities; physical space is never taken for granted, and that is why I have this bias against sports requiring extensive land.

Religion and Its Affiliated Institutions

As we have seen, church structures, even in the midst of an urban landscape consisting of a myriad of building types, public spaces, and subsequent histories, are unlike any other buildings. To pretend otherwise would be foolish from my standpoint. Churches are unlike other institutions in society. They fulfill multiple roles while conducting their aspirational missions, including entertaining an audience—and this cannot be overlooked.

Historically, these institutions reflected society's priorities, as manifested by their physical structures, for using material resources in addition to their religious, social, and cultural aspirations (Buringh et al., 2020). In fact, religion, and its institutions such as schools, played a significant role in the settlement of many immigrant groups in this country. These structures have symbolic meaning far beyond their physical prominence in these communities.

Scholars may argue that "religion is a foundational aspect of American society" (Allen, 2019, 2020), with structures unlike any other, and ones that stand out in any landscape. There is little wonder that the birth of religious congregations has drawn its share of research and scholarship, taking on a symbolism of a birth of a star. The birth of a church generates excitement and high hopes for communities and society in general, particularly for those facing social justice challenges and seeking hope for a brighter future.

Similarly, the closing of houses of worship can be compared to the death of a star. Closures have not drawn anywhere near the level of excitement or scholarly attention they deserve. A wide range of well-known figures have weighed in on the "death of religion." Mark Twain argued that its death had been exaggerated; Max Weber predicted that secularization was inevitable because of modernization (Jordan, 2023). Although religion is certainly not dead, it is "on the ropes."

Religiosity can be defined as an embrace of "an organized system of beliefs, rituals, and practices that are oriented toward the sacred" (Parker et al., 2023, p. 153). Such a vision also carries over to its buildings (Russell, 2019):

> Although the popular song "We Are the Church" sings, "The church is not a building," a church building is the vessel that expresses, supports, and shelters the mission, spirit, and community of a church. A building can be a powerful sign and witness to the presence and ministry of God's spirit at work in the community through the church. Church buildings can also be an issue, creating difficult decisions and situations for congregations.

Historically, church literature has been dominated by an emphasis on growth and prosperity. This stance is morally uplifting and creates hope and excitement, and may be understandable when religious affiliation and attendance are strong and growing. However, the "decline and death" of houses of worship has been largely overlooked, considering the significance of churches: Church closings represent major social-cultural events for communities and the country. Unfortunately, much has not changed during this period to give hope for those waiting for a better day.

Crises are opportune points to start bold projects such as repurposing to fulfill new missions (Omezzine et al., 2022). Urban scholars, with sociologists and geographers standing out, began to critically study adaptive reuse by the late 1970s, a period characterized by industrial decline and inner-city recolonization and gentrification (Lynch, 2022). This is also a period known for its emphasis on "urban renewal," an initiative that caused great destruction and resident displacement. Why the term "Negro removal" is associated with "renewal" needs no further explanation!

That is beginning to change due to the increase in church closures. Closed church buildings represent a key force or indicator in urban economic development and the state of the community (Netsch, 2019). The longer these structures stay closed, the stronger message to community members that the area is in decline and they are not valued, standing as a testament to how society views them.

Meaningful repurposing of U.S. churches can be traced back to the 19th century, but until recently the process has been slow to gain popularity. It is estimated that by 2010 there were 210 successfully repurposed religious buildings and schools, falling into seven categories: 52 residential condominiums, 22 apartment buildings, 43 retail buildings, 26 office buildings, 42 cultural buildings, 24 schools, and 1 industrial building (Simons & Choi, 2010). The range of outcomes for these churches will only expand in the immediate future.

Housing, however, is often the outcome of repurposing or excess land made available, as readers will see with countless examples throughout this book. Minnesota recently passed a law allowing houses of worship to build on their property shelters for those lacking secure housing. Atlanta has a plan to have 2,000, or 10% of housing units to be developed by churches, synagogues, temples, and other religious institutions; the city's Faith-based Development Initiative will offer technical assistance to faith organizations interested in making affordable housing available on their properties (Bolan, 2023). The Atlanta initiative has 40 institutions taking part in this initiative, with almost a dozen positioned to do so in the immediate future. Atlanta, it is important to add, had 33 congregations leading affordable housing projects between 2010 and 2022; the average development had 78 units, most serving low-income families, seniors, people with disabilities, and those with earlier unhoused experiences. Again, and this is a theme about church repurposing, zoning restrictions are often identified as the major barrier in starting these housing initiatives (Bolan, 2023).

Church closings and repurposing have accelerated over the past decade, with all indications that this trend will only gain speed in the coming decades. A balanced view of church openings and closings better reflects why and where these trends are unfolding, helping us to develop an understanding and portrait of these phenomena. Trends rarely unfold in a smooth and highly predictable manner, with pockets defying the trend, and this is true with church closures and repurposing.

Buildings are society's largest manufactured and expensive products and symbols, shaping daily life in visible and invisible ways, with churches often the largest structures within a community. Buildings, too, can represent symbolic and prominent physical manifestations of a community's pride—or shame, as the case may be. (The latter might include perceived or actual crimes against the community, as in the case of sexual abuse.)

Historical churches can dominate the vista of a community—"The higher the spire, the closer to God"—with their imposing physical structure casting a shadow that moves slowly as the day unfolds. Barucco (2023) reminds us that "historic churches stand as community landmarks, reminding us of the investments of previous generations and adding a rich texture to the tapestry of our neighborhoods." These buildings stand out in their grandeur against what can often be a drab and colorless landscape.

We cannot imagine this country's urban architectural landscape without houses of worship. Old and dominant houses of worship in major U.S. cities, for example, required large structures to both accommodate a large membership and to cast symbolic shadows on their surroundings, highlighting their social, cultural, economic, and political importance. But many of these cities and their "magnificent" churches are experiencing dramatic demographic changes, including reductions in their traditional church-going groups.

Architecture is referred to as the "art of meeting human needs" (Hassan, 2023). Buildings, sacred or otherwise, must be responsive to the changing circumstances where they are found, whether demographically or environmentally. The repurposing of churches is not exempt from these forces: These buildings must be prepared to evolve to meet a range of community needs that may well change over time as congregations age.

Churches seek to fulfill a multitude of instrumental and lofty expressive needs in their communities and society, so it is a challenge for any field to capture their significance when they close (Kinney, 2018):

> A church is many things. Churches are places of worship. They are community centers and gathering places. They represent Christian faith and our-biggest-asset-changing-communities-by-repurposing-buildings/congregations. They can be beautiful, historic, and beloved by generations of United Methodists who have called their sanctuaries home. These same churches can be old, in disrepair and underutilized. Their maintenance and repair can financially burden the congregations who use them for worship. They can become imposing monuments that are less than warm and welcoming to the community and their outdated facilities less desirable for the community and sometimes even impossible for the disabled and elderly.

Churches do not age well without necessary upkeep. They are exposed to weather, such as harsh winters and hot summers, and due to their size and location, it is impossible to ignore when they start their journey of physical decline. All structures become obsolete over time due to physical, economic, and functional limitations, and churches are no exception. In some cases demolishing a building rather than repurposing it brings certain benefits; recovering materials and recycling are always options (Assefa & Ambler, 2017). Although repurposing can be very expensive, it brings environmental and social benefits for communities and society, in addition to preserving local history when undertaken with a vision of what is best for a community based on the community members' perspectives.

Philadelphia, a city that will receive considerable attention in this book, has faced pressures to demolish buildings such as houses of worship; an estimated 79% of demolitions are attributed to development pressures, particularly in areas of the city that are gentrifying (Hildebrandt, 2016). Between 2009 and 2016, 28 religious buildings were demolished. Why were they not repurposed? According to Hildebrandt:

> I suspect that a congregation's connection to its building and history plays a role in the decision-making process once its leadership, either at the level of the congregation or judicatory, depending on the faith tradition, has decided to downsize, merge, or close. If this is true, it means that religious buildings that no longer house their original occupant may be in greater danger of being demolished as opposed to adapted.

If this conclusion is proven correct, it has obvious ramifications for other cities' efforts to repurpose rather than demolish churches. This developmental history, if we wish to call it that, requires targeted interventions to focus on this stage with specialized efforts to enhance the likelihood of repurposing.

We must never be under the illusion that repurposing is easy, predictable, and inherently successful. Further, repurposing is far more than a practical or technical process: It is complex, time-consuming, and political; it requires a specific set of skills; and it can be very expensive, with no guarantee of success (Lynch, 2022). Doesn't this sound exciting from a project standpoint? Therein lies the challenge and the reward!

Repurposing is one of society's greatest challenges, but one that can potentially have a tremendous return on investment and commitment. This strategy is built on the premise of a "healthy and environmentally friendly approach" (Stone, 2019). Repurposing is an emerging strategy (Plevoets &

Van Cleempoel, 2019) and is expected to play an influential role in the urban rejuvenation movement, particularly when considering environmental concerns such as carbon emissions, for example. Construction accounts for 40% of total energy consumption, an activity largely responsible for greenhouse gas and carbon dioxide emissions (Grecchi, 2022).

Churches can be liberating physical-spiritual places and spaces, particularly for marginalized communities. Unfortunately, they can also be oppressive places and spaces, as with the Catholic Church's sexual abuses, for instance. The Church's practice of reassigning serially abusive clergy to Latino-serving churches, and the silencing of victims with threats of deportation and further violence, alienated the Latino community and especially undocumented immigrants (Reynolds, 2023a). The sexual abuse claims and legal verdicts against the Catholic Church may have spurred efforts to shield its properties to avoid financial claims from lawsuits. For instance, in 2010, the Roman Catholic Diocese of San Diego owned 421 separate properties, making it a major land owner in the county. However, in 2022, that number was reduced to 56 (Morgan & Schroeder, 2023). The property transfers were made in the autumn of 2019, several weeks before "Gov. Gavin Newsom signed a law opening a three-year window allowing lawsuits alleging sexual abuse that happened years ago—long after the legal deadline for filing such lawsuits had expired." The diocese said the timing was purely coincidental; the move had been planned over a decade before.

Newman's (2018) book *Desegregating Dixie: The Catholic Church in the South and Desegregation, 1945–1992* chronicles the tension and complex role of White, non-Latino Catholics in the South fostering segregation and the embracing of a progressive social-racial civil rights agenda. Desegregation shook many congregations, but in rare instances genuine integration occurred.

Significant membership declines can cause pending closures, and vice versa. In 2021, 47% of Americans reported that they were members of a church, the lowest percentage Gallup has ever measured in its 80-year history. In Orlando, Florida, for example, 42% of residents reported that they had stopped attending church services over the past 25 years (J. Graham, 2023). Hopefully, a "come to Jesus" moment will occur through church itself that becomes a community guiding light.

Church repurposing has started to attract attention from the nonprofit and business sectors. *Forbes* (Clontz, 2020) published an article exclusively devoted to church repurposing, pointing out its potential economic benefits for investors and communities. I must be honest: The more I hear about the economic profits that can be made from church repurposing, the more I worry that this field can be transformed in a manner detrimental to marginalized communities.

Repurposing churches is a worldwide phenomenon. Almost 25% of the churches in the Netherlands closed (Remøy & Wilkinson, 2022), and 2,000 U.K. churches closed over the past decade (Pfeiffer, 2022). Internationally, church closings offer a wealth of data and case examples of repurposing projects, helping communities and the field. Historical context is very important; we can use the knowledge gained from other countries' experiences, with necessary modifications to take into account our own unique historical circumstances.

Closures of any kind—businesses, colleges, theaters, local newspapers, for instance—rarely bring celebrations that look back on their history and accomplishments, and church closings are no exception. They can be associated with sadness or even depression about an era gone by and concerns for what the future holds in store. The religious marketplace—yes, there is such a concept—is dynamic, as argued by Dougherty, Maier, and Lugt (2008). Readers, I am sure, get the picture. The birth and death of churches, as addressed in this book, is similar to that of other institutions, but we should never forget their uniqueness in society: They are not like any other structure.

Tyler's (2000) named four types of intervention for repurposing/adaptive reuse, helping us to better understand the challenges before us: (1) preservation; (2) restoration; (3) reconstruction; and (4) adaptive reuse. The first three approaches keep the original building's purpose but also involve serious cost and maintenance considerations. This book focuses on repurposing in situations in which the other three options are considered economically and environmentally unfeasible, and it will offer the most promise of meeting local needs while addressing environmental concerns.

Reinhard (2022a) paints a graphic picture of what churches mean for downtown areas and the far-reaching consequences of church closure. Closed churches often remain structural eyesores for years:

> The closure of religious houses creates headaches for Main Streets in rural and big cities alike, fundamentally changing the fabric of a downtown, whether it be through gaps between storefronts or increased density of office, residential, or retail units. Imagine the impact of these projected closures on Rome, Georgia (population 36,000), which has 15 churches in its six-by-four-block Main Street area or Orange, New Jersey (population

31,000), which has 16. Vacant buildings that once housed faith institutions in the middle of America's big cities are being scooped up by developers as if there's no tomorrow. The First Methodist Church of Seattle, for example, sold its 19th-century property to developers for $30 million. Like other trends that affect the built environment of Main Streets, it is important to understand the causes of this phenomenon, as well as the challenge and opportunities.

As the real estate saying goes: "Location, location, location." For example, Orange City, New Jersey, population 31,000, has 15 churches in its small downtown area located several blocks from the New Jersey Transit Station, from which commuters can reach Midtown Manhattan (Reinhard, 2021c). It does not take a real estate genius to realize the worth of these Orange City properties on the open market! Further, it does not take an active imagination to appreciate the widespread impact that church closings have on their immediate environment, even more so in smaller geographical areas where they may occupy a vital and oversized role in the community's social and economic dynamics.

Like other business sectors, churches are most prone to closing at times early or late in their histories, what are called "danger zones." Looking at religion through such a marketplace lens may be viewed as cold and calculating for those who are very religious (Grose, 2023). Thinking of religious institutions using a supply and demand perspective, however, helps us better understand their openings and closings, allowing a level of rational thought process and predictability to enter an analysis of what is surely to be a highly emotional time for a congregation and the community.

Beltz (2005) predicted an immense wave of church closings almost 20 years ago, and this continues to materialize today:

> Get ready, America. Get ready for the huge collapse from within that is soon to result in the locking of hundreds and then thousands of church doors across our country—all from the inside. The trend is already well underway . . . in Roman Catholic circles. Mainline churches, like the Methodist church in my neighborhood, will not be far behind. Denominational treasuries simply aren't up to the task of sustaining ministry personnel and facility upkeep.

A somber prediction, to put it mildly!

Why an entire book on church repurposing and community practice? Why not an article or even a book chapter? That is because no series of articles or chapters can capture the journey, size, complexity, and importance of this topic. Church closings bring profound changes for church members, the communities where the churches are situated, and society at large. Religion historically has been viewed as a critical "glue" keeping communities together, even when congregational members do not share a common ethnic or racial background. Some proponents of religion may well argue that the United States would not be the United States without the glue that religion provides in bringing disparate groups together to form a national identity.

Why should church closings ("congregational death") be of concern for community practice? That is because churches are much more than just physical structures no longer meeting spiritual needs that must be torn down or repurposed in the name of safety or progress. These buildings often occupy physical and profound symbolic roles in a community and their history. They can house the soul of a community and thus cannot be viewed from a narrow brick-and-mortar standpoint. They have profound histories and meaning transcending metaphysical realms!

Broadening our vision beyond the spiritual helps us understand the social, cultural, economic, environmental, and political ramifications of church closures, which is why practitioners from different professions and contexts (urban and rural) must come together and play a key role within communities experiencing church closures. The U.S. church closure trend is national in scope, not regional or highly localized, making it a salient agenda, and this trend can be grounded internationally, too.

We can also view church closures from a climate change perspective. Some regions of this country have faced particular ecological challenges. Summer heat affected both the southwestern and the northeastern portions. Turning away from organized religion is the equivalent of global warming.

McRae (2023) discusses church closures in Canada:

> The 1950s and early 1960s were the high-water marks for church attendance for major Christian denominations in Canada. The loss of congregants from the mid-1960s onward usually didn't lead to the closure of churches. Churches continued to hold services as fewer and fewer people sat in the pews. There were some mergers and churches shared ministers or priests but things still chugged along for decades. Since then churches started to close.

The strategies used to address this crisis have a familiar ring and can be found throughout the United States, as readers will see. Canada's outcomes are eerily similar to ours, too. Canada has an estimated 9,000 churches likely to close over the next several decades. The United Church of Canada, for example, expects to close a congregation a week. The Anglican Church of Canada expects to close its last congregation by 2040; finally, the Roman Catholic Church, Canada's largest religious denomination, has closed 20% of its 2,500 congregations (Daly, 2023).

In Holland, rural church closings represent the source of potential best practices for the field (Netsch & Gugerell, 2019). An estimated 20% of Dutch churches have lost their original mission in the last two decades due to declining religious affiliation and secularization.

The Church of Scotland is in the midst of selling 40% of its properties between 2017 and 2027 due to decline in membership (Miller, 2023).

In Germany, churches are being closed due to decreasing attendance—over half a million people left the church in 2021. The Catholic Church, too, faces closures of a third of its properties (they will be demolished or repurposed) due to dwindling membership and revenue loses (Luxmoor, 2023). A projection to 2060 has 40,000 rectories, community centers, and places of worship facing closure. One key challenge facing Germany's Catholic and evangelical churches is that 80% of its 42,500 churches are officially listed as architectural monuments.

Spain has experienced a dramatic decline in church membership over the past several years, with an estimated 27% of the surveyed population describing themselves as non-believers in God; only 16.4% fall into the practicing believer category—in other words, they attend Mass every Sunday and on most important holidays (Statista.Com, 2023). In 2011, 70% of its population considered themselves Catholic, a figure that dropped to 57.6% in 2022. Only 2.9% practiced other religions (Statista.Com, 2023).

In France, the number of Catholics has declined dramatically from 81% in 1986 to 47% in 2020.

Finally, in Belgium, religious attendance is taking its toll on its churches (Meller, 2023):

> Statistics paint an alarming picture for churches, with attendance plummeting over the past 50 years. At the beginning of the 1970s church attendance in Brussels was around 25 percent, 50 percent in Flanders and 35 percent in Wallonia. By 2010 all regions recorded church attendance of

around five percent and the numbers continue to decline, according to figures from the Church. No surprise then that churches both large and small are being closed for worship. Last year 35 Belgian Catholic churches closed their doors to their parishioners for the last time, according to church statistics.

Belgian's church attendance decline and corresponding closures, with repurposing around the corner, paints a picture eerily similar to that of other European countries and the United States. These trends are familiar in the United States (Cuperus, 2019; van de Kamp, 2022), translating into four church closings per week (Thomson & Pojani, 2019).

Reinhard and Elisara (2022) draw on Jane Jacobs's scholarship to make important observations on how urban churches often view their mission as singular in nature, with implications for their repurposing once they close down:

> In *The Death and Life of Great American Cities*, urban guru Jane Jacobs outlines four major attributes that make for a great city: mixed use, walkability, old buildings, and density. Houses of worship may be old, but most have none of the other three attributes: Most are single use; they act as "beached whales" amid the urban fabric—large pieces of property with fences, large parking lots, and most doors locked shut; they're low density. Turning a house of worship into a mixed-use, walkable, higher-density property can help restore life to a community, while targeted adaptive reuses, developed in conjunction with stakeholders, meet prioritized community needs.

Repurposing requires attention to local needs, assets, and appreciation of local history if is to play a transformative role shaping community dynamics. Religious spaces, just like other spaces, are not fixed in meaning and purpose and need to respond to changing social circumstances to remain relevant (Kilde, 2022).

There is an important relationship between churches and their public spaces that bears closer examination (Arboix-Alió et al., 2023). Repurposing churches into housing, for example, also transforms the spaces surrounding these institutions. This perspective does not diminish the sadness of their closings for members, but we can certainly rejoice that they have found a new mission that enhances people's lives, building upon a legacy of social concerns. That realization helps soothe the sting of having a beloved church close. It had a good life; maybe it can even have a good afterlife, too!

The United States has approximately 600,000 unhoused people (New York Times, 2023)—almost the number of people who live in Detroit. This nation has a severe housing shortage, which can be partially met through repurposing. Converting vacant churches into housing is one approach among many needed to address housing insecurity.

California, with an estimated 36,000 unhoused residents, accounts for 30% of the nation's unsheltered population (Anderton, 2021):

> And we need more housing. A national shortage continues to drive up prices across the country, squeezing out those with the least means. In California alone, an estimated 3 million to 4 million new dwellings are needed to address the crisis. Los Angeles is short at least 455,000 units... [O]ver 12,000 new housing units alone have been constructed in downtown Los Angeles through reliance on adaptive reuse.

Expensive cities, such as Los Angeles, have an imbalance between unused dwellings and unhoused people. It has more than 93,000 vacant units, with almost half not in the housing market. Why? Thousands of luxury units are empty, being second homes or investment properties.

According to a 2020 study by the UC Berkeley's Terner Center for Housing Innovation, California has almost 38,800 acres of land—the size of Stockton—owned by religious institutions and suitable for housing development. One faith-based social justice group in Los Angeles comprising 20 congregations hopes to build 2,000 apartments (Wagner, 2023). A key barrier to repurposing churches to dwellings in Los Angeles is their high probability of being found in areas with zoning restrictions: For instance, 42% of religious land suitable for affordable housing is in areas zoned for single-family homes. Senate Bill 4 (Chapter 1) seeks to ease these repurposing efforts. Repurposed churches will not solve this nation's unsheltered problem, but they can be influential in localized efforts helping to solve the problem. Bethel AME Church and SDS Capital Group built a project on church property in South Los Angeles for 52 unhoused people (Beech, 2022b).

L.A. Harvest Tabernacle Bible Church existed for 45 years at the corner of Holmes Avenue and East 55th Street in Vernon (Beech, 2022a). The congregation moved and co-occupies space in another church due to a loss in membership that made it impossible to keep its own structure. The hope is that the move will be temporary until it expands its membership, allowing a move to nearby spaces. The church was demolished and replaced by a multipurpose building with apartments, communal living spaces, a rooftop garden, and a grocery store. The grocery store highlights the need for new businesses to meet residents' needs.

In a final example from Los Angeles, the Los Angeles Church of God in Christ (Serlin, 2023), in that city's Crenshaw community, started a project to develop 168 apartments, 17 units set aside as affordable housing (Serlin, 2023). It will have 40,000 square feet of ground-floor retail space. The site is a 1.3-acre property formerly in the West Angeles Church's North Campus; congregants are served from its south campus location. An active mission to embrace social and economic justice can have a prominent place alongside spiritual goals.

When discussing community economic development, we usually focus on wealth—money, property, investments. When we frame church closings in this manner, they translate into community wealth/assets or capital lost (and this can be compounded when what replaces these churches bypasses the community's wishes and needs). But when we think of religion and spirituality as worth or capital, they can actually be viewed as "cultural wealth" (Park et al., 2020). Embracing this view enhances our understanding of wealth within marginalized groups and communities, as with urban Blacks and Latinos. Spiritual capital can rightly take its place alongside other forms of capital (assets) in marginalized communities (Yosso, 2005): (1) aspirational; (2) familial; (3) resistant; (4) linguistic; (5) social; and (6) navigational capital. Further, we must eschew seeing churches as standalone institutions rather than part of a collective of major urban landowners, with property often found within prime geographical locations. Viewing church property as wealth from an economic standpoint allows an assessment of their wealth, broadening an understanding of who owns the most property in low-resource urban communities.

Community practice thrives when it creatively addresses problems, meaningfully embraces local engagement in seeking solutions, and mobilizes local assets. Kim, Newman, and Jiang (2020) conclude that community engagement must never be an afterthought; in fact, it must be integral in any venture, in our case repurposing closed churches: "Most studies reveal that the importance of community engagement process in terms of understanding the problems and potential value of vacant land, redevelopment process, financial support, regulation, and neighborhood organizations participation for vacant land projects." Closed churches remain community assets. Pushing practice boundaries requires an expansive vision of this field so that all possible options can be entertained. Practitioners must recognize the past, understand the present, and take a futuristic view; all three perspectives are integral parts of any repurposing equation.

Church buildings occupy unique perches in societies across the world, yet they mysteriously remain an "invisible" aspect of our urban geography (Thomson & Pojani, 2019). These institutions bring local histories (social, cultural, political), making them integral to the history and identity of their communities (Mirza-Avakyan, 2013, p. 13): "Churches and other religious buildings are special because they often represent the values and historical identities of neighborhoods and communities in a similar magnitude to important municipal buildings or universities."

"Heritage buildings" like churches give identity to cities and their communities, representing traditions that hold great local significance (Yazdani Mehr, 2019). Unlike Europe, which has embraced an "historical-cultural heritage" stance on repurposing, the United States, because of its comparatively brief history, usually does not have that hurdle to overcome in shaping how repurposing unfolds (Della Spina, 2020).

As mentioned earlier in the chapter, this role can be conceptualized as a glue uniting communities, particularly during periods of crisis. However, it has little meaning to new residents (Phillips, 2017): "Church conversions are most often architecturally stunning and therefore quite appealing to a younger/more affluent buyer. In many instances, church conversions take place in transitional neighborhoods, which leads to consideration of gentrification and changes in community identity."

This observation will be proven over and over again in this book. Further, churches serve a key social function of connecting various parts of the community, including different age groups. This is a function they are uniquely positioned to carry out if they enjoy a history of embracing social justice goals (Cook, 2022, p. 46):

> Houses of worship often operate as a social adhesive, helping keep parts of the community bound together . . . different kinds of locale, visual appeal, and architectural style and, in so doing, give a sense of the variety and veracity of place-making efforts . . . The visible, vernacular particularity of these spaces and places speaks outwardly to the lifeways, determination, and struggles of those whose time in the area appears to be short.

When churches help craft the social fabric of a community, they cannot be easily replaced when closing because their history is integrally interwoven with that of the entire community, not just parishioners.

Churches play a significant role in the socio-cultural-political life of communities, reaching far beyond the spiritual domain to encompass the political sphere and creating community identity. Attending church is strongly associated with higher neighborhood commitment, illustrating both the reach of religiosity beyond the confines of the church building itself and the role it plays in community-building (Dougherty & Mulder, 2020). Many U.S. houses of worship were constructed during periods when people walked to worship, so parking lots were not needed in most cases. When churches with parking lots eventually closed, they became even more attractive for repurposing, as seen in the Boston case illustration in Chapter 3. Increased use of cars and the dispersal of congregations away from cities to the suburbs made churches dependent on new residents, who may have had different demographic and religious affiliations.

Church closures are around us if we take the time to look. I seriously doubt that there is an urban resident who does not encounter a closed/repurposed house of worship over the course of a week. One newspaper reporter's observation captures the saliency of today's church closings (Thielen, 2023):

> It used to be homes, businesses listed in real estate ads. Now these familiar classifications of real estate have added a new category—churches. Until the last few years, I had not seen churches being listed as property the public could buy and repurpose into a new function. From my research as a writer of parish history books, I had known them to burn, be torn down to make way for a new model, be repurposed by the parish as a convent or a parish hall or even to be moved into a neighboring town to begin a new parish. I had not encountered the church that was sold to become a dental office or low-rent housing unit.

Church closures are integral to the American landscape and will be so for the near future, with two key questions remaining: (1) Are the new establishments replacing or occupying church buildings what communities want or need, or does the economic marketplace dictate their new identities? (2) Which side of community history will these new establishments be on?

There is greater general awareness of how the built environment shapes public spaces and the well-being of residents, including engendering feelings of safety, connection, and welcome (Delgado, 2023). The nation's cities are challenged in achieving built environmental equity goals, a key force shaping daily existence. A cross section of professions are vested in influencing the ultimate outcomes.

The built environment has a defining role in global greenhouse gases and raw material extraction (Joensuu et al., 2020). Viola and Diano (2019) named three major built environment challenges with implications for church repurposing: (1) economic; (2) social; and (3) environmental. Churches will undoubtedly occupy a prominent seat in this movement, along with other structures.

Substandard housing, for example, is often accompanied by substandard physical surroundings, so that opportunities to improve surroundings are very limited. This includes affordable housing and recreational spaces, and converting vacant lots to meet other community needs. When an opportunity presents itself, as in church closings, which are sizable structures, these events are too important to ignore in channeling political will and resources to alter the physical environment.

Over 40 years ago, Burchell and Listokin (1981, p. 1) defined "adaptive reuse," and their definition still resonates with a community practice stance. Although broad, it offers a useful window for viewing church conversion projects: "neighbourhood revitalization strategy which employees a series of linked procedures to plan for, inventory, acquire, manage and reuse surplus or abandoned real estate." This term's simplicity hides its complexity: It appeals to capitalists at one end of the continuum and to a social justice stance at the other end.

Shipman and Siemiatycki's (2022) publication on church closings and their community development potential, although focusing on Toronto (The United Church of Canada), has lessons for the United States. Their spatial analysis of church real estate activity points out opportunities for using church-owned land to develop inclusive redevelopment projects. They also found barriers, including limited development experience/expertise and the uniqueness of each project, making it difficult to generalize and set parameters.

We tend to associate repurposing of buildings with urban areas, but this phenomenon is not confined to cities. Cataldi (2023). Cataldi (2023) focused on repurposing of a variety of structures in the Catskills and the Hudson Valley in upstate New York. Lefrak and Meyer (2023) looked at church closings in Vermont:

Like many churches across the U.S., some of Vermont's are facing dwindling congregations and financial pressures. This hour, we ask, what should happen when a church closes? Some of Vermont's churches are getting repurposed as community centers, apartments, art galleries—there's even a brewery. Others are being torn down. And some sit empty, as developers, preservationists and clergy debate next steps.

A church in the Vermont village of North Thetford is getting new life as a community center reaching out to people of color (Krupp, 2023), an example of repurposing a church for a socially inclusive mission.

We attach emotional significance to many structures, not just churches (e.g., libraries, schools, gyms, hospitals). Although this book focuses on church closures and repurposing, schools are facing similar challenges. Almost 2,000 schools are closed annually across the United States. Like churches, school closures often bring many strong feelings, with these two types of cultures treated as separate events (Green, 2017; Syeed, 2019). Closings in major cities such as Chicago and Philadelphia stand out and are highlighted throughout this book (Nuamah, 2021), including community efforts to fight against these closures (Johanek, 2023). The reasons for these closings parallel those of church closings—failure to meet performance expectations, demographic trends, under-enrollment, deferred maintenance, and budget deficits.

In 2013, Chicago closed 50 public schools (generally in the South and West Sides), resulting in 46 vacant buildings, of which 26 remained closed (16 are still publicly owned but vacant, and 10 were sold but have remained vacant). However, 20 were repurposed, with most becoming housing, offices, or private schools. A few were repurposed for the community's good (Chicago Sun Times, 2023): "What actually happened was predictable: In parts of the city with strong real estate markets, buildings were snapped up at multimillion-dollar prices, destined for luxury apartments and private schools."

It is certainly understandable why the closing of schools and churches can elicit neighborhood fears. Conversion of schools into residential real estate exemplifies the fears that many marginalized communities have that these efforts "exacerbate uneven access to quality education while furthering destructive processes of gentrification, displacement, and uneven development" (McFadden, 2023, p. 128). The success or failure of repurposing school buildings, as in Chicago's West Town, a gentrifying neighborhood, depends on how well local leaders can find a delicate balance between economic and community goals (Garcia, 2019).

School closures, as with churches, can be viewed from a spatial justice standpoint because they disproportionately affect marginalized groups and communities like Blacks and Latinos (Tieken & Auldridge-Reveles, 2019). Both school and church closings are sensitive to demographic trends, emphasizing the importance of listening to community concerns and engaging local leaders in the decision-making process (Good, 2022).

Arfa, Zijlstra, Lubelli, and Quist (2022, p. 148) advance a 10-step framework that aids repurposing heritage buildings that readers may find useful in conceptualizing this process: initiative, analysis of heritage buildings, value assessment, mapping level of significance, definition of adaptive reuse potential, definition of design strategy, final decision-making, execution, maintenance, and evaluation after years. Each step progressively sets a foundation for the next step.

Altering physical surroundings brings both expected and unanticipated benefits, such as improving the health and well-being of residents, for instance (Delgado, 2023). We cannot expand land, but we can expand the functions of buildings, transforming spaces and making them better meet residents' needs since church closings may be due to changing community demographics.

Urban communities must ensure that these buildings do not become the landing site for gentrification, because there is a tendency to do so. Brooklyn's St. Vincent de Paul Church, for example, a 19th-century building, was repurposed into "The Spire Lofts," consisting of 40 luxury apartments, with one-bedroom units renting for as much as $4,812 per month (Merritt, 2018). This is not affordable housing stock! Repurposed churches can make an important contribution toward this nation's need for affordable housing (Bandlamudin, 2022). Church repurposing for affordable housing, however, faces many of the same financial challenges as does repurposing for luxury housing.

Church buildings may be used by another religious order as community demographics change, going from Episcopal to Baptist to Methodist to Pentecostal, for example, and interrupting what eventually might become a death spiral. Such transitions rarely go smoothly, however, but the physical structure of the building still supports its original purpose.

Houses of worship have historically occupied exalted positions in society, influencing all segments and regions of the country directly and indirectly.

According to Bruce (2023, p. 95): "Classical sociologist Emile Durkheim equates the idea of 'church' to a 'single moral community' conjoining religious adherents together. In showing that the idea of religion is inseparable from the idea of a Church."

We cannot fully understand the United States without realizing that religion and churches were critical in shaping its character, both historically and today. Their significance (symbolically, spiritually, and materially) is manifested by their structures, which cast imposing physical and metaphorical shadows (Jordan, 2023): "The challenge of repurposing deconsecrated spaces has been the subject of studies by both architects and heritage professionals, concerned about inappropriate or destructive reuse of sites that continue to carry symbolic meaning, memory and community value." Churches are often geographically well located, occupying physical and social spaces where residents live so that they have easy access without having to rely on cars or even public transportation.

Sarason (1974), half a century ago, argued that one of the primary goals of community interventions is to create or reinforce a sense of community as a fundamental building block to any meaningful and lasting change. This creates a climate fostering mutual support and a psychologically significant sense of identity based on feeling valued and belonging. This is still the case today and serves as the basis for social agency. This perspective reinforces the important role of churches in serving as "third places" and why their repurposing must keep this quality. Such places can be considered sanctuaries for marginalized members in society, such as Blacks and Latinos, among others.

"Third places" are defined as spaces that, like churches, fall between home and work (Oldenburg, 1989). DeGroot (undated, p. 15) discusses this critical point:

> Churches have a natural opportunity to serve as a Third Place. By not rushing people through the building, we invite them to stay and get to know the church and its people better. And the more comfortable people feel at church, the more likely they will be to continue on their spiritual journey.

Converting churches into new third places is not a conceptual stretch, highlighting their importance if successful! They take on greater urgency in places in desperate need, as in low-resource communities. The closing of churches, however, is only part of a trend of closures of third places across the nation, bringing consequences for collective health and well-being (Finlay et al., 2019). The presence of fewer third places emphasizes the importance of those that remain.

Mendez and Deeb-Sossa (2020) documented the importance of creating a welcoming place and space for Latina immigrants by using public activities to engender attachments to place and to promote belonging and feelings of "being at home." Successful churches foster belonging, which is essential for a vibrant organization. If a church cannot create this sense of home and safety for an uprooted population group, an excellent opportunity is lost to build for a future, and without a practical substitute to take its place.

Lopez et al. (2022) discuss how religious leaders can serve Latino newcomers and the multifaceted roles they must occupy to be successful, similar to social workers, for example. Ministers are expected to meet the instrumental and expressive needs of their members, including setting up collaborative roles with formal service providers and organizations. These roles share parallels with Black counterparts. Latino religious leaders living in areas with an anti-immigration stance, as discussed in Chapter 6, find themselves in difficult positions.

Churches help communities to address a range of social, economic, and public health needs, with implications for urban community practice (Hodge, 2020). The ripple effects of church closings often go far beyond their members and the building itself. A building is often much than a physical structure prominently occupying a public space; it cannot easily be replaced by another structure. An estimated 90% of church attendees are not actually members of the congregation, since these institutions often house various community programs, such as day care centers (Beers-Altman, 2023). Because churches can serve as community service/educational institutions, integral to residents' well-being, closure means that these programs are dislodged and must move or close. Further, this "traffic" into churches illustrates how these institutions often play a central role in the life of a community, taking their place alongside other institutions of note.

Cleveland and Philadelphia Church Closures: A Snapshot

Cleveland, Ohio, and Philadelphia, Pennsylvania, provide excellent case examples of the major trends of church closures and mergers that we have discussed. Many other snapshots will be presented throughout this book. These examples illustrate many themes discussed in this book, introducing readers to the interplay of social and economic forces that cause church closures and the ramifications that follow.

Nagel (2011) raised a familiar theme of urban church closures in Cleveland, before there was greater recognition of this national movement. In 2009, the bishop of the Cleveland Catholic Diocese announced a significant reconfiguration of the diocese involving a reduction of 52 parishes over an estimated one-year period; 23% of that city's parishes were either eliminated or combined. The ripple consequences on respective communities are not hard to imagine. The Latino community, for example, bore the brunt of these changes, and the closures created a glut of shuttered buildings with all the associated problems. The success of repurposing these buildings is greatly dependent on the community, the degree of their involvement and commitment, and stakeholder buy-in, among other significant factors. These churches can serve as valuable anchors for newcomer groups, often filling an existing vacuum in their lives.

In 2023, the Columbus Catholic Diocese announced that it will close 15 more churches in response to a two-year study entitled *Real Presence, Real Future*. The Ohio church closures and mergers result from the major socioeconomic forces outlined throughout this book—shifting demographics, a dwindling priesthood, aging infrastructure, and financial shortfalls, for example. Only 15 young men were training to become seminarians. The diocese's "pastoral plan" significantly overhauls the structure of its 105 parishes spanning Ohio's 23 counties (Walsh & Marshall, 2023). Further, two K-8 Columbus schools will close, following a pattern found in other cities undergoing a wave of church closures.

These planned mergers may involve two, three, and even four churches, dramatically altering the character and composition of these churches and their respective communities. Combining worshipers from different communities is not an organic process that automatically results in unity; in reality, it may increase tensions and even cause disengagement from worship services, undermining a primary benefit of belonging to a congregation. Historically, U.S. churches catered to the ethnic groups patronizing their respective ethnic churches, serving as an entry point into a community and this country, and fulfilling a variety of social and political functions beyond religious needs. A "Polish" Catholic church, for example, might be found in a community that was historically Polish. Italians who moved into the parish would not feel comfortable or welcomed in the Polish church and would rely on "their own" church. Cities with long histories of being home to European newcomers, such as Boston, Chicago, New York, and Philadelphia, for example, typify this phenomenon.

There are about 3 million Black Catholics, making up 6% of this nation's Catholic population (Diamant et al., 2022). When they attend Mass, they tend to do so with White, non-Latinos:

> Just 25% of Black Catholics who attend Mass at least a few times a year report that they typically go to a Mass where most other attendees are Black. That compares with 80% of White Catholic churchgoers who worship where most attendees are White and 67% of Hispanic Catholic church attenders who worship where most attendees are Hispanic.

In contrast, 68% of Black Protestants say they typically worship where most other attendees are Black. Attending services with other worshippers who look like them has psychological benefits that are integral to the worship experience.

Another example of an urban church closure is Philadelphia's St. Peter Claver (the "Mother church" for the city's Black Catholics), which is located in a Black but gentrifying neighborhood and draws Black Catholics from throughout the city. In 1910, there were seven churches in South Philadelphia; in 2023 there were three, primarily serving the Black community. It does not take a crystal ball to predict what the future has in store for Philadelphia. Two additional notes: 16% of Black Catholics are converts to the faith, representing a potential growth area for the Catholic Church if it wished to pursue this strategy. More Black adults have left Catholicism than have entered the faith: 4% of Black Americans saying they were raised Catholic but no longer identify as Catholic, whereas 1% are converts to Catholicism. St. Peter Claver's declining membership and closure coincided with gentrification forces, a theme in this book worth watching for predicting future church closures (N. Brown, 2022):

> As the Black Catholic community spread to many areas of the archdiocese, [St. Peter Claver] became utilized by fewer and fewer people over the years, and Mass was being offered on a monthly basis and was attended by fewer than 15 people... The former Saint Peter Claver Church building has been sitting vacant as an unutilized asset for some time. The recent decree and

a potential future real estate transaction will allow for greater support of ministry to the Black Catholic community in the archdiocese.

The financial capital needed to repurpose churches is largely determined by the building's location and condition, goals, and local costs, and often involves significant external funding and competing for local needs (Chernick, 2017), particularly if local governments are unable or unwilling to assist. The political nature of this decision-making process is undeniable.

The closings of Catholic churches in Philadelphia have drawn scholarly attention. Gambino (2022, 2023a), for example, examined the history of Catholic Church's decline, actively starting in the 1970s, and changes in the Roman Catholic Archdiocese of Philadelphia from the 1970s to 2010, which significantly shaped the practice of Catholicism. Readers interested in this city's early church history, particularly its first Catholic church devoted to Black residents, should read Gambino's (2023b) "Advancing 'Catholic Truth and American Equality': Black Self-Determination in Philadelphia's First Black Parish and the American Catholic Church." Demographic changes alone do not explain this decline, introducing the role of institutional systems of support and disinvestment in causing eventual church mergers and closures.

McIntosh (2021) discusses gentrification, churches, money, and neighborhood identity in Philadelphia. Gentrification (for instance, the Fishtown neighborhood) is a polarizing force, and houses of worship are caught in this wave (McIntosh, 2021). St. Laurentius Church, which was built in 1882, formally closed in 2014, and demolished in 2022, symbolizes this church closure movement (Associated Press, 2022).

Community identity, with churches as critical symbols, is in flux as new groups enter and displace established residents. Building a multiracial church brings rewards for parishioners and communities (DeYmaz, 2017, 2020). Readers wishing to learn more about Philadelphia's Catholic church closures and revitalization efforts should read Welch's (2012) article on this trend and new models of revitalization to appear through a community development corporation that is part of the Archdiocese of Philadelphia.

Urban planners, for example, embracing practice as conceptualized in this book must contend with social forces looking to demolish rather than repurpose, largely driven by economic motives and a total disregard for local histories. Community Development Corporation (CDCs), land banks, and municipal governments have a stake in repurposing. Unfortunately, city planning has historically been more focused on demolition as a primary strategy, with repurposing only relatively recently gaining importance. This shift will require an embrace of a broader mission, and that can be said for other professions, too, including my own social work profession.

Trauma and Houses of Worship

Trauma and houses of worship can be closely linked, particularly related to sexual abuse but certainly not limited to these experiences. For some community residents, churches are symbols of oppression and abuse that they have experienced firsthand. These feelings are heightened when the trauma has gone untreated; such feelings may manifest as wanting to tear down these institutions rather than repurposing them for some worthy community purpose. On the surface, these attitudes may come across as heartless or less than caring and counterproductive to a repurposing project. However, for these residents, the church may represent traumatic experiences that may be very difficult to discuss with others. Thus, dealing with trauma may just be part of the job of undertaking church repurposing, even though community practitioners are not trauma specialists or therapists in the conventional sense of the word.

Book Goals

I have no architectural training or ability, nor aesthetic sense, for that matter! This book does not offer opinions on design. Readers interested in an architectural perspective should read Merlino's (2018) *Building Reuse: Sustainability, Preservation, and the Value of Design*, which discusses sustainable design predicated on reusing and reimagining existing buildings.

The word "church" signifies a primary focus on a building structure, but other dimensions will be covered to ground the repurposing movement. Also, this book focuses on Christian churches, but mosques and synagogues also open and close and play significant roles in their communities, and their closures are felt by both adherents and non-adherents. Our focus on Christian churches does not change the significance of this book, because non-Christian groups represent a small percentage of religious institutions. Nevertheless, this "limitation" needs to be acknowledged.

This book has five goals:

1. Provide a trend and statistical profile of church closings and repurposing in the United States, with a focus on cities and communities of color, particularly Blacks and Latinos
2. Examine the social, cultural, political, demographic, economic, environmental, and religious forces shaping these closings, including their histories, to ground repurposing efforts
3. Provide case illustrations of various lengths highlighting conversions, with rewards and challenges for community practice
4. Draw implications for professions with strong urban missions, such as the arts, public health, social work, recreation, medicine, and community education
5. Provide research, educational, and practice recommendations for urban church repurposing.

In addition, I hope that this book sparks projects and scholarly endeavors to move this field forward (Inform Magazine, 2022):

The heart of communities in the West has always been the church, where congregants have not only worshipped and found greater meaning in their lives but built their social lives around this hub. However, in recent decades, changing demographics and secularization have depreciated the church's position as the social locus of society. This phenomenon is particularly conspicuous in Europe where its large, historic cathedrals have become progressively more vacant.

This book focuses on urban centers. However, practitioners in cities and rural settings must guard against stereotypes of the other. An urban/rural bias is counter to professional social/spatial justice missions. One is not better than the other. They are certainly different, influencing how methods are conceptualized and implemented, but that does not equate to a hierarchy with one on top and the other at the bottom from a worthiness standpoint. We must not see church attendance decline as solely an urban phenomenon, with "country folk" keeping their religious tradition and "city folks" losing theirs. Rural demographic trends, too, show population declines, affecting communities and their churches (Perks, 2020). These changes bring corresponding negative outcomes (Herbkersman, 2022).

This book focuses on urban community practitioners in social work, public health, community education, recreation, religious studies, planning, policymaking, and foundations, illustrative of this field's broad appeal. Companies are appearing with specific missions on church repurposing, such as Baltimore's PraiseBuildings Religious Property Brokerage. Repurposing will continue to gain appeal across a wide segment of professions. For some readers, this field of practice is a first-time entry into this new world; for others, there is an "it's about time" yawn. This field is big enough for all!

Conclusion

This chapter grounded readers in the journey they are undertaking while issuing a series of warnings on the challenges they will meet. Houses of worship transcend earthly domains, and repurposing occupies a privileged position within this field. Readers have learned about the emerging church tsunami this country has been slow to recognize and now have a roadmap. They also understand why I have taken a particularly expansive view of this subject, with all of its perils.

The future is shaped by our actions today and is built upon past decisions. We are not helpless in shaping our destiny and surroundings. The following chapter introduces urban community practice and church repurposing, and why this field of practice will open new and exciting doors for those selecting this realm of practice.

2
Urban Community Practice Realm

Introduction

I elected to position a chapter on urban community practice early in this book to ground why church closures and repurposing are so important for urban communities. I hope this will help readers see themselves in these repurposing initiatives and potential roles, and as part of an extensive network of like-minded colleagues. Chapter 3 will provide a detailed case illustration uplifting community practice.

Preserving an empty closed church for historical purposes per the wishes of its parishioner community, beautiful as it may have been at one time, is not economically tenable. Thus, a fundamental decision will need to be made: Tear the building down and erect a new structure, or keep the building and repurpose it for a new mission. If repurposing is the answer, will the new structure be considered a "respectful" and "welcome" addition to the community, or will it have a purpose that is considered "disrespectful," such as a bar or a music venue? Community practitioners can help communities during this deliberative process as they formulate their desired goals for a former house of worship.

This chapter provides a lens for understanding and responding to church repurposing. Community practice principles, however, must permeate our thinking and actions and must not be relegated to one time period or set of actions. Community practice is like the air we breathe: ever constant, and we cannot do without! This worldview of practice emanates from a core belief system.

It may be tempting to discuss church closings and repurposing in the abstract, without relation to their geographical location. However, contextual grounding is key to community practice. For example, not all cities are facing demand for vacant property, and those with low real-estate demand will find it easier to develop closed churches into affordable housing. This is a sad observation because it directs affordable housing to certain sectors of a city when it should exist throughout and should not be limited to undervalued areas.

No one wants problematic properties dominating an urban landscape, emphasizing the importance of turning these properties into productive entities. Seeing cities as social and cultural hubs (Naheed & Shooshtarian, 2022) will help us to realize how churches manifest these qualities. Sustainability must embrace the built and cultural environment. Houses of worship are part of a community's social and cultural scene, both historically and currently. Church closures take on even greater significance because of how dramatically the lives of parishioners are altered.

Readers will be able to apply a wide variety of perspectives to church repurposing that are applicable to the field of urban community practice, such as regenerative strategies to the built environment and sustainability (Camrass, 2022). This is exciting from a practice standpoint, certainly, but it can also complicate explaining why and how we wish to pursue church repurposing. I stress the role and significance of social justice as a guiding light in helping in the decision-making process.

It is difficult to explain what urban community practice entails. That may seem odd to readers new to this field, but those with long histories in this field can attest to this challenge. One practitioner described it as a "state of mind followed by a 'toolbox' with all sorts of tools!" Readers may find this definition unhelpful, but it does evoke a particular worldview, reminding us that the methods we use must be responsive to the urban context, helping us invest in communities, too! I often associate the word "passion" with this work. Yes, it is a professional role, but it is so much more!

Community practice is indeed a big toolbox, with its compartments holding tools related to advocacy, assessment/research, capacity enhancement, fundraising (proposal and grassroots), brokering, organizing, management, policy analysis, and systems change, for example. Some aspects of community life are not off-limits. This is the adventure of breaking new ground and pushing boundaries to achieve social justice goals, with church repurposing but the latest example!

Community practice is shaped by context, and it has expanded over the past several decades to include such areas as environmental-spatial justice, fighting racism, dance and theater, entrepreneurship, friendship development, reducing gun violence, youth programs, improving vacant lots, celebrations (such as fairs, festivals, and parades), public art, establishing sanctuary cities, small business development, and, in the case of this book, repurposing church structures. Clearly, community practice is an expanding universe.

Viewing community practice within an urban context and with a focus on people of color opens the door for the introduction of new and exciting concepts. Urban church repurposing can be viewed from a resiliency and sustainability stance, two concepts with saliency to both the urbanization movement and community practice (Zeng et al., 2022). Sandra Braman (p. xvi), in an introduction to Costanza-Chock's (2020) book *Design Justice: Community-Led Practices to Build the Worlds We Need*, splendidly describes the richness and vastness of the community practice field and the built environment through a focus on responsive design when guided by a social justice stance:

> It's about design, social justice, and the dynamics of domination and resistance at personal, community, and institutional levels. In essence, it's a call for us to heed the growing critiques of the ways that design (of images, objects, software, algorithms, sociotechnical systems, the built environment, indeed, everything we make) too often contributes to the reproduction of systemic oppression. Most of all, it is an invitation to build a better world, a world where many worlds fit; linked worlds of collective liberation and ecological sustainability.

This quotation serves as a valuable backdrop to this book on church repurposing. Social justice, liberation, and design are intertwined, forming a philosophical vision of how repurposing can bring meaningful and lasting change in marginalized communities. Design justice meets community practice justice, creating a more socially just world.

Readers can see that we are embracing the potential relationship between social justice, church repurposing, and urban community practice, introducing a brave new world for the field in the nation's cities. This repurposing wave, which has many different motivations, has saved many historical churches from demolition, and they have emerged as totally new entities, distant memories for former parishioners and the community.

Those who believe that closed churches should not be saved or repurposed argue that the churches died because they did not respond to changing times and the needs of their constituents. As one critic noted (Beres, 2018): "There's nothing in the Bible that requires ornate houses of worship. Centuries of church leaders building ornate monuments to ego instead of using the funds to care for the poor are not something to be celebrated. Followers of a man who said to give your second coat to the poor shouldn't be obsessed with buildings." Readers may find this stance to be overly harsh, but nonetheless it can be found in all communities and must not be ignored in any repurposing undertaking.

Those who venture into the urban church repurposing field, and the built environment in general, will find it exciting and terrifying at the same time. We rejoice in our successes and wallow in despair when we fail, but I have found that I can learn more about a person by how they handle failure than by how they handle success. Learning from our successes and failures will shape our future undertakings. Creating a cadre of urban academics and practitioners examining, collaborating, and writing about these undertakings, including presenting at forums to share experiences and ideas (synergistic impact), will help move the repurposing field forward.

This field brings excitement and great promise for those embracing social justice values because it has the potential to spill over into other community projects. Needless to say, it is not a field for everyone. Finding our niche in life is a process of honesty and discovery that will be rewarding professionally for those willing and able to undertake this journey, and we must have an openness to take in information and undertake a reality-based self-assessment.

Definitional Parameters of Community Practice

Defining any field brings inherent challenges, and community practice is no exception because of how national boundaries shape perspectives. I prefer to define community practice as "the use of structured activities premised on an explicit set of values emphasizing the value and worth of residents, and their abilities (agency/assets) to create positive change in their lives and their communities." In my case and in this book, urban areas represent the context where it occurs.

This definition is simple and broad concomitantly, involving the multitude of goals, programs, and activities needed to repurpose churches. I view community practice as an expanding universe, bringing both excitement and the wonder of discovery along with great trepidation about what we will encounter. It also raises implications for evaluation, comparing different programs and contexts to grasp the significance of an intervention across time periods, demographic groups, geographical settings, and particularly church closings. Community practice, at least from a scholarly viewpoint, tends to be associated with cities, although it is not limited to them.

Dividing community practice into three perspectives will help us form an operational definition. Each view has a set of assumptions, allowing a cross-professional view and local circumstances to emerge. Banks (2010)'s distinct perspectives of community practice were activity, occupation, and discipline (Banks is based in Great Britain, but these perspectives are relevant to other countries as well). For instance, a social worker can practice alongside an urban planner, a community educator, or a public health worker, with each bringing particular knowledge and skillsets to the project while sharing a philosophical social justice stance. Further, a social worker can specialize in working with certain groups, such as children/youth, people with disabilities, and older adults. In my case, it has been community practice with youth, although it's important to note that effective youth-focused interventions lead to engagement of their families, including adult members.

The distinctions between these viewpoints help clarify how this field can successfully evolve to create interventions for different audiences—practitioners, practice academics, foundations, policymakers, social scientists, and residents, for example. All of these audiences are interrelated, but each brings needs and specific views of community practice. Bringing these groups together can be symbolic, powerful, and essential, too, for the field. Enlisting a variety of professions to address a church repurposing project increases the likelihood of success.

The community practice field knows no national boundaries, although it goes by many different names in different countries. The term "community work" has found favor in European English-speaking nations. "Social pedagogy," which is situated between the fields of social work and education, has found favor in non-English-speaking European countries, with strong national and regional differences (Úcar et al., 2020).

Using the metaphor of a universe helps when discussing community practice. An expanding universe is exciting, always filled with the hope of new discoveries that can enrich our lives and those of future generations. In studying the universe, we are looking at the past to understand the present and project into the future. Again keeping with the universe metaphor, there are competing theories, or epistemologies, that shape our journey in the community practice field. These tensions should actually be welcomed because they occur only in important fields, not in uninspiring ones.

Bringing another international perspective, the Australian Community Workers Association (2017) defines "community work" as:

> A diverse profession that covers over 50 occupations. For this reason, practitioners are often distinguished by the client area within which they work. These can include aged care, disability services, Indigenous and multicultural support, asylum seekers and refugee services, mental health, child and family services, counseling, schools, emergency relief, youth, justice, housing, and community development.

Readers should be impressed by the breadth of this field. It embraces a wide spectrum of practitioners and academics, as well as residents of all ages, which is exciting and challenging at the same time. But with this breadth of practice comes the challenge of deciding what are the most meaningful boundaries of practice. With an expanding universe, to use this metaphor again, comes great anxiety about the unknown. We start off with theories and quickly need to adapt them to new circumstances we were not prepared for. In essence, what are the boundaries of a field of practice? Must there be boundaries? Is formal education a prerequisite for practicing?

One challenge in grasping the boundaries and depth of this field is understanding the extent of terms used to describe it, as with community social work practice. Sathyamurthi's (2017) literature review found six key terms often associated with this social work field: (1) social work practice with communities; (2) community-oriented social work; (3) social work in communities; (4) social work community practice; (5) community-based social work; and (6) social work approaches in community practice.

This book will draw upon the international scene to broaden the context of community practice. Church closures, as noted earlier, are not restricted to the United States, allowing an international brother/sisterhood to appear in terms of best practices, offering valuable lessons. Ways in which this practice is defined and practiced reflect national and historical biases, but they also share a common stance, as the case in Cuba before and after its revolution, for example (de Urrutia Barroso & Strug, 2016).

The United States has a history of community practice in a variety of social spheres, in various population groups, and at various levels—a micro level (individuals, families, and groups), a mezzo level (community and organizational level), and a macro level (policy practice)—over a period covering several decades. Church closings represent a new frontier, bringing together a variety of professions to repurpose these buildings.

This field consists of many professions sharing traditions of innovative approaches and participatory democracy. This practice addresses some of this nation's most intractable problems using approaches such as community arts, banking, celebrations, corrections, dance, education, medicine, mental health, nursing, nutrition, pharmacy, policing, psychology, public health, recreation, rehabilitation, safety, small business development, sports, theater, and worship, for example. It does so while embracing values of community-centered engagement/empowerment but using different terms to capture and explain this phenomenon.

As a social worker, I am well aware that other professions, too, bring their own gifts to the community practice field. Focusing on urban marginalized communities needs a team approach, with each profession supplying particular perspectives and contributions. Community activists, too, have some of these tools and the vocabulary to describe their goals, strategy, activities, and tasks. A "Rosetta Stone" to aid in translating concepts across disciplines/professions, however, is much needed.

Community practice's venture into the built environment highlights how and why it has contributions to make that will find us meeting new professions, such as regulatory bodies and construction, for example. Converting churches falls within the community practice realm, following a distinguished tradition of pushing boundaries when community is central in its mission. Community practice meets a range of emotional and instrumental needs, including venturing into the built environment realm such as vacant lots (Delgado, 2023).

These practice spheres bring unique histories, techniques, terms, strategies, and research findings, along with their share of rewards and challenges (García, 2019). Converting closed churches requires all three levels of interventions to be successful, particularly when the community is central in these interventions. We cannot say that all practitioners have ignored church closings. Christian social work community practitioners, for example, have recognized how churches and religious belief systems help their community, proposing the use of a settlement house model to enhance the role of churches as providers of social and health services (Polson & Scales, 2020). In fact, after the government, religious congregations are the second most significant social service providers in the country (Hodge,

2020). Although Thorp's (2023) description is about Protestant churches, it is applicable to other religious groups:

> Protestant pastors and small churches face a threefold problem embedded in the context of the local church mission: a lack of resources to provide mission-based educational programming, a decline in people not joining or affiliating with local church congregations, religiously unaffiliated persons in communities that pastors and churches need to address according to their church mission.

Providing afterschool programs, for example, helps extend a church's mission to younger people while further integrating them into the social fabric of a community, and possibly investing in a future generation of churchgoers.

Health and human service ministries may help struggling churches to attract much-needed new members (Russell, 2017). Cnaan and McGrew (2004) found that 90% of Philadelphia churches supplied at least one social service, highlighting their multipurpose functions that transcend traditional views of worship and congregations as only focused on spiritual salvation. Please do not get me wrong: A spiritual worldview is immensely important in the lives of countless number of people, but more earthly needs, too, deserve to be considered by a congregation. Examples include afterschool care, day camps, food pantries, homeless shelters, recreational programs, soup kitchens, and tutoring. Churches that run these programs take on more of a social service role than is widely acknowledged, playing a significant role in the health and well-being of low-income/resourced urban communities. When these churches close, the community loses not only a church/spiritual center but also a social service agency with a long-established tradition of service.

Anti-Urban Sentiments

Urban practice faces many of the same challenges of any intervention looking to make significant social changes. However, strong prevailing national anti-urban sentiments, even though the nation is highly urbanized, will continue well into the future.

Cities have historically been excellent scapegoats because they tend to house high percentages of people of color and newcomers to this country.

Anti-urban federal and state policies disadvantage cities in addressing resident inequities (McGahey, 2023). National attitudes towards cities need grounding historically if we are to appreciate the depth of these sentiments (De Sena & Krase, 2015; Hyeon, 2013). Practitioners must be cognizant to the prevalence of these narratives, including their influence on perceptions and broader support of their work. These narratives often highlight marginalized groups that historically made cities their homes, with implications for their urban church closures and repurposing. All states have major cities, but how these cities are viewed from a state government perspective may relegate them to a second-class citizen status. Such viewpoints will shape responses to church closures in urban centers, whether considered salient or latent in importance.

Consider, for instance, how popular music sings the praises of a rural lifestyle (Cimaglio, 2011, p. 1):

> Country lyrics have often described an idyllic "Small Town USA" where "we still wave Old Glory down at the courthouse," where "everybody knows me and I know them," home to "picture perfect postcard[s] of America" like kids at a lemonade stand. This nostalgic rural imagery of the Norman Rockwell variety has been central to those who, like McCain and Palin, have located authentic Americanness in "small town people," "Middle Americans," "working people," or "flyover people," labels that refer to white middle-income Americans who live somewhere other than the urban centers on the coasts. Country musicians claim to speak on behalf of these people, hold them up as "real" Americans, and, importantly, mark them as "small town," "country," or "rural."

My intent in highlighting this quotation is not to pit country versus urban from a cultural standpoint. But you will rarely, if ever, hear "urban" music criticizing rural/country life. Rather, it emphasizes urban challenges and joys.

Steven Conn's (2014) *Americans Against the City: Anti-urbanism in the Twentieth Century* notes that an anti-urban bias is not new; in fact, its origins can be traced to the founding of the nation. An historically strong anti-urban sentiment complicates current-day views (Delgado, 2023):

> The relationship between immigrants and cities, particularly taking into account this nation's love-hate relationship with this geographical entity, is

in large part the result of how this nation's founding fathers distrusted and simply disliked cities, based in large part on their experiences in Europe . . . Nevertheless, urban places and spaces have resisted these negative perceptions and have offered counter-narratives that are resiliency and social justice based, including the presence of hope and sanctuary from governmental forces seeking to do them harm.

We cannot separate immigration from cities historically, currently, and into the future. The great waves of immigrants to cities in the United States created controversies about how they might change the nation; anti-Irish sentiments in Boston come to mind, for instance. Donald Trump worsened these long-held anti-urban sentiments with his derogatory comments about cities such as Chicago and San Francisco; even New York, his hometown, did not escape this criticism! Davidson (2017) ties anti-city bias to present-day politics with implications for urban community practice, illustrating the long reach of this historical bias and its influence across a variety of sociopolitical spheres:

> The Trump administration's disdain for urban culture has a rich bipartisan pedigree. Thomas Jefferson formed his view of nationhood around a belief that the countryside was not only preferable but morally superior. "I think our governments will remain virtuous for many centuries; as long as they are chiefly agricultural; and this will be as long as there shall be vacant lands in any part of America," he wrote to James Madison in 1787. "When they get piled upon one another in large cities, as in Europe, they will become corrupt as in Europe."

Over the past several years this anti-urban bias has intensified for marginalized groups, such as LBGTQ+ persons, immigrants (documented and undocumented), and other groups historically finding refuge in the nation's cities.

The historical existence of an anti-urban stance does not necessarily translate into an emergence of a counter-narrative stressing the importance of cities rather than having them be a drag on the nation. Western world cities have historically had their share of death and misery associated with industrialization, for example. These histories and experiences have changed dramatically over the past century (Glazer, 2014). But the past continues to influence present-day urban narratives, feeding into pervasive anti-urban sentiments. This is relevant to church repurposing because, due to these prejudices, urban church closures may have difficulty attracting repurposing resources in a manner that will meet major group needs.

Community Practice and the Urban Setting

The word "community," when grounded in the urban studies field, for example, is conceptually vague (Blokland, 2017). However, this ambiguity opens the door for innovation and excitement; it also opens the door for great caution. I compare "community" to a cloud in an otherwise cloudless sky. We can see, describe, and follow it across the sky—but try grabbing it! Yet, community exists and, depending upon the viewpoint, it means different things to different people.

Community is central to people's lives, and churches represent an important glue, bringing together people on a weekly basis to share and belong. Another view, participatory in nature, defines community as a place where people connect and where democracy gets practice for the greater good. The "greater good" is key, and repurposed churches may assume a prominent place in fostering this good.

Trust and Community Practice

Community practice relies on depths of relationships and trust as key elements in successful interventions. Being courageous helps to build trust with groups that have histories of betrayal and hence have difficulty trusting professionals and outsiders. Healy's (2017, p. 7) comments, although they spotlight social work, are also applicable to community practice:

> The question of trustworthiness is important for two reasons. The first is longstanding and centres on the relationship-based nature of social work practice. This feature means that gaining and sustaining the trust of others is central to the work we do ... Importantly, the capacity to engender trust, although obviously important to direct practice, is also relevant to our relationship with other stakeholders, such as team members, governments, nongovernment community services, community members, other service funders, and collaborators in political activism ... The second reason for the

focus on trust is that our profession, like many human service professions, emerged and continues to practise in institutions that were sites of poor practices and, in some instances, the gross violations of human rights.

Urban community practice requires being courageous and speaking truth to power. Trust is key in being courageous; embracing truth, however, may put us at odds with our organization when it does not share this value to the needed extent.

Any seasoned practitioner or academic will understand why this was done. Social workers, for example, are well versed in the importance of mutual trust and respect in the development of effective working relationships. That applies across the entire spectrum of interventions, from therapeutic to community, social change, and working with different age groups.

Connectedness is an essential element of being in a community, one where you are valued and you, in turn, value others. This hunger for belonging is not restricted to any single group, with shared values helping to establish connectedness (Vogl, 2016). Community practitioners understand the immense value of feeling a sense of belonging.

We can think of "belonging" as a two-fold concept—social and spatial. If viewed from a community standpoint, it brings a greater perspective. The same can be said about belonging from an organizational standpoint. It is very hard to function effectively if one is not valued. The concept of "organizational citizen" comes to mind. A "community citizen" is a resident who has a personal stake in where they live and is willing to act to ensure it. Trust helps with engagement and relationship building, which are essential aspects of belonging. Social cohesion, another aspect of belonging and trust, can be integral to community practice even when community members share similar backgrounds, as with Latinx newcomers moving into established Latinx communities (Plenty & Jonsson, 2017).

Community projects cannot succeed without social trust (Häkli, 2016; Walker et al., 2010). Trust is similar to the foundation of a house; a house without a strong foundation is not likely to exist when the first storm hits. The importance of establishing relationships based on mutual trust is well proven in micro-focused strategies (Livingstone & Gaffney, 2016s). Trust also plays a key role in urban community practice because it is an essential part of the glue bringing groups together.

Trust is enhanced when the practitioner and community share similar life experiences and socio-demographic characteristics. Our micro-focused colleagues are well attuned to the interplay of these factors in helping develop relationships built on mutual trust. The same principles apply to community practitioners, including whether or not we live in the communities we serve. My personal experiences stand as an example.

I lived in Cambridge, Massachusetts, and worked in Worcester, approximately 40 miles west. I worked with a primarily low-income and low-wealth Puerto Rican community, and I shared their background. This shared background helped improve both communication and comfort level in working with this community. I spent approximately 10 hours a day in my work capacity, and my heart and soul, so to speak, was there, too, but I did not live there; at the end of the day, I would drive back home. I was not from the community and never would be unless I physically lived there.

Because of that, one segment of the community never fully trusted me because they considered me an outsider. I learned to accept this but always needed to be prepared to have my loyalty tested because of this factor. I spent five years working in Worcester, by the way, and life certainly got easier from a loyalty standpoint. However, I was never a resident. Living in a community 24 hours a day, seven days a week, is different than working in a community 10 hours or so a day, regardless of one's ethnic, racial, and cultural background and the number of languages one speaks.

Churches as Communities

It is not a conceptual stretch to view a church as a form of community (Plekon, 2021). In fact, it is not unheard of to hear the term "church community." Working with these communities requires paying attention to relationships and capturing the stories (lessons learned) of church leaders who have revived congregations that were near death. What did they do to attract members to attend and reinvest in their church? Church structures have compelling historical stories to tell (DCG Strategies, 2015):

> Churches used to be the cornerstone of a growing town. Oftentimes, they are the oldest buildings in a community, and the setting of a city's most famous moments. These seemingly weary old buildings, though, usually have a very valuable hidden asset: a good story. Here lies opportunity. A crumbling, old church building has a good chance of being torn down. Sadly, when the congregation closes its doors, the spark tends to run out

of the place. A former church can become just another old building with a leaky roof and boarded-up windows on a list for demolition. For those who remember the good times, it can be [painful] to see. On the principle of historic preservation, the case can be made that a building with a story not only has sentimental value, but a monetary one as well. This story can be the architecture, associated people or even the objects inside it.

Thus, repurposing efforts should not focus just on saving a building. We should also try to save their stories, and to do so we should enlist those with the skills to record, save, and share these stories for future generations. This will allow former churches to continue to live well into the future.

The concept of "ReStory" provides the field with a framework that churches near closure can use to exercise legacy options, particularly in the case of repurposing, but also restarting or reallocating resources. Churches near closure can share their stories (past and present) in helping other churches through three critical questions: "What story are we telling ourselves now? What story did we live in the past? What story does God dream for our future?" The answers can help craft an important narrative to be shared within and between communities. This storytelling activity serves to increase ownership outcomes among church leaders and members (Youngman, 2022). Development of this church closure narrative, and capturing its unfolding, is discussed as part of the various stages of "dying" outlined in Chapter 4.

These stories or lessons can be seen through a spiritual frame and also understood using a community practice frame but with a different language, and we do not need a Rosetta Stone to aid in this translation. In the case of closed churches, we must learn the language used in religious circles (important religious terms, belief systems, tensions, and worldviews) to aid in communication—no small matter! This knowledge is rarely learned in any formal education for practice in this arena.

Churches as Targets and Vehicles for Social Activism

We often think of houses of worship starting and being associated with social justice campaigns, but the reverse is also true. Social change campaigns highlight the need for churches to save not only the spirit but also the body; sermons on social justice can be a call to action, opening the door for community practice from within. Church occupation, much like other "Occupy" campaigns, introduces a different dimension in making these institutions more responsive to community social justice concerns. Churches actively embracing social justice issues are better positioned to attract new members, particularly younger ones looking for this commitment from a church.

The Catholic Church, for example, can assume a national activist role aiding major groups that are part of its membership. Sharp (2021) discusses the social activist role that this Church played in Indianapolis, Indiana: The Church took on a high-profile advocacy role on behalf of the Latino community, leading to an increase in Latino membership. A church by and for the people gains the support of the people! Latino activist role on churches and their challenge to their power has not received the attention it calls for. If these churches close, they leave a critical void in the community, while sending a message to the broader religious community about their responsibility to parishioners and respective neighborhoods.

Church Buildings as Community Assets

Thomson and Pojani (2019, p. 1) conceptualize churches as community assets, which fits well with the central thrust of this book: "Today, churches are considered as assets in terms of their architecture and heritage values, as social and cultural institutions, and as community facilities." Churches can also be conceptualized as community anchors, and probably no more so than in communities of color struggling to meet basic human needs. Churches are probably the largest community structures, and these physical assets can be repurposed and mobilized in service to a community, opening the possibility of community practice projects being shaped by local needs.

Urban communities are dynamic entities, and so are their buildings in responding to changing times and local needs, not to mention the looming climate crisis. This is exciting and can have a cascading effect, drawing much-needed attention, resources, and hope for a community struggling to meet a range of current and future needs, particularly if local preferences for repurposing these new public spaces are taken into account. The new lives of former churches can be inspirational for their own and other communities and can serve as a shining model on a hill.

Current infrastructure initiatives offer great promise in generating local jobs, a benefit that is key in low-resource communities with high unemployment rates (Harvey & Bogle, 2023). Every $1 million spent on repurposing creates 5 to 9 more construction jobs and over 4.5 community jobs than the same amount of expenditure on new construction (Propmodo, 2021).

Locally spent funding translates into local investment with circulating dollars. If repurposing churches embraced local job creation, a property would become more significant and repurposing would become more widely embraced. This creates circulating money as one direct benefit, increasing ownership of the final building structure by locals. Community job creation causes seismic waves touching every sector, from small businesses to tax revenues. Further, and it is difficult to put a dollar figure on this, local residents who helped build this structure can rightly point to their contribution to the community.

Further, repurposing churches allows "greening" to be introduced in areas where it is in short supply or nonexistent, for example. This become even more important when communities are rapidly changing in terms of composition and newcomers have greening or gardening in their cultural heritage. Greenery improves the environment and the health of residents, as extensive research has shown, while fostering community engagement and pride, too.

My interest in church closings was sparked (Delgado, 2023) while writing *Urban Gun Violence: Empty Lots, Green Spaces, and Other Ecologically Focused Interventions*. One of the case illustrations used in that book (United Neighborhood Initiatives, Southwest Detroit) focused on All Saints Neighborhood Church, which closed but gave birth to a new community-centered organization embracing a social justice and community participatory agenda. All Saints Church has a history that parallels many of the church closures covered in this book, including how changing community demographics (in this case the introduction of large numbers of Latinos with high percentages of undocumented immigrants) and the broader social forces outlined in this book came together to cause this church's closure.

The former church building was converted to the All Saints Neighborhood Center. Churches often bring with them land that can accommodate parking and other needs. Eight vacant lots, in turn, were eventually transformed into the Springdale Green Play Lot. Further, and arguably more importantly, this church's closing gave birth to an organization with a built environment and social justice mission centered on youth of color and their families.

When congregations resist inevitable church closings, they need to be open to new purposes that will allow the building to continue functioning as a church by introducing innovative ways of using unneeded spaces, such as renting them out to community groups. These buildings/land are hyper-localized resources and represent opportunities for mobilizing communities to tap as newfound assets to meet current and future needs, but not without a price! We generally cannot expand the size of a neighborhood, but we can influence how that space is transformed and used.

When viewing churches as communities, we must strive to mobilize assets and opportunity points for positive change. Churches that are eventually successfully converted offer valuable lessons for urban centers. They create practical options and concurrently engage a range of academic and service professions to collaborate with. Collaborations are a noble but difficult goal to achieve, but we must still strive to undertake these types of initiatives, with communities as central partners.

Social work has largely ignored religion and church closings, with notable exceptions as in the case of dual-degree programs with religious schools. Urban planning, too, has largely overlooked this phenomenon, limiting its importance for this field to move forward in the future (Manouchehrifar & Forester, 2021): "Urban planners—whose disciplinary focus is the local, the spatial, and the practical—have been largely indifferent to the significance of religious difference in urban settings and seemingly unable to understand why religious diversity presents both problems *and* opportunities for the modern city." Urban planners and other practitioners must be prepared to play a key role in church repurposing with a new mission guiding its unfolding and requisite support to help ensure its eventual success.

In a *New York Times* article entitled "New Spirits Rise in Old, Repurposed Churches," Nierenberg (2020) chronicled outcomes for abandoned churches, illustrating their potential to meet a variety of local needs given the proper expertise and financing:

> These "different congregations" sometimes look *very* different from a house of worship. An Episcopal church in Denver founded in 1880 became a dance club called "The Church" (real original). In Troy, NY, a former Catholic church was bought by the Phi Sigma Kappa fraternity. The frat brothers made an agreement with the town when they bought it that they would keep it alcohol-free, but if they've done so, then they would be the first college fraternity to do so, well ever. Second Presbyterian Church of Newark, NJ, became the headquarters of Audible, a digital audiobook and podcast provider. While in San Francisco, a Christian Science Church founded in 1923 is now home for an archive of everything ever posted on the internet.

Local forces shape building outcomes regardless of where they are located in the country, but generalizations are difficult to make without grounding efforts locally, including the potential to attract a range of professions (Nierenberg, 2020).

There are other community-centered outcomes for abandoned structures, illustrating their flexibility and potential to meet a variety of local needs, and pointing to how urban community practitioners can assume a prominent role in their repurposing by helping communities envision alternatives to better meet local needs (Rockwood, 2017):

> For many neighborhood stakeholders, the best of both worlds means more than simply maintaining the look of these structures—it's about making sure conversion projects are enriching the community. In Baltimore, a US $8 million project is underway to convert a former Catholic church into a health center for low-income residents of the neighborhood. In Chicago, Illinois, Stas Development is turning St. Boniface Catholic Church into 15 residential condos. It partnered with the Chicago Academy of Music to reserve a handful of those units at affordable prices for students or guests of the academy. These projects may hold wide appeal. Closed churches need major physical repairs due to deferred maintenance and may be thought of as "money pits." This will need major infusion of funding, however.

Preparing practitioners is not solely the responsibility of institutions of higher learning. It must be shared across a wide spectrum, including governmental and nongovernmental institutions through the sponsoring of conferences, institutes, and workshops. Repurposing—and not just church repurposing—is an environmental strategy increasing in significance because of the saliency of the ecological movement and global warming.

Social interventions rest on key values and principles. The more transparent we are about the underpinnings of an intervention, the easier it is to explain our actions to ourselves and others—with church repurposing, communities and requisite authorities. Readers need clarity on why they undertake this type of work. Having this understanding helps us weather the inevitable trials and tribulations of urban community practice.

Although I tend to romanticize community practice, it is far from romantic. The hours are unpredictable, competing interests need to be reconciled, and it may not even follow a logical path—one step forward, two steps back. However, this practice is still enormously consequential, never more so than when we uplift voices that have long been ignored or silenced. This realization is never easy or painless but is still critical, particularly if we wish to learn from our mistakes and make our practice meaningful.

Repurposing, State Government, and Religious Attention

Multi-use development is an attractive outcome of repurposing houses of worship (Roach, 2023). Municipalities, for example, may wish to sponsor repurposing projects that combine tax-generating businesses alongside non-profit service providers. Who has not attended an activity at a house of worship that had nothing to do with its religious purpose? Churches often have unused spaces and are well situated to sponsor public community events. Closed churches lend themselves to projects using these spaces as theaters—for example, they can be rented to production companies as a revenue-generating stream (Anzani & Capitani, 2022).

Capitalistic elements can find a home within church spaces, although profits must not take priority in terms of event sponsorships. Church space is rarely 100% used daily during a typical week. Programming, such as renting out kitchens for micro-enterprises or sponsoring artistic studios and exhibitions tapping community talent, both supplies a revenue stream and increases the relevance of these spaces to non-church members.

The emerging popularity of repurposing as a field of practice, in turn, has led to the issuing of manuals/reports by a variety of governmental entities. Florida published *Eyesore to Asset: Building Housing Affordability + Sustainable Communities: A Guidebook for Adaptive Reuse of Vacant Retail*. The federal government (Fannie Mae, 2020, p. 4) published a report entitled *Eyesore to Asset: Building Housing Affordability + Sustainable Communities: A Guidebook for Adaptive Reuse of Vacant Property*, with the following as a guiding theme: "This guidebook suggests that local leaders can, and should, look to vacant or underutilized properties as a resource in catalyzing positive local momentum. These properties represent an opportunity for creative adaptive reuse for affordable and equitable housing that is physically and programmatically tied to on-site workforce development systems."

These governmental entities have taken note of repurposing as a force, which bodes well for this field because of the role they are expected to play in shaping initiatives. Other local and national foundations will hopefully follow suit, helping to further shape the church repurposing field within a wide variety of geographical contexts through funding special initiatives.

Catholic Church closures, too, have been subject of study. Mankowski's (2016) book *Catholic Parishes in Transition: Creating Viable Parishes Through Mergers, Closures and Collaborations* provides a multifaceted view of churches making the transition to new configurations; this journey resembles a grieving process much in line with this discussion throughout this book, with all of the requisite sensitivity and attention it warrants. A wholehearted commitment to transparency is vital throughout this journey to increase the chances of success; withholding information compounds an already-arduous process.

Key Competencies and Community Practice

Urban practice involves a fundamental embrace and understanding of the challenges that we will undoubtedly encounter. Values and knowledge are critical in community practice, and translating them into skills is the bottom line. Four competencies are highlighted here because of their central significance to church repurposing. Readers will bring their own set of competencies, too, and will not have trouble finding other frameworks better suited to their values and unique circumstances.

Enhance community competencies

A successful outcome for a repurposed church weighs heavily for urban practice, and particularly for its marginalized community residents. The magnitude of this undertaking brings potential long-lasting influence for the life of a community, placing a tremendous amount of pressure on practitioners to be successful. For many, this is the bottom line. For entities interested in economic impact, such as real estate developers, it makes enhancing competences not as attractive, however.

The journey is as important as the destination, because along the way residents are made more self-confident, knowledgeable, and competent. Having explicit or implicit objectives enhancing resident competencies pays prodigious benefits for all involved. This, however, may upset current political arrangements, particularly when the city government is playing an important role in these endeavors.

Finally, helping participants assess their competencies aids in future community undertakings—an inventory of skills before and after their participation will serve the community well. Initiatives, in turn, can be planned to further build on these newly acquired skills and knowledge for those wishing to continue future pursuits in this area of practice, eventually resulting in a critical mass of practitioners in the church repurposing arena.

Incorporating local culture into initiatives

On the surface, incorporating local culture may seem obvious from a practice standpoint, with few practitioners not publicly embracing this goal. However, a "cookie-cutter" approach is doomed to fail because no two church repurposing circumstances will be identical. Its importance, as a consequence, needs uplifting for specific attention. A Penn State Extension Service report (undated) addresses how local culture can shape initiatives:

> The culture of a community significantly shapes debate and action. Local culture also presents unique options for locally based economic and other development. Local understandings and interpretations of a community's history reflect past events that feed into, and are partially driven by the demands, sentiments, and interests of those in the present. This makes it crucial for community development practitioners to consider the importance of culture in efforts to improve local well-being. By paying attention to, and incorporating unique cultural values, traditions, and related factors, more efficient and effective development efforts can be achieved.

Culture is never static, because for it to remain practical it must respond to changing circumstances. Thus, understanding culture is easier said than done. Practitioners are never presented with a booklet identifying key community cultural values. Practitioners must be keenly aware of current cultural values as well as how they are dynamic, too, particularly among subgroups such as youth versus older adults, for example.

Community decision-making as central

Readers with extensive practice histories are well versed on how terms such as "community participation," "community input," and "community power" are used quite freely in discussing the importance of community engagement. It is critical that decision-making is not token but rather meaningful. "Genuine" community decision-making, unfortunately, is rare in our society.

These challenges must not dissuade us from focusing on the central feature of community practice—namely, that those who must ultimately live with the proposed changes must be instrumental in shaping outcomes. Communities must not only be at the table of decision-making but must also decide the seating arrangements, menu, guest list, and music! Practitioners can offer opinions, but the ultimate decision is made by the community, because they will be the ones living with the outcomes.

There are various conceptualizations of what this means. One popular approach consists of three developmental stages (Kahila, 2022):

Informative participation: Systematic efforts are made to inform the community of a project through various formal or informal channels.
Participatory and planning participation: Community members are formally incorporated through web-pages, local news sources, and updates at formal gatherings, for example.
Decision-making participation: This is the most consequential form of engagement, with members being the decision-making body of community groups with personal stakes in church repurposing, including youth—and not as "junior" members, but as full voting members.

The first two approaches allow local circumstances to dictate the most appropriate form of participation for each stage and the time and resources needed. Tensions and disagreements are to be expected and worked through, whether we are discussing a highly spiritual structure or a factory, for that matter.

Multifaceted interactive skills

Interactive skills are a critical glue in any intervention, covering the range from micro to macro. Having a range of these skills allows practitioners to enhance their position within a project. Hardcastle, Powers, and Wenocur (2011, p. 2) highlighted the importance of interactive skills in community practice: "Community practice calls for interactive, public information, collaboration, and interorganizational tasks such as networking, social marketing, and public information." Readers will have no difficulty in grasping the important role these interactive skills will play in brokering projects in other practice arenas.

Skills related to public speaking, collaboration, and conducting meetings, to highlight only three, are indispensable in navigating the worlds between residents, elected officials, and religious organizations, for example, and are key tools in the proverbial toolbox that practitioners bring to an assignment. Most of these skills, however, will not be learned through formal education, so in-the-field experiences must build on the knowledge and skills obtained through formal education. Further, these competences are by no means exhaustive or can guarantee success. Practitioners equipped with those covered in this section, however, are more likely to achieve success in repurposing churches.

Characteristics of Successful Community Practitioners

What characteristics mark a successful urban community practitioner? My rural community practice counterparts may see many parallels with this list. Context is important. I, for one, hate getting lost in a rural section of the country. The markers I rely on, without using Google Maps, for example, focus on street signs, building shapes and heights, level of foot traffic, and so forth. Those markers do not exist in rural America (but they have their own, of course).

I have colleagues who can tell me the time of day by looking at the sun; I get blinded looking at the sun! Urban sounds ground me and, probably most importantly, bring comfort; rural sounds frighten me. I cannot tell the difference between east and west, nor south and north! Readers, I am sure, get the drift of my argument. A match between the geographical context of practice and the comfort level of a practitioner increases the chances of projects achieving success because the practitioner is grounded.

Before addressing desirable community practitioner qualities, I want to point out the similarities between practitioners and religious leaders.

I cannot help but think of our discussion of a life-cycle view on church closures (see Chapter 4) in describing leadership roles. Church leaders bring different personal histories, strengths, and qualities, making them well suited for various stages in a congregation's life. One can even think of them as "religious community practitioners," because they, too, must assess and interact, taking into account goals and the forces helping or hindering them in the quest to achieve results. A congregation's birth requires a leader with a vision, competencies, and a magnetic personality with a vision that attracts members and motivates them to make the requisite commitments to become members. A maturing congregation requires a leader with competencies to keep a church open when the initial novelty and excitement are gone. At the end of a church's life, a leader is needed who can keep the remaining faithful attending, along with dealing with grief, facilitating the transfer of attendees to other churches, and planning for the orderly deposition of church property and eventual building closure.

Seven characteristics of community practitioners are covered in this section, setting a context for the rest of this book. These characteristics need to be viewed on a scale of 1 to 10 rather than from a simple "yes/no" standpoint. Further, personal characteristics interact with organizations and communities, and represent one dimension, with the remaining three dimensions: (1) personal characteristics, (2) ever-present, and (3) dynamic.

Feeling comfortable in our own skin

We must like who we are! It is impossible to like someone else if we cannot say that about ourselves. This quality may seem strange for some readers, but my hope is that upon closer examination, readers understand the intent of this quality.

Learning about others and their religious beliefs requires that we know our position on this subject. The more I learn about other people, the more I learn about myself. That, mind you, can be both good and bad. That journey is always a work in progress, so to speak. Church repurposing initiatives require us to confront our feelings about religion in our own lives, and we must be open to the beliefs of others and what their religious institutions mean to them. We must remember that trauma may be associated with religion and its institutions, as touched upon earlier in this book.

The quest for learning never stops

Once we are finished with our formal education, we must continue to learn and grow, and not necessarily from books, journals, or continuing education courses. I am fond of saying that the more I learn about a subject, the more I realize how little I know about it. That applies to church closures and repurposing! Discovery is a wonderful experience and must never stop. Community practice requires that we must continue to learn as we venture into new fields, as with church repurposing. This learning is not limited to classrooms but can also be acquired in community settings.

Optimism as a genuine world outlook

Believing tomorrow will be a better day is not just dreaming or a song theme. This outlook is contagious. Of course there will be bumps in the road and rainy days will enter into our practice, but the central disposition remains the same. We must have a fundamental belief that tomorrow will be better than today in a search for social justice. It is impossible to convey optimism if we are not optimistic and cannot inspire others to think in similar ways. Those whose practice involves repurposing churches should epitomize optimism about the future for these new structures and their missions to serve their communities.

A genuine like of people

I am sure readers have heard the phrase "people who like people." Community practice rests on our ability and willingness to connect with people in different settings and from different backgrounds, and we must welcome learning about others. However, there are many necessary behind-the-scenes tasks (research, for example) that do not require elevated levels of people contact.

A genuine like of people requires meeting them where they are—in houses of worship, in their homes, where they work, where they eat, and so forth—and not in a formal office. Very little of my consequential work has been done in the confines of an office; it was often achieved in homes, parks, streets, and the most unlikely of settings. It was not restricted to 9 a.m. to 5 p.m., Monday through Friday. Church repurposing, too, requires us to undertake this adventure without restrictions to circumstances. We must plow along, because the mission is too important.

Every day has a new lesson to share

Learning is a lifelong process and a great motivator to continue living. This stance means practitioners will be more knowledgeable tomorrow than today. Learning new knowledge or skills is empowering and essential in church repurposing. This growth can be manifested through experience, cognition, or even emotional maturity, meaning that a practitioner is growing and helping communities in the process. If we are not growing, then we are stagnating! That simply is never an option when discussing community practice.

Embrace the thrill of the adventure

Urban practice involving church closures and repurposing is new to many of us, and we may have minimal or no formal preparation for this area. The enthusiasm we bring to the task is contagious. I learned this lesson early in my career as I ventured into unchartered territory in the practice field, pushing the proverbial envelope in the process. Yes, it can cause anxiety. However, it also brings the thrill of a new experience.

How can we expect a community to be enthusiastic about a venture if we are not? Many of the people involved in this undertaking, too, are new to this field. Acknowledging the potential rewards and challenges of these ventures helps create confidence in the journey, including unanticipated twists and turns. Being able to share these lessons with others, too, is rewarding, since we are all part of the journey together, casting us into teacher/mentor roles.

Ability to bounce back from failure (resiliency)

I prefer to learn from success rather than failure, and I guess that is human nature. However, I have learned more from my failures, I must confess. These experiences stay for a lifetime, too! Weathering setbacks and learning from them is essential in community practice. Practice is never about success followed by success and so on. Community practice is broad, constantly testing our abilities to problem-solve situations that we were totally unprepared for regardless of how well we planned.

One or two of the above items may resonate for readers. As practitioners, however, we need to think about how we personally relate to our work. Work has a prominent place within our identities, and not just in community practice. Venturing into the church repurposing field will test us in predictable and unpredictable ways, and that brings excitement about the future for this arena of practice.

Importance of Participatory Approaches

The importance of participatory approaches is self-evident. We will uplift this value relatively early in this book and will address it throughout. Engagement of community residents in projects can go by many different names, with "civic engagement" receiving wide recognition across different fields of practice (Mohr Carney et al., 2023).

Viola and Diano (2019) advocate for the value of a participatory approach to practice: "A bottom-up, community-driven perspective increasingly connotes the design approaches. Knowledge-intensive, based on the perceived identity and collective creativity, the community-centred vision aims at extending the life cycle, driving built settlements' transition towards prosperity." Dukelow and Murphy (2022, p. 517), in turn, challenge the field to embrace a democratic process in ecosocial projects:

> Such research must reach beyond academic circles as part of a transformative politics. An ecosocial welfare architecture must also be informed by active citizenship, and participative and deliberative democratic processes that inform, educate and give voice to different public interests, complementing representative democratic processes and mediating the inevitable political conflict in bringing to life an ecosocial post-growth world.

Participatory democracy is a theme because religious/spiritual outlets are central to the well-being of countless people of all ages. Reopening in a new configuration ensures a church's continued life, but in a different form—reincarnation if you wish.

Potential Community Practice Roles and Church Repurposing

What can community practitioners do to address the immediate and long-term consequences of church closings? The answer is a great deal, I am happy to declare! The following are seven examples of roles they can play, covering a range of interests, knowledge areas, competencies, and goals, which should not be surprising to both the uninitiated and those actively engaged in this work (Reinhard, 2022a,b):

1. **Know your houses of worship.** It is never too early to develop an inventory of church properties in your neighborhood. This inventory must be comprehensive, covering large and storefront churches, including the identities of religious leaders and their contact information. A comprehensive understanding of their worshippers is also in order so that you can assess their motivations for attending and the concerns they may have about continuing to do so. This will require reaching out to and developing relationships with clergy and lay leaders, particularly in key locations. Creating this inventory will be labor-intensive, but once developed, it will become easier to update.
2. **Create strategies on zoning, codes, and taxes that encourage, rather than prevent, houses of worship to become dense, mixed-use developments.** A knowledge base and skillset helps mixed-use church repurposing to meet a range of community needs by introducing flexibility as to which projects are needed. This knowledge is highly specialized and cannot be easily obtained through formal schooling. You will need to reach out across the state and country to learn about the latest advances in the repurposing field.
3. **Establish and demonstrate a willingness to aid small, but growing, houses of worship.** This recommendation can be controversial and shaped by local social and political circumstances. Churches serving parishioners of color and immigrants take on greater importance from a social justice standpoint, which means they represent community segments needing extra attention. These churches can be valuable conduits for health and social service programs. Local government can help these efforts, bringing in needed ability for addressing local concerns.
4. **Develop access to a capital resource library that is specific to the adaptive reuse needs of a religious building.** Knowledge is power,

including knowledge about various forms of housing (affordable, low-income, or senior housing, for example) and how religious organizations can conduct their mission by transferring property. Making necessary resources more easily available through a local library or online enhances the potential success of this field by democratizing knowledge.

5. **Help enterprises providing human services to find a new location.** Churches often offer a range of social and support services/subsidies to the community (an average of $150,000 per church every year). When the church closes, these services may be at risk as well if they cannot find suitable new spaces (physical, logistical, and psychological). Finding the "right" location (one perceived as safe and non-stigmatizing) takes on great significance for those currenting receiving these services.

6. **Work on each house of worship reuse project individually, but also keep the door open for holistic collaboration and coordination.** Church closings can occur in groupings, bringing shared forces, concerns, and opportunities. Political will associated with a crisis can be created if the forces are understood and appropriately addressed. Brokering coalitions can lead to using existing resources and sharing spaces. Mind you, sharing space can extend beyond conventional boundaries, as in the case of a Montreal Anglican church that shares space with a nonprofit circus company (http://stjax.org/en/home), a refugee advocacy organization, and other entities, allowing local circumstances to dictate tenants.

7. **Serve as facilitators between and among houses of worship and developers.** Effective facilitators are worth their weight in gold because of their extraordinary talents. A broker role leads to efficient use of time and resources and minimizes turf concerns, decreasing the risk of strained relationships after a decision is made. This skill requires legitimacy across all parties to be effective. There is ample scholarly literature on gentrification and how it dramatically changes communities, including interpretations of its value. There is no disputing that it is a major secularizing force in neighborhoods, speeding the forces that displace population groups, including churchgoers and, chances are good, also long-term residents.

These roles are multifaceted, requiring a range of analytical and interactional skills to stem church closure consequences, as well as significant "buy-in" rom all major interested parties. No practitioner has all of these skills, so a cadre of staff will be needed that can cross conventional boundaries and engage with wide audiences, bringing flexibility for engaging experts as needed.

We must first show that repurposing churches is a "legitimate" form of practice or specialty and is important for communities and society. Putting a spotlight on the multiple roles these projects can play in a community will attract future practitioners and scholars, including research funding to document the process and outcomes. Popular media and local news coverage can move this field forward by informing residents of plans for these buildings. This attention will attract new funders for initiatives centered on community well-being goals.

All practitioners have their favorite intervention phase but must also engage in other phases, because we rarely have the luxury to specialize. I favor assessment (assets and needs) as a foundation for an intervention; to guide this phase, I try to discover what a community's assets are rather than asking whether there are any assets. I enjoy wrestling with the ambiguity and challenges of this phase, including enlisting local support. Other practitioners may prefer searching for funding sources and writing proposals, for example. We cannot be a "one that is skilled in one area" to be successful in bringing projects to fruition by mastering all of the phases.

Chapter 2 offered a conceptual and historical foundation and a unifying set of values for achieving transformative outcomes in communities with vacant church buildings. Further, we've provided readers with guiding principles that can help to bridge differences between professions. Church repurposing brings rewards and challenges for educating and supporting practitioners and the general public.

Pushing practice boundaries is a perennial goal. We can create new interventions and challenge conventional views by repurposing closed churches, facilitating small business development, fostering local festivals and parades, and converting vacant lots, for example. Expanding the world of community practice means being open to critiques, facing challenges, and being willing to embrace innovative ideas and theories—pushing the envelope! Pushback is to be welcomed, causing us to question ourselves, too!

Campbell, Svendsen, Johnson, and Landau (2022, p. 713) discuss creating urban stewardship groups (claims-making on space and caretaking of place), with implications for church repurposing: "Stewardship groups both marshal and redirect material flows as well as transmit knowledge, beliefs, and practices through social networks, and are thereby able to impact social infrastructure locally and at-a-distance via these networks." Readers can appreciate these groups when they are representative of community's stakeholders.

Conclusion

There is no debate about the potential of community practice for bringing together a team of professionals and community residents in pursuit of a common goal: repurposing urban churches. The vastness of this field allows it to embrace a multitude of important concepts in creating repurposing projects of various kinds. The latest urban community practice view, for example, has the potential to bring together the built environmental field with urban church repurposing, continuing the expansion of this field into new areas of practice.

The position we occupy—be it in City Hall, a nonprofit, or even a university, for instance—offers a vantage point from which we can make contributions to communities. The qualities outlined in this chapter can be tested as we embrace the transformative power of urban church repurposing. Readers understand the significance of urban church closings and their repurposing. Knowledge must be converted into action, with and on behalf of marginalized communities, with church repurposing as a brave new frontier.

3
Boston Case Illustration
The Blessed Sacrament Church

Introduction

At this point in the book, readers will be better able to appreciate a more detailed case illustration, highlighting various dimensions and concretizing key themes raised earlier in this book. This case illustration, in turn, will set the stage for better understanding and appreciating the multifaceted aspects of church repurposing that we will cover in the forthcoming chapters.

Case studies and illustrations help bring abstract concepts to life in a manner that is more easily grasped, allowing readers to apply key concepts to a real-life situation. A good case illustration supplies concrete examples in a narrative and more digestible form to enhance readability, allowing readers to absorb key points or lessons learned and making it more likely that they will be carried out in practice, which is the bottom line in a practice-oriented book. A case illustration, it is important to clarify, does not have the depth of detail (qualitative and quantitative) of a case study. Nevertheless, it supplies sufficient details to allow a detailed picture to appear. Lengthy case studies can provide a wealth of details and analysis, but limited page space does not allow their use, particularly when looking to paint a national perspective.

Church repurposing involves many nuances that cannot be captured in a single case study. Case illustrations of successes and challenges help to bring abstract concepts to life, including highly nuanced points. Case illustrations can help readers develop a deeper appreciation of nuances under different circumstances. Shorter case illustrations, or snapshots, have been interspersed throughout the book. However, the Boston illustration that follows offers greater details than these other cases while tying together themes from the literature.

Further, a case illustration that is based upon a well-known city or community allows readers to bring their prior knowledge of the site to their appreciation of the key points raised in an illustration. I believe readers will enjoy this particular case illustration because the repurposing of the Blessed Sacrament Church in the Jamaica Plain section of Boston was undertaken by an urban practitioner (a social worker, in this case), and the project is still active as this book goes to press and will not be completed for several years after it is published. Thus, readers with a particular interest in this repurposing project can follow along to see its ultimate outcome, including detours along the way.

In the interest of transparency, the fact that I am based in Boston and have an historical relationship with the Hyde Square Task Force (HSTF) and Dr. Celina Miranda (Executive Director) as a colleague facilitated access, making this project a natural for inclusion in this book. This organization was a subject of another book (Delgado & Staples, 2008), another factor that made this selection easy. I usually avoid using Boston for case illustrations in my writings because I look to bring attention to other parts of the country, increasing the national relevance of a publication. However, the HSTF's church repurposing initiative made it an ideal illustration, particularly since it sought to accomplish a range of goals integral to community practice, along with the fact that there was extensive documentation through reports and media coverage of this initiative.

This Boston illustration captures the breadth, depth, and potential of this field, providing examples of how local conditions have a tremendous influence on the success of a project. Church repurposing has huge potential for achieving good results, but if done improperly, harm can come to urban communities of color. The Boston case highlights key analytical (theoretical) and interactional (political) considerations that increase the likelihood of achieving repurposing success and will provide readers with insights into this process.

Brief Historical Overview

Boston's history is similar to that of other older East Coast cities, such as New York City and Philadelphia. Its role in American history is well secured, and the city is often credited with playing an instrumental role in the American Revolution and the birth of the nation. However, using a racial and ethnic lens brings with it a different view of this city's history, helping us understand the role of religion, and more specifically the Catholic Church, in shaping its character, and thus explaining the significance of church closures and the repurposing that happens once their doors close.

Boston's first Catholic parish was established in 1789, taking its place in American history in the year that the Constitution was adopted. The Diocese of Boston was established in 1808, and its first bishop, Father Jean Cheverus, was a refugee from the French Revolution and was appointed by Pope Pius VII. Bishop Cheverus is credited with making the church more welcoming to Europeans. By 1850, the Irish were the largest ethnic group in Boston and remain so today. It is important for readers to understand that Boston's archbishop has historically wielded unprecedented power compared to those in other cities (Columbia University, undated):

> Boston's archbishop presided over an extensive network of parishes, schools, seminaries, convents, and hospitals. The job title alone conferred significant power, and for most of the 20th century, Boston's larger-than-life archbishops had expanded the scope of the office to wield power well beyond the church, and well beyond Boston. "The Boston Archdiocese is a uniquely American Catholic institution," wrote a Minneapolis newspaper when the head of the archdiocese there was under consideration for the Boston job. "It is to the church what the New York Yankees are to baseball, Carnegie Hall to music, Broadway to theater."

The political power and prestige of the Boston Catholic Church provides an important backdrop for the repurposing of the Blessed Sacrament Church. As consistently addressed throughout this book, politics and religion go hand-in-hand—no more so than in Boston.

The Boston Catholic Church is no stranger to protests. For instance, in 2004, almost 25% of the city's Catholic churches were slated to be closed (Reynolds, 2023b), impacting an estimated 28,000 parishioners. Community protests managed to avert the closure of St. Mary of the Angels, "a small, eclectic, basement-level church" in a Black and Latino neighborhood in Roxbury. This historical memory set the stage for long-time residents to engage in social activism.

As an aside, the Catholic Church initially was confronted with paying an $85 million settlement to survivors of the sexual abuse scandal that rocked the Boston Catholic community and soon spread across the country and internationally. By 2007, the amount had increased to $615 million. A "perfect storm" materialized, with three forces converging for the Archdiocese: legal fees, payouts to victims, and fewer parishioners and decreases in offerings.

Cardinal Patrick O'Malley strongly denied that the parish reconfiguration plan was related to the abuse crisis and stated that no proceeds from the sales of parish property would fund this settlement. Even so, the settlement was seen as compounding the closings, and the Church was perceived as "closing ranks" against the abused and parishioners (Seltz, 2011), causing great consternation among congregations.

Boston Demographic Profile Overview

According to the 2020 U.S. Census, Boston is a "minority-majority" city. It is 44.0% White, non-Latino, 23.5% Black/African-American, 19.8% Latino, and 9.70% Asian, with 3.00% other. Boston has a long history of segregated neighborhoods, often with clearly drawn lines; for instance, the Jamaica Plain neighborhood that is home to the Blessed Sacrament Church is currently heavily Latino and is experiencing gentrification. This history of segregation drew national attention with the busing of students and the acrimony it engendered in the 1970s.

It is impossible to separate Boston and the Catholic Church from the history of the Irish and Italian immigrants to this city and country. These two groups brought with them a lengthy historical grounding in Catholicism. Demographic trends will show similar experiences across the country in which Catholic churches have been closed or multiple parishes have been merged. These actions invariably disenfranchised groups of color in the process, further worsening tensions related to church closures.

Religious Beliefs and Church Attendance

Massachusetts is at the forefront of the national decline in church attendance, tied with New Hampshire. Boston is no exception to the rapid and significant national decline in Catholic membership: In 2007 it stood at 44% and by 2017 it had declined to 32%, a drop of 31.9%. Decreases in church attendance have been felt throughout the Boston area, largely led by "Nones" (those not affiliated with any religion). Thirty-two percent of Massachusetts residents identified themselves as Nones.[1] Among first-generation immigrants, 10%

---

[1] Readers interested in a detailed report on Boston's "Nones" should read the PEW Research report *Adults in the Boston Metro Area Who Are Unaffiliated (Religious Nones)* at https://www.pewr

were Nones; in second-generation immigrants, 21% were Nones; and in third-generation and later immigrants, the figure was 69%.

Blessed Sacrament Church Closure

The Blessed Sacrament Church is considered one of New England's finest examples of Italian Renaissance Revival church architecture and is an imposing structure in the neighborhood, standing tall and dominating the vista (Figure 3.1). Its soaring dome (10 stories high) served as a symbol of Jamaica Plain's Hyde Square neighborhood. Construction started in 1890 and was completed in 1917 at a cost of $115,000. The church had seating for 1,200, and it included 15 stained-glass windows. The church was part of a compound of buildings catering to different constituencies: Two buildings housed priests and nuns, and two other buildings were middle and high school schools. The compound originally covered 3.2 acres, a considerable parcel of land in a highly congested urban neighborhood. The church was originally built to meet the needs of Boston's growing German and Irish population. However, by the 1980s and 1990s, it accommodated the neighborhood's burgeoning Latino population.

As shown in Figure 3.2, the church's outdoor space served as a staging area for summer performances, allowing residents to attend and local talent to perform. Such a space is especially important in high-density communities where there are few outdoor venues for community gatherings.

In 2004, the Archdiocese of Boston closed the Blessed Sacrament Church in an effort to combine Catholic parishes throughout Boston due to dwindling attendance. Further closings or mergers of Boston Catholic churches followed. In 2012, the archdiocese approved a plan to merge 288 parishes into 135, a reduction of over 50%, matching similar efforts across the country. The closings and mergers resulted from the continued dramatic decline in membership, a projected priest shortage, and financial challenges that left 4 in 10 parishes unable to pay their bills. The ramifications of these closures and mergers were extensive and caused an adverse political reaction, which was only to be expected when decisions are imposed on communities without their involvement in decision-making.

---

esearch.org/religion/religious-landscape-study/religious-tradition/unaffiliated-religious-nones/metro-area/boston-metro-area/.

BOSTON CASE ILLUSTRATION   83

Figure 3.1 Blessed Sacrament Church, front of church. (Photographer: Greg Cranna)

Figure 3.2 Blessed Sacrament Church, outdoor performance. (Photographer: Mark Saperstein)

Since it was shuttered in 2004, the Blessed Sacrament Church has had several owners. Well-intentioned nonprofits tried to redevelop it, but with limited success. The church was initially slated to be converted into luxury condominiums, but this effort met with significant community opposition (Boston's Jamaica Plain Section Hyde Square Task Force, 2020). The nonprofit Jamaica Plain Neighborhood Development Corporation (JPNDC) and New Atlantic Development bought Blessed Sacrament's three-acre campus from the archdiocese in 2005 and built around the church itself, including a mix of luxury and affordable housing and what is now the headquarters of the HSTF (Bay State Banner, 2020). This campus has seen redevelopment over the years; for example, the rectory building was moved and converted into condos. The convent eventually became housing, and one of the schools was converted into 21 housing units. The HSTF is housed in the Cheverus building. Figures 3.3 and 3.4 show that despite some deterioration, the church had retained part of its majesty but also represented a vacant building waiting for a new purpose. Readers, I am sure, can use their imagination to see its potential for housing, a performance stage, and other uses that could benefit the community.

The Boston archdiocese made three stipulations for the property: (1) a school could not be built on the site (there was speculation was that it did not

Figure 3.3 Blessed Sacrament Church, broad view of internal deterioration. (Photographer: Joni Lohr)

Figure 3.4 Blessed Sacrament Church, focused view of internal deterioration. (Photographer: Joni Lohr)

want competition for its own schools); (2) abortions could not be performed on the premises, limiting the types of healthcare organizations that could occupy the space; and (3) no other denomination would be welcomed. Also, the unique architecture of historical churches limits the options for repurposing; in the case of the Blessed Sacrament Church, the limited window openings made it challenging to convert to housing or commercial uses.

Boston's church conversions are best understood and appreciated within the broader Boston real estate scene (Sader & Maldonado-Estrada, 2021):

> The story of church conversion in Boston mirrors the way our city has changed over the last 30 years—the gentrification of neighborhoods, the dwindling rates of church attendance, the reckoning with widespread sexual abuse in the Catholic Church, the skyrocketing rent, construction, and housing costs. As more churches come on the market, and many are slated to become luxury condos, it is important to understand the options for and restrictions on repurposing and preserving these beautiful and historic but often prohibitively expensive-to-maintain buildings.

In 2014 the HSTF purchased the property from the JPNDC for $880,000, with the goal of turning the church into a community and arts center. This, however, required carrying $500,000 in debt. The costs and expenses for the building totaled $100,000 annually, a considerable onus for a nonprofit, particularly when viewed from a long-term perspective. (The HSTF's annual budget is approximately $3 million, making it a medium-sized nonprofit organization.)

When the church had been closed in 2004, the stained windows, pews, and all remaining items had been removed; essentially, the church was left empty.[2] Deferred maintenance also meant that a considerable infusion of funds was needed to keep the church from further deterioration while its final fate was being decided.

The HSTF board considered three practical options: (1) renovate the church, which could cost millions of dollars when all was said and done; (2) demolish the church and build a new facility, which would also cost millions; or (3) sell the property. The HSTF board voted to sell the building to an entity they could work with to carry out a set of social goals and repurpose the structure. In the wake of the COVID-19 pandemic's impact, much like countless other nonprofit organizations in Boston and across the country, HSTF faced a series of unprecedented financial and organizational challenges.

HSTF eventually selected Pennrose, a Philadelphia real estate development company established in 1971, as its partner because of its past experiences and its stated goal of "profoundly impacting the lives of working families through the development of affordable housing." Pennrose, although it was a national organization, also had local representation and extensive experience with affordable housing projects, a key factor because of the HSTF and local Jamaica Plain goals. A neighborhood 200-person performance space and capital support to help pay off the HSTF's property debt on the church, and consideration in the naming of the new building, sold this development firm on the project.

Eventually, there was a consensus that the church would house 55 new mixed-income housing units, with over 50% being set aside for affordable housing (20 units at 120% of average median income, 16 at 60%, 8 at 50%, and 8 at 30%). The eligibility standard is much better than Boston's minimum standard, which calls for 13% of new units to be affordable. However, community activists worried that the definition of "affordable" was too high, at 60% of the Boston-area median income.

---

[2] It is important to note that before a Catholic Church is closed and sold, items of particular significance, such as the tabernacle, the vessel holding the consecrated Eucharist, alter, relics, art, and bells, are removed (Fazio, 2019).

Almost 15 months passed before significant movement toward converting this church happened, illustrating the slow pace of decision-making (Woodard, 2022, p. 8):

> But the aging church remained untouched. Its owners proposed to convert the property into luxury condos, but affordable housing advocates objected. In 2014, the Hyde Square Task Force purchased the site for $880,000. The nonprofit had ambitious plans to transform the parish into a state-of-the-art performing arts center. But weather and time took their toll on the old church, and project costs kept climbing. Moreover, the task force was carrying an approximate $700,000 mortgage on the property. Then last year, the nonprofit sought proposals for the property, hoping to find a redevelopment partner. "Hyde Square Task Force is very good at youth and community development," said Mark Saperstein, the nonprofit's board president. "But development is not our expertise."

Development expertise is often in short supply in repurposing projects, and this needs to be remedied by equipping community practitioners with the requisite knowledge and skills. This will involve formal education in the nation's colleges and universities, and in the field through workshops and conferences.

The repurposing project involved an estimated building area of 63,235 square feet, which when developed would become a multipurpose/performance space (6,475 square feet operated by HSTF) and 55 residential units (56,764 square feet) plus management, maintenance, and community spaces to be operated by Pennrose.

It is easy to get lost in the myriad of details of this Boston case illustration, but it's important to remember that church repurposing is not just a cultural or social phenomenon: It is also political and economic in nature. Repurposing, particularly in the case of mixed-use projects, and even more so when including housing, is quite complex and consequential, requiring a broad discussion and inclusion of a variety of expertise. For example, I had no exposure to the field of financing in my formal education, and that is a very specialized skill that practitioners must either own or have access to if they are to be successful. Repurposing is a team effort on both sides of the negotiation, even more so when we actively want community input and decision-making in this process.

This compromise represented a long journey with community input and countless deliberations and political compromises along the way, which is typical of successful repurposing efforts. In 2023, Blessed Sacrament was designated a Boston landmark. The conversion was well documented and covered by both print and television media, and reflected the organization's active mission to seek community input, which resulted in both concerns and praise. Other urban centers across the country pursuing these types of repurposing initiatives can learn from this illustration.

Lessons Learned for the Field of Urban Community Practice

Lechtchiner's (2023) study of Boston's affordable-housing development through the use of church repurposing, which focused on the Blessed Sacrament Church and the St. Katharine Drexel parish in Roxbury, found that repurposing had different outcomes and involved different forms of coalitions. The former involved a cross-section of advocates and residents; the latter entailed a partnership between church leadership and the Planning Office for Urban Affairs, the affordable-housing developer of the Archdiocese of Boston. Demographics, too, were different: The Blessed Sacrament Church had a heavily Latino population and the St. Katharine Drexel parish had a heavily Black population.

The former did not seek collaboration with the City of Boston for the Catholic Church; the latter did. Both projects involved actors with differing motivations. In the case of St. Katherine Drexel Parish, the Catholic Church looked to maximize its economic benefits; the Blessed Sacrament Church developers, in contrast, sought maximum participation and a multifaceted use of the property. Mind you, one is not "better" than the other; they simply reflect different properties based on local needs.

Eight lessons stand out with the Boston repurposing effort that aid the field of urban community practice. Readers may identify other lessons with particular relevance to their local situation. These lessons are not listed in any particular order of significance, and readers can rank order them according to their own circumstances.

The more ambitious the project, the more time, money, and expertise will be needed, which may not be in house

The HSTF project spanned over 10 years, involved considerable sums of money and countless meetings, and required an ability to continue to conduct a mission while also juggling a massive project. This is in addition to meeting the challenges faced by any community-based organization with a social justice focus. The organization was pushed to the brink.

Organizations pursuing capital-intensive repurposing projects will need ready and trusted access to highly specialized input and skill sets. For instance, technical expertise, such as the knowledge needed to obtain an historical designation for a building (thus preventing it from being demolished), is a skill that few community practitioners obtain in their formal schooling. Boston had the resources locally to assist in this endeavor, but other cities may not be so fortunate.

Closed churches cannot be easily or cheaply repurposed into new structures

Because of the physical dimensions of the Blessed Sacrament Church, repurposing had to be multifaceted rather than having just a single purpose (housing, for example). The size of the structure, including the land, introduces multiple options for a project. Having multiple options for repurposing a church brings both advantages and disadvantages for an organization and community practitioners. For instance, it allows for multiple audiences to weigh in on how repurposing can best meet their needs. A building with a multifaceted capacity involves greater challenges than one with just a single purpose. Having multiple options means that multiple pressure groups will be looking to influence the project. Again, this is exciting because it will attract many groups advocating for their interests. Nevertheless, the costs, time demands, and finding the right development partner all factor into the final decisions on the future of a former church building.

Multipurpose church repurposing involves being able to negotiate with varied interest groups

Reaching different audiences, such as different age groups, requires dealing with various subgroups, with their specific interests guiding negotiations. For instance, older adult activities must be weighed against youth activities, and older adults may have access considerations that are not relevant with younger groups. Communities consist of different age groups, and one is not more important than the other. Likewise, people interested in housing might not have the same interests as parents seeking children's educational or recreational outlets.

Negotiating with these groups requires staff with various competencies, and few nonprofits have this range of expertise in house. Brokering competing interests is to be expected. Nevertheless, the process is as important as the outcome. The former must be explicitly articulated to facilitate input and decision-making.

Repurposing based on the past

Honoring and respecting the past while establishing a foundation for the future is a goal of most church repurposing projects that are community-centered. Maintaining a physical space and a place for future generations that builds on the history and legacy of a church carries symbolic and practical ramifications for repurposing projects. For instance, a church repurposing initiative that covers a period of years (which is often the case) opens the door for an increased number of interest groups to share their opinions, particularly those who weighed in during the early periods of organizing to save the church for the community.

Simply put, there are no shortcuts to seeking input and obtaining community buy-in to a repurposing project, particularly one with such symbolic meaning. Seeking community input and ownership is a theme in this book that is well illustrated by this case example. Any reader with a construction background will attest to how building projects seem to have a life of their own, and I am not even making reference to weather! Repurposing a church can easily become a major project for practitioners and their organizations, competing for the time and attention with other projects. It is not a sprint; it is a marathon—and readers do not have to be runners to know the difference between these two races.

Time is an enemy of repurposing

The costs of a repurposing project will increase the longer the church remains idle, not to mention the increased likelihood of vandalism, further compromising the project. These increased costs are not just related to inflation; they will also vary based on the deteriorating physical conditions of a building subject to the elements. The quicker a project comes to fruition, the less expensive it is. However, if community participation is sought, repurposing will definitely not be an expedited project.

Church repurposing involves a different definition of time for community practitioners. Patience was a virtue in the case of the Blessed Sacrament Church project. The Boston example is a rarity because the project leader's tenure has spanned over a decade. This has allowed HSTF to have a stable leader who could stay focused on the repurposing project. Staff turnover, including leadership, is not uncommon in our field. Although a natural occurrence, it nevertheless interferes with continuity of focus, which is essential because there are so many moving parts.

Municipal support is essential

Municipal government, as we will argue in Chapter 4, can help or hinder a church repurposing project. The first stages of this repurposing process did not benefit from municipal support, with leadership sitting on the sidelines. However, when city leadership changed—specifically when Mayor Michelle Wu was elected—technical and financial support was forthcoming and proved invaluable in moving the process forward promptly.

The moment municipal government is enlisted in a repurposing project, both analytical qualities (theory) and interactional skills (political) are needed. A change of mayors—in this case of woman of color (Asian) replaced a White, non-Latino male (Irish-Catholic)—proved helpful to the organization and its leader (Latina) and helped to break down potential barriers. In Boston, racial dynamics cannot be ignored in a repurposing project, least of all one involving a former Catholic church.

All views are welcomed

On a final note, according to Dr. Miranda, church repurposing is challenging:

> I think it's important for readers to understand that the repurposing of churches is complex, especially when the group redeveloping the property is trying to meet the needs of multiple stakeholders. The Church has been referred to as the "jewel" of the neighborhood, so any project that

came to the building needed to be one that resonated with the interests of the community and that it did not feel like another win for the forces of gentrification.

Thus, a key lesson in this Boston illustration was the importance of seeking community and stakeholder buy-in, which required careful planning so that major constituencies had an opportunity to weigh in on major decisions, as well as sufficient time for a consensus to emerge. A church with a long history draws its share of people who are attached to the structure, each segment bringing distinctive and important experiences and opinions.

When repurposing decisions are extended over time, the door is open for input from participants throughout this entire period. Early newcomer parishioners, for example, remembered the significance of having a Catholic church where they were able to worship in Spanish. Balancing distinctive views was challenging because of the Church connected distinct repurposing opinions. The HSTF recognized the importance of this history and planned to collect these stories and share them with the general public. The nature of this project has not yet been decided as this book goes to press, but it's important to remember that the repurposed church belongs to multiple generations.

Expertise when needed

Expertise in many fields is essential in church repurposing projects because of the unique challenges they present. Readers may ask: "Isn't that always the case?" The answer is "yes." The economics of church repurposing is complicated, and few practitioners have this training, complicating decision-making when finances wield such importance. Ready access to this expertise at the local level, if available, is vital, along with an understanding of the broader regional and national scene. Without this, the organization will face incredible challenges crafting immediate and long-term solutions.

Thus, organizations should have access to a range of expertise they normally would not require to carry out their operations. For example, it is not easy to bridge the worlds of human services and construction within an organization. This requires venturing into other "worlds" and having the necessary language to ask for very specialized help. Establishing internships with local schools of social work, urban planning, and architecture, for example, can help organizations with needed tasks while also serving as a way to create a cadre of future repurposing practitioners.

Conclusion

This Boston case illustration highlighted what happens when the dreams of achieving a social good come into a contact with the reality of day-to-day life in a community fighting against gentrification, within a city also struggling to provide housing and services to its population, and one with a checkered history of racial dynamics brought to life through the busing crisis of the 1970s. I would have loved undertaking a case study rather than an illustration, but time and space were serious considerations.

Repurposing a church requires patience, foresight, thick skin, the ability to forgive, fortitude, vision, intelligence, and a deep and unwavering commitment to a social justice vision—saint-like qualities, if you ask me! The HSTF experience described here illustrates the complex process of converting an historical Catholic church and the current-day social forces operating that are shaping its future as a new entity. The Blessed Sacrament Church story is evolving as this book goes to press. It remains to be seen what further twists and turns this project will take.

4
Social Forces Shaping Church Closing Trends

Introduction

We must have a comprehensive grasp of urban church closings before embarking on repurposing interventions, as illustrated in the previous chapter. We need an in-depth knowledge foundation and concrete examples of these special buildings because of their complexities and symbolism in society. Capturing the extent of destruction of a moving tornado is certainly challenging, but that is what this book is trying to achieve. Grasping this urban environmental movement cannot be done in isolation from other ecological facets of the topic operative within and outside the United States, or from just a Snapchat moment in time.

Exceptional readers will rejoice in reading statistics; I, however, do not fall into that group. Nevertheless, I have a strong respect for statistics when backed by qualitative data to give them meaning and requisite grounding. This chapter provides a plethora of data on a major movement in this country gathering strength and refusing to pause to allow us to understand its significance, much like an active tornado. Readers are warned that putting together these data is similar to putting together a puzzle consisting of several hundred pieces with a not-too-detailed picture!

Unfortunately, I could not find a national database of properties owned by religious groups. This is consequential in a nation as big and diverse as the United States. Consequently, comprehensively determining the extent and distribution of vacant churches is impossible from a national perspective. Creating and maintaining such a dataset would be a terrific endeavor for a national foundation to undertake while serving a leadership role in this emerging field.

Readers wanting a glimpse of what an abandoned church looks like after many years of neglect can see the example of Detroit's St. Agnes Catholic Church and School (https://www.onlyinyourstate.com/michigan/detroit/abandoned-church-detroit/), which should satisfy their curiosity. These photos capture the church's grandeur and the devastation of the ravages of time, including vandalism, although nothing can replace the in-person experience. Conversely, readers wishing a visual display of repurposed churches should read and view the photographs in Fedderly's (2019) *Architectural Digest* article, "A Wealth of Historic Churches in New Orleans Have Been Beautifully Repurposed."

This chapter offers a multifaceted view of church closure trends and the major social forces shaping them, signifying its broad national reach and implications for congregations and their respective communities. Readers interested in Black and Latino church closures will find these covered in the following two chapters in greater specificity, although attention is paid to these institutions in this chapter. Church closures reshape major segments of the religious community and cities in the process. They leave remnants of a bygone era when religion reigned supreme and its buildings served as testimony of their power and influence locally and nationally, as in the case of the civil rights movement, for instance.

We cannot read this chapter, regardless of religious beliefs, and be untouched by the fundamental changes occurring to religion and worship—and I am not just referring to worshipping online, largely the result of the COVID-19 pandemic. Disengagement from religiosity is a particularly salient force, with implications for undermining society's social fabric and drawing the attention of multiple audiences—religious and non-religious, local government, lay, and academic, for example.

Another example is the rise of Christian nationalism, which, it pains me to say, has found a foothold among Latino males, counter to the importance of a social justice stance for this and other communities of color (Molina, 2023). Burke, Juzwik, and Prins (2023) summarize four key assumptions guiding Christian nationalist views in this country:

> (a) that the United States was founded as a Christian nation and is divinely chosen and blessed by God; (b) that a rigid and clearly defined societal hierarchy should be maintained under the dominion of this Christian God (e.g., males above females, adults over children, Whites over other racial/ethnic groups); (c) that preserving God-given freedom is of paramount importance, but only for the White Christian men atop the hierarchy; and (d) that for all others, authoritarian and, at times, violent forms of control and governance (rather than deliberative democracy) are needed to maintain proper...

A welcoming church for all will not find a home under Christian nationalism, a counter-movement that is gaining strength and fueling electoral politics. It is an antithesis to a social justice embrace, and an anti-urban force, too.

Schools historically have been important vehicles for socializing youth to become contributing members of society. Churches function in similar ways for a cross-section of a population. Schools sponsored by churches, however, are closing at an alarming rate, diminishing the role of religious-based education and further eroding support for sponsoring churches, since these two institutions are closely tied together.

Statistics and Caution

Statistics wield tremendous power in helping us understand the forces leading to church closures, so it is important to spend a moment focusing on what church closure statistics mean. Belief systems are extremely sensitive, playing a vital role in shaping the life of believers and their immediate social networks. Religion, as with politics, is highly charged, with belief systems going to the core of an individual!

Statistics allow us to paint a broad portrait of church closures and repurposing. Quantitatively inclined readers can attest to the power of numbers; our qualitative readers, however, take a different viewpoint, valuing the narratives (stories) behind the numbers to improve understanding. There is a place for both perspectives in painting a nuanced portrait of this movement.

We can easily get lost in church closing statistics. Statistics and charts show critical trends. We must, however, not lose sight of how church attendees' lives, too, become dramatically altered, including their immediate social circle in the process. Nevertheless, statistics allow us to situate individual narratives. It is irresponsible to cast all vacant churches into one large and all-encompassing category from a statistical point of view. That would be simplistic thinking without considering contextual forces. No two churches are alike; neither are two communities, for that matter!

Cleveland State University's study of over 200 religious facilities and schools conversions between 1984 and 2009 found that condominiums were the dominant repurposed category, illustrating the power of economics in the field of repurposing (Wisniewski, 2023). This tendency to convert to condominiums or rental units makes sense because of the relative ease of converting internal rooms of various sizes to take into account distribution of space.

In booming real estate markets, developers will quickly snap up vacant churches and convert them to luxury and market-rate housing. Closed churches in economically depressed areas will find the nonprofit sector as an attractive route for repurposing initiatives, calling for research using local and regional contexts. This analysis may need aid from municipalities or local institutions of higher learning. These locations, in turn, open the door for social and human service-related initiatives, such as housing.

Demography as Destiny

If demography is destiny, what does that say about urban church closings? The answer is that they are in for challenging, if not tumultuous, times, with the reversal of closures nowhere in sight! These closures fly under the national radar, but we need to spotlight this phenomenon because of their importance and centrality in the well-being of this nation's communities. Demographic forces shape society's institutions, particularly those requiring participation and appealing to a cross-section of age groups. Society does not mandate religious beliefs, affiliation, or church attendance. It is an institution and a belief system attuned to social forces and membership needs to ensure that congregants return on a regular basis and economically contribute to the process.

U.S. church membership was first systematically measured in 1937 and stood at 73%, with the 60 years following showing minimal national decline (70%). However, there was a steady decline from the start of the 21st century (Jones, 2021). A recent estimate has the decline continuing since 2020 among Protestants (44% to 40%) and Catholics (37% to 30%), two of the largest faith groups in the country (Berg, 2023).

A Gallup poll conducted between 2018 and 2020 among adults found U.S. church membership falling below majority for the first time (particularly in the eastern part of the country), with a distinctive trend of each generation seeing a membership decline among groups stating affiliation with a specific religion. Among Black adults, it stood at 59%, or a 19% drop. Latinx church membership was the lowest of all subgroups at 37%.

Davis, Graham, and Burge (2023) argue in "The Great Dechurching: Who's Leaving, Why Are They Doing It?" that the reasons for this decline can be discovered. They take a different approach to the decrease, and why millions of Americans have disengaged from attending church over the past several decades. They argue that the attendance decline is caused by the multifaceted demands society makes upon people and the importance of achieving financial and professional success, leaving limited time for other pursuits such as church attendance. Church membership and attendance needs a commitment of time and energy that is in short supply. The full answer is far more complex, however, particularly when introducing changing age and racial demographics, particularly in cities (Zouves, 2023).

This decline has been significantly experienced by major denominations, with some sectors more so than others. Church closings are national phenomenon, increasing their importance. Small towns and cities, too, have not escaped church closings. Half the churches in Ottumwa, Iowa (population 25,000), for example, have closed, even though its population remained largely unchanged. Jordan (2023) refers to the decline in religious beliefs as the "Western-centric disenchantment model." The urban scene stands out in grounding this decline for the reasons discussed earlier in this book.

The U.S. United Methodist Church, for example, is projected to lose a million members by the end of 2025, falling to approximately 5.2 million (DiPaolo, 2022). This signals further church closings: "Empty church buildings can be expensive. While there are valuable properties bishops can turn into cash, there are also many others that will be hard to sell and expensive to maintain and insure." The locations of these churches will have a significant influence on the options available to them. The Adventist Church, too, has experienced dwindling membership and church closures, with a slow uphill climb projected in this decade, for example (White, 2023):

> The Adventist Church originated as a church planting movement. The church had significant and sustained growth until about 30 years ago. In the past decade, the growth rate of our global church has averaged about 2.3%, with the average since 2019 being 0.77%. This alarming drop in growth has resulted in 75% of our churches having either plateaued or declined in the last few decades, with many church closures... To help combat this decline and grow the future, the North American Division has developed Plant 1,000, a vision to have at least one church for every 25,000 people across North America.

I like to say that to plan is human, but to implement is divine. However, hope is a not a plan. Time will tell how well these plans bear fruit for the church planting movement. Nevertheless, there is no denying their importance, and they bear watching.

The Seventh Day Adventists launched a special Latino outreach initiative. Fifty percent of Latino church plants over the last 30 years have been Spanish-speaking ministries. In fact, one church was planted to specifically serve second-generation Latinos in both English and Spanish, recognizing their unique needs, challenges, and assets (E. Brown, 2023). Time will tell if other religious groups follow suit with specific goals of engaging younger generations of Latinos.

Not all church closures are similar from a repurposing or community standpoint. It would be a mistake to lump them together, increasing the importance of grounding these efforts locally. Centralized efforts may miss key factors, translating to successes in some cases and failure in others. Those generalizations are challenging to make, with no "one model" standing out, for instance. That may be frustrating for community practitioners, but localizing our efforts reigns supreme in the field of community practice.

There is a call for the U.S. United Methodist Church, for example, to aggressively address the coming tsunami of church closings by exploring creative ways to use land and buildings, such as sharing, repurposing, and rebuilding (Lee, 2021). Not all empty churches should be repurposed; indeed, tearing them down may be the best way to make room for a more responsive structure and to meet local needs more effectively. Making a correct determination ultimately requires research, analysis, and the resources developed for this endeavor—not to mention political considerations.

Church membership is strongly correlated with age; for example, 66% of "traditionalists" (U.S. adults born before 1946) belong to a church. This compares to 58% of "baby boomers," 50% of "Gen X," and 36% of "Millennials." Why is that so important? It's not a leap of faith (pardon the pun!) to say that increasing age is a key demographic factor does not favor church membership growth because of its wide reach across all segments of society. To thrive, churches must receive sustained and increasing support from a cross-section of groups. The call for a ministry reaching out to multiple generations is not a novel idea, as shown by McIntosh's (2002) book *One Church, Four Generations: Understanding and Reaching All Ages in Your Church*.

Anderson (2014) emphasized the importance of churches reaching Millennials, identifying three values that must be recognized and addressed: (1) "I want to be heard"; (2) "I want to contribute"; and (3) "I want to be accepted." Those values are not restricted to this generation and can easily apply to other generations. Churches, as a result, would do well in embracing these values to help build a future.

Church leaders understand they exercise minimal control over members' chronological age, although they can add features to be particularly attractive to particular demographic segments. However, they do have greater control over church size and financial matters—how big do they want their churches to be? That answer will set the marching orders for clergy and their congregations, bringing economic requirements in the process!

Rainer (2020, p. 115) identified seven ways in which church leadership can weather closures, which can exist in various permutations and combinations: (1) acceptance of responsibility for facing closure; (2) overcoming the trap of adhering to traditions; (3) paying attention to worship attendance, donations, and conversions; (4) adherence to the power of prayer; (5) willingness to confront toxic members who undermine leadership; (6) understanding there is no magic solution—it requires commitment and hard work; and (7) "Membership has meaning. Membership means sacrificing for the greater good of the body. Membership has clear expectations." These recommendations create an organizational climate that can help a church to address challenges that can lead to closure if poorly handled.

In 2000, there were 343,000 religious congregations in the country: 3,727 synagogues, 1,209 mosques, and 338,000 churches (Carter, 2022). Krejcir (2007) supplied another historical perspective. In 1900, there were 27 churches per 10,000 people. At the turn of the 21st century, there were 11 churches per 10,000 people. In half of all churches fewer than 65 people attend weekly service, leaving little latitude for losing attendees before a church enters a death spiral. This statistic illustrates how even a minor change in attendance can start a downward spiral that eventually results in the closing of a church.

Declining U.S. church membership (Jones, 2021, pp. 1–2) results from the interplay of decreased religious affiliation and generational differences. These are disturbing trends from a religious standpoint and have together played an instrumental role in threatening or closing churches:

> Over the past two decades, the percentage of Americans who do not identify with any religion has grown from 8% in 1998–2000 to 13% in 2008–2010 and 21% over the past three years. As would be expected, Americans

without a religious preference are highly unlikely to belong to a church, synagogue, or mosque, although a small proportion—4% in the 2018–2020 data—say they do. That figure is down from 10% between 1998 and 2000. Given the nearly perfect alignment between not having a religious preference and not belonging to a church, the 13-percentage-point increase in no religious affiliation since 1998–2000 appears to account for more than half of the 20-point decline in church membership over the same time.

Shifts in church membership from predominantly White European to groups of color, for instance, created a significant void that could not be closed. This "perfect storm" led to vacant church buildings, with ramifications for the communities where these buildings were located.

This demographic trend must be grounded within broader demographic shifts occurring in the country, which is increasingly becoming more of color, particularly in older industrialized cities. This trend may bode well for churches in these communities, but that is not always so. Analysis is needed of how local forces shape churchgoing behaviors, including the services provided to congregations and communities and how they must be replaced or augmented to ensure continued relevance.

Finally, mass secularization received international attention in the 1960s when Cox (1967) published *The Secular City: Secularization and Urbanization in Theological Perspective*. This book proclaimed (p. 4) "[t]he age of the secular city, the epoch whose ethos is quickly spreading into every corner of the globe, is an age of 'no religion at all.'" This viewpoint has garnered considerable strength since the publication of this book.

Finally, according to one prediction only one or two of the dominant denominations will be left after mergers and continual declines over the next 50 years (Easum, 2018). Dallas (2023), in an article titled "What will American religion look like in 50 years?," predicts that Christians will not long enjoy the status of being in a majority; instead, "Nones" will become the majority. Christians will represent only 35% of all Americans by 2070. To say that this is a seismic shift is not an understatement.

Predictions that far into the future are best left to the brave. If this one comes to fruition, however, it will cause major upheavals to the religious scene in this country, with cities bearing the onus of these closures. It does not take an active imagination to wonder what will happen when a community experiences multiple church closures at the same time. Readers may ask whether God is dead. Some may argue that God does not need a building to find legitimacy and is alive and well, allowing us to practice religion without needing a church to do so. A church is just that—a building made of earthly materials! Nevertheless, we cannot deny the association between religious belief systems and church buildings, and this relationship's personification.

The Urban Church

There is no such thing as an urban or rural church; there is simply a church! This may seem obvious. However, it is superficial, if not dangerous, to examine Black and Latino churches without a geographical and historical grounding. Urban church leadership, too, must reflect a congregation's ethnicity, race, and lived experiences to increase success in attracting and keeping a viable membership. A religious leader with a rural background is challenged when assigned to an urban center; the reverse is also true. The same conclusion can be made about any profession.

"Urban imaginary" is best shaped by lived experiences and not book knowledge. Church leadership simply cannot imagine urban living without having experienced it themselves, as in the case study of Chicago's Downtown Church struggles (Barron & Williams, 2017). Inequities must not be replicated in the House of the Lord if it hopes to survive. Churches, regardless of denomination, cannot simply decide to diversify their memberships and undo decades of practice to ensure survival. That decision entails a deliberate undertaking.

I concur with Berrelleza's (2020, p. 750) assessment on the paucity of urban life and religious research, which significantly affects Black and Latino churches and their struggles for survival:

> Scholars have devoted relatively little attention to the study of religion in modern, urban life. Religion is often seen as a relic of the old city, not a factor of the new. Studies along this line of reasoning highlight the higher religious disaffiliation of the gentrifying middle classes as evidence that religious institutions are doomed to fail . . . These scholars assume religious decline is inevitable in the modern turn—a hypothesis promoted by secularization theorists before . . . To be sure, urban religious institutions are bound to change along with their neighborhood—they are, after all, neighborhood institutions, but they have not vanished from these urban centers.

When religious practices are contextualized, it uplifts the intersection of religion, race, and space. It cannot separate out Black and Latino churches from their operative reality, including the challenges they face.

Increasing the participation of younger generations will require new strategies to be introduced. Dolloway (2023), for example, proposes a revitalization plan for Christian churches in Queens, New York, targeting younger generations and providing them with leadership roles in the church. Investment must not be relegated to one segment of society, however.

Psychology and Repurposed Structures

The consensus is that repurposed buildings have a potential to meet a range of human needs, particularly in low-resource urban communities, with psychological concepts emerging to guide the unfolding of this process. Embrace of a "positive psychology" buildings approach has gained currency, although there has been effort linking this movement to the environment (Grant et al., 2019). It is not odd to see old churches from a building life-cycle perspective or a "cradle-to-grave-to-reincarnation" cycle and part of the environmental sustainability capability movement (Fnais et al., 2022; Hasik et al., 2019). "Reincarnation" being a newly repurposed structure, introducing other perspectives that may resonate for readers.

Another approach uses Maslow's human needs hierarchy, which fall into five categories, with each having applicability for church repurposing: (1) physiological needs; (2) safety needs; (3) love and belonging needs; (4) esteem needs; (5) and self-actualization needs. Higher needs appear only when people have met the prior ones. Zheng, Heath, and Guo (2022) apply Maslow's hierarchy to architectural spaces (in their case industrial buildings) by explaining how repurposed structures can meet a range of human needs:

> [T]he basic needs are evaluated at the level of the building infrastructure, advanced needs are about humanistic care, and challenging needs are about the distinctiveness and attractiveness created through their own characteristics. The evaluation shows that ... the basic needs of the contemporary building are of high quality; the challenging needs could be seen as the driving force behind making the project unique and attractive; however, the advanced needs are probably the most neglected. More importantly,

the issues of the project that have been exposed in this evaluation are well placed to guide the direction of the project's future development.

Readers may enjoy applying Maslow's hierarchy to the role residents can play in shaping church repurposing goals and how programming can address their needs. For the built environment to be successful, it must be guided by human needs rather than making a profit!

Religious Practice Trends: A Window into the Future?

It is fair to start this section by sounding the alarm on the crisis that awaits houses of worship. A. Walker (2023) has over the past several decades sounded the alarm about the existential crisis facing Western Christianity:

> All across the Western world, traditional churches are teetering on the brink of collapse. [I specifically added the word "Western" to this seemingly outrageous claim.] There is a different story about Christianity in parts of Africa and Asia . . . The members of Western churches pretend they care. They delude themselves that they want to turn things around. They "talk the talk" for change and growth. But they delude themselves. I worked as a full-time priest in the Anglican church for 38 years until my retirement in 2021. I tried everything I knew to turn the ship around.

An alarm is ringing, and quite loudly, too! Churches do not have the luxury of waiting to see if the trend reverses itself—the choices are institutional life in a greatly different state or death, and neither outcome is attractive.

Christian churches will find themselves increasing their reliance on new patrons from parts of the world that they are not accustomed to. Blake (2023) offers a counter-argument to the decline of Christianity in the United States, drawing upon the symbolism of Easter: "Both Christian symbols are bookends to the Easter story. One symbolizes the tragic execution of Jesus while the other represents the Christian belief in his resurrection, and the claim that death does not have the final word on him or his followers." How? The wave of newcomers to this country offers a life preserver for Christian churches that can adopt these new congregants.

Churches are closing at a record pace across religious affiliations. Krejcir (2007) noted the yearly trend had more than 4,000 churches closings, but only 1,000 new church starts! A more recent estimate has between 6,000 and 10,000 churches closings in the United States each year, or 100 to 200 each week (Morton, 2019). These closures are not evenly geographically distributed across the country, with some areas having more than others.

In 2020, a study by Faith Communities Today found that the average membership of a Christian church was less than half of what it was in 2000, falling from 137 to 65. Further, one-third of churchgoers were 65 or older, "double that age group's slice of the general population" (Yahoo News, 2023), raising alarm about the future viability of churches. These reductions are not restricted to just one region.

U.S. Christians historically constituted the majority of the nation's church-affiliated population (90%), but in 2020 that figure declined to almost 64%; if the current trend continues, in 2070 they will represent only at 35% to 46% (Eisenberg, 2023), with more church buildings closing. The greatest declines in attendance occurred between 2020 and 2022 among those under the age of 50, with a college degree or less, Latino Catholics, Black Protestants, and White mainline Protestants (J. Brown, 2023).

Scholars note that religious practices are changing, and churches cannot ignore this trend. Inglehart's (2020) book *Religion's Sudden Decline: What's Causing It, and What Comes Next?* discusses this country's church membership decline, particularly among younger members. The decrease is largely due to the convergence of macroeconomic and sociocultural changes linked with modernization, and a significant decline in religious emphasis within households. The influence of these forces does not bode well for future attendance; strategic initiatives will be needed to stem this trend if churches are to remain a part of the modern city.

Readers may wish a greater understanding of the historical roots of religious practices, setting up a foundation for the present-day phenomenon of turning away from organized religion. K.S.'s (2023) book *Escape the "Gods": All of Humanity Worships Ancient Cults* provides a critical assessment, laying the groundwork for why people turn away from church attendance.

One recent estimate had approximately 4,500 Protestant churches closing in 2019 (the last year for which data are available), with almost 3,000 new churches opening (Gabbatt, 2023), or a net loss of 1,500 closings, or 29 per week. Another estimate, although dated, shows that church building sales, a different dimension, increased by almost 100% between 2010 and 2015 (Rockwood, 2017).

In 2014, there were 3,700 Protestant church closures compared with 4,500 in 2019, signifying a disturbing escalating trend (Shimron, 2021). In 2020, another estimate found that there were over 300,000 Protestant congregations in the United States, with 60,000 expected to close in the next 18 months (Gray, 2020). In 2020, 3,850 to 7,700 houses of worship closed per year, or between 75 to 150 congregations per week. The person on the street may not be alarmed by this number until it happens to them and that part of their world, figuratively or literally, crumbles.

One proposed solution is to have churches convert their spaces to mixed use or to set aside portions of their land for housing or other purposes. We must not forget that each closure is a traumatic event for parishioners and neighborhoods. By broadening their mission to meet other instrumental needs in their community, churches can help ensure their relevance and potential survival.

Another solution is to merge with other churches, a "brave new world" for increasing attendance. In communities undergoing rapid population displacements, due to shrinking cities, and facing the influx of new ethnic groups, such as in Buffalo, closing churches will be prone to "takeovers" by new groups with different religious affiliations (Krishna & Hall, 2019). These churches will retain their original spiritual purpose or mission, although under different auspices.

Readers may see a similarity to business takeovers. The selling of a church building by one religion under duress to another can cause public dissension and backlash. In fact, some closing churches may specifically forbid this, as discussed in Chapter 6 with Boston's Catholic Church. This phenomenon is not new in the United States, as Kilde (2013, p. 3) points out: "While each instance of a religious building changing hands seems to garner public attention in the contemporary period, such transfers of real estate among religious groups have been common in American municipalities for close to three centuries." The difference today is that they are occurring with greater frequency and over a shorter period of time, making it a movement.

Combining congregations can lead to greater efficiency, but with limitations. It leads to larger "flocks" to minister to and a higher likelihood of declining vocations to the priesthood (Jones, 2023). With larger congregations, priests are limited in their connectedness to parishioners; attendees, in turn, have limited access to their priests, leading to increased dissatisfaction. Further, massive influxes of new parishioners due to mergers raise critical issues for congregations and their leadership.

Although this topic may seem distant to the central thrust of this book, I must touch on what happens when there is an introduction of multiracial church pastors, as with Black, AAPI, and Latinos. These religious leaders are known as "estranged pioneers" because of how they shape the religious experience (Edwards & Kim, 2019, p. 457): "They leave the familiar to explore a new way of doing church but their ventures are not valued or celebrated as something that will potentially benefit the communities they come from. What's more, their sense of identity is challenged or destabilized in the process. Alienation characterizes their journey."

What happens to these churches? Do they thrive or not, eventually lead to closure, being torn down, or repurposing? Only time will tell. The implications, however, have a place in this book. The significance of multiracial church leadership holds valuable lessons for the religious community across the country, not to mention other spheres of society.

Much needs to be learned about what happens when two churches merge, particularly when one is racially or ethnically homogeneous (White, non-Latino) and the other consists primarily of parishioners of color. There is the potential for segregation in the new structure if the influx is not well planned (Berrelleza, 2020). This further marginalizes members of color and their communities. Mergers are increasingly used to save a congregation (Tomberlin & Bird, 2020).

Yet another estimate projected that 100,000 out of 384,000 churches and other houses of worship, or almost one-third (31.4%), would close in the next few years at a rate of 3,750 to 7,500 per year, or 75 to 150 per week in pre-COVID times (Reinhard, 2021a, 2022b). These closures do not consider affiliated buildings, which can be significant. Closures have extensive consequences across the country, particularly in urban areas as these buildings become available for a second life to meet new needs.

Church closings are not a recent phenomenon spurred by COVID-19, for example. U.S. church sales increased by almost 100% between 2010 and 2015, with Catholic parishes declining in number by 4% from 2010 to 2016 (Rockwood, 2017). In 2014, New York State's Catholic Church, for example, announced its largest church closing initiative in 150 years, with projected closures of 112 in 2015 (Santana & Blanco, 2014). The Catholic Church is a major U.S. landowner. The remaining membership would merge into 55 parishes to address attendance and financial shortfalls (Otterman, 2014), and this is a common strategy. The social-religious outcomes of these mergers need further research to help us better understand what factors enhance the likelihood of success and what success actually looks like, including avoiding road bumps. These mergers will undoubtedly increase in frequency in the near future to starve off closures, calling for research recording their outcomes.

These closings caused considerable political controversy because they happened in communities experiencing population growth, such as among Manhattan's East Harlem neighborhood, a predominantly Latino community where three churches were to be closed or merged. Population growth signified a need for these churches to remain open. Further, Homan (2022) traces these and other closings to broader macro-demographic changes in New York City and more specifically in Manhattan, home to an estimated 13,222 churches, with each having an average of 643 members, as a backdrop to viewing these closures (Dolloway, 2023).

The Church of the Lady of Guadalupe, Manhattan's first church specifically created for a Latino congregation ("Little Spain"), was slated for closure after a history spanning over one century (Gill, 2023). New York City's Latino population numbers 2.5 million, or 29% that city's population.

Interest in saving funds at the expense of marginalized groups and their worship needs means that churches were needed to accommodate larger and larger memberships, with costs being the guiding principle. These closings occurred against a significant backdrop of Catholic Church closings of 2,222 parishes nationwide over an approximately 25-year period (1988–2014), a disturbing continuing and broader trend to the present that is projected to continue.

Chicago's Catholic churches are facing significant closing challenges, with a third fewer parishes today than five years ago, with increased costs of supporting aging buildings and diminishing numbers of attendees (Namigadde, 2022). Pittsburgh's Catholic community, too, has confronted the reality of church closings, with a reduction of 188 parishes to 57 by 2023, or almost 60% (The Editors, 2018). These closings are in response to a 40% drop in attendance since 2000 and are not shared across all ethnic and racial groups, calling for a more nuanced study of this trend when discussing communities of color.

As expected, the number of diocese priests is also projected to fall from 200 in 2018 to 112 in 2025, which is a dimension of church closings that has not received the attention it warrants. Thus, there is also a labor crunch. Fewer priests are also expected to be available in coming years. Seattle's archdiocese (early 2023), for example, had 80 pastors for 174 locations. By 2036, it expected to have 66 pastors, a 17.% reduction (Capitol Hill Seattle, 2023).

The priest shortage took time to unfold and to be recognized as a serious matter. In 1965, with U.S. Catholic population estimated at 50 million, 95% of the country's 36,467 diocesan priests were engaged in active ministry. In 2022, 73.5 million Catholics were being served by 66% of the 24,110 priests, with most of the other 34% being retired. Ordinations dropped from 805 in 1970 to 451 last year, including religious-order priests (Catholic World Report, 2023). The Catholic Church is also facing the challenge of a shortage of native-born priests, with foreign-born priests from sections of the world new to this country—Africa, India, and the Philippines, for example (Shaw, 2023a, 2023b). This phenomenon is not new. Historically, foreign priests have found their way to the United States from Ireland and Italy, paralleling the ethnic composition of their parishioners.

An analysis of religious staff is beyond the scope of this book but nonetheless is worthy of attention to grasp a holistic view of religion in our society, and the role that church staff play, including their building closures. We must keep in mind that church staff are not just those who have official functions and are paid, because there are countless lay members fulfilling important roles but not being financially paid. The drop in religious personnel on a national scale illustrates one challenge for the Catholic Church, with local implications. The U.S. Catholic Church (Smith, 2022) had almost 161,000 religious sisters in 1970, but only 41,000 in 2020. The problem is that the Church still has housing for 120,000 religious sisters.

California's Sisters of the Holy Family followed this pattern. These Catholic nuns have aged and were not being replaced; at their peak they numbered 250 sisters, but in 2022 there were a little over 40 members (Smietana, 2022). Fewer than 1% of U.S. Catholic nuns are under 40 years old, with the average age of 80 years (Cullen, 2023). This demographic profile does not bode well for a thriving future for Catholic nuns in this country.

A similar story holds true for Catholic priests and religious brothers. Nationally, in 1970, there were 59,000 priests and 11,600 religious brothers, but in 2020 there were 35,000 priests and 3,800 religious brothers. In 1975 the Archdiocese of Chicago had approximately 2,400 priests, including diocesan, religious order, and retired priests. In 2022, there were 1,200, a significant reduction of 50%. Parishes also showed a precipitous drop from 344 in 2018 to 221 in 2022, or almost a 36% reduction. We cannot separate a drop in the number of priests from a corresponding drop in the number of churches. We must not forget that individuals who have devoted their lives to a religious mission must move to other facilities. Disrupting their lives and needing to re-establish new connections can be quite challenging.

The Catholic Church is expanding internationally, which is an important development. This calls for coverage in the Church's efforts to prevent closures and to expand more acutely in the United States, but is indicative of a significant shift in the future parishioner base of this religion (Llywelyn, 2022):

> In February 2022, the Vatican released statistics showing that in 2020 the number of Catholics in the world increased by 16 million to 1.36 billion. That means that 17.7% of the world's population is Catholic. Of this total, 48% are in the Americas, with 28% living in South America. Following recent trends, the Catholic Church grew most rapidly in Asia (+1.8%) and Africa (+2.1%) with very slight growth in Europe (0.3%).

In the United States that is not the case, which is why Catholic Church repurposing is a destined to be a prominent phenomenon with far-reaching consequences for the country and its urban centers.

The majority of the world's Catholics do not live in the Global North, with projections that by 2050, 75% of them will live outside the West. I leave it to readers to assess the long-term consequences for both the United States and its cities, for instance, and in the countries where they are expanding.

Catholic Church Righting the Ship Against Prevailing Winds

We need to follow up on the earlier section on the Catholic Church, which is highlighted in this book because of its size and influence in urban areas, and because its efforts at countering prevailing winds have failed. This caused a significant decrease in worshippers, with corresponding church mergers and closures. I am not "Catholic-bashing," mind you, but their sheer influences in this book require extra attention, particularly among urban-based Latinos, historically and today.

The Catholic Church is starting various efforts to right the ship, so to speak, internally and externally. The metaphor of this church as a big ship is apropos of the situation they find themselves in. Shifting directions for a cruise liner requires foresight because dramatically changing course cannot be done quickly, in similar fashion to a car, for example. The Catholic Church needs to have considerable foresight as to where and when to turn.

Solutions countering membership decline are appearing, as with Detroit's efforts to increase Catholic Church membership. There is a call for the Church to make amends for past policies and actions that violated the rights of groups of color (White, 2022). Will the decisions lead to renewal or continued decline? Either direction will bring seismic repercussions for parishioners and their communities.

It has been suggested that the Catholic Church start outreach efforts, even going out into the streets rather than waiting for the faithful to re-engage; this would be a change in basic assumptions and strategy (Pearson, 2023): "This past Saturday, members of Detroit's Resistance chapter spent some time speaking about the Faith with passersby in Plymouth, Michigan's Kellogg Park. Evangelization is something all Catholics are called to do in whatever capacity they are able." Time will tell whether these efforts will spread and be successful in refilling Catholic Church pews, averting consolidation and closure efforts.

Counter-prevailing winds are ever present, and in this case, it is how new Catholic priests view their vows and mission, and whether this poses a significant lacuna with parishioners and their expectations, potentially causing an even greater rift (Pearson, 2022):

> The discord is driven in part by a generational shift . . . "The fact that younger priests tend to be more traditional or more conservative than the ones who are now 60 or 70 is a global trend. In the United States, it's much more extreme," said Faggioli. "It is very hard to imagine what will happen to liberal Catholicism in this country, because it's not producing a new generation of clergy that can sustain it." Many young priests are embracing a return to forms of worship that pre-date the Second Vatican Council reforms of the 1960s, he said. These new traditionalists are alienating some older church members accustomed to priests who welcomed the reforms and gave lay members a greater role in shaping their parish.

Priests are the face of a church. and their actions stand for its theological and policy stance. How they act, and the reasoning undergirding these decisions, is what local communities must respond to—staying with the church or leaving it! The latter causes church closures and diminishes their influence in local matters and achieving an inclusive climate.

Readers wanting an in-depth analysis of burnout in the Catholic Church are recommended to read Plante's (2023) article "Principles for Managing Burnout Among Catholic Church Professionals." This trend bears close watching if the Catholic Church is to reverse declining membership and to avoid mergers and closures, particularly in cities attracting newcomers with different visions of church services, including how younger priests ("New Traditionalists") conduct services. If the Catholic Church does not fully recognize the need to change its course to address this challenge, it will experience a more dramatic clash in the near future, particularly when looking to attract newcomers settling in cities.

The academic literature needs to catch up with its popular press counterpart regarding the embrace of conservative views and practices among the American Catholic priesthood. This is particularly so when examining moral opinions on who should or should not be ordained, including politics and theology (Vermurlen et al., 2023). These views are most pronounced when taking into account whether priests self-identify as gay and/or hold more liberal social views when compared to their heterosexual counterparts, for example.

In late 2023, the Vatican concluded a highly anticipated and much-watched month-long meeting called by Pope Francis without reaching any agreement on moving forward on issues such as LGBTQ+, allowing married priests, and having women potentially assume roles as deacons or priests (Horowitz & Povoledo, 2023):

> But progressives who had high hopes that the meeting would create real momentum for change said the final document had failed to move the institution at all. Before the meeting, a variety of sensitive topics were on the table, including the blessing of same-sex unions, reaching out to L.G.B.T.Q.+ Catholics and the possibility of allowing married men to become priests. Those basically vanished.

There is no disputing that the Catholic Church is confronting major social issues within its walls. How these social issues are dealt with will have long-term ramifications for the Church and how it navigates its role in society. A ban against LGBTQ expressions of pride in Catholic schools, as in Cleveland, for example, illustrates the reach of this ideology that counters a social justice stance, and one not restricted to religion (Morris, 2023). This ban prohibits the display of flags and rainbows, and also prohibits same-sex couples from participating in school dances. Readers can no doubt visualize how this contentious social issue influences perceptions and behaviors within Catholic schools and in its churches.

It bears noting that the Catholic Church is not the only denomination struggling with how to address LGBTQ+ members, as addressed throughout this book (R. Graham, 2023):

> America's second-largest Protestant denomination is in the final stages of a slow-motion rupture that has so far seen the departure of a quarter of the nation's roughly 30,000 United Methodist churches . . . At issue for Methodists is the question of ordaining and marrying L.G.B.T.Q. people, a topic that has splintered many other Protestant denominations and which Methodists have been debating for years.

One-fourth (5,641) of U.S. United Methodist churches have received permission to leave the denomination because of disputes over its LGBTQ-related policies. These policies fail to "enforce bans on same-sex marriage and the ordaining of openly LGBTQ persons" (Audiq, 2023). Also in 2023, the Southern Baptist Convention, which is the largest Protestant denomination in the United States, voted to expel women from the role of priests and a number of churches for having female priests, causing great consternation and making national news. The immediate and long-term implications of these struggles remain to be seen but bear watching from a repurposing standpoint.

Land Owned by Churches

Most readers probably have never thought about this topic, but its importance sets a foundation for viewing church buildings as economic assets, including assigning dollar amounts to their holdings. The term "landlord" obviously elicits a range of responses, depending on whether one owns property and one's experiences with them. In undervalued communities landlords are rarely associated with positive thoughts and feelings, or even within religious institutions, for that matter.

We often think of a property owner as an individual or a real estate corporation; we rarely think of churches as property owners, but they are. The land owned by churches ("God's acres"), including buildings, is a form of capital, with all the characteristics associated with this asset, and is worthy of attention from a macro standpoint. This understanding sets a broad parameter on why these buildings and land (public spaces) play such a vital role in cities and why church property ownership cannot be ignored.

Multiple ways of viewing church land/property ownership can help us think creatively about practical strategies for church building repurposing. This section focuses on the Catholic and Mormon churches, two major U.S. landowning churches. However, land owned by other churches scattered throughout the country must not be overlooked, particularly in cities experiencing housing insecurity because of high rents/real estate costs. The United Methodist Church, for example, is estimated to own $50 billion in real estate across the nation—no small amount.

Reinhard and Elisara (2022) discuss church closures in downtown Rome, Georgia, where there were 15 churches within a six-block-long and four-block radius, with church properties representing a substantial part of developable land. These authors note that how these properties are viewed and addressed shapes the future of their communities because of their social and economic influence:

> What will happen to the 15 church parcels in Rome's small downtown may determine the city's success over the next 30–40 years. Rome is one of thousands of cities, towns, villages, and neighborhoods facing the disruptive storm of closing and closed houses of worship. New urbanists need to build bridges with faith communities to reuse and redevelop houses of worship.

The new urbanist movement cannot ignore such a vital segment of an urban community if it is to remain viable in the future. Land is so limited in urban centers that ignoring church-owned properties translates to professional malpractice.

Other ways of viewing church property illuminate the challenges they face in staying afloat (Reinhard, 2021a): "A denomination in one state owns an estimated $1.4 billion in real estate to serve 50,000 weekly worshipers—a hefty $28,000 in property per attendee. Many churches have found themselves spending half or more of their operating budgets on real estate and owning assets that are 80 or 90 percent composed of illiquid real estate. Many congregations report being 'one new roof away from closing.'" Turning illiquid assets into cash to pay immediate bills and possible reinvesting in other projects can entail a lengthy process and requires access to experts.

A parcel's economic value is shaped by an interplay of its size and location, with a property in an urban neighborhood usually generating a higher price than one in a rural area. This makes locational context key in calculating the worth of a property, making the following statistics of limited value. Nevertheless, data on church holdings, when readily available and current, play an important illustrative role in helping us to understand church repurposing and economics, including the symbolic value of land within religious circles.

Nguyen (2023) offers an important perspective on the wealth of religious organizations, of which land and real estate represents a major portion "When people say, 'more money than God,' what might be a real number for that amount of money on Earth that God has? I'm thinking of the entire income and assets for all faith organizations, including houses of worship, faith charities, etc. How might we estimate that and compare it to large nations' GDPs, the world's wealthiest billionaires and our national debt?" The amount, as readers have seen, is a significant sum of money.

Land is widely considered the ultimate commodity, which is why we pay attention to it in this book. "Who Owns More Land: Bill Gates, McDonald's, or the Catholic Church?" is an article by Budzyn (2022) that readers may wish to read. Bill Gates is alleged to own 270,000 acres, mostly in the United States; McDonald's has 47,037 acres of land around the world; and finally the Catholic Church owns 177 million acres across the world, making it one of the world's largest landowners. Another estimate has it owning Church property 227,000 square miles, it bears noting, this covers a vast terrain. If all its land were combined (a sizeable country), it would be among the world's top 50 landmasses (Schuster, 2017). To provide another perspective, these land holdings rank behind the Kingdom of Saudi Arabia and the British royal family, who own more land.

Another example highlights the Catholic Church's wealth in addition to its land holdings (Posner, 2015). For instance, the 26 museums in The Vatican house thousands of works of art from some of the most recognized artists in history, estimated to be worth over $1 trillion American.

Owning large tracts of land in an urban setting carries with it immense political influence, and to think otherwise is foolish and ignores "the elephant in the room" when discussing church holdings, mergers, closures, or other important decisions, as often mentioned in this book. Practitioners will be well served by being aware of the presence of political winds when church property outcomes are being considered, and no more so than when it is counter to the wishes of the community.

California has approximately 38,000 acres of religious land suitable for housing development (Wagner, 2023). In Los Angeles, there are efforts to end the unsheltered crisis (20 congregations with a goal of creating 2,000 apartments). All church denominations combined own 20% to 25% of U.S. land, which has historically been largely fueled by their tax-exempt status. Why are we including all of these estimates? Because church structures are property, allowing their closures or portions closed to be viewed as transactional, or "the cost of doing business." In short, churches wield considerable power beyond influencing their congregations. Their economic holdings, as manifested through land ownership, speak for themselves.

A 2020 (McKnight & Dodge, 2022) study of the real estate holdings of the Mormon Church (Latter Day Saints) found that it owned 1,754,633 acres across the country, with a market value of at least $15.7 billion. This translates into a total of 15,963 parcels; almost 50% of the parcels are zoned for agricultural use, with the remaining half primarily zoned for commercial or religious use. In 2013, the Mormon Church became the largest private landowner in Florida, for example, signifying its potential political, social, and economic influence when viewed from a regional standpoint. Church land ownership is not unique to the United States: the Church of England's religious structures, for example, are valued at £925 million, with £112 million a year spent on repairs (Chartres, undated).

Owning property compels owners to "do well" by their property and tenants. Having the privilege of owning property—even more so with churches because of their moral and spiritual mission—means that life after the death of a church can be just as meaningful as when a church was alive and thriving. We must remember, though, that owning property in a low-demand area does not carry the economic clout of owning land in an area with a high demand. Closed houses of worship in low-demand areas face a future that is dismal, and the buildings pose a safety challenge for their communities if left to deteriorate.

Vacant Church Buildings and the Urban Landscape

Churches represent a distinct architectural type within urban landscapes, bringing along historical linkages between generations. Let's face it, churches usually stand out for good reasons! When they are well kept, they can add to the majesty of a landscape. But when neglected, they become eyesores, detracting from the landscape and even becoming dangerous! Closed churches cannot be ignored in daily interactions and serve as constant reminders of their former life, for long-term residents even bringing back memories of the glory days.

This book emphasizes church closures due to dwindling membership, but natural disasters, such as tornados, earthquakes, fires, and hurricanes, can also be cause for a closing. These "acts of God" can be viewed as a "calling" to reshape a church's mission for a broader social good. Unfortunately, depending upon the health of the church, it can also mean the end of its mission. Churches that are damaged by one of these acts require immediate attention due to public safety concerns. If a congregation does not have resources to rebuild, then these churches will be demolished, causing disruption of congregations and resulting traumas. In all likelihood, vacancy results from declining enrollments and financial shortfalls, making rebuilding challenging.

Hurricane Fiona (2022) destroyed the Calvary Church in Charlottetown, Prince Edward Island, Canada. The rebuilding project added two apartment towers with 400 housing units (Yarr, 2023). Broadening a church's mission to actively embrace earthly needs, such as housing, opens the door for creative rebuilding/repurposing projects that address the needs of a current generation.

The declining church membership in the United States as a major social-religious force in church closures makes it appropriate to introduce a quote on repurposing historical buildings (Amayu, 2014), grounding us in this complex yet exciting and highly rewarding process:

> The adaptive reuse of old church buildings generally involves repurposing these historic buildings for economically viable new uses while concomitantly preserving the heritage elements of the buildings. Adaptive reuse therefore offers a creative and sustainable solution for economically revitalizing neighbourhoods and preserving the heritage of old church buildings once they stop functioning as places of worship. However, undertaking a successful adaptive reuse of an old church building is a complex process as it is influenced by several planning policies and regulatory requirements.

Church buildings are not your typical buildings. Stained-glass windows (considered works of art in many circles), for example, may have artistic and symbolic value but play no practical significance in most plans for the future of these buildings.

Church closure is a profound and drastic action from a community resources standpoint, including law enforcement, fire departments, and healthcare facilities, and is rightly a concern to a wide variety of entities, religious and non-religious, depending on which side they stand—mourning the loss versus salivating over the potential of economic gains from development. Churches that are left vacant for extended periods of time create public safety concerns and the opportunity for vandalism and other criminal activity, affecting local law enforcement personnel. Fire departments face challenges of fighting fires in these buildings, more so in gentrifying neighborhoods. Church fires present fire departments with building-specific challenges. Burned-out buildings are a magnet for mischief and raise safety concerns. Local health centers and hospital emergency rooms, too, must deal with the injuries that occur with unlawful entries into unsafe buildings.

Hoevelmann (2019) notes that fire departments face particular challenges fighting large structure fires, with churches falling within this category:

> For the large majority of us, our bread-and-butter fires are the single-family home. Our curriculums, our training programs and our tactics are, for the most part, based on this fire. The videos and photos we go over are also mostly single-family structure fires. Our apparatus are set up with hose lays that are common lengths that will reach the farthest point in a residential-building fire. It's what we do, and we do it well. Every now and then we are faced with a fire that challenges the norm. We have considered most of these fires, but have not done much specific training for them. They could be commercial occupancies like strip malls, eating establishments, warehouses and industrial areas... History tells us that these fires are dangerous and can kill firefighters. We have lost and injured firefighters in some pretty historic church fires. Each had its own challenges and problems created by the building style and difficulty in getting to the seat of the fire.

Not all church fires are similar, of course, particularly when falling into either a "legacy" or a "modern" category due to building materials and design, two key aspects. Another dimension addresses the emotional reactions of firefighters responding to the blaze, particularly if they have a personal history with the church that they are called to save.

Predicting Church Closures

A community's ability to predict short- and long-term closures in their midst is important for strategically addressing these pending closings, and helping to shape the church's future. Data on church attendance can help us decide on the likelihood of church closures. Categorizing churches using weekly attendance is a typical way of thinking about their viability. One study found the following attendance distribution (Rainer, 2022): (1) under 50 (31%); (2) 51 to 99 (37%); (3) 100 to 249 (24%); and (4) 250-plus (8%). Thus, almost one-third of these churches are in a potentially critical stage, with closure around the corner if they do not have the financial reserves to ward it off.

An estimated 20% of the nation's religious buildings are in "critical" condition, with 40% in "serious condition" (Clark, 2023). This assessment will only get worse without immediate capital infusion. With 60% of the nation's churches falling into these two categories, the handwriting is on the wall, with repurposing one strategy when these churches close. When these congregations consist primarily of low-income members, the financial strain can be considerable and unavoidable.

Adaptive reuse of churches may be as old as history. The subject has taken on new urgency over the past several decades, however, raising the importance of focused attention from government, communities, and academic/helping professions. It is a trend we cannot ignore, regardless of our religious beliefs, because houses of worship look to address multiple needs in our society and cannot easily be replaced by another institution. Their uniqueness makes them an integral part of a community's social-cultural-economic system.

There is a disturbing national decline in church membership within religious circles, as mentioned frequently in this book. This trend has lasted several decades, as already noted, with no end in sight. The national church membership decline is at a crisis point and can be best appreciated when viewed historically, including how far it has dropped and why it has caused extensive church closings across the nation (Keller, 2023):

> The American church after World War II seemed strong and flourishing. In 1952, a record 75 percent of Americans said religion was "very important" in their lives. In 1957, over 80 percent said religion "can answer today's problems." Church affiliation during the 1950s jumped from 55 percent to 69 percent. From 1950 to 1960, the U.S. population went from 150 to

180 million, a record growth aided by the post-war baby boom. In the late 1950s, almost half of all Americans were attending church regularly. This was the highest percentage in U.S. history.

It is not surprising why churches are increasingly becoming vacant eyesores in the urban landscape. Rebuilding membership requires a plan, resources, time, and commitment, with great clarity as to who is the "ideal" recruit. This strategic decision requires a plan. Time and weather will not wait, and without action communities will have to contend with disintegrating empty physical structures.

The decline in church membership and corresponding church closures can be viewed from a statistical point of view, allowing for a broader portrait to appear. But we must not forget that this decline and church closures have real-life implications (Neuman, 2023a):

> When Pastor Douglas Theobald steps to the pulpit at Struthers United Methodist Church this Sunday, it will likely be the last religious service in its 112-year history. Over the years, Struthers UMC has weathered the boom and bust cycles of the Youngstown, Ohio, suburb. In the 1960s, when the steel industry was at its height, it was common to see as many as 250 people in the pews on any given Sunday. But Theobald, who started preaching there in 2009, has presided over a congregation in slow decline. Today, services attract only a few dozen, mostly older, congregants.

A slow decline can also be conceptualized as a slow death, bringing with it all of the same characteristics and ramifications. Nevertheless, the very slowness of the process can allow for interventions to revive a church and give it new life if this condition is recognized early.

Although it is understandable to focus on closed churches (those that have died), we must not lose sight of those on life support with death imminent, awaiting an infusion of worshippers. Assessing how many new congregants are needed to keep a church viable is necessary. For example, over a year, for every 100 attendees, you can expect to lose 1 to death, 7 will transfer to another church, 9 will move, and 15 will simply stop attending for unknown reasons. This translates into 32 out of 100 attendees lost in a year, or almost one-third of a congregation! When viewed in those stark terms, it translates into urgency for active recruitment and retention initiatives.

Churches must replace 32 attendees to break even (Phillips, 2017), preferably younger ones who will be around for an extended period and ideally will provide strong financial support, too. This project needs religious leaders who are keenly attuned to their congregation's expectations and needs and able to address them in a meaningful manner, with the constant need to look out for new members. New member recruitment cannot be a seasonal activity—there is no recruitment season but rather a recruitment year!

Closings of Black churches, as in Charlottesville, Virginia, may not follow a predictable path, so it is difficult to make broad generalizations about this phenomenon. A church congregation can outgrow its physical structure, which is exciting but presents its own challenges. It might have to abandon one structure for a bigger one somewhere else, which means it would no longer have a community presence (Berry & Hutchins, 2023):

> A white church with green trim has sat on the corner of 10th Street and Grady Avenue in Charlottesville since 1939. In the 84 years that have passed since it was erected there, the church has served as a community center for one of the city's few remaining historically Black neighborhoods, a home to pioneers in the civil rights movement and, of course, a place of worship. Then, in 2018, the old Trinity Episcopal Church was purchased. The new owners, the locally based Stony Point Development Group that redeveloped the Dairy Market food hall next door, poured more than $600,000 into renovations at the church, got the necessary permits from the city and reopened the building last year as an event space.

For churches with lengthy histories, this might not be the first closing or near-closing, pointing to the importance of tracing the church's developmental history. An up-close view is needed to understand the forces behind these closures.

The birth of a church is associated with hope and expectations of a bright future, but the death of a church elicits pain and sorrow. It has been compared to the death of a loved one, particularly for longtime worshippers. A retrospective journey recalling the "good old days" is never a foundation for a "good new day." As we have said repeatedly, church closures have wider implications beyond church members, involving the whole community.

Brubaker (2023) used Elizabeth Kübler-Ross' five stages of grief in describing the reactions to church closures: (1) denial (temporary decline);

(2) anger (particularly at religious leaders); (3) bargaining (changes that can be made to attract worshippers); (4) depression (remembering the good old days); and (5) acceptance (emergence of creative thinking and bold new ideas, such as gifting the building to a local and widely respected nonprofit). Brubaker concluded, "There is indeed life after death for those congregations that have learned to die well."

A staged view of closures from research and practice standpoints is in order. Each stage requires clear demarcation lines, assessments, and specific interventions to maximize existing resources and increase the chances of success or better predicting the eventual demise of a church, including when it will occur as accurately as possible.

What are the characteristics of dying/eventual church closures? Why is that important for community practitioners to recognize? Understanding these forces is critical in grasping the challenges before us and dictating strategies likely to succeed in repurposing these structures. Reader, as quoted by Bartholet (2013), found six influential factors shaping closings:

1. Financial shortfall, which results in little, or no money spent on outreach and significant deferred maintenance of the building and grounds.
2. Steadily declining attendance over the last few years.
3. Ministry styles and offerings not in keeping with the community (e.g., outdated worship style).
4. An average age significantly older than the demographic of the community.
5. People in the church typically "driving in," with few participating from the community around the church.
6. Internal power struggles between board, pastor, and people, with large portion of pastor's time being taken by working hard to keep everybody happy.

Any permutation or combination of these factors will force closings, with only a question of time before it occurs. Financial shortfalls and shifting demographics ascend in significance and will invariably be part of any equation predicting and causing closings.

Although Wiens and Turner (2018, p. 10) do not conceptualize their approach as a life-cycle model, we can certainly think of their approach as such. They focus on the importance of church plantings (opposite end of the cycle), which will increasingly see greater attention in the coming challenges of church closings. They note that there are limited resources devoted to understanding both the church restarting process and the church closure process:

> Over the last decade, we've been encouraged by an increasing focus on church planting. It has been one of the few positive signs in a period when the local church has suffered severe decline in North America. Estimates vary, but of the 300,000 Protestant congregations in the United States, 240,000 to 270,000 of them have plateaued (Level 2) or are in attendance decline (Level 1). This book dares to dream that God hasn't given up on those 270,000 Level 1 and Level 2 churches. We believe there is hope, but we're also quick to say that the pursuit of this hope will likely require great risk from both leaders and their churches.

This typology allows assigning a status of a church, serving a heuristic function by simplifying a problem-solving approach on closures. Level 5 churches are multiplying churches.

Church attendance is often used as a key measure of religiosity (Martyr, 2022), because with more people there is a corresponding likelihood of increased financial support through weekly donations, not to mention special funding requests for particular projects. Significant attendance decreases, particularly over an extended period, have a significant negative impact on financial support and also lower the morale of attendees, who see the handwriting on the wall for the future of their institution.

Empty or nearly empty church buildings will not wait for political will, innovative initiatives, and demographic trends reverse to fill the pews again to sustain them for another generation. Action plans need immediate responses and future planning. A strategic vision, and the tools to bring it to realization, must be integral to training future religious leaders; being well versed in the Scriptures is no longer sufficient! Marketing and retention lessons are in order, too. Religious leaders wear many hats, and this role has gained prominence.

COVID-19 and Church Closings: Black and Latino Churches

No understanding of church closings over the past several years is complete without attention to COVID-19's enormous impact. A 2023 study found that overall church attendance was down an average of 9% below worship size before the pandemic (Lisi, 2023). Median attendance at local churches numbered 60, representing a decrease from 65 in 2020, or a 9% reduction; 30% of churches had a significant decline, 24% had a slight decline; 12% remained unchanged; 11% had a slight increase; and 22% noted dramatic growth (Smietana, 2023). This pattern (half of churches reporting a decline and a third reporting growth) follows a similar pre-pandemic pattern of attendance.

Key institutions within communities of color, particularly those in highly dense urban areas, felt its spiritual, social, cultural, and economic consequences the most, with many churches going virtual or even closing their doors. COVID-19 accelerated the trends unfolding at the time, and other pandemics can appear again in the near future.

Latino churches, such as Pentecostal ones, like their Black church counterparts, faced serious challenges during the COVID-19 epidemic (Estrada III, 2020). The pandemic was particularly significant for Black and Latino worshippers, dramatically reducing in-person attendance, with financial ramifications for the institution and its abilities to meet its own economic needs and those of its congregations, too. These churches tended to be smaller, without the necessary finances to weather storms of any kind, much less the hurricane that COVID-19 represented!

According to the Centers for Disease Control and Prevention (COVID-Net, 2023), Latinos and Blacks were hospitalized at almost three times the rates of White, non-Latinos. Latinos were 36% more likely to die than their White, non-Latino counterparts, with Blacks being 99% more likely than White, non-Latino whites to die. The disproportionate impact of the pandemic on these groups required special initiatives to aid them and their institutions (Gourley et al., 2023). There is no disputing that a Black church closing is a significant loss for that community.

Although church membership had been decreasing for decades across the country due to the confluence of various major forces, COVID-19 accelerated the process. No sector or segment escaped its devastation. It had a particularly immediate and long-term impact on urban communities of color and the institutions serving them, including houses of worship. Churches have historically been a refuge for those seeking solace during trying times, and COVID-19 certainly falls within this category (Bentzen, 2021). We can go back to the 1918 influenza epidemic to see parallels with present-day consequences and responses (Pockras, 2020, p. 12):

Quarantine. Wearing a mask. Keeping safer at home. Pandemic. No public worship. Closing and reopening. Many of us think of these far more often than we did a year ago, since we have never experienced anything comparable to COVID-19. But many of us have heard about the great Spanish Flu pandemic at the end of World War I, and we know that a lot of these concepts were important then.

Church closings were consequential then (Gamble, 2010) and now, particularly when churches lack the cash reserves to invest in modern technologies and to serve a congregation with immense personal needs of their own.

Blacks suffered disproportionate rates of COVID-19 infections, deaths, and health complications (Peteet et al., 2022). The institutions they supported, too, were affected by this pandemic. Their socio-ecological system will take a long time to recover before returning to pre-COVID-19 times, if they are able to hold on until then. Thus, the next several years will be critical for Black church survival. A national discussion is needed to confront this challenge and to discuss what can be done to prevent this coming calamity. The potential of another wave of COVID-19 infections will find these institutions even more vulnerable to closure.

When these institutions can no longer offer solace or meet the basic human needs of worshippers, or at least in the conventional way, attendees might disengage from formal worship and other church-centered activities. The interpersonal dynamics of attendees changed, too, as noted by the pastor of a St. Louis Black church (Brown Jr., 2022):

> Before the pandemic, Pierson said his church had about 200 members. "That number is now less than 40. It impacted our attitudes toward one another with everybody wearing masks and flying out of the doors after service, going straight to their cars," ... Pierson said, adding, "There's no camaraderie anymore. People who do come don't have the same friendly fellowshipping spirit. They don't want to get too close to anybody. They're not hugging and embracing like they used to. They're throwing kisses from a distance."

That church closed in late 2022, with similar experiences found throughout the country, and with no end in sight. These closings can be sudden or can follow a slow and painful process. Either way, the end result is a closure, and a community left to struggle with what to do with a vacant structure.

We have focused attention on how COVID-19 caused tremendous harm to Black church congregations. However, we must also acknowledge the COVID-related deaths of Black ministers and bishops, which had a devastating impact on institutional leadership as well as the broader community, because religious leaders often fulfill community roles that transcend their religious duties. Their deaths, too, made their respective churches more vulnerable to closures (Bunn, 2021):

> Bishop Nathaniel Wells Jr. of Muskegon, Michigan, who led his congregation at the Holy Trinity Institutional Church of God in Christ for more than 40 years, was a consistent advocate for affordable housing, education, transportation and child care. Bishop Gerald O. Glenn of New Deliverance Evangelistic Church was described as a bridge builder by community members in Richmond, Virginia; he even helped broker an agreement among the NAACP, the Daughters of the Confederacy and the Sons of Confederate Veterans about how to acknowledge the city's history.

Bishop Wells cannot be replaced by his congregation or Richmond, for that matter. His death cannot be relegated to a statistic! There lies the challenge for community practitioners—embracing the bigger picture without losing sight of individual lives.

If churches recognize this challenge, crises can bring hopes of a better future ("a shining city on the hill") and opportunities for creative institutional responses, such as starting public health outreach initiatives (Brand, 2019; Brown et al., 2022; Peteet et al., 2022) and food programs, and making outdoor property available for recreational purposes, for example (Hartford Institute for Religion Research, 2021). The integration of these institutions into the social fabric and life of an urban community is the ultimate goal of a community-centered house of worship.

Community practitioners, too, are in propitious positions to encourage or enhance these efforts by setting up collaborations with churches and developing models that can be replicated across the nation. Local experiences can inform national models; national models, in turn, can inform local experiences. Few practitioners actively seek the role of being a "broker" due to challenges in balancing competing interests.

Language Used in Church Closings and Repurposing

How we use terms to frame church closings goes beyond semantic considerations because of the social, political, cultural, and economic dimensions associated with these actions. How we label something also reveals our underpinning values, including our motives behind a set of actions under consideration, rationalizing church closings and what follows in their place.

One way to conceptualize church closures is to view them as the result of church leaders failing to exercise leadership in supplying options for communities. Congregational life cannot be separated from social responsibility if a church wishes to be relevant in communities struggling to achieve social and economic justice, and churches are often expected to weigh in on local social justice matters. As practitioners, we cannot succeed if we detach projects from social justice goals. Remember, these institutions are about peace and justice, not manufacturing wickets!

How we label church closings wields significance in understanding the values held by the entities closing these institutions, in addition to helping academic disciplines and professions undertake research on this topic. Readers, particularly those in England, will come across the term "redundant churches" to describe closed houses of worship (Purcell & Tweedie, 2023). This simple term conjures images of an item that has outlived its usefulness.

Several terms stand out in the literature, such as "repurposing," "reuse," "property rehabilitation," and "historic redevelopment," with repurposing having saliency in this book. More terms will appear in the future on the church closure phenomenon, such as "renewing the local church," and we must be prepared to assess what values underpin them. These terms illustrate the philosophy and values undergirding these actions, including political considerations. Is there a difference between a dying institution and one struggling to stay alive? I think of the terms used by the business sector such as "downsizing," "right-sizing," "reconfigurations," "retrofitting," and "staff restructuring"—all of which mean staff cutting!

Economics of Church Closings

Readers may be surprised by the presence of a section specifically devoted to the economics of houses of worship and earlier references to it. DeStazio

(2023) argues that churches are associated with "deaths of despair," such as alcoholism, suicides, deadly accidents, and overdoses, to list several, thus helping to explain the decrease in religious participation levels because of their association with pain and sorrow.

Church economics covers an extensive terrain. We will try to take an expansive view whenever possible in the hopes of capturing the breadth of this concept and its importance. Nevertheless, we will also make an effort to delve deeply into the relationship between church economics, closures, and repurposing, to better understand the forces shaping when and how closures unfold.

Although generally not recognized, religious organizations wield significant influence on local economies. A recent spatial distribution study found higher levels of churches concentrated in areas with lower incomes, higher economic inequality, and higher unemployment (Cheng & Meng, 2023). These plantings, from a marketing standpoint, are strategic, much like businesses being opened in geographical areas with plenty of potential customers.

Su, Yan, and Harvey (2022) spotlight how religious congregations represent a significant portion of the nonprofit sector and cannot be ignored in any comprehensive assessment of this system of care. According to estimates (although dated), houses of worship represent almost a quarter of all nonprofit organizations in the United States; they employ 1.3 million paid staff, representing approximately 11% of employment in the nonprofit sector. Yet minimal research exists to help us better understand church finances, which takes on saliency since finances are such a critical factor in church closures.

The consequences of church closures are multifaceted: cultural, spiritual, social, economic, and political. Some effects are highly visible and others are invisible. They might affect every member differently, based on their personal experiences. The consequences can be immediate as well as long-term. It is easy to see why closings are worthy of special attention in our society and therefore a specialized arena for practice.

Readers will be hard pressed to find scholarly material on closed churches and how they may elevate local crime rates. There have been studies related to gun violence in churches (Denney et al., 2022), but I was unable to find studies on this subject related to closed churches. A literature search on crime and place will find a plethora of studies on bars, street lighting, lack of "eyes" on the street, and other factors. Urban vacant houses have been found to increase crime (Porter et al., 2019), nevertheless, and so do vacant lots (Delgado, 2023; Kvit et al., 2022). Closed churches are subject to arsons, which bring repercussions for a neighborhood, including spreading toxins into the atmosphere. Vandalism, too, is increased, bringing its own set of consequences for altering public space and conveying a negative message to the immediate and broader community. Closed churches involve both empty structures and vacant land; thus, development and repurposing can bring a decrease in crime.

Vacant property reduces a sense of social connectedness within a neighborhood, which translates into increased feelings of isolation and insecurity, and possibly serving as a magnet for criminal activity. This can further curtail local activity in public spaces, although there is a need for more research on this topic, as in the case of Detroit, for example (Kagawa et al., 2022). It is easy to imagine a desperate downward spiral for these communities.

How gun violence affects church attendance is an under-researched subject in high-violence urban communities. Neighborhood violence and drug activity can cause churches to close or move to another neighborhood, as in the case of Redemption Church in Spokane, Washington (Funch, 2023). Church closures can accelerate neighborhood disinvestments, translating into business closures near the closed churches.

Church denominations cannot hold on to empty buildings for an extended period, assuming they can financially support them until the real estate market improves. That is an insult to the communities where they are situated and politically untenable. An empty building is a magnet for trouble and safety concerns (just ask anyone on the street), calling for a more nuanced view of crime and empty buildings (Moroni et al., 2020), including empty churches (Reinhard, 2021b).

Empty churches also affect local economies in both hidden and overt ways, further expanding their community influence. Viewing church worship through an economic stained-glass window has started to garner attention from scholars. We often think of these institutions as having "cultural wealth," but we can also ascribe "economic wealth" to them, wielding important influences at the local level (Park et al., 2020).

According to a 2016 Religious Freedom and Business Foundation report, religion contributes $1.2 trillion of economic value to the United States, which would make it the 15th largest national economy—greater than that of almost 180 other countries and territories. This sum falls into three broad categories: (1) $418 billion from religious congregations; (2) $303 billion from other religious institutions (universities, charities, and health systems); and (3) $437 billion from faith-based, faith-related, or faith-inspired businesses (Grim, 2021). Schools that are part of many of these congregations, in turn, employ 420,000 full-time teachers and train 4.5 million students each year.

Homes within a half-mile of a large church have a 6.27% increase in property value. Another perspective: In 2016 the value of religious organizations was greater than Apple, Amazon, and Google combined (Dallas, 2016)! These statistics, although dated, convey religion's impact on this nation's economy, making these institutions economic as well as spiritual engines.

Churches affect local economies. The average urban church generates over $1.7 million annually in local economic impact (C. Gerber, 2023), or almost $141,000 per month, a considerable sum that may surprise most readers. The authors of this report group church economic contributions into four categories: (1) congregations themselves; (2) faith-friendly businesses; (3) religious institutions; and (4) benefits to individuals (services provided to individuals that can be classified as social services).

Further, this dollar figure takes into account the value of programs offered, recreational facilities, space sharing, and direct local spending. Spending one dollar locally translates into spending $1.80 as this money circulates throughout a community. Inflation, too, is a dimension of church economics that needs to be addressed, particularly during crisis periods. A 200- to 400-member congregation, for example, generates $4.2 million annually in area business. Larger churches (3,000–4,000 members) generate $11.2 million annually. I imagine that most readers would never think of churches as community economic engines; they may have various amounts of horsepower, but economic engines they are!

Viewing houses of worship as viewed as million-dollar, if not multi-million-dollar, economic engines broadens our view and increases our respect for their impact when they close. It is important to remember that communities of color generally have small businesses with small economic impact. Churches, in these instances, stand out in terms of their economic influence and are part of a broader community wealth terrain, making them prime economic engines within communities of color.

The economic impact of churches, however, is not limited to urban centers. One study of rural churches in North Carolina found that they have a $735,000 economic impact each year on their local communities (Haertsch, 2023). The following statistics are over 10 years old yet paint an impressive picture of how churches affect the local economy. It is very easy for the general public to overlook the costs of services provided. An average-sized church supplies the equivalent of $115,000 in community services (Haas, 2013).

Capitalism enters into the picture of repurposing churches. Investors may be attracted by potential savings on building costs; profit may be the bottom line without regard to social value. There is a call for new metrics to capture denominational resources more accurately and to help us understand their role in defining and shaping a "successful" church.

The lower on the community economic ladder, the quicker the closing of its churches, as in Manchester, England (Peacock, 2023), which Purcell and Tweedie (2023) addressed in their report *Is the Church Losing Faith in Low-Income Communities in Greater Manchester?* This same question should be asked about other cities as well, because urban churches in low-income areas have historically contended with the vicissitudes of an economy that runs hot and cold.

Cutbacks in local donations to various church-supported causes and businesses, too, must be acknowledged. These can involve buying food from local businesses, sponsoring local events, hiring local residents to do maintain buildings and grounds, buying food baskets for those in need, buying flowers for those hospitalized, and helping to pay funeral expenses.

With inflation, the costs of goods, services, maintenance, and utilities, for instance, have increased, putting financial strains on parishioners and churches. Salaries for pastors and staff, too, have not kept up with inflation (McConnell, 2023). Limited purchasing power restricts the impact of funds set aside to aid parishioners in financial need as well as the local economy, for instance. Church members who need food vouchers and/or direct financial help in marginalized communities represent a further impact on limited reserves.

Church closures also mean the closures of various community services they provided. These are often invisible to the external community, as experienced in Chicago (Neuman, 2023a), but are vital to their immediate community. Such services can make daily life tolerable for those who are marginalized:

> Corpus Christi Catholic Church in the Bronzeville area of Chicago is an example of what happens to those community services when a church falls into decline. The church, like many Catholic institutions, ran a soup kitchen for years. It also once operated a thriving school. Both are now

gone. The church itself closed in 2021. Its congregation merged with three other parishes to form Our Lady of Africa parish.

There is no set formula for analyzing the ripple ramifications of church closures, so each closure needs to be individually examined to assess its impact on the immediate communities. Local circumstances will dictate which spheres are important. A broad-stroke picture must not come at the expense of local circumstances.

Critics argue that the influence churches have in creating social change is vastly overrated. They argue that when churches engage in supplying services, such as soup kitchens, allow residents to stay in their communities, helping to slow the process of gentrification, is still a noble pursuit (Kresta, 2022). Not everyone has the vision, disposition, time, and talent to pursue macro changes, however. That, mind you, is not a criticism. Rather, it is a reality check.

Addressing the root causes of hunger may not be part of this agenda, for example, and this is why some critics see these programs as merely "putting a bandage" on systemic problems rather than trying to make major social justice changes. It is actually possible to do both at the same time! Nevertheless, we cannot view the Black church—or any other church—in a political vacuum. Whether a house of worship embraces a social justice agenda or not, it is still a political actor in society.

Dutra (2021), although not specifically focusing on Black churches, takes a radical view of church closures and sees a positive aspect that can create hope for the "poor, marginalized, and disenfranchised." There are varied options for churches in distress, such as leasing property, merging, and selling their property. These decisions are framed as "crossroads," and not "dead ends." Underutilized property increases the likelihood that the church will die, and not a dignified death! The degree of community participation in making these decisions will go a long way toward determining the level of success that is possible. Simply "dropping" a decision on a community is not likely to result in success.

The Black church is a vital economic engine. We think of the Black church as an institution primarily serving religious, social, and political goals (Wilson, 2017), so its economic role has largely gone unrecognized. Its economic role increased in significance when the Black community and its businesses were restricted to certain geographical sectors through segregation. The Black church formed close relationships with and supported these businesses and they, in turn, supported the churches. An embrace of self-help in the face of past and present racist practices reinforces the support of Black economic enterprises by the Black churches (Edwards & Oyakawa, 2022). These efforts often go unrecognized by the outside world and thus are not considered assets.

The subject of church economic viability is increasingly receiving scholarly attention. Kresta's (2021) *Jesus on Main Street: Good News Through Community Economic Development* and DeYmaz's (2019) *The Coming Revolution in Church Economics: Why Tithes and Offerings Are No Longer Enough, and What You Can Do About It* symbolize shifting thinking on the economic life of these institutions and communities, and why this aspect must be uplifted and reinforced to stem the tide of church closings.

Corrêa et al.'s (2022) research on the importance of ministers having an entrepreneurial orientation uncovered two critical factors: (1) an innate quest for the discovery of opportunity, which has found prominence in the literature; and (2) an ability to overcome inherent challenges associated with the quest for day-to-day survival. This latter quality stands out because many urban congregational members, too, are struggling to survive on a daily basis. Ministers with this quality and experience can more easily connect with members.

There is a call to make churches "recession-proof," like essential businesses such as car maintenance, food markets, and healthcare, for example (Matt, undated). The 2008 recession, for example, caused over 500,000 church staff layoffs or reduced salaries, speeding the steady church decline (Subsplash, 2022). When these staff live in low-resourced communities, it further compounds the economic problems of their community.

Staff layoffs and reduced salaries caused by COVID-19 are yet to be fully understood but have similar, if not more devastating, consequences. Much as in 2008, requests for church financial help increased dramatically, adding to church's financial distress. One example is the work done by Detroit's Church of the Messiah, which developed and runs over 200 affordable housing units in that city (Jackson, 2020), making housing an integral part of their social mission.

A recent survey of pastors found that the current economy is hurting Protestant churches (Earls, 2022). More specifically, it is hurting small churches (memberships of under 50), with 61% of ministers saying that donations were down. In contrast, pastors (63%) of large churches (250 or more members) said that donations were higher than last year's offerings.

Does this translate into "bigger is better"? It appears that smaller churches are more vulnerable to the vicissitudes of the economy and congregational wishes, which means that churches serving marginalized communities face a greater threat of closures because they cannot increase income from current membership.

Smaller churches cannot help but be extremely sensitive to economics because they rarely have a cash reserve to draw upon during turbulent times, including the need for major repairs due to delayed maintenance, for instance. Boston's Four Corners section, for example, one of the toughest neighborhoods in Boston, had 29 churches, with most being storefront congregations and within a half-mile of each other. However, most attendees were not residents (McRobert, 2005). Low rents made it economically feasible for churches to rent space in this neighborhood. Although the study is almost 20 years old, the findings are largely unchanged today. Attendees are often relegated to the margins of society, making fundraising a difficult undertaking.

Storefront churches, if successful, eventually move to larger structures, bringing increased costs, which can be offset by larger congregation giving. Black storefront churches are not necessarily headed by men. Women can occupy roles as originators and founders of these churches and as pastors, signifying their exalted status (Crumbley, 2012). Repurposing a storefront will not wield the same significance as repurposing an imposing physical structure such as a longstanding church. Nevertheless, church members and family will still experience upheaval and significant loss, with potential long-term ramifications.

Economic alternatives to relying solely on tithes and offerings have been advancing this decade due to the financial viability of this approach, making churches part of local economic enterprises. Moon (2020, p. 19) created the acronym MINCE, highlighting five nontraditional approaches that churches can use to withstand periods of financial uncertainty: "1. Monetize existing church resources. 2. Incubate new businesses. 3. Nonprofits form mission arms of the church. 4. Co-vocational pastoring opens multiple income streams. 5. Entrepreneurial churches locate church inside the marketplace." This thinking will only gain greater saliency during the rest of this decade, bringing churches more into the economic life and activities of their communities.

We must pay particular attention to a declining membership to understand the economic forces at work in church closures. Not all parishioners are created equal, although this may seem unholy to some readers. "People in seats put dollars in the place" may no longer be correct axiom when talking about the economic viability of churches. Maybe there is a stratification of seats, with "premium" seats bringing in more dollars. This may seem crass, but it has a grain of truth. Some parishioners are able and willing to contribute funds to a church generously. Others may not be in a similar financial position; indeed, they may have needs that far outstrip what they can financially contribute. They may still contribute in countless ways other than financially, and we must not dismiss this form of wealth, but that form of contribution does not pay the electric bill. Sound church economics requires keeping up with a changing demographic and developing a realistic marketing plan, much like the business sector (DeYmaz & Michel, 2023):

> Here's the problem. If a 65-year-old attending your church dies or moves to a different state and their giving goes away, how many millennials will it take to replace that giving? Nobody has done a study on this, but every time I talk about it, people say "Maybe 10." Let's just say it takes 10 millennials to replace that 65-year-old's giving. Then, what is the customer acquisition cost? What do I have to spend as a church to attract a millennial versus what I have to spend to attract someone who is 65? When you say to that 65-year-old, "We teach the Bible. We're exegetically sound. We love and care about people," they say, "Hey, that's good enough for me." And they'll show up. But the millennial will ask, "What else do you do? What about your social justice side? What about your compassionate work? How about your children's programs?" And all those things cost. Now I've got to buy a laser light show and a smoke machine. I've got to wow everybody, and that costs the church money. Right now, we are like hamsters on a wheel. We're chasing more people, but with that chase comes the expenditure of more money to attract them, and you'll never catch up.

Readers may take issue with this economic or marketing analysis and the practices needed to increase demand for religious services. But funding is an integral part of supporting a church, even more so now because of the demanding times we live in.

Demographic shifts mean that churches need to rethink how they offer religious services and to pursue multiple streams of revenue to support a vibrant mission, including a cash reserve ("rainy day fund") for unforeseen events. A failure to recognize the realities of the marketplace increases the likelihood of failure and closure, leaving a critical void in the community that could have been averted with better planning.

Rasmussen (2020), although focusing remarks on Denmark, has issued warnings about how the "marketization of religion has become embedded in the institutions within the Church to the point where it has become a cultural dominant." Religion is not a product that can be thought of in a conventional manner, including monetization. This warning, of course, can easily find a home in the United States.

Organizational Efforts to Repurpose Churches

We need to discover and honor the motivation undergirding the "real" impetus behind a repurposing project, particularly when it is undertaken because of a "mission" rather than an economic imperative. This will help all involved to weather the turbulent winds invariably associated with any community venture. What may be considered "proper" and "welcomed" in one community may not be so in another community or municipality. This may be frustrating for those wanting a high level of predictability, but that is the operative reality we must take into account.

A decision to repurpose a structure is dependent on its (1) purpose, (2) location, (3) heritage, (4) architectural assets, and (5) market trends (Bullen & Love, 2010). These factors may at first appear easy to assess, but each one is complex and, when taken together, will challenge community and practitioner ventures into the church repurposing field, whether urban, suburban, or rural. Historically, the repurposing of churches has been undertaken by religious orders, which bodes well for advances in this field because there is a body of work to draw upon, although the outcomes of these ventures have been mixed at best.

The Catholic Church is facing considerable challenges in supporting viable memberships. Catholic Charities of the Archdiocese of Chicago Housing Services (CCAC-Housing) is one of that city's largest providers of affordable housing for seniors and veterans, which may surprise readers, as it did me; in addition, it supplies housing for unhoused individuals and families. Catholic Charities (Van Tessle, 2022, p. 2) published a report on its viability and the steps that need to be taken into consideration when converting church structures into affordable housing:

> Converting surplus church property can occur with little or no "out of pocket" funds and can result in valuable and highly appraised affordable

housing projects. These projects often add value to parishes and the diocese and provide quality housing to low-income households. There are many types of surplus church properties, including but not limited to: closed churches, schools, vacant convents, donated land, and bequeathed structures. Finding alternative uses for surplus church property, including conversion to affordable housing, is not a new concept.

This report offers examples of various approaches for selecting a locally based housing development organization. This is key in increasing the likelihood of success because of their knowledge of the local scene and the embrace of a socioeconomic justice mission.

There is no single model for repurposing, allowing local circumstances to determine what is the best choice. That may seem complicated and challenging to practitioners in general. Nor is there is a speedy approach. Any repurposing project will be time-consuming and expensive, and underestimating the challenge condemns any effort to ultimate failure. Some readers may say, "Isn't that obvious?" I am afraid not, particularly in cases where grants have a time limit but communities simply do not subscribe to this perspective. A community's clock moves differently than that of a grant funder, as any seasoned practitioner will attest to.

The National Housing Preservation Foundation (Burns, 2018) views church repurposing from a win–win viewpoint for faith-based organizations and developers (private or nonprofit). This group is "a not-for-profit real estate organization dedicated to preserving and creating sustainable, service-enriched multifamily housing that is both affordable to low- and moderate-income families and seniors, and beneficial to their communities."

Faith-based organizations can develop long-term income streams and not be burdened by a disintegrating physical structure, allowing critical investment in new initiatives to attract parishioners and expand their membership. Communities can increase their housing stock, with vested parties winning through investment in their communities and increasing resident stability, which is key in any community wishing to thrive into the future with a stable population base from which to build.

Stable communities have residents wanting to stay and invest in their surroundings; communities in flux do not have the luxury of investing where they live because they would rather invest where they are going to eventually settle in the future. Businesses, in turn, want to invest in stable communities.

Investments go far beyond economics and transcend all aspects of people's lives, including the political sphere. They generate local taxes that can then be reinvested in the community.

A Brief Glimpse of Chicago

Trends show local population increases causing Latinos to take over the closed churches of other groups. There are exceptions to this trend, as in Chicago, where a Mexican American church was scheduled to close (Amezcua, 2021). Within the past decade, Catholic churches in neighborhoods historically dominated by Latino Catholics have started to close. In 2015, there were seven parishes in Chicago's Pilsen neighborhood, but five years later the number was down to three (Kanter, 2021), a disinvestment on the part of the Church in this community. The empty churches, in turn, become symbolic of the worth of the community within the broader city. This signals another important trend: In 2013, almost 50 public schools in Chicago closed (Preservation Chicago, 2019). Readers can imagine what emotions such church and school closures elicit, engendering concern about a neighborhood's future.

The Archdiocese of Chicago once was the largest and most populous diocese in the country in terms of the number of parishes, and had the distinction of having the nation's largest parochial school system. The Chicago area, with 2.2 million Catholics, has one of the nation's largest concentrations of Catholics. Chicago's Pilsen neighborhood was originally home to Polish residents and is now predominantly Latino, but it still honors religious symbols from the past (*New York Times*, Bosman, 2022):

> Their mission was about more than the statue. For the Polish members of the group, the church and the statue were monuments to their ancestors and a reminder of their ties to Pilsen, which was once an entry point in Chicago for Polish immigrants. For the Latinos, the fight was to preserve community anchors including churches, as the neighborhood becomes increasingly gentrified and working-class Mexican families are being forced out by rising rents.

Two groups with immigration histories in different historical periods found commonality in this neighborhood and its Catholic church. The church became a "rock of salvation," helping them to make the transition to life in this neighborhood and nation.

An overview of Chicago's history with Catholicism helps us to appreciate what church closures symbolize in that city. The late 19th and early 20th centuries saw a massive influx of Catholics from Italy, Ireland, Germany, Poland, the former Czechoslovakia, and other countries. They, in turn, built their own churches and schools (Fenner, 2014):

> But Chicago, as if you needed reminding, is different. It's the city whose first European settler was a Catholic priest. Run for decades by Catholics. And continually flooded with Catholic immigrants, at first from Western Europe and these days mostly from Mexico and elsewhere in Latin America. More Catholics live here than do members of any other single religion.

Readers interested in Chicago's Catholic Church and the Latino community are recommended to read Fernandez's (2012) *Brown in the Windy City: Mexicans and Puerto Ricans in Postwar Chicago*. This book provides insights into religion's role in helping these groups to settle and connecting them to the city and its neighborhoods, setting the stage for current-day efforts to save Catholic churches and schools.

Rhode Island is the "most Catholic" state in the nation, with 44% of residents identifying as such. In terms of the "most Catholic" cities, Boston (see Chapter 6), New York, and Pittsburgh are tied for first place, with 36% of residents identifying as Catholic. Chicago and Philadelphia are tied for the second most Catholic cities in the United States, with 33% of residents identifying as Catholic. Los Angeles and Miami, with 31% each, round out this list. It is no coincidence that several of these cities have high percentages of Latino residents.

In Chicago, the closure of Catholic churches involved community protests, raising ethical or moral questions about the proceeds from the selling of church property (The Pillar, 2022):

> Five Chicago Catholics were arrested Tuesday, as they protested the removal of a Pietà statue from a shuttered local Catholic church. The arrests came after months of protests, as demonstrators have tried to prevent both a sale of the St. Adalbert's church building in Chicago's Pilsen neighborhood, and the removal of a large Pietà statue, which was relocated Tuesday to a nearby parish church... In a statement to *The Pillar* Tuesday, the group

said that "St. Adalbert's was paid for through the great sacrifices of Polish immigrants who came to America in the late 19th and early 20th centuries, people who made it their highest priority to conform their wills to the Will of God. Churches such as St. Adalbert's testify to that. It was created to last forever." The statement continued: "Cardinal Cupich recently sold the parking lot at his Holy Name Cathedral for over $100 million . . . Could some of this not be used to preserve the historic epicenter of Chicago's Polish Catholic culture? If not, can't we at least be given the opportunity to fund its preservation through other means?"

How Chicago handles this crisis can serve as a model for what can be expected in other large cities with significant numbers of multi-racial/ethnic population groups, setting the stage for future church undertakings.

The history of Chicago's St. Adalbert Church in the Pilsen neighborhood (Wisniewski, 2023) parallels the city's immigrant influx:

St. Adalbert's is a symbol of a looming aesthetic disaster in Chicago—the closing and possible demolition of historic churches. Changes in religious practice and in the city's population have driven down church attendance, and the Archdiocese of Chicago, individual parishes and the heads of other denominations have found they can no longer afford to keep many of their buildings open.

There certainly are significant parallels with other cities across the country.

Readers wishing more information on this church and the community's effort to save and repurpose the building are advised to view a short PBS video (https://www.pbs.org/video/st-adalbert-church-one-step-closer-to-landmark-status-zcx5c0/). The closure of St. Adalbert Church and efforts to repurpose it illustrate community involvement. Repurposing efforts such as this lend themselves to visual coverage to bring these efforts to life.

Currently, St. Adalbert Church's grandeur is best described as faded glory and represent a physical threat in a neighborhood facing daily safety concerns, as noted in the following description (Wisniewski, 2023):

Seen on a gray, rainy morning, St. Adalbert Church in Pilsen looks haunted. Scaffolding wraps its 185-foot-tall Baroque towers like a parasitic plant. At the church entrance, eight rose-colored granite columns are blocked by dirty plywood, on which are hung Polish and Vatican flags. Behind the plywood, someone has pitched a tent—the only comfort currently offered by the 109-year-old building.

We invariably view church closures from a physical/structural standpoint. However, they bring an aesthetic dimension that makes them an integral part of a community's beauty and character, qualities we usually do not associate with communities of color.

Church structures remain while a community's ethnic/racial composition changes. In the case of St. Adalbert, Mexicans are the latest immigrant group replacing Poles, as in the case seeking landmark status in Chicago. In 2023, the Archdiocese of Chicago had 23 properties for sale, with 15 on the South or West Sides or in the southern or western suburbs, illustrating the immense challenge facing the Catholic Church.

St. Adalbert's shares a similar financial profile with other churches across the country facing closure—it had a $1.6 million debt and monthly upkeep of $15,000 a month; weekly collections brought in approximately $5,000 a month. The cost of repairs was estimated to be $5 million. Selling church property, as in this case for $100 million including St. Adalbert, raises ethical and practice questions about what happens to those funds; for instance, are they reinvested in the community? St. Adalbert almost closed in 1974, with its parochial school not escaping closure.

Houses of worship have often enjoyed a lifetime of tax-free existence because of their special status in society. In old industrial cities, for example, more than 50 percent of properties are tax-exempt (Main & Reinhard, 2023), creating financial pressures to have repurposed properties generating property taxes. Readers may rightly ask why churches are exempt from paying property taxes (Brunson, 2023):

> Why are churches exempt, anyway? Fair questions. One reason is history—religious exemptions from taxation go back at least to the Bible. When Joseph imposed a 20% tax on Egyptian land, he exempted the priests from the tax. Jump forward to the United States: while it hasn't been a straight line, the exemption of at least some religious property from the property tax goes all the way back to Colonial days. And churches have been exempt from income taxation since the introduction of the modern federal income tax.

Taxpayers who are not church members have a say in the outcome of repurposing initiatives because they have shouldered the tax burden of churches over the years. Further, as with the Pilsen church closing, a food pantry was also lost. How do we put a price tag on that?

Churches with a community-centered mission provide a wide range of social services to the broader community, and that is certainly the case in Black and Latino-centered churches. These services must find new homes that remain psychologically (non-stigmatizing) and geographically accessible to current patrons in order to minimize disruption in their already precarious lives.

Extent of Church Closing Challenges

Repurposing is so much more than a technical or practical construction application. This is especially true when the new structures change the functional classification of a building, creating new regulatory conditions that may entail rezoning approval (Fisher-Gewirtzman, 2016). There is a consensus that zoning and land use regulations, for instance, play overly influential roles in shaping housing availability and prices, and they certainly do so with church repurposing. Reinhard and Elisara (2022) comment on the challenges that zoning barriers pose when undertaking repurposing projects:

> A municipality can have zoning and code regulations that make it difficult if not impossible to turn a single-use house of worship into a mixed-use development, especially one involving affordable housing. Neighborhood associations can be a drag on innovative ideas as well. Local finance officials, hungry for revenues, often swoop as soon as a house of worship is closed to levy large property taxes against an empty house of worship, adding to a project's financial burdens.

Anyone who has ever undertaken a rezoning effort will attest that this is best attempted only by those who are knowledgeable of the process, which is very technical, and who have a great deal of patience. Further, historical design and outdated infrastructures make repurposing more challenging because of its complexity.

Why is church repurposing so attractive for such diverse types of development? Developers of repurposed churches, for instance, can cut demolition costs and minimize new building costs, which can be considerable, bringing increased economic profits and ecological benefits. However, there may be challenges (Propmodo Research, 2021, p. 4): "Being able to take an old building, with blueprints that may or may not be intact and legible, and craft it into an entirely new use is not for the faint of heart. Furthermore, it requires a real impetus, not just the simple capacity." This commitment must be steadfast to be successful.

Repurposing encompasses social, cultural, economic, political, ecological, design, structural, and spatial dynamics found throughout the world and part of an evolutionary movement of the built environment and its offshoots. Consequently, its potential is only limited by our imagination and capacity to mobilize needed political will to achieve positive community change.

Repurposing can entail a range of time periods based on a project's size and budget and the socio-political-economic challenges involved. It can also be exciting for communities, bringing hope, often associated with any birth, as well as potential concrete outcomes, opening the door for innovative and substantive projects that are welcomed and can reverberate across the neighborhood. These projects assume even greater significance when churches are simply waiting for the time when their death is unavoidable, with time, progress, and hope diminishing every day.

Why should church buildings be exempt from a natural process of urban renewal that is operative across the nation, and the world for that matter, including a natural evolutionary process? This question is not meant to be provocative. Rather, it is intended to sharpen our thinking of how the urban landscape is expected to change due to changing times and demographics, for instance. Are churches exempt from these market forces? Of course not; they are a dynamic and integral part of the built environment while supplying a service that meets a series of primary or secondary needs to survive. An inability to grow and change relegates these institutions to the relics of history, but without the benefits that come from becoming a tourism site.

Why did I write a book on urban church closings and repurposing rather than combining them with school buildings, banks, libraries, or fire stations, for instance? Churches clearly stand out against a backdrop of other buildings. They will rarely be confused with other buildings. When closures are clustered, however, they have exponential effects on communities.

A church repurposing project can cause a ripple effect with wide-ranging local, regional, and even national benefits. Many of these are unanticipated and are important to catch, record, and analyze.

Repurposing initiatives can extend to other institutions (such as libraries, for example, in India; Vinayaraj, 2022), illustrating how this strategy can easily expand to other types of institutions/structures we typically do not associate with this arena of community practice. Library closures due to budget cutbacks can also mobilize communities to protest, particularly when there are fears that these institutions will be converted into businesses or housing (at market rates) and not in the community's best interest.

Libraries do not have the symbolism of churches but are nonetheless significant in a community's life and are often considered "special" places. I remember growing up thinking of the library as a "safe zone" where I did not have to worry about my safety. Safe public places are rare in high-violence communities and therefore precious to patrons. Closing a library can cause a seismic reaction that will surprise outsiders unfamiliar with this community. The same can be said about libraries within schools, for example (except, perhaps, in states where efforts are under way to ban books).

As already noted, churches occupy a unique perch in our society, and further attention is needed to develop a clearer picture of the challenges they face (Betz, 2022):

> Get ready, America. Get ready for the huge collapse from within that is soon to result in the locking of hundreds and then thousands of church doors across our country—all from the inside . . . The trend is already well underway, of course, in Roman Catholic circles. Mainline churches, like the Methodist church in my neighborhood, will not be far behind. Denominational treasuries simply aren't up to the task of sustaining ministry personnel and facility upkeep for neighborhood "franchises" that can't carry their own weight. When the 25 elderly people who gather now each week dwindle to a dozen, someone will have to pay the piper. And someone will have to mow the lawn of the church that isn't being used anymore.

The above scenario is common, raising critical questions about the future or these buildings and their potential to transform residents' lives in a new manner, if done in a thoughtful and participatory manner.

Churches expecting the coming closure tsunami ("church death tsunami") must confront their often-overbuilt real estate and the legacy they hope to leave their communities and need to plan for collaboration on redevelopment/repurposing (Reinhard, 2021b). Repurposing outcomes shape local communities in the short and long term as buildings are recycled to meet new needs. That requires imagination and a solid grounding on local needs.

The repurposing of churches looks different from industrial repurposing, and not just because of their spiritual mission and physical structure, thus bringing unique challenges for community practice (Aranđelović et al., 2022). This type of project calls for approaches taking into account building structure, building and zoning codes, local geography, and history. Industrial settings, for example, are often found on city outskirts, although in older cities due to expansion over time they no longer are. Historically, churches often occupy prominent places in communities because they were set up for that specific location. For repurposing to be successful, it must be responsive to local circumstances. That can certainly be the case with any successful community intervention.

How extensive are church closings nationally? The answer is difficult to ascertain, but it is worthy of analysis because it touches many audiences and geographical settings (Bacon, 2022a):

> But what has happened to the churches—to the people who used to populate the pews and to the pews and the buildings that housed them? Answering these questions is important and complicated. The number of churches affected almost certainly is higher than those identified by *21st Century Christian*... their story is important, not just for them, but for us.

There are various and wide-ranging U.S. estimates on the extent of current or projected church closings, making it challenging to accurately estimate the need for repurposing these structures. I know of no serious efforts to systematically collect data on these closings.

Churches of Christ as a Case in Point

Churches of Christ have a relatively brief history when compared to other denominations covered in this book. They trace their origins as a separate religious body to 1906, when they consisted of 2,649 congregations with 159,658 members (an average of 60 people per church). In 1946, they had increased four-fold to 10,089 congregations and 682,172 members, or 68 per church (Fillinger, 2021).

Churches of Christ reached their membership apex around 1990 with 1,684,872 adherents and 13,174 churches (128 members per church), or seventh most in the country, and they were found in all 50 states. However, the past 30 years saw a decline to 1,447,271, or 14%, with congregations falling to 11,965, or 9% (Bacon, 2022b). Michigan's Church of Christ, for example, had a membership decline from 31,314 in 2009 to 23,805 in 2019, a nearly 25% decline over a 10-year period (Krause, 2021), with membership on a downward trajectory with corresponding church closings.

Five Southern states—Alabama, Arkansas, Oklahoma, Tennessee, and Texas—account for over half of the membership, bringing a heavy regional dimension. More specifically, Texas and Tennessee had over one-third of this total. There have been 200 church closings since 2014, with at least 30 in each of these two states. This number might not seem alarmingly high, particularly in Texas, a big state in terms of both area and population, but these closings took place alongside other church closings as well.

Church Repurposing from a Life-Cycle View

We often associate a life cycle with human beings, but churches, too, go through a life cycle, as do other organizations (Weins, 2018). There are countless ways of conceptualizing these stages, as in the following examples that may resonate with readers. This perspective helps local communities analyze whether there is a high likelihood of a church closing in their midst.

Rucker (2023) proposes what can also be viewed as a life-cycle viewpoint:

> As churches transform through construction, disrepair, and destruction, the community it caters to transforms as well, and best land use projects must be adapted. When architecture succumbs to time, the emotions and identity represented by that physical dwelling produce feelings of joy and pain. It is a fact that all things go through some form of physical transformation and spiritual transition as they age.

Morgan (2023), too, addresses the importance of a church's life cycle and named seven distinct phases, with each stage having unique characteristics, rewards, and challenges: (1) launch; (2) momentum growth; (3) strategic growth; (4) sustained health; (5) maintenance; (6) preservation; and (7) life support. The "life support" phase does not necessarily mean that death follows. A phase 8, rebirth, can be added, bringing hope, with corresponding energy and drive! The grief stage may stand out for some readers. If so, Irwin's (2014) *Toward the Better Country: Church Closure and Resurrection* will prove of interest. The process of replanting a church necessitates considering how best to replant its ministers, too (Gleason, 2023).

A life-cycle frame lends itself to a proactive action plan that will bring challenges and rewards (Morgan, 2023):

> Once a church has reached the life support phase, they can no longer survive without a form of strategic relaunch. The church must embrace a new mission and relaunch into a new lifecycle through one of three options: firing themselves, hiring a new pastor, or giving the keys to their building to another church. Ultimately, there must be a consensus that the church will never drift back into health, and that a new plan of action is required.

This moment of reconciliation in moving forward can be expected to cause great consternation, however.

A developmental stage perspective brings unique rewards, excitement, and challenges for community practice. An organization's birth is associated with excitement and high energy; no two days are like. Maturing organizations have institutional procedures and run like well-oiled machines under the best of circumstances. A mature organization has its own traditions and "way of doing things," making it harder to institute innovative strategies for fear of "rocking the boat."

Religion has not been extensively discussed from an organizational and management practices standpoint (Van Buren III et al., 2020), and this lacuna is most obvious with church closures. We hope that as more professions and academics "discover" churches and the repurposing movement, our understanding of closures will be greatly enhanced, introducing new viewpoints to integrate into urban research and practice in this field.

Catholic Schools Caught in the Closing/Repurposing Movement

We cannot view church closings through a narrow lens because it limits development of a comprehensive view of the consequences of closure.

Catholic school closures, for instance, require a greater depth of coverage (Miserandino, 2019); quite frankly, the subject deserves its own book. Nevertheless, its coverage here will hopefully spark the interests of community educators, for instance.

Catholic school closures cannot be separated from urban demographic trends, as with their church counterparts. Glazer (2014) draws attention to three factors not generally covered in this analysis of closures:

1. The costs of operating these institutions have increased.
2. Catholic schools no longer can count on nuns, their traditional teaching force, because fewer young women are taking up the religious life. Thus, administrators have needed to hire more expensive lay teachers.
3. Catholic churches are "territorially fixed" because they are associated with a geographically defined parish. Thus, they cannot move away and follow their constituents, as with other religious congregational schools.

The parallels between church and school closings allow further insights into the decision-making process, which is largely fueled by a precipitous drop in the number of students and resulting financial shortfalls. School closures, like church closures, have consequences for their neighborhoods. The declining enrollment in Catholic schools and the resulting school closures have garnered increased attention over the past several decades, so this is nothing new (Miller et al., 2022). Parochial schools and churches are intertwined, and when one closes, it is only a question of time before the other does, too. (See the Boston case illustration in Chapter 6.)

Readers wishing an in-depth coverage of this topic would benefit from reading Brinig and Garnett's (2019) book *Lost Classroom, Lost Community: Catholic Schools' Importance in Urban America*. This book provides an analysis of their importance to the community, highlighting a critical statistically significant relationship between Catholic school closures in Philadelphia and Chicago and community crime rates. Their presence, simply put, decreased crime rates. These authors emphasize the ways in which Catholic schools serve to stabilize communities and point out the importance of leadership within schools, as in parishes, in shaping outcomes.

Suburbanization (Zhang & Park, 2023) or "white flight," impacts Catholic churches and their schools. Like their church counterparts, Catholic schools have played an instrumental role in their communities by serving as invaluable social anchors, particularly for newcomers to this country, helping children and their families make a successful transition.

Enrollment in U.S. Catholic schools, again like their church counterparts, has experienced a steady and downward decline over the past half-century, with implications for their communities and the nation (Wodon, 2019). These schools have increasingly become more of color, with greater numbers of Blacks and Latinos. In 1965, 5.2 million children were enrolled in Catholic school; that number has since declined to 1.7 million students, almost a two-thirds reduction (Wodon, 2022). The past decade witnessed an acceleration of closings, an ominous sign for congregations and their communities (Miserandino, 2019):

> The Catholic school system in the United States is undergoing significant changes in size, populations served and the funding models which have traditionally supported such schools. The closing of many schools in urban areas in the last 10 years in conjunction with the rising costs of schooling suggests that unless a new approach to funding schools is developed, the future of Catholic education in the United States is seriously threatened and with it the American Church.

School buildings and their church counterparts represent attractive structures (in terms of size and location) for repurposing. These structures are often well situated geographically, increasing their economic value for repurposing because there are more options for the buildings and land. Unlike their church counterparts, which historically consisted of just buildings, schools bring with them land (e.g., playgrounds) that can accommodate tenants with cars, making them attractive in highly congested urban centers.

When churches and schools close at the same time, it is a seismic event, leaving a critical vacuum within the neighborhood that is difficult to fill and affecting children, adults, and older adults. The amount of land these two institutions occupy, often in close proximity to each other, leaves a huge void that will be challenging to fill promptly. In high-violence communities, this void invariably attracts efforts by gangs to control it, and a community-stabilizing institution is lost. If left unattended, these structures will deteriorate, casting a prominent dark shadow on their communities.

Potential Municipal Governmental Repurposing Roles

Local municipal governments can be a facilitating or hindering force in finding new purposes for closed churches. They have a vital stake in church closing outcomes and must, as a result, have a say in any sustainable solutions because of the immediate and long-term consequences for these spaces. Cities with high real estate demands will often view church closings with great anticipation; however, dread will be the prevailing sentiment in cities with low demands. For the latter, another empty structure dotting the landscape will represent a physical reminder of the daunting task ahead for these cities.

Examining church closings within an urban and multifaceted context allows us to draw on the scholarship of a variety of urban scholars, helping increase our understandings. Reinhard (2023) turns to the late Jane Jacobs in challenging municipal governments to address church closures: "Cities need to prepare for a wave of declining houses of worship. While faith institutions, at least the Christian ones, have been asking WWJD (What would Jesus do?), municipalities need to get them to ask another question: WWJJD (What would Jane Jacobs do?). Doing so might create a new model for true community houses of worship."

Regardless of how municipal governments view closed churches, they must undertake a yearly inventory, assessment, and planning for the future of these structures and spaces, particularly when the churches historically played critical roles locally and are vulnerable to closing. This inventory must be periodically updated if it is to have value.

The role of municipal governments in church repurposing has started to appear. Amayu's (2014) study of the effects of planning regulations on adaptive reuse of church buildings in Kingston, Canada, for example, found four regulations that helped repurposing and are applicable to the United States:

(1) The City should take a more proactive role in facilitating church adaptive reuse projects. (2) The City should develop new funding initiatives aimed at encouraging adaptive reuse projects. (3) The City should streamline the existing Zoning Bylaws and provide more flexibility in meeting zoning requirements; and (4) The City should develop specific designation criteria.

These and other recommendations in this section are critical in shaping the church repurposing field now and in the near future. Some will be easier to carry out than others, as expected. This area of practice is too important to expect it to remain stagnant in the near and distant future.

Having a typology to rate the health of these institutions is one step toward understanding their state of existence from a community-wide perspective and having advance warning of potential church closures in the near or distant future. These institutions represent key economic anchors in the community and, because they typically provide a variety of social services, are also important in the health of the community.

Having this profile helps distribute needed resources in a planned and prompt manner. However, it is tempting for local governments to see closings as quick ways to increase tax revenues, for example, by making these buildings and spaces commercially available, even when local groups oppose doing so. When this occurs, an opportunity is lost for community engagement. Church properties may not hold a special place for municipal governments, making repurposing for the social good difficult and representing an opportunity lost (Reinhard, 2021):

> Unfortunately, most municipalities and denominations treat church redevelopment—whether for affordable housing or other civic uses such as community and arts centers or even office and retail space—not strategically but like a whack-a-mole game, touching one house of worship at a time with no real advocate in either the bishop's office or the mayor's office. In hot real-estate markets, private developers target struggling houses of worship, often taking advantage of inexperienced negotiators and building whatever the market demands.

The absence of a strategic plan hampers both planning for these closures and fostering purposeful development. Residents' opinions stand on closures and what is to follow must also be systematically elicited and recorded.

Municipalities that are attuned to significant trends within their communities will never be surprised by a church closing. Anticipating brings greater rewards and less pain than simply reacting! Religious communities, real estate experts, and potential funders, for example, must all be at the table with municipalities to start coordinated efforts to repurpose churches (Reinhard, 2021):

Is an empty church—or a church that wishes to become multiple- or mixed-use—a problem or an opportunity for a municipality? On the one hand, no municipality wants an empty building dominating a prominent intersection, especially an empty hulk that is difficult to reuse or to demolish. An active house of worship often serves as the site, if not the sponsor, for considerable social-services programs: food pantries, clothes closets, child-care centers, health clinics, and 12-step groups (such as Alcoholics Anonymous and Narcotics Anonymous). These initiatives often are taken for granted by municipalities, which may be forced to find alternative sponsors and alternative spaces if a church closes its doors. On the other hand, most municipalities would welcome the opportunity to take a prominent property that has been off the tax rolls and get it to generate local property taxes. Perhaps just as important is to take a prominent property that has seen limited use—perhaps one or two days a week—and turn it into a mixed-use activity generator.

When well attuned to community needs, municipalities can broker church repurposing projects to meet community needs. However, if municipal officials act as a barrier, the repurposing process can be even more complicated.

Municipalities must carefully weigh their options using a deliberative process because their decisions have long-term ramifications and cannot easily be reversed (Reinhard, 2021):

> Many municipalities are looking at the properties of houses of worship as ideal sites for needed affordable or low-income housing. However, alternative uses may be the highest and best use. Municipalities should be wise to the fact that what is best for a religion and their institutions may not be best for the community and should be prepared to negotiate.

Municipalities must balance analytical challenges and socio-political forces in making their decisions. They must if communities are to receive needed support and repurposing opportunities are maximized!

Kim, Newman, and Jiang (2020) focus attention on municipalities that encourage community participation in repurposing vacant land, with implications for shaping how vacant churches are to be addressed:

[They] should have to provide adequate information about vacant land conditions and their potentials in terms of ecological and social value. Code enforcement and tax foreclosure are efficient ways to control vacant land and the abandoned building problem. Tax incentive systems, such as high taxation rates on land but a low rate or no tax at all on infill development on vacant land, tax credits on vacant land forest structure, and rehabilitation abatement on abandoned buildings can increase public investment in vacant land. Local governments should support such efforts by creating community involvement groups, such as neighborhood coordinators, civic leaders, CDCs (Community Development Corporations), and other community-based nonprofit organizations.

These authors capture the spirit undergirding engaging communities, but municipalities must be prepared to take the lead due to their unique vantage point and sources of political legitimacy and access to resources. In essence, it is their job!

Governmental entities can offer tax credits and other financial incentives so that repurposing projects can meet local strategic goals (Filisko, 2023). Examples of governmental resources are highlighted throughout this book. Weighing financial options is known as "capital staking," and readers interested in this topic should read Filisko's (2023) article "Show Me the Money for Financing Do-Overs."

Mirza-Avakyan (2013) explored outcomes of adaptive reuse of old religious buildings in two cities: New York City, which typically involved market-rate condominiums or co-ops, and Pittsburgh, which entailed community development, neighborhood regeneration, and commercial establishments. Comparing these two projects highlights different outcomes and the role local circumstances shape how repurposing is conceptualized, whether for profit or not for profit. These two approaches result in dramatically different outcomes, as expected.

Urban regeneration initiatives, particularly those resulting in gentrification, have avoided examining the role of religious groups in these undertakings, either easing or hindering this movement (van de Kamp, 2022). However, once a regeneration effort targets churches, it places these groups squarely in the political mix. If done right, repurposing can increase a sense of belonging and place-making. This is critical in a project's success and makes these buildings responsive to local needs and circumstances.

Resident stability is an essential element in creating a thriving community. Having a core group as an anchor allows for both absorption of new groups and the ability to plan for a future based on collective good as a guiding force. How these changes are made or managed goes far toward being a model for other stability goals, as with businesses, for example.

Church closings take on symbolic and practical meanings and outcomes. Closed churches become physical reminders of a community in decline, with church shadows casting a wide influence on community dynamics and often sparking discussions of a bygone era. When community histories incorporate buildings, churches often take on prominence in these discussions, particularly among long-term residents with life-long experiences/stories related to that institution. Passing these histories to the next generation helps connect generations, creating a common community identity.

Municipal governments must assume meaningful roles in slowing or curtailing church closings, and/or easing the repurposing process if they have the requisite expertise and institutional legitimacy to do so. Top-down decision-making is unhelpful because it ignores the will of the people. Reinhard (2021) found five potential ways that municipal officials can be instrumental in facilitating this process, with implications for community practice roles, too:

1. *Researcher*: Research plays a significant role in any repurposing movement, religious or otherwise. Researchers help communities gather data on houses of worship (their size, value, and condition) and their congregants (such as their health and goals), creating an open-access inventory and information depository. By providing examples (case illustrations) of repurposing, researchers can help the visioning process to unfold.
2. *Mediator/broker*: Municipal officials can work with the various stakeholders in a project, who might have different agendas and might even speak different languages. Municipal officials can become translators/mediators, assuming they have institutional and expertise legitimacy to fulfill this role.
3. *Policymaker and implementer*: Repurposing churches for a new societal mission requires a person or team with the requisite legal background to help interpret zoning and building regulations, which can be quite complex. Institutions of higher learning, unfortunately, have a

long way to go in producing practitioners and academics with this area as a specific focus of expertise.
4. *Grant- or loan-maker*: Municipalities have personnel with the time and expertise to write grant proposals and can tap their financial resources to hire consultants with real-estate expertise. They can help to fund the redevelopment, in part or totally, of the building and site. This role takes on more significance because, as already noted, financing of repurposing projects is complicated.
5. *Purchaser and project manager*: Municipalities are well positioned to kick-start a church repurposing project by buying the structure and serving as project managers. Purchasing buildings and "flipping" them is a new dimension, and bureaucracies are often very reluctant to expand their missions into new and untested areas. A concerted effort to buy and hire locally is one way of circulating money within a community.

Readers can see that these potential municipal roles helping repurposing are congruent with community practice, which is reliant on the trust levels and relationships that municipal governments have with their communities—parishioners, religious leaders, community leaders, and local organizations. The concept of "it takes a village" by definition requires community members to gather and be actively welcomed as part of the project. When present, this "glue" unites church members and community members who are not, but still respect those who embrace this stance. We share the same community; it's where we go to school, work, play, worship, and live. Mutual respect and responsibility are essential.

State Legislatures and Repurposing

The role that government can play in facilitating church repurposing cannot be overlooked in any analysis. Although local government stands out in significance, state legislatures are also important. Legislators are increasingly making office-to-housing conversions easier to undertake, so the topic has saliency on the national landscape, with the goal of finding solutions to local problems through local resources (Fabris, 2023c). However, state legislatures will increasingly be drawn to church closings when they become more widespread across their geographical purview and constituents raise alarm; they can also help to shape the repurposing efforts that follow. However, their involvement "politicizes" this process even further.

New York and California, two key states with national influence, illustrate this involvement, which can be expected to increase in prominence in the near future. These two states wield tremendous national influence in shaping trends and represent barometers of how this nation will conceptualize and respond to church repurposing, particularly in states experiencing high rates of church closings.

In New York, a state senator introduced a measure that would lead to parishioners having a greater voice in the closing or merging of houses of worship (Reisman, 2023): "The bill addresses an existing part of the law that sets out parameters for some denominations when considering mergers. The law includes a specific provision for Methodist church members to be able to vote before a merger occurs. The measures would add Catholics to the provision." Involving elected state officials adds political considerations to the process of church closure and repurposing.

For instance, San Francisco has over 160 religious bodies, and repurposing could provide space for hundreds of housing units. Efforts to help religious organizations convert houses of worship and religious schools into housing, such as Senate Bill 4 (signed into law in October 2023), are under way in San Francisco involving the California State Legislature (Brinklow, 2023), and these efforts will gain saliency in the immediate future. This new law allows religious organizations and institutions of higher education to build affordable housing without requisite public hearings or the need to obtain special approval from cities (Senator Scott Wiener, 2023): "Senate Bill 4 streamlines the building process for faith-based institutions and non-profit colleges that want to build affordable projects for low income families by allowing them to build multifamily housing, regardless of local zoning restrictions." Church closings and mergers bring consequences that impact residents, be they parishioners or neighbors living near these soon-to-be-closed churches.

Interestingly, closed or merged churches are often called "churches in transition." "Transition to what and where?" is the key question, however. Church closings will become impossible to ignore in the near future, and state policies governing the process should be established. It remains to be seen how state legislatures throughout the country will act on church closings and their repurposing when voters put political pressure on them, although the tradition of separation of church and state will weigh heavily on them and the decision-making process.

Megachurches: Where Do They Stand in the National Landscape?

There are an estimated 2,000 megachurches in the United States, and they are gaining strength and representation across the country. Their success is largely due to their ability to attract new members in an increasingly competitive religious marketplace (Priuses, 2023; Wellman Jr. et al., 2020). Megachurches are worthy of our attention because they have largely avoided the closure phenomenon, offering a stark contrast to the many community churches facing challenges in staying open.

Megachurches (which are often nondenominational) have a high profile in society, giving the impression that they are expanding and countering the church closure trend. Melton (2020) estimates that there are approximately 1,600 megachurches across the country, a number that pales in comparison with the Catholic Church, for example. Nieuwhof (2023) puts forth an interesting perspective on these churches that readers may find thought-provoking in terms of the state of organized religion is in this country:

> While many might think the mega-church is dead, it's not. And while others think mega-churches are awful, there's nothing inherently bad about them. Size is somewhat irrelevant to a church's effectiveness. There are bad mega-churches and bad small churches. And there are wonderfully effective mega-churches and wonderfully effective small churches. We will likely see large churches get larger. Multisite will continue to explode, as churches that are effective expand their mission.

The size of a church's membership is not an inconsequential factor, influencing whether a church is thriving or dying. The size of the congregation, combined with income, expands a church's programming options. Architectural integrity or classification is inconsequential to worshipers; the symbolic meaning of a church in their lives is!

Melton (2020) suggests four important factors for analyzing these churches: (1) denominational affiliation; (2) their location relative to the nearest urban complex; (3) number of churches and membership; and (4) contrasting theological perspectives. Most megachurches followed a developmental path toward growth, starting out in rented facilities, hotel meeting rooms, or public school auditoriums. As they increased in size and budget, they eventually moved to a permanent site, such as a newly constructed facility or a former church that could comfortably accommodate the congregation.

Neuman (2023b) describes Liquid Church, a megachurch in Parsippany, NJ, capturing what it means to be a part of such a church:

> The average Christian congregation in the U.S. is in precipitous decline, with just 65 members, about a third of whom are age 65 or older, according to a 2020 pre-pandemic survey. By contrast, a separate 2020 study found that three-quarters of megachurches were growing, many at a rapid clip. Experts say these trends have continued since the start of the pandemic. Liquid Church claims 6,000 members, 84% of whom are under the age of 55, with most younger than 35. About a quarter of members are Hispanic/Latino, 13% Asian and 8% Black.

Clearly, a congregation like this is different from what the typical reader may have seen through church membership or as a guest. This highlights how difficult it is to make broad generalizations, as tempting as it may be, about this movement.

Megachurch congregations are one of the most racially integrated worship gatherings in the country, which is a profound finding considering that churches tend to be racially homogeneous. The Hartford Institute for Religion Research (2021) predicted that Latinos will be increasingly drawn to worshiping in these ethnically and racially diverse churches, which will have a significant impact on community churches. If this trend unfolds, it will have immediate local ramifications, drawing worshippers away from conventional churches, for example.

The physical structures of megachurches have more in common with theaters than small storefronts, and the spaces they occupy are increasingly significant within the landscape of churches in this country. These spaces have high maintenance costs and expensive worship technology (e.g., sound systems), meaning that sizable portions of their operating budget cannot be used for missionary pursuits. They still supply a range of important social and recreational services, though, aiding ministries in carrying out their mission.

Megachurches are usually Protestant congregations with a minimum of 2,000 weekly attendees. They find fertile grounds in the following areas, according to: "(1) where a large, closed evangelical community exists; (2) where a large upward oriented Christian immigrant community exists; (3) and in tolerant (and educated) areas—in conjuncture with the presence of a larger community of Protestants." U.S. Protestant megachurches generally share a conservative theology and are found in suburban areas of "rapidly growing sprawl cities" (e.g., Los Angeles, Dallas, Atlanta, Houston, Orlando, Phoenix, and Seattle). Marketing research must play a prominent role in the "church-planting" decision-making process, much like any other startup venture that hopes to succeed in the long run.

These churches draw audiences that are not bound by the geographical restrictions customary in conventional houses of worship. They often have elaborate fundraising operations staffed by experts rather than relying on pastors to lead these efforts. (Fundraising is typically an activity that pastors learn on the job, not as part of their religious training.) Parishioners are only expected to commit a limited number of hours, one day per week. This model is dramatically different from one that may require participation on multiple days per week over extended time periods!

Estimates show that 33% of all megachurches are nondenominational, and 25% are Baptist. Over half are evangelical, opening the door for a wider variety of ministries to emerge. These churches, for example, have found fertile ground in the Black community (Hall & Park, 2022; Williams et al., 2019). This point needs greater scrutiny, particularly on how they affect the viability of smaller churches.

Finally, "mega" applies not just to membership but also to land holdings. Many prominent churches occupying land tracts of 50 to 100 acres with major traffic thoroughfares nearby, also making these tracts economically valuable from a development standpoint. The extent of church land ownership is a theme in this book and is certainly manifested with megachurches.

At the opposite end of megachurches are "micro-churches," congregations of 25 to 30 members formed as a strategy to counteract church closings (Gray, 2020). Readers may also come across "mini-churches" with memberships in the single digits (Corrêa et al., 2022), highlighting the importance of "planting seeds."

Repurposing: Not an "Either/Or" Proposition

Church repurposing is not an all-or-none proposition, opening the door to a more nuanced—and complicated—view. The First Baptist Church in Jacksonville, Florida, was once one of Florida's largest Southern Baptist churches. In 2019, however, it had to sell most of its real estate. Its membership over the course of a decade declined by almost 70% (10,000 to 3,200), severely reducing its income. The maintenance budget consumed $5 million, or almost one-third of its operating budget, with deferred maintenance of more than half ($7.6 million) of its annual budget. The reasons for membership decline are not a mystery (Rose, 2020):

> First Baptist's financial crisis is unusual only in its scope and scale. All of Downtown's churches are experiencing declining membership and a drop in revenue. There are several factors. People are attending suburban churches rather than driving Downtown. And fewer people attend church, especially millennials, and when they do attend, they give less money than previous generations.

A similar story holds true for other churches in downtown Jacksonville. These church closures, including those of other religious groups, were not sudden and therefore were anticipated. This allowed for proactive planning of an intervention.

Where were the elected leaders, municipal governments, institutions of higher learning, and local foundations as this major event was occurring? The same question can be asked across the country. Indianapolis-based Lilly Endowment, for example, has taken on a national role in making significant grants helping communities in repurposing churches. However, it remains to be seen if other foundations will weigh in as this trend continues, which it surely will.

Land Banks and Church Properties

Land banks represent another quasi-public entity entering the church repurposing movement. The Syracuse, New York, Land Bank purchased the 134-year-old Delaware Street Baptist Church (Moriarty, 2023) and will seek a developer to turn this former church into affordable housing units. Churches can buy land from land banks to develop affordable housing, supplying an option for repurposing rather than just walking away (Click On Detroit, 2019).

Houses of worship with extensive land holdings represent a form of land banks. In Denver, Colorado, for instance, houses of worship own 500 undeveloped acres in the five counties surrounding the city (Kenney, 2018). How did this happen? Older established churches bought land on the urban fringes when it was relatively inexpensive, and as cities grew and land became more accessible, it increased in value.

Land banks are uniquely positioned to shape the transformation of closed churches at the municipal level. Although their primary goal is often preserving existing buildings, they are positioned to engage in church repurposing, too. Venturing into this field requires deviation from the usual practices land banks are accustomed to. Land banks, too, can be gifted with church property, providing a potential repurposing possibility. In 2020 in Toledo, Ohio (WTOL11, 2020), the Lucas County Land Bank entertained proposals to redevelop the historical St. Anthony Church, which had been donated by the Diocese of Toledo in order to save the church from demolition.

The first land bank was established in St. Louis, Missouri, in 1971. These banks responded to "growing inventories of tax-foreclosed properties stuck in legal limbo because the taxes and penalties owed on properties far exceeded their fair-market value, making them impossible to sell" (HUD, 2014). Special circumstances lead to special initiatives, as in the case of this urban church repurposing book.

Religious Organizations as Real Estate Developers

Readers may not think of religious organizations as real estate developers. Nevertheless, it is a "brave new world," and this role is increasingly finding a place in this field as repurposing gains prominence. Religious groups can develop housing on their property as a revenue stream if they have the requisite real estate expertise (Stiffman, 2023):

> For cash-poor congregations that face declining revenue and member participation and rising maintenance costs, developing housing can offer a financial benefit while also expanding their social mission. Most faiths embrace helping the vulnerable, and faith-based organizations have long provided housing. But it's rare that religious leaders have real estate development expertise and resources to navigate the often-challenging financial and political barriers that come with planning and building apartments and houses.

When we cast churches within a real estate movement, we broaden our vista on their potential to take on new identities. Some of these new identities will resonate with communities; others will not.

Churches bring unique histories that must be considered in how we view their future. These histories are informed by their communities. Nevertheless, society must be dynamic if it is to progress into the future, and so must its institutions—including its religious institutions. Introducing real estate developers is bound to raise eyebrows in the nonprofit world and concerns for their communities as to what the future holds.

This venture will bring reactions from real estate interests, too, who may not want competition in this potential lucrative and expanding arena. When tax-exempt churches sell their property to a for-profit business or engage in for-profit development, they must seek to make restitution to localities to compensate them.

New Model for Priest/Pastor Deployment: More with Less?

As we have noted, membership decline is key precipitating factor in church closures, but losing religious leaders is also a factor. So who will lead church revivals? Churches are responding to these challenges by using new models for deploying priests/ministers to maximize their availability, while acknowledging that this is not ideal or often welcomed by congregations.

In the Catholic Church, for instance, the number of priests is diminishing, with no signs of abating, at least in Western societies. According to a 2022 report by the Georgetown University Center for Applied Research in the Apostolate (CARA), the United States had 34,344 priests (24,110 diocesan, 10,234 religious) and 452 priestly ordinations, serving 16,429 parishes and 66.5 million "parish-connected" Catholics (Christian, 2023). However, only 66% of the diocesan priests engaged in active ministry, or one active priest per parish. That is not a winning formula for a thriving religious institution.

Churches are experimenting with deploying priests where churches are closing or merging to meet the remaining parishioners' needs. The Catholic Church, although not alone, is experimenting with a priest deployment model: (1) a single parish with a resident pastor (conventional approach); (2) two or more parishes with independent finances but sharing a pastoral team and staff; and (3) two or more parishes merging into one, also bringing unique challenges (Bernhard, 2023a). Unfortunately, low-income parishioners of color, particularly Latinos, are disproportionately affected. This trend will prove difficult to ignore because of the importance of the Spanish language and cultural needs historically addressed by a local parish. This model is also taxing (in terms of time and focus) for priests. Thus, closures represent an increasingly attractive choice for the Catholic Church (Bernhard, 2023a, 2023b). Other worship models will need to appear if churches are to weather the storm, but these will at best slow the inevitable tide and are likely to fail if not carefully planned.

Conclusion

This chapter addressed religiosity and church closings, highlighting the vastness and richness of this field, including its complexities. We have seen that it is foolhardy to make simplistic assertions. Church repurposing involves so much more than just repurposing buildings. Community practice has a key role in church repurposing. Vacant churches will numerically increase in the near future, so this situation is impossible to ignore!

We are at a stage of understanding the trends on church membership and closures. Trends are never static, responding to socio-environmental forces. Church closings are a national and an international phenomenon. Giving church closings/repurposing the attention they need will expand our vision of the community practice field. The following two chapters will focus on Black and Latino churches, giving readers a window into these two highly urbanized communities.

SECTION 2
BLACK AND LATINO CHURCHES

Section 2 focuses on Blacks and Latinos, two groups often occupying the same neighborhoods and struggling to get their voices heard and acted upon. Religion is prominent in their lives, although there are distinctive trends that have ramifications now and well into the not-too-distant future. These two groups, although diverse in backgrounds, bring significant similarities and differences shaped by historical and present social, cultural, economic, and political forces. Church closures, and their eventual repurposing, affect both cases. Nevertheless, nuances exist, with implications for community practice that must be highly responsive to local circumstances.

5
The Black Church

Introduction

Few, if any, racial or ethnic groups in the United States are more identified with religion and churches than Blacks. The Black church occupies a unique perch in this nation's religious landscape and history. Blacks historically had to set up their own cultural institutions because of society's racist policies and practices (Subramanian, 2023): "For persons of African origin, the Black church has functioned as a beacon of resilience, spirituality, and social strength, building a sense of community and justice." We need to work hard to understand this institution and the challenges associated with its closures, particularly in urban communities.

The historical and current-day significance of Black churches in urban America is undisputable. The future of Black churches, however, is open to debate and represents a cause of alarm for these institutions and the communities where they are situated due to a series of significant crosscurrents. We need to embrace a broad perspective beyond a narrow theological stance because of how the Black church permeates a community's social relations (Dates, 2021):

> The truth is the Black church is not a monolith and will never fit neatly in the progressive or conservative binary ... How the Black church has thrived this long, feeding the hungry, giving scholarships to its young, nourishing young families, preserving the wisdom of the elders, building schools and health centers while proclaiming an undying hope is a clue as to the clearest picture of the future of the Black church ... We have an answer for America's future because our sense of justice is not merely in the passage of laws, though important that is. Fundamental to our sense of justice is that love overcomes evil, that right will prevail over wrong, that hate cannot reign forever and that God will come through for us somehow.

This quotation provides a stark explanation of the importance of the Black church, connecting the past with the present and setting a foundation for the future of this institution and its worshippers, not to mention the geographical areas where these churches are located.

Ferguson (2023), too, broadens the meaning of the Black Church beyond its walls: "The role of the Black church in the lives of Black Americans has much to teach all American Christians—first of all, why there needed to be a 'Black' church at all. But is it time to look beyond self-segregated institutions in the hope of forming one multiracial, multiethnic institution? 'White,' on the other hand, is a mere legal category." The Black church is a "cradle of entrepreneurship," with a reach far beyond its walls into an area few of us think about.

Subramanian (2023) highlights why the Black church holds such prominence, particularly among older members, and its uniqueness as an institution in this community and society:

> The history of the Black church may be traced back to when enslaved Africans were forcibly carried to the Americas . . . Africans took refuge in their faith and spirituality despite the anguish of enslavement and the loss of their cultural heritage. They developed their distinctive forms of Christianity, fusing African customs with Christian teachings, and established their worship communities. Amid persecution, these early Black churches were places where Africans could openly express their faith, retain their cultural identity, and feel community.

The closing and potential repurposing of these impressive institutions cannot be done without carefully considering their history to parishioners and the community at large.

Finally, Lincoln (2011, p. 96) argues that the Black church *is* the Black community—they are one and the same and have great influence and significance within this community:

> To understand the power of the Black Church it must first be understood that there is no disjunction between the Black Church and the Black community. The Church is the spiritual face of the Black community, and whether one is a "church member" or not is beside the point in any assessment of the importance and meaning of the Black Church. Because of the peculiar nature of the Black experience and the centrality of institutionalized religion in the development of that experience . . . the Black Church, then, is in some sense a "universal church," claiming and representing all

Blacks out of a long tradition that looks back to the time when there was only the Black Church to bear witness to "who" or "what" a man was as he stood at the bar of his community.

Clearly, the Black church is unique and critically important in the Black community and society, too! Anyone wishing to learn more about the Black church will not have difficulty in finding articles, documentaries, governmental/foundation reports, and scholarly literature on the subject. Much of this coverage is very positive, and for good reason.

The Black church and its community are inseparable. Struggles for social justice make it so, although there is a fracture occurring that is a cause for alarm. If Blacks join predominantly White, non-Latino churches, it brings its own challenges. If congregations become racially integrated, as with new Black parishioners, it challenges host churches and their religious leaders to foster a climate celebrating this racial diversity, a noble but challenging goal.

Guhin et al.'s study (2023) of 102,000 sermons from more than 5,200 pastors found that preacher messaging can be an effective mechanism for decreasing prejudice only when pastors can ideologically reconcile their potential role in economic inequality—examining their own privilege. White Evangelical pastors rarely preached on social justice issues. The context of preaching matters. When congregations have a greater share of Black attendees, they are less likely to address justice issues. And when they actually addressed them, they ideologically avoided critiquing these systems. Blacks who worship in predominantly White, non-Latino churches, as in the case of the Latter Day Saints Church, for instance, must socially navigate racism while worshipping (Wood et al., 2023).

The Catholic Church, for example, recognizes the challenge of attracting and keeping Blacks historically and currently. However, the challenge is particularly formidable when racial justice is expected to be a prominent part of their religious experience, and this viewpoint, too, is missing for Blacks in similar fashion to their White, non-Latino Evangelical counterparts (Massingale, 2021):

> The answers lie in a different direction. More than three fourths of Black Catholics say that a commitment to racial justice is an essential or important dimension of their faith, versus only 13 percent of Catholics overall. Three quarters of Black Catholics want and expect to hear sermons that are relevant to the distinctive struggles of Black people in America, yet less

than a third of those who worship in predominately white parishes heard sermons addressing last summer's massive protests over the nation's callous indifference to Black lives.

It is clear that what transpires within a church will determine whether Black parishioners feel their plight in life is significant to the congregation. If it is, they will feel validated and welcomed. If it is not, leaving for another congregation that better understands their life situation is a practical alternative.

Conner (2022) discusses the Black church as instrumental in defining the Black American experience, helping engender interpersonal relationships and creating critical relationships between this institution and the community it serves. The Black church has filled critical gaps in education when public schools have ignored or distorted Black people's historical contributions to society. Current efforts to revamp the teaching of Black history in Florida's public schools is a 21st-century example, calling on the Black church once again to fill this critical gap about their history.

The Black church is certainly diverse beyond the skin color of parishioners and their experiences with histories of enslavement and oppression. Nevertheless, it represents a rare safe space for sharing aspirational dreams, as well as sorrow and pain. It has been instrumental in the past and looks to continue to be so well into the future, despite the ominous clouds looming on the horizon.

When viewing church membership as a community, we must expect that changes will occur as new members enter who may not share the ethnic, racial, and life circumstances of existing members. As in any vibrant community, we must expect that there will be moments of joy, tension, and conflict. How these differences are recognized and addressed dictates whether the church will thrive or die. The church community brings a cultural context that can be viewed from an assets perspective (Park et al., 2020).

This institution has a long and distinguished history, but its future is not predetermined and is currently a source of debate in academic and religious circles. Cudjoe-Wilkes (2022) calls for the Black church to embrace innovation as an intentional form of practice—a "calling," if you wish—if it is to remain relevant, attractive to congregants, and practical in the future. Readers will see some examples in this chapter and throughout the book.

This chapter's focus is purposely narrow in scope. We will examine church challenges and closures and the key trends and reasons shaping these outcomes, setting the stage for repurposing closed church buildings into new forms for serving their communities. A number of significant factors shape these trends, and some may be surprising. The Black church can be considered the "canary in the coal mine for churches of all races and denominations" (Stephens, 2023).

According to Ecclesiastes 3:1–2 (TLB), "There is a right time for everything: A time to be born; A time to die; A time to plant; A time to harvest." This quote offers a life-cycle viewpoint with saliency for church closures and repurposing. Churches do not close on their own or because of a divine power; earthly reasons are the cause! And earthly actions, in turn, can reverse this trend.

In Corpus Christi, Texas, a thriving Catholic church was torn down because of structural safety concerns, despite parishioners' willingness to make the needed modifications (Gibson, 2022). In this case, church members could not fight the Catholic Church or City Hall.

In Montopolis, Texas, the New Jerusalem Baptist Church, a Black storefront church (Asher, 2023), was demolished due to building code violations; municipal officials determined that the only viable alternative was demolition. The spouse of the pastor noted: "This is our place. God blessed us with this area. We paid for this. We didn't have no lawyers and doctors in our congregation—we were a small congregation, we stood together, and everybody worked together." These small churches do not enjoy the benefits of highly influential members like more advantaged churches do.

Major social forces have come together to create conditions that make it untenable for some churches to stay open. For example, Black Christians have expressed a strong preference for attending racially diverse congregations (Brumley, 2022). The Black church's composition has more than half of its congregants in all age groups but still contending with shrinking membership (Stephens, 2023).

These forces start as small waves that go unnoticed. As they gather strength, they become noticed with some level of apprehension. But they will eventually become a tidal wave, destroying everyone and everything in their path. As we noted in Chapter 1, the church closing trend has been gathering strength for several decades, generally flying under the radar. Stopping this trend will require creative interventions to ensure that the new structures and missions are responsive to community needs and goals.

There is no denying the importance of urban Black church closings and why this topic has a special place in this book. It is impossible to understand the Black community without also understanding their church because of their interdependence, particularly from historical and social justice viewpoints. Black Church attendance is positively related to membership in a social support system, helping congregants to weather turbulent times (Nguyen et al., 2019). The church is a place where Blacks can obtain instrumental and expressive services without being stigmatized; these services are provided by someone who looks and speaks like them and shares their lived experiences.

Urban practitioners must be prepared to address the Black church (and, as discussed later on, the Latino church) if they hope to have any significant degree of influence within this community because of its prominence as a community institution. It is not a question of "whether" but rather "how." How this engagement happens depends on local needs and circumstances and is simply too significant to ignore.

What Is Meant by "the Black Church"?

The term "the Black church" is often used without any specificity attached to it. After all, the mere mention of "the Black church" will at once conjure up images for anyone on the street. Thus, it is important to note that the Black church is not monolithic, and no two Black churches are similar when contextualized to the local scene.

When we talk about "the Black church," we are typically referring to one of the seven major Black Protestant denominations: (1) National Baptist Convention; (2) National Baptist Convention of America; (3) Progressive National Convention; (4) African Methodist Episcopal Church; (5) African Methodist Episcopal Zion Church; (6) Christian Methodist Episcopal Church; and (7) Church of God in Christ. Where pertinent, we will name the specific church denomination; otherwise, we will use the generic label to ease the unfolding of a narrative. The same principle applies to "the Latino church."

It is estimated that 60% of Blacks who attend church do so at Black churches, 25% attend multiracial congregations, and 13% attend White, Non-Latino/Other congregations. The prominence of the Black church within rural and urban communities shapes every major aspect of Black parishioners' lives, particularly those in urban communities where few institutions are controlled by the Black community.

To understand the nature of Black faith today, three points should be kept in mind to avoid stereotypical or overgeneralized thinking (Turner, 2022): (1) Black churches are constantly evolving and changing; (2) in Black churches, politics consists of far more than conventional electoral engagement; and (3) Black churches are not just or even best visible through the pulpit; we need to consider a broader view of their mission. Cunningham Stringer (2023) calls attention to the role that Black women clergy and lay leaders play in fighting against state-sanctioned violence and why their importance to the Black church must not be overlooked.

The Black church, like any other church, cannot remain static if it is to survive in the 21st century. However, the prominence and centrality of the Black church necessitates that it further embrace a dynamic social justice agenda—at the risk of alienating parishioners who do not share this perspective. The Black church brings an undeniable historical legacy, but it cannot rest on this history to remain viable in the 21st century. Middleton (2023) proposes a model that relies on a co-vocational ministry framework; this would address the challenge that Black urban churches face in fostering and keeping leadership, including preventing burnout and ineffective mission mobilization, by engaging millennials in leadership roles.

The Black church has a dually important and heightened purpose of spiritual formation, serving as a platform for social and economic justice (Harrison, 2021). These congregations represent multifaceted systems of support crucial to the well-being of their members and neighborhoods while also addressing the spiritual needs of their members (Azzara, 2019). I like using the analogy of a multi-service agency! Such an exalted position makes the closing of a Black church so much more consequential than the closing of any other building or establishment.

For readers unfamiliar with the Black church, there is no uniformity between urban and rural settings, which should not be surprising (Spencer, 2022, p. 2):

> [Black churches] situated in urban city environments differ from those situated in rural country locales. They serve different socioeconomic levels, divergent political ideologies, and separate cultures. Furthermore, as strange as it may seem, there are also divisions within the Black Church that distinguish between color lines, educational attainments, and economic status.

Their contextual grounding and histories are also different, making comparisons and broad generalizations difficult and increasing the importance of having initiatives that are well grounded within their respective communities.

A regional perspective, too, is essential in grounding and understanding the role that these churches play. For instance, Southern Black churches provided newly freed enslaved people a place in society where they were welcomed, and they served as a base from which to fight racism and exclusion (Harrison, 2022). The social, economic, political, and cultural importance of the Black church in the South makes this institution of great significance. When Blacks migrated north, many moved away from the Black church and joined other churches that were open to welcoming new groups. This process has continued to this day, posing a threat to the Black church's basic spiritual and physical survival.

Readers may ask: "Why must Black churches worry about closing their doors? After all, there shouldn't be any serious competition." That is not the case. A Pew study of the Black church (Weber & Lee, 2021) found that 4 in 10 Blacks attend a non-Black congregation—including half of Millennials and "Gen Z." Further, 6 in 10 said that when they were church shopping, it was not important for them to find a congregation where most attendees shared their race. Finally, two-thirds identify as Protestants, but only one in four identify with historical Black denominations. This translates into a dramatic shift in terms of where it is best to worship, a trend that raises concern for the Black church.

A 2021 study of ministers found that churches of color were being challenged, with Black pastors (20%) noting that the economy was having a negative impact on their churches; they were more likely to say that their donations were lower than budgeted (48%), and below 2019 levels (50%) than White, non-Latino pastors (31% reported that giving was below budget and 34% said it was down from last year) (Earls, 2021). Black churches often operate with a thin operating budget, a precarious state of existence that often parallels that of their parishioners. Some Black church gatherings have addressed the importance of fundraising activities to help them carry out their missions (Partners for Sacred Spaces, 2021).

According to the Pew Research Center (2023b), in 2021 an estimated 25% of Black households and 15% of Latino households either had no wealth or were in debt, compared to 10% for the nation as a whole. Being in a financial precarious position makes it difficult to make sustained financial contributions to churches.

Evangelical pastors, in turn, were more likely than their mainline counterparts to say that giving in 2020 was higher than budgeted (23% to 14%). Evangelical pastors were also more likely than mainline pastors to say that giving was above 2019's offerings (32% to 19%). Pastors in churches with worship service attendance of 250 or more were increasingly more likely than pastors of smaller churches (fewer than 50 people) to report increases in giving from 2019 (32% to 23%).

For readers who have not attended a Black church service, it is unlike any service I have ever attended. These services can go on for multiple hours; they involve singing and testimonials, with food and eating as part of the experience;. You leave these churches energized but also exhausted if the experience is new. One cannot help but appreciate the diversity of ways in which people worship. Being a church member may involve attending several times a week. The same experience can be found when attending a Latino storefront church, I would add. In essence, it is quite different from attending a Catholic mass or a Church of Christ service, for example!

It would be a disservice to associate church closures with majestic buildings standing tall and proud, symbolizing a bygone era. When small storefront churches close, they, too, shake a neighborhood in a way that far exceeds the size of their building and congregation. Kostarelos (1995), in *Feeling the Spirit: Faith and Hope in an Evangelical Black Storefront Church*, examines storefront churches in Chicago and supplies a vivid account of their worship services and why they occupy such prominent places within their communities. The description by one attendee at a Baptist storefront church helps capture their importance from a sociocultural standpoint (Kutty, 2020):

> There was a difference between the church that I left (in Prescott) and the Baptist church here. This church wasn't, what should I say, it wasn't as warm. The church I left in the South, everybody knew everybody else, and we were one to another. The Baptist church here, well it seemed that more emphasis was on what you had on. You know, everybody dressed fine in that church and they didn't reach out to you. When I was there, I barely knew the people. You know, I'd go to service and I'd go home. That was just about it.

Readers can appreciate how a church's social climate can make members feel either welcomed or unwelcomed. No one church can accommodate all attendee expectations. Thus, being acutely aware of congregants' needs and expectations is essential for a thriving church.

When these churches close, it is difficult to find a ready and easily accepted substitute to take their place, leaving an incredible void in the lives of parishioners and their community. In other words, a church is not like a big-box store; they are not interchangeable and we can't easily replace one with another. Storefront churches are not limited to Black urban communities; they can also be found in Latino and Asian American and Pacific Islander (AAPI) communities, and similar consequences occur when they close. They churches introduce a different dimension to what we typically think of a church repurposing.

Each church brings unique histories and dimensions that are highly dependent on the relationship between ministers and congregations, as well as the history of their community. We must avoid viewing church closings from a simplistic grouping or categorical standpoint, tempting as that may be, because no two have the same history and circumstances. We must, too, have a broad understanding and deep appreciation for the closure trend without losing sight of each church's specific meaning for its community.

Between 2012 and 2022, 120 Harlem faith-based organizations closed, or 12 per year. The following narratives goes beyond these numbers, capturing how each church closure brings a unique history and a range of outcomes (CBS New York, 2022):

> A vacant lot now sits on Amsterdam Avenue where Childs Memorial Temple Church of God once stood. It was the site of Malcolm X's funeral. Its sale and subsequent demolition is currently under investigation by the state. A soon-to-be condominium building on Madison Avenue in East Harlem was once Metro Community United Methodist Church. As an historic landmark, St. Luke's cannot be torn down, but it can be repurposed... St. Philip's Episcopal Church has successfully leased part of its property to a school, which Rev. Canon Terence Lee said is helping with much-needed repairs to the sacristy. "I don't think that has been renovated since this church was built in 1911," Lee said, "so that's a challenge. And then, of course, you always have roofing issues." St. Philip's once boasted a congregation of thousands. It is now down to fewer than 200 dedicated parishioners, but Lee leans on legacy to help.

When churches close, their unique histories and narratives are relegated to history books, if they're lucky. The communities where they once stood risk losing the wisdom of these churches and stories about how they shaped countless lives.

Being based in Boston, I am used to seeing plaques commemorating where an historical building once stood and why it was so important to the neighborhood, the city, or the nation for that matter. Low-resourced communities rarely are able to share this history with current occupants. People of color have hardly ever been in a position to record their histories for future generations, and houses of worship are no exception.

The interior design of storefront churches is simple, and due to limited budgets they may have only 500 to 1,000 square feet to conduct their missions (Kutty, 2020). Worshipping in a small physical space is a very special experience, and not just because of the physical proximity between each worshipper and the religious leader. Despite their small physical size, they are part of a community's built environment and are important to both the congregation and the neighborhood. Closure can bring with it immediate and long-term social and emotional consequences, much like their larger church counterparts. However, it is rare for local media to cover these closures.

Churches that actively embrace financially struggling members in their social justice mission will not be able to escape financial challenges by simply recruiting more members. This precarious situation needs fundraising expertise. Thriving churches (the fastest-growing, largest, and most financially stable), with notable exceptions, are invariably located in this nation's affluent suburbs, predominantly White and non-Latino.

Mattis, Palmer, and Hope (2019) observe that Black urban life in general, and faith life in particular, is more expansive and nuanced than commonly understood, calling for a careful analysis of how church closings affect their life and that of their communities. I would stress the importance of a multidisciplinary perspective, because church closures provide an important social, economic, cultural, and political window into the Black community's well-being and public space.

Are Blacks Losing Their Religion?

This question is not meant to be provocative. Rather, the topic of Black religiosity, as measured by attendance as an expression of beliefs, is a critical force shaping whether their church is thriving or dying. Standing still is a rare choice because it is only one tragedy away from falling into the dying category. Black churches, too, are facing a future that can be conservatively categorized as challenging! What about the communities where these churches currently stand or once stood?

The Episcopal Diocese of North Carolina, which counted 60 such churches, found only 12 remaining, and only 3 had full-time clergy. Full-time clergy are key to ensuring a thriving church (Shimron, 2018); "part-time" clergy will not have the time, energy, and creativity to maintain a congregation while seeking to expand it at the same time! Making clergy part-time can be an interim move to save money and help rebuild church membership. It can also be seen as a cold and desperate step before closing a church.

In Lawton's (2023) study of Black church closure and economic outcomes, almost 60% noted that participation had a positive impact on their socioeconomic status by tapping bridging social capital, particularly among parionshioners with more frequent (weekly) religious attendance. Church attendance meets instrumental means concrete; expressive means emotional and serves as a critical dimension of being "religious." Religion is a source of social capital; losing confidence in religious leaders and the church's moral leadership undermines houses of worship and weakens the critical "glue" that keeps a congregation together.

A relationship was found between the frequency of religious participation and the likelihood of receiving a scholarship or grant funding from religious organizations (Kristof, 2023):

> Ultimately, the literature suggests that the church plays a vital role in creating and sustaining social capital in the African American community. By providing a space for community members to come together, share experiences, and build relationships, the church contributes to the economic and social well-being of African Americans.

Black Church closures can undermine the economic foundation of parishioners and the community where they spend their money, another dimension worthy of further study.

Generational Importance of a Social Justice Agenda

The economic wealth of some religious organizations is considerable, and how this wealth is used to further a social justice mission of the congregation requires scrutiny. Saint Ignatius of Loyola said it well from a social justice standpoint: "If our Church is not marked by caring for the poor, the oppressed, the hungry, we are guilty of heresy."

Understanding the attendance decline at Black churches, particularly among younger members, requires discussion of congregational views of social justice causes and their centrality to their mission. "All talk and no action" causes consternation among activist members. The Black church's role in social activism, as noted by one Black minister, has diminished over time (Stephens, 2023):

> While Davis agrees, he warns that there are differences between activists of the original civil rights movement and their more contemporary counterparts. "The difference is this: I think that Grandma and Great-Grandma had a theological grounding that had a dependency on God in this process of social justice," Davis said. "When they were marching, it was a God force. While they were protesting, there was God's protection. What has happened, in this new movement, they don't see God in that. They see social justice, they see it in light of their own strength."

Black youth, for example, have more outlets for engagement in racial/social justice than their grandparents and parents did, decreasing the centrality of the Black church in this movement. The Black church is still significant, but is experiencing competition for its membership.

A toxic church climate, any minister and/or congregation's greatest fear, cannot be ignored when it affects Millennials and "Gen Z," who represent the future of any church's survival (Soul Thursdays, 2023):

> It's important to recognize that no church is perfect. Unfortunately, some churches create toxic environments that are not about connecting with God, but instead focus on prosperity preaching and pastoral salvation. This can be especially problematic for Black churches, given their history and the potential for discomfort within a polarized society. When Black churches fail to consider this history and its implications, it can lead to people feeling disconnected and ultimately stopping attendance altogether. This trend is particularly evident among Millennials and Gen Z, who display declines in religiosity.

More research is needed, with answers and corresponding actions playing an instrumental role in ensuring the continued survival of this church.

Some critics of the Black church, for example, argue that its future will largely be decided by how it addresses the subject of LGBTQ+ members. In all fairness, this controversy is not unique to the Black church, but it is nonetheless considered to have a significant role in shaping the future (Crowley, 2021).

A social justice agenda like the Black Lives Matter movement, for example, can be a strong dividing line in a Black church. Some parishioners may leave the congregation in order to move to one that actively embraces this cause, introducing a generational standoff that carries immediate and long-term implications (Mathis, 2020):

> Leaving one's church represents a personal loss for the individual, but the institution also suffers when parishioners decide to take their valuable perspectives away from the flock. It's still too early to quantify exactly how many Black churchgoers nationwide have made such a decision, or how many might still leave their church if their concerns aren't addressed ... It's not uncommon for people of color who attend multiracial churches to hear very little about racism ... Instead of supporting systemic change, some white Christians view racial reconciliation as a matter of fellowship among churchgoers of different races—something that can be achieved through interpersonal relationships. As a result, churches may not perceive the need to acknowledge or lament racial injustice. Others might hesitate to endorse Black Lives Matter, because of ideological differences with the national organization and its founders. But Black parishioners' desire for recognition doesn't mean they're ideologically aligned with the national group—they just want to know that their congregation values them. If more Black Christians leave their church, their absence threatens to tilt congregations' demographics toward the segregated status quo.

The complexity of a social justice cause requires a deliberative process. If handled poorly, it can have important consequences; either an exodus of current members or an influx of new parishioners can occur, depending on which side the church stands on (Mather, 2023).

The challenge of embracing a social/racial justice agenda and vision is not unique to the Black church. Los Angeles Archbishop Gomez, Head of the United States Conference of Catholic Bishops, made a speech in 2021 at the Congress of Catholics and Public Life in Madrid that offended Black Catholics, lay and clergy alike. His speech included "ill-advised, ill-timed remarks about social justice movements being 'pseudo-religions.'" He argued that social justice movements are political religious movements and represent "replacements and rivals to traditional Christian beliefs" (José Horacio Gómez). This stance highlights the disconnect that can exist between the Catholic Church leadership and racial justice in the United States, and will not endear this church to Blacks and other groups of color and their allies.

A Black Church's Vision Beyond Ministerial Duties: A Case Illustration

Black churches can and must expand their service vision to community pastoral efforts, incorporating this vision in their mission. In Louisville, Kentucky, for example, a pastor's vision resulted in a 30,000-square-foot facility called "The Village at West Jefferson," also known as MOLO Village, which means "welcome" in the southern African language Xhosa (Holznagel, 2021). This facility offers social services in addition to housing and has space for local businesses, with 35 Black- and Latinx-owned ventures signed up, making it a mixed-used facility meeting a range of social and economic needs:

> "When you look at the media and all the things that define who we are as Black people, it's not good," Christopher said. "All the attention that MOLO Village is getting is because of the fact that Pastor Ferguson brought all the community together and said, 'Here's who we are. This is what we look like.' For the folks at Beecher Terrace to see a beautiful building like this—it speaks volumes. It's everything."

By reaching out beyond conventional borders, Black churches become grounded in the social, economic, and political fabric of their communities, increasing their support within and outside of the church.

COVID-19 and Black Church Closures

COVID-19 had a devastating impact across the nation, particularly within urban communities of color and their institutions. One of the long-term consequences was slower growth in cities and even decreases in population because of fears of how population density might affect health and well-being (Tavernise & Mervosh, 2020). The pandemic significantly and dramatically altered church attendance and continues to do so—there is a symmetry to "six feet apart or six feet under" (Moore et al., 2022)!

Black churches are not immune from the national forces causing church closings. Washington, D.C., has experienced a Black population decline of 19% since 2000 (largely due to gentrification), causing decreases in congregations at Black churches (Major, 2022a). More specifically, Washington's Black population decreased from 59% to 41%, largely due to an influx of Latinos and Asians, inflation, and increased rents. White, non-Latino median household income is three times higher than for Black residents (Major, 2022b).

COVID-19 played an influential role in changing worshipping patterns, increasing the number of church closures, and reducing congregation sizes due to health concerns and deaths (Levison & Segall, 2020; Makridis, 2022). However, this the church closing trend was clear before the pandemic started (Bacon, 2022b). Legal factors, too, weighed heavily in the decision-making process about church closures—for example, the fear of lawsuits resulting from unsafe building structures.

D.C.'s Lincoln Congressional Temple United Church of Christ

The demographics and church closures covered in this book can certainly benefit from more in-depth attention, including historical views, to describe the process and painful outcomes of a church closure. In this case we focus on one in the Black community, Washington, D.C.'s Lincoln Congressional Temple United Church of Christ, which closed in 2018. Founded 149 years ago by formerly enslaved people, it played a pivotal role during the 1963 March on Washington (N. L. Brown, 2018). This fact that this closure occurred in the nation's capital brings added symbolic value and significance.

The church, which was listed on the National Register of Historic Places in 1995, occupied 10,000 square feet, seated 1,200 attendees, and was once home to thousands of parishioners. However, as it approached closure, at any given service there would be only about 12 attendees; the last service drew only 9. Decisions had to be made about whether to donate the church's pipe organ and its furniture and whether to sell the building, which was assessed at $3 million. These decisions weighed heavily on the congregation and members of the general public, who rarely witness these deliberations.

Why did this church close? Changes in community demographics between 1990 and 2010 in the historically Black Shaw-Logan Circle area of the city were dramatic: The Black population plunged from 65% to 29%. As young White millennials flooded into the community, the church made efforts to attract new members, such as Saturday evening concerts, but they were not successful. Another factor in the closure was the fact that many members who had moved away needed to drive to the church; however, parking was inadequate, compounded by fears of getting parking tickets and cars being towed.

The Black Church and Other Urban Centers

This discussion about Washington, D. C., serves as a good lead-in to examine other cities. These statistics are best understood and appreciated against a broader backdrop that takes into account demographic trends. A recent Baltimore-Washington Conference of the United Methodist Church (2022) report on Black church closings noted that between 2012 and 2018, a total of 13 churches were sold (an average of 1.9 per year). The average sales price was $334,000, generating $4.3 million in proceeds. From 2019 to 2021, church sales tripled to an average of 5.7 churches per year, generating $5.9 million in total proceeds. This is an indicator of a disturbing trend in the Black church community.

New York City (Ransome et al., 2022) also offers important insights for the country. According to one estimate, 120 faith-based organizations closed in Harlem between 2012 and 2022. However, not all Harlem churches experienced these loses. First Corinthian Baptist Church, for example, is increasing in membership, with the onsite mental health clinic proving extremely popular (CBS News, 2022). Churches often carry out service missions that further integrate them into the social, economic, and political heartbeat of a community, making them particularly indispensable in highly economically and socially marginalized communities. Offering these services, in turn, increases the likelihood that they will survive major events such as COVID-19 or a severe economic downturn, for example.

Church closings, in part due to aging parishioners, decreases in religious importance, and the impact of COVID-19 (deaths and decreased attendance), raised alarm in public health circles because of the multifaceted role these institutions play in Black communities (DeSouza et al., 2021; Major, 2020b). Gentrification, in turn, is a powerful force ever-present in urban communities that are close to downtowns or other highly attractive areas of a city—as experienced in Harlem, for instance (Solis, 2017). The possibility of gentrification brings fears to these communities, and rightly so.

Neuman (2023a), in quoting Reinhard, notes two outcomes that do not meet local needs:

> "In New York, San Francisco, Miami, developers are chomping at the bit to come in and get their hands on urban church properties and to turn them into luxury condos or . . . offices," Reinhard says. However, "in poorer communities and in rural communities, often churches just sit there and nothing happens to them."

Unfortunately, closed churches become magnets for vandalism and fires, creating an unsafe situation that can harm a community in a variety of ways.

There is a plethora of scholarly literature and governmental/foundation reports on gentrification ("urban renewal") and how it dramatically changes the composition of communities. There are diametrically different opinions on its value for this nation's cities. However, there is little dispute that it is a major secularizing force in urban neighborhoods; the socioeconomic forces that gentrification brings displace major population groups, including those who are church-going and, chances are good, also long-term residents.

In 2023, the National Association of Realtors issued a report, *Repurposing Smaller Buildings*, noting that churches represented a significant portion of the available pool of buildings (Clark, 2023). Nonprofits and community practitioners, it is important to emphasize, must be at the table when church repurposing is being discussed. We cannot let for-profits dictate the repurposing agenda. Yes, they belong at the table, but the table must be wide enough to include other entities with differing agendas, including municipalities, for example.

Outreach as a Mission: Two Dimensions

Outreach is a strategy that is near and dear to me. Churches increasingly need to develop outreach initiatives, if they have not done so, because congregations are dynamic rather than static entities (Barnette, 2023). Reaching out to new immigrants from other countries is one means of helping to buttress a church's current membership and ensuring its economic viability and survival, as in Aurora, Colorado (Neiss, 2019), while serving a broader social agenda, allowing houses of worship to take on multifaceted goals. These efforts, however, can cause a backlash and controversy among current parishioners, which can spill over into other sections of a community.

Another viewpoint suggests that Black churches should reach out to engage the Latino community because of demographic changes in communities. These two groups often occupy the same neighborhoods and confront a similar range of social justice issues that marginalize them. Two interesting initiatives concerning the Black church focused on the initiation of outreach initiatives.

The New Birth Missionary Baptist Church's efforts to target the Latino community, which grew from Latinos in the community seven years later, signifies a distinct trend (Haines, 2007). This initiative was multifaceted, including employing a Latino band, adding Spanish-language Sunday services, learning Spanish, and even hiring a Latino pastor. The Church motto, "Our house is your house," was translated into Spanish—"Nuestra casa es su casa." I could not obtain further information on this initiative's success or failure, but the very nature of this initiative suggests the bold efforts that can be taken to expand a congregational base of support.

St. Stephen Missionary Baptist Church, based in La Puente, California (Sweas, 2016), is another example of outreach to Latinos. St. Stephen, a 4,000-member church with a 51-year history, responded to the changing demographics of La Puente, which went from primarily Black to 85% Latino and only 2% African American. Sizeable numbers of longtime church members moved farther into the Inland Empire region east of Los Angeles, but a large number of Black parishioners undertook the commute back to attend religious services. The jury is still out on whether younger members will continue this practice, however. Rev. Dockery said it in a way that addresses a key theme in this book: "It's important for the church to be relevant to its community as well." An inclusive church is a surefire way of being relevant!

Churches that have community service missions stand out in their communities, and this can serve as a way to recruit new members. Harper (2005) found an emerging trend within vibrant Black churches of taking leadership in community redevelopment by exercising "authentic spirituality," addressing both body and soul. When these churches fail, they are greatly missed and cannot be easily replaced by repurposed establishments.

Blackwell (2022) argues that the Black church can play a transformative and enhanced role in creating economic stability and wealth within their community by embracing an entrepreneurship spirit as ministry practice, which is exciting and daunting at the same time. The Black church's centrality to the community has a long history. It has continued to the present and can continue well into the future, if concerted efforts are made to right the ship.

Black and Latino churches fulfill multiple critical roles in our society, and observers argue that they simply cannot be replaced. However, we live in a segregated society (even though progress has been made to decrease this), largely the result of where we live and the institutions we patronize, including churches (Berrelleza, 2020). Multi-racial/multi-ethnic churches take on greater importance by bringing together community institutions seeking to fulfill this critical role (Munn, 2019).

When these institutions close because of declining members and corresponding financial challenges, replacing parishioners becomes immensely important and challenging. In all likelihood, the businesses that replace these institutions will have economic goals guiding their mission rather than goals of bridging racial divides and social justice, for instance. Institutions that can carry out this goal are extremely important but often in short supply, as in the cases of churches.

The Black Church as a Living Institution

The Black church has grown in significance over the past two centuries, including playing an influential role in this nation's civil rights movement (Johnson, 2019). This church is considered the oldest institution established and controlled by the Black community. According to the National Trust for Historic Preservation (2023), it represents a "living testament to the achievements and resiliency of generations in the face of a racialized and inequitable society." Of the more than 95,000 entries in the National Register of Historic Places, only 2% focus on the Black experience (Cep, 2020), although this community represents 13.6% of this nation's population. The ability to view and preserve Black history through their churches and other buildings brings forth an urgency to save these structures.

The Black church can be envisioned as a special place and space that meets a range of community needs beyond the spiritual, while serving as an anchor for initiatives extending beyond the walls and stained-glass windows of this institution. As well noted by Claytee White, director of the Oral History Research Center for UNLV Libraries (Strott, 2022),

> "One of the things that the Black community can control—one of the only things—is a church," White went on to say. "When you think about not being able to get loans for a house, not being able to get [Small Business Administration] loans for business, one of the things that you can control in your neighborhood is a church."

But what happens when this is no longer the case? Can the community control what replaces its former church building? The answers have immediate and long-term consequences for this community.

Urban churches, particularly those that have extensive local histories of serving as havens or sanctuaries, are associated with ethnic groups and identities. They represent a critical means for socializing newcomers to this country and helping them meet their instrumental needs. Increased research and other scholarly efforts have focused on how urban churches can be revitalized (i.e., membership, money, and morale) by embracing a multifaceted mission integrating social justice, prophetic preaching, missional stewardship, intergenerational ministry, and progressive pastoral leadership.

It takes an exceptional church leader to balance all of these goals to be successful. In fact, it can be argued that it takes a team! External support is essential, such as consultants and trainers, to enhance leaders' knowledge and skill sets. Embracing this stance takes the Black church from an inward vision to one encompassing a multifaceted outward mission, as noted by a Black minister/scholar (Harrison, 2021, p. 2): "I believe the faith community can potentially serve as a catalyst of change that ushers in spiritual renewal, economic development, social uplift, civic engagement, and leadership development in the same disinvested communities in which they are located."

Inward and outward missions must be in harmony for the Black church to thrive. Supporting this balance is one of the foremost challenges facing this church and its leadership. Latino churches, too, have started to shift in similar fashion in response to changing local circumstances, with much to learn from their Black brethren (Hinojosa, 2021).

The Black church has served as the training ground for many of this nation's major social activists/leaders, occupying a unique and prominent position in our country's social justice landscape from an historical context. As noted by Dr. Lerone Martin of Stanford University (McKinney, 2023): "African American churches have played the role of gathering place. A place of community. A place of harnessing talent and resources and labor. Also, a place of advocacy." When these churches close, these spaces and their activities are lost to communities, if repurposing efforts do not meet the lacune left behind for residents.

The subject of burnout in the Black clergy must not be overlooked, as well as the culture that may avoid and even frown upon addressing their emotional needs, thus denying their humanity (Brandon, 2022). It does not take a mental health professional to know that suffering in silence can interfere with sound decision-making when responding to environmental stressors; the result can be membership declines, eventually causing the church to close.

Hunter (2022) makes an important observation that the Black church has historically been centered on its people and social justice events, providing an invaluable forum for exercising self-control and self-determination. However, minimal scholarly attention has been paid to the physical buildings ("sacred Black spaces") that house parishioners and these events; this represents a serious gap in our knowledge base. Mission and structure cannot be separated because expanding services to various family members to have the feel as they are being heard and their needs being addressed in response.

Black Millennials and Church Closures

It is important to end this chapter with attention to demographics and why Black Millennials are leaving the church. Challenger (2016) sees Black Millennials as the future of the Black church, and suggests that one approach to keeping them engaged in the church is to establish mentoring relationships, giving license to their questioning, exploration, and discovery. Walker (2022) proposed five key reasons for this exodus:

1. **Judgmental and unaccepting stances:** Millennials may be put off by a church's resistance to having women as pastors and viewing same-gender relationships as evil, two positions that effectively disempower

a sizable part of a congregation. (Readers are recommended to read St. Clare's [2022] article for a rationale for this policy.)
2. **Choosing traditional spiritual paths:** Millennials may be attracted to more traditional spiritual practices that can be traced back to African belief systems, counter to the more conventional views practiced by a church.
3. **Anti-intellectual/closed to new information:** Millennials may consider the Black church to be too dogmatic and traditional ("ancient") in conducting its mission, which makes it difficult to respond to changing times.
4. **Apolitical** (in "church speak," we are "in this world but not of this world"): Millennials may find the church too focused on life after death and not focused enough on life on earth (daily living) and the struggles of the community.
5. **Peers missing:** Older congregants may not share the life struggles that youth do, pointing to the importance of having all ages represented in a congregation.

To remain viable, the Black church must target younger generations while holding on to traditionalists, a delicate balancing act. Hiring youth ministers is one strategy that can help break these generational barriers. Such ministers can develop activities specific to this population group.

More research is needed on how the Black church can attract different age groups, among other demographic groups, to create a multigenerational congregation and decrease the likelihood of decline and closure. Having more women ministers resonates with many, and having their voices uplifted rather than suppressed also stands out (Mitchell, 2023). The Catholic Church, for example, has resisted ordaining women, hindering their efforts to recruit more parishioners. This policy has remained a source of great controversy (Hibshman, 2023).

The Black church has played an instrumental role in our nation's history, politics, and the quest for social justice (St. Louis American Staff, 2023): "The centerpiece of Black communities starts with the Black church . . . Black churches are exceptionally important in American democracy, not only for their legacy in civil and human rights but also for their role in uplifting civic identity and community empowerment." The Black church is one of the very few institutions controlled by the Black community, as argued throughout this book.

Black religious leaders may argue that their church transcends a physical space; its ventures into community service represent such an example, as evident during periods of crisis. COVID-19, which certainly qualified as a crisis, threatened these efforts and rocked smaller churches to their very foundations, causing many to close. As membership numbers diminish to a critical point, congregations may be forced to close for economic reasons, even if there is significant community opposition to doing so (Shapiro, 2022). Leaders of any church, regardless of its congregational composition and location, must carefully consider the costs of supporting the church, including assessing the prospects of obtaining new members and the infusion of needed funds in the immediate future. When thinking about making institutional changes to attract new members, leaders must consider that such changes might alienate existing parishioners, who might leave the church. A delicate balancing act is needed during these moments.

The increased cost of managing aging real estate is a key factor in church closings, even more so when major repairs have been deferred due to a lack of funds and poor decision-making by leadership. Reinhard (2022a) notes that if we estimate costs of $5 per square foot, and the typical church consists of 10,000 square feet, it will cost approximately $70,000 per year, or the equivalent of having a 100-member congregation paying $20 for 35 weeks per year to support the costs of a non-tax-paying church. Mind you, that does not consider any other expenses. If the average membership is under 100, which is considered a sizeable congregation in many circles, it is easy to see the financial challenge facing congregations that are steadily losing members.

Declining Black church membership raises the important question of who is leaving—men, for example (Lampley, 2017). Stressors for Black pastor, and how they address dwindling congregations, have been understudied. This must be remedied to reverse a key element in the trend toward closings and to help find solutions (Rogers, 2022) or the proverbial "glue" that holds together a congregation.

Black Americans are more likely than other racial/ethnic groups to see a sharp decline in church attendance. This is particularly significant for urban neighborhoods and the historic social justice role played by their institutions. In 2019, for instance, 45% of Black Americans attended religious service regularly. By 2021, attendance had dropped to 30%, a difference of 15% points. The decline among other groups was between 5% and 6% (Wang, 2022). This precipitous drop in the Black community has accelerating the closing of churches. Attendance decline is an indicator that social scientists see as critical in predicting church closures.

Waning interest in Black church affiliation and attendance can be summed up in the following assessment by Cotson (Cep, 2020): "The first generation is fired up, enthusiastic and dedicated to God.... The second generation goes through the motions. The third generation doesn't care." It does not take a statistician to see the cliff that awaits this community and the need to engage younger attendees to join and maintain church affiliation. Decreased church attendance by the younger generation is part of a broader trend in this country, which only increases the challenge.

We must view the Black church from a multigenerational perspective. For instance, Sunday school provides children with educational instruction, including important socialization and connectedness (Harris, 2020). Closing churches means that classroom instruction will also cease, affecting current and future generations. When Sunday school spaces are also used for community activities, it's easy to see how a church closing can also affect the broader community.

A Pew study found that most Black church attendees attend Black congregations, but generational patterns are changing as to who attends (Mohamed et al., 2021). Approximately young Blacks are not affiliated with any church, and this trend is most pronounced among members of Gen Z and Millennials (Mohamed et al., 2021). Over the past decade, the number of Black Americans without a religious affiliation ("Nones") rose more dramatically than among White, non-Latinos, Latinos, or Asians (Burge, 2022), which does not bode well for their churches.

Another Pew study captured the rapid decline in Catholicism among Latinos, from 67% in 2010 to 2020, with the proportion of "Nones" tripling to 30% over a 12-year period (Hardy, 2023); this is similar to trends among their Black counterparts. Readers might be interested in reading Burge's (2023) book, *The "Nones": Where They Came From, Who They Are, and Where They Are Going*, one of many that can be expected to be written in the future. Espinosa (2023), however, raises concerns about the methodology pertaining to Latino religious identity and Nones. Estimates have approximately 43% of Latinos as Catholic, a dramatic drop from 67% in 2010 (Long-Garcia, 2023).

A demographic breakdown has men more likely than women to be part of this group; more specifically, people without children. Baby boomers represent about 20% of Nones, Gen Z 45%. However, there has been a call for the use of "the 3 B's" (belief, behavior, and belonging) to obtain a nuanced understanding that goes beyond demographics. Future research will be needed to shed light on this ever-growing group.

A study of New York City church closures between 2013 and 2019 found that the highest rates occurred in communities with the highest percentage of Blacks (Magee, 2022), highlighting how the national trend toward closures has not bypassed this community. The rapidly gentrifying peninsula in Charleston, South Carolina, home to several historically Black churches, is experiencing church closings; Greater Macedonia AME, for instance, was left behind when the congregation built a new and larger church in West Ashley (Dennis Jr., 2022). No region of the country has avoided the trend of church closings and their consequences. How closings are planned and managed, as with decaying shuttered buildings, presents an opportunity for community workers to meet and enlist local groups in solving pressing community needs.

Sadly, Black church closings can also provide opportunities for embezzlement: In Harlem and Brooklyn, New York City, several religious leaders have been charged with taking almost $2 million in secret payments (bribes) from a developer in exchange for selling seven predominantly Black churches to him (Gerber, 2022). These church closings bring extra pain for their community.

Repurposing Black Churches as Housing

It is fitting to end this chapter by discussing ways in which closed churches can be repurposed into community housing, which has been discussed in various forms throughout earlier portions of this book because of its significance within this community. The process of repurposing aging buildings can be started by the Church itself rather than outsiders or municipalities; often, strategic creative solutions can be found to meet their own needs and those of the community (Roewe, 2023).

Church leadership must seek the active and meaningful involvement of parishioners, residents, and community leaders when planning and implementing these projects to ensure that they meet salient local needs, helping to ensure a smoother transition in a building's purposes. Decisions made in far-off places, such as the Vatican, limit how local voices are solicited and acted upon. Centralized decision-making is generally a barrier to repurposing projects that are responsive to local conditions.

Church buildings can be extremely attractive for housing developers, not just because of their distinctive architecture and size but also because of their strategic community location and potential to minimize costs to attract investors. However, as outlined by Mian (2023), Black churches are called upon to respond because of high housing costs in cities across the nation:

> Black churches are responding to these shifts in religiousness, population change, and lack of housing by working to change land use regulations and asking how church property can serve a different function in the community. Black churches in Seattle; Oakland, California; and Washington, D.C., among others, are building coalitions and working with city government and other organizations to create pre-development studies, participate in capacity-building programs, and develop housing on their own properties, and advocate for changes to housing policy and zoning regulations. These efforts and initiatives are intended to soften the impact that gentrification and displacement have on low-income neighborhoods and communities of color as the cost of housing increases.

Although Black and other churches have joined coalitions to address a range of community concerns such as violence (Rhea, 2019), there is still a need for them to join together to address the crisis of church closings in their midst, and to shape plans for the projects that will fill the void caused by their closure.

The Boston case illustration in Chapter 3 spotlighted a central theme in this trend, including potential rewards and challenges for communities, with lessons for urban practice and education. Churches occupy a prominent place in cities and are often integral to the way in which a city's historical narrative is shared in history textbooks and classrooms, bringing meaning to future generations. History, it is important to emphasize, is also embedded in buildings, and one does not have to visit this nation's historical cities to understand their practical significance and symbolism.

Initiatives to Save the Black Church

There are current efforts to address the challenges the Black church faces along a variety of dimensions. Seattle's Nehemiah Initiative (https://www.nehemiahinitiativeseattle.org/), for example, shows how Black communities can address church closings using a faith-based community development organization working with Black churches and other Black organizations to develop their properties:

> The Nehemiah Initiative seeks to empower the African American community in the Seattle region and beyond to support the retention of historically Black institutions by advocating for development of real property assets owned those historically Black institutions . . . The Nehemiah Sustainable Church Initiative is designed to help churches and ministries to learn innovative and creative ways to disciple their congregations, including entrepreneurs and marketplace leaders while enhancing the church's ability to sustainably achieve its mission.

Institutions with urban missions need to address church closings because of their unique circumstances and prominence within their communities, requiring staff with requisite knowledge and competencies to advance their missions. This expertise does not need to be housed within these institutions, but having access to it at a local or regional level is essential. We can no longer ignore these closings because of the unique potential repurposing presents for meeting local needs.

Despite the fact that they are an integral part of the built environment and played important roles in history, closed churches can become neighborhood artifacts that are taken for granted (American Institute of Architects, 2020, p. 5): "The built environment is an archive of culture and history. It manifests the aspirations and needs of society in a particular time and place, creating a record of who we are." The closure of churches that played a prominent role in shaping a community's identity takes on even greater significance for a community.

Saving and restoring Black churches across the nation has drawn philanthropic interest; for instance, Lilly Endowment Inc. donated $20 million to the National Trust for Historic Preservation's African American Cultural Heritage Action Fund and its National Fund for Sacred Places. Although this is a significant amount of money, it is only a drop in the proverbial bucket due to the sheer magnitude of the challenge.

External funding will help attract the interest of research institutions in documenting and evaluating these endeavors, with lessons for this emerging field. Foundation funding, for instance, can serve as seed money for a more comprehensive assessment of this realm, attracting other funding, including in-kind donations, and broadening participation in the process. Having a national landscape of church building salvation or repurposing will help us understand how local forces shape these interventions, providing lessons learned in different national regions.

Repurposing churches, with requisite community support, buy-ins, and needs in mind, enhances a community's visible and invisible wealth, which is a new way of thinking about these acts (Simons et al., 2017). Repurposing projects bring hope for communities. Black churches often sit on valuable real estate, considered a major source of wealth within the Black community. Seattle's Black churches, for instance, own property appraised for over $100 million. These churches are also well positioned to empower their communities by tapping Black capital (assets) and preventing resident displacement by providing education, training, and resources to meet Black organizational needs.

Not all Black churches need to assume a leadership role in their community to address the problem of closed churches or any other pressing community concerns; this is a tremendous burden to put on any institution, including a multitude of challenges among parishioners. A model in which one or multiple churches assume a coordinating or collective leadership role and serve as resources in their areas of expertise holds great promise (Hamilton, 2022) in community practice undertakings.

The Nehemiah Initiative, for instance, partnered with the University of Washington's College of Built Environments graduate students, introducing collaboration with local institutions of higher learning. Black church/university collaborations, too, can strengthen both parties (Owens et al., 2020). Institutions of higher learning are valuable resources that need to be mobilized to aid local institutions, including supplying field placements, as with social work, for students interested in pursuing careers in this area.

Conclusion

The Black church, as highlighted in the chapter and this book, has a history of survival against incredible odds, reflecting the resiliency of its congregants and leadership. That quality of survival must never be underestimated because it is impossible to imagine where the Black community would be without the "Black" in its history. However, the challenges facing the Black church today are unlike any it has ever faced in its illustrious history. The forces are formidable and unprecedented, and not a passing fad. The Black church's ability to pivot to consider contextual forces and to respond accordingly is critical in shaping how it will fare in the future, and whether it will rise to prominence once again. Of course, it still holds prominence in communities across the country, but from a collective standpoint, it has arguably lost its power, including facing competition from other groups.

The Black community and its churches must never be separated from their past. The past is not necessarily a prelude to the future, but it certainly serves as a foundation. The Black church has instrumental and expressive roles to play in the future of urban America, alongside its Latino counterparts sharing the same urban spaces. Blacks control relatively few institutions, with their churches standing out. Saving these institutions will help their community not only survive but also thrive and meet future stormy headwinds.

The following chapter on Latinos furthers our understanding of church openings and closures and builds upon the Boston case illustration in Chapter 3. Readers will see similarities and differences between these two groups, even when they occupy the same communities. A focus on Blacks and Latinos, however, will continue in the rest of this book, bringing together urban demographics, historical forces, church closure, and repurposing initiatives.

6

The Latino Church

Introduction

When I initially contemplated authoring this book, I intended to combine the Black and Latino churches in one chapter. Thanks to the wise advice of an external reviewer of this book's proposal, I realized how ill-advised this would have been. Not only would it make for a very long chapter, but it would ultimately minimize these two distinctive houses of worship. Due to the different histories of these two communities, separate chapters were needed to do justice to them, even though they face common social justice challenges and often occupy many of the same urban neighborhoods. The Boston case provided in Chapter 3 provided a concrete illustration that is helpful in examining key trends and challenges. Latino church closures and their repurposing projects present practitioners with unique challenges in addition to those addressed earlier in this book because of the language, cultural, and legal status issues in many communities.

It is significantly more challenging to find reports and scholarly material on Latino churches than it is on Black churches, although that will no doubt change as their population increases over the next several decades. These increases in population will make it impossible to ignore them and their institutions.

The Latino community will undoubtedly be a significant presence in the future of the United States, with their presence felt throughout the country, and that applies to their churches as well (Sanchez, 2022). Despite this population increase, the Latino community still faces a religious crisis, with church closures as indicators of this situation. The Boston case illustration in Chapter 3 illustrates this observation.

Like the Black church, the Latino church is not monolithic. Although the two churches share broad similarities, each presents unique challenges and rewards in terms of church closures and repurposing. They both have a significant urban presence, but differ in terms of demographics, history, culture, language, and immigration status.

The role of the Catholic Church is distinctly different in the two groups (Foster-Frau & Hatzipanagos, 2023): "Catholicism and Latino culture are tightly intertwined, with many of its cultural touchstones based on religious figures—including la Virgen de Guadalupe, the rosary, or even, Rios said, the word 'adios,' which means goodbye in Spanish but also literally 'to God.'" Difficulties can arise when the makeup of a Catholic congregation does not match that of the community where the church is found. In San Diego, California, friction occurred between worshippers at St. Anne Catholic Church and the Latino community (Logan Heights) surrounding it (Lopez-Villafana, 2020). This church holds Mass in Latin seven days a week. The tensions were, in part, the result of parking issues, the racial composition of attendees (White, non-Latino), and concerns some congregation members raised about Black Lives Matter signs near the church. One resident summed up neighborhood concerns:

> Angelica Padilla, who lives in the neighborhood, said she believes there is tension in the community because people who go to the church are mostly White and some have Trump bumper stickers on their cars. She said the church hasn't made an attempt to reach out to residents who raised concerns. Padilla is one of them. In April 2018, she wrote a "one-star" review of the church on a Facebook page named St. Anne's Catholic Church. She wrote that people who attend the church have "rude, bigoted (and) hateful" bumper stickers and take up residents' street parking.

This church has been there for many decades and once even held Mass in Spanish. However, Bishop Robert Brom proclaimed St. Anne as an "extraordinary form" parish, allowing Masses to be celebrated in Latin, drawing parishioners from throughout San Diego. It stopped reflecting the composition of the neighborhood, becoming a physical reminder of "better days" for residents.

The Catholic Church, arguably more than any other church, stands at the forefront of the dramatic demographic changes gripping the nation when discussing Latinos. U.S. Latinos constitute almost 40% of this country's Catholic population and represent 71% of all Catholic growth since 1960 (Huckle, 2020). It is not surprising to find that Catholic Church plays a prominent role in this chapter and throughout this book, and at times it has received highly critical coverage because of the immense influence it has had both historically and today, with profound implications for its future.

One study of thriving U.S. Evangelical Latino congregations found five key factors were operative, countering a perspective that "church growth and vitality strategies can be one size fits all" (Grusendorf & Acevedo, 2022): (1) trusted pastoral leadership; (2) the presence of a distributive leadership model; (3) the use of biblical literacy as a means for development; (4) a relationally oriented community; and (5) the presence of salient denominational attributes. These qualities, with the exception of biblical literacy, also apply to a service organization.

In the interest of space, I will only elaborate on the first factor—trusted pastoral leadership. Several aspects stand out. Longevity allows religious leaders to develop relationships with and to know their parishioners. These pastors display authenticity by sharing their flaws and shortcomings (humility). They also engender a positive vision for their congregation, in the present and in the future, bringing hope and a sense of direction.

These personal qualities are not surprising. Pastors must not stand above their congregations; instead, they should bring earthly personal quantities as well as experiences with heavenly visions and aspirations. The ways in which they have confronted earthly challenges are just as important as their mastery of the Bible! Even the music one hears at a Latino church, as in the case of the Evangelical Spanish-language Latino churches of Oregon, will challenge the uninitiated, reflecting both the diaspora and social agency of the Protestant Church (Berhó, 2020).

Of course, these are qualities that should apply to church leaders of all backgrounds, Black, Brown, or White, non-Latino! Pastors with these qualities become endearing by showing their vulnerability, making them more human and relatable for a congregation facing daily challenges.

For spiritual practice to resonate with urban youth and young adults, religious leaders must be prepared to walk in their steps so that their spiritual message reflects the operative reality of this age group. This knowledge must be obtained first-hand rather than through books or formal courses, particularly if a spiritual mission is to resonate with the realities that youth experience, as in the case of South Central Los Angeles, for example, a neighborhood with a long history of racial and economic challenges (Goodlow, 2023).

As noted by Romero (Christianity Today, 2022), what makes Latino churches attractive is their ability to acknowledge and feel the pain of the congregants: "Latino churches are proximate to the pain felt by communities; they are often first responders in crisis situations like COVID or immigration cases; and they are a vital, though often overlooked, partner in the social safety net." Understanding and feeling this pain helps unite a congregation with its leadership in pursuit of a consensus-based action plan. As the saying goes, there is no "I" in "team"!

Although this book places heavy emphasis on the Black church, attention has also been paid to Latino churches because their religious beliefs have a bearing on church plantings and closings. Non-Christian religions represent an exceedingly small percentage of the Latino community (Pew Research Center, 2023a). The Latino church has been called a "Brown church" to differentiate it not only from its "Black church" counterpart, but also from other smaller Protestant churches, but of color (Romero, 2020).

Tensions can be found in communities that are experiencing outreach from non-Catholic churches. For example, churches, when occupied by community activists, as with Latinos, because of their social justice neglect of the communities they are purported to serve, can be an important community base for undertaking social justice campaigns, as seen in Chicago, Houston, Los Angeles, and New York City (Hinojosa, 2021). It is no mistake that those cities had among the highest concentrations of Latinos in the nation.

The Church and Latinos

Readers interested in the Latino community from a religious standpoint can find an increasing amount of literature to draw upon, but nowhere near what is required. K. E. Nabhan-Warren's (2022) book *The Oxford Handbook of Latinx Christianities in the United States* will be of interest due to the breadth of coverage it offers on a topic that is so dynamic; it brings a multifaceted and up-to-date view of this growing and highly complex group.

Morello, as quoted by Guzman (2023), makes a social observation about the role of a church in Latino communities:

> Latinos tend to have a different engagement with religion than Anglo-Saxon communities. While Anglo communities are socially involved outside of their church through things like volunteer work or charitable giving, Latino churches tend to function as community centers as well as places of worship by offering services like food pantries and immigration services.

This multifaceted mission makes their presence—and disappearance—critical to a community's well-being for reasons beyond spiritual salvation.

Readers wanting a glimpse of Latino religious services (Catholic and Protestant) should read Ricourt and Danta's (2003) book *Hispanas de Queens: Latino Panethnicity in a New York City Neighborhood*. Although over 20 years old, this book provides an excellent description of how churches are grounded in the social fabric of Corona, Queens, a New York City neighborhood bordering the better-known Jackson Heights. It is impossible to separate these two worlds, giving "living together" a whole new meaning. "Little Caracas" is the latest enclave of Latinos (Venezuelans) establishing a foothold in New York City; Venezuelans represent one of the fastest-growing immigrant groups in that city and the nation. It will be interesting to follow this community in the near future to see how religion plays a role in their settlement (Hu & Vilchis, 2023).

We must remember that geographical displacement is not an alien experience for Latinos and other people of color in this country. One has only to witness what is currently happening at the border between Mexico and the United States: Thousands are attempting to enter this country, and those who succeed are being bussed or flown to another destination, such as Chicago, New York City, and even Martha's Vineyard. Establishing roots in a neighborhood takes on practical and symbolic value, and for these new residents churches serve as important anchors in the life of the community.

When these anchors become untethered, however, the ripple effects are felt throughout the community, not just among parishioners. Florida provides as an excellent example. The in-migration of Latinos, predominantly Puerto Ricans from Puerto Rico and northern states such as New York and New Jersey, to Orlando, Florida, and its surrounding areas have transformed this part of Florida, including its religious institutions (Delerme, 2023). Church membership declined dramatically in Puerto Rico over the past decade, with an estimated 400,000 residents moving to the mainland United States. Three thousand churches were badly damaged as a result of hurricanes, and that statistic is dated (Shellnutt, 2018), with many relocating to Florida.

Political winds at the local level will affect Latino church membership. Latino evangelical church leaders in Florida are facing the challenges of Gov. Ron DeSantis's harsh anti-immigrant policies. For example, Tampa's Iglesia Jesús es la Vida (Jesus is Life Church) usually has a congregation of 70 members, but 10 of its families left the state once the law took effect (Chavez, 2023b). Florida churches will no doubt experience more departures of their most vulnerable members. It remains to be seen how many of these Latino churches will survive a mass exodus of parishioners, and the situation bears watching, including the ramifications at the local level.

The argument that "come Sunday, churches are the most segregated spaces in the country" is borne out by a 2022 study by the Public Religion Research Institute (Contreras, 2023). According to this report, almost half of Latino Protestants (47%) say their churches are composed mostly of Latinos, 26% say their churches have mostly White, non-Latino members, and 20% attend mostly multiracial congregations. In contrast, over three-quarters of White, non-Latino Christians say that their churches are mostly White—80% of White mainline/non-evangelical Protestants and 75% of White evangelical Protestants.

The majority (74%) of Black Protestants state that their churches have mostly Black members. Among Latino Catholics, 74% say their church is mostly composed of Latinos, while only 12% attend mostly multiracial churches. This statistic reflects changing community demographics across segments of the country, particularly cities, which can be expected to continue into the near future.

If we had to summarize the modern-day narrative of American religion, we would say that it is in decline using a variety of standard measures, with one significant exception—Latinos (Mulder et al., 2017). This makes for an excellent backdrop on examining how religion is faring in this country. According to predictions of Latino Protestant growth, numbers will increase from Latinos who call themselves Protestants by 2030, doubling in 10 years (Mulder et al., 2017). According to estimates, there were 10 million Protestant Latinos in the United States (Berhó, 2020).

What Is Meant by Latino Religious Beliefs and Practices?

This question makes me smile because there is no simple answer; the statement "it all depends" comes to mind. Latino religious beliefs and practices may not fall neatly into a denominational category, which further complicates any analysis and development of action plans (Ramos et al., 2018):

> Conversions to Protestantism are not free of challenges. Some converts, particularly Mexican immigrant and Mexican American converts, find it difficult to navigate tensions with their deeply Catholic families. Yet other Latinos sidestep these tensions by retaining a Catholic identity while

attending Protestant church—a seemingly paradoxical dynamic. Such an ironic religiosity has been similarly documented among Latino Buddhists... We also know that Lutheran and Episcopalian churches with large Latino immigrant populations have adopted some obviously Latin American Catholic iconography, like that of the Virgen de Guadalupe, in order to make visitors and members from Catholic backgrounds more comfortable.

Churches with a Latino presence, regardless of denomination, must alter "business as usual" if they hope to attract and keep them as members. Worshipping is a dynamic activity, often with long histories and unique rituals, and those denominations able to adapt will likely increase in number; those unable or unwilling to do so will face challenges, including potential demise.

The Growth of the Latino Church

Christians are the fastest-growing segment of American evangelicals, and this is not a recent phenomenon, even when religious affiliation is facing many challenges. The growth of the U.S. Latino church is in large part due to active recruitment by these institutions. The Catholic Church is historically the primary religious group in the Latino community, here and throughout Latino America (Winter, 2021). However, this dominance is being threatened as Latino Catholics are encountering concerted recruitment by other denominations while disengaging from any formal religious affiliation, as seen in other denominations.

Episcopal Church leadership, for example, is recommending planting churches in areas that have a significant Latino population, and in growing towns or cities; these new churches should have strong lay leadership, a preschool, and requisite funding (Petersen, 2022). The recommendations for having strong lay leadership, reflecting the racial/ethnic composition of the community, and having a preschool point to the influential role of demographics in church affiliation. This is needed if it seeks to grow in the future.

Demographic Distribution and Projections

Why an emphasis on urban churches? Fifty percent of all Latino churches are in cities with populations of 100,000 or greater, with 31% in cities under

100,000 (Lifeway Research, 2023), illustrating their heavy presence in the nation's cities. Seventy-eight percent of Latino congregations are in the southern (48%) and western (30%) regions of the country. Just over half of these churches were established in 2000 or later. This community comprises 46% Mexicans and 22% Caribbean Latinos. Fifty-eight percent were born outside the United States, 24% were born in this country to parents who were born outside of the United States, and 17% were born to parents born in the United States.

Latinos are a highly diverse and growing group in this country, and they are increasingly central to any understanding of religion and churches (Nabhan-Warren, 2022), particularly in cities. We must view them from multi-generational and acculturation perspectives to appreciate their impact on church attendance, activities/services, and the dynamics of church openings and closings. There is no simple way to present their composition other than as a mosaic of countless pieces.

Churches that are looking to expand rather than close must set up and enhance generational bridges rather than barriers, similar to what we discussed with the Black church in Chapter 5. The youthfulness of the Latino community lends itself to such an approach, although not without the challenges already discussed that are involved in attracting the younger generation.

A Pew Research Center (2023a) poll of Latino religious practices found that 72% view themselves as Christians (48% Catholic, 19% Evangelical Protestants, 5% Mainline Protestant, and 1% Mormon). The remainder were of non-Christian faiths. Thirty-eight percent attend church at least once a month, 35% attend once a month, twice a month, or a few times a year, and 28% seldom or never attend. These numbers are important because attendance is a key barometer of a church's viability.

The departure of Latinos from the Catholic Church is a significant trend with long-term implications. Latino Catholic members stood at 43% in 2022, down from 67%, a drop of almost one-third from 2010. Evangelical Protestants, in turn, saw an increase from 12% in 2010 to 15% in 2022 (Guzman, 2023). Although modest in number, it is still a counter-trend to the Catholic Church, which means it bears watching. Assimilation forces, too, are present in attracting Latinos to religions other than Catholicism (Shaw, 2023a).

Over three-quarters of Catholic Latinos attend churches that are primarily Latino or White, non-Latino. Thus, when the Catholic Church closes churches in Latino communities, these congregations feel that they are being targeted because of who they are. Further, Latino Catholics are socially progressive on many of the issues in the forefront of society (Elie, 2023):

> Of all the groups surveyed, only among Hispanic Catholics was there a majority (fifty-six per cent) that wished for more leaders of color. How about more women leaders? Sixty-four per cent of Hispanic Catholics surveyed want this (the highest of any group). More L.G.B.T.Q.+ leaders? Thirty-nine per cent of Hispanic Catholics want this (the highest of any group). Trans rights? A third want this (the highest). Open discussion of political divisions in the U.S.? Three-tenths want this (again, the highest). So Hispanics who remain Catholic are, by a clear margin, the progressive wing of the Church.

These findings certainly surprised me, raising important questions about the upcoming clash between Latino church members and priests who hold orthodox views on these issues.

Another significant shift, and one experienced among other religious groups, is the growth of Latinos who are not affiliated with any religious denomination. In 2022, 30% of U.S. Latinos were unaffiliated, an increase from 10% in 2010; younger Latinos were less likely to be Catholic and more likely to be religiously unaffiliated than older Latinos. This is consequential because it might lead to the closure of more Latino churches, Catholic and non-Catholic alike, and is a finding that is receiving recognition in academic and non-academic circles.

Evangelical Protestants can be recruited from different Christian denominations (Bell & Lehto, 2019), with the growth of Christian churches in the Caribbean and South America providing fertile grounds for outreach and conversions. Churches are brought to the United States through migration, while adapting to local circumstances to remain relevant and continue making inroads into these communities and new surroundings.

Leadership roles in Protestant churches are often occupied by Latinos, much like Blacks in the Black church; however, this is not necessarily the case with Catholic churches that have high percentages of Latino worshippers (Mulder et al., 2017), and those who teach in their schools, for that matter. Having someone up front who looks and talks like you, and shares similar life experiences (representation), helps to make worshippers feel understood and welcomed and shapes how sermons are delivered.

Much like their Black counterparts, there are differences between Latino Protestant churches (Barba, 2022). Ramos, Martí, and Mulder (2022) note that it is a mistake to see them as monolithic. This complexity makes it more challenging to paint a picture of growing and shrinking churches in this community; it is also more difficult to understand the characteristics of churches that close or thrive, including their repurposing and how well these new structures are accepted or rejected by the community.

As Latinos enter and become an increasingly integral part of U.S. economic, social, and political life, particularly in its cities, the church serves as a bridge to help them make this critical transition, including providing help when bumps are encountered along the way (Lopez et al., 2022). This is much like the role of the Black church and how well it is integrated into the social fabric of the Black community (Holmes, 2017).

Appreciating the consequences that the closing of a Latino church has on its community requires a nuanced analysis. A church closing provides an opportunity for the community to "own" this space and plant the seeds of a project that can grow with the community, as well as an opportunity to take stock as to why their church had to close. The discussion of storefront churches later in this chapter helps readers conceptualize this key point.

Latino churches, it is fair to say, can be described as family-centered and often offer a range of instrumental and expressive services to help immigrants make the transition to this country (often including help with immigration issues). The church becomes part of their lifestyle and represents a natural social support system. Geographical movement has been a significant part of the Latino experience over the past century, and religion and churches represent constants and serve as valuable anchors in this country until permanent settlement is achieved. What the future holds in store at that point remains to be seen. However, the outcomes will be critical for parishioners and their communities.

If this is one of their goals, churches can promote physical activity among members—for instance, a group of Catholic churches partnered with their local parks to encourage parishioners to exercise in the park, further embedding themselves into the life and well-being of their community (DeRose et al., 2022). Enhancing parishioners' health, a key theme in many urban churches, increases the instrumentality of this institution. When it closes, not only spiritual needs but also instrumental and expressive needs may go unmet, with immediate and long-term ramifications.

Similar to the way that Blacks migrated from southern states to northern cities, Latinos, too, moved from the south—although much further south! Hope was an instrumental part of this mass migration for both groups, and churches turned this into action, economically, socially, and politically. This is another reason why the death of their churches has significance in their communities and the country. Latinos are not in a position to own or control very many institutions in their community, so Latino churches represent a major stakeholder in this country. When they close, the support they provide is lost, opening the door for external sources to fill this vacuum.

Age Demographics and Latino Churches

One recent survey of Latino Protestant churches found that attendees are young and first generation (58%), and growing numerically as church members (Earls, 2023). Latino churches are not experiencing church closures to the same extent as their Black counterparts, even in the same communities, and demographics are playing a key role in their growth (Earls, 2023). In Latino churches, 35% of parishioners are under 30 (with 18% of parishioners under 18), 38% are age 30 to 49, and 28% are age 50 and above (Kellner, 2023). Nevertheless, when closures do occur, their impact is as significant as with their Black counterparts.

Currently in the United States White, non-Latinos constitute almost two-thirds of the country (64%), but this group will become a representational minority in the next three to four decades. This demographic shift has spawned the contentious replacement school of thought in far-right political circles, has gotten the attention of Christian Nationalists, and has largely fueled an anti-immigrant stance across the country, particularly in the southern and western parts.

The Latino population will continue to grow, doubling from 54 million (17% of the nation) to an expected 106 million in 2050. This increase will affect all sectors of the country, and major cities will often become the final destination for newcomers to this country. The Catholic Church needs to recognize this demographic trend and embrace its challenge if it hopes to remain a vibrant force within this community (Bruce, 2017). There is also an urgent call to celebrate and embrace this diversity rather than ignore or undermine it to stem parishioner losses (Mulder, 2017). This will involve having religious personnel who look similar to and reflect the background of this community to increase the relevance of the Church as one key dimension.

Religious organizations that wish to remain viable in the near and distant future need to reach out to the Latino community, particularly sowing the seeds among youth (Jones, 2020). When this space is closed and the replacement consists of people who do not share the demographic profile of the community, a sense of betrayal takes on greater significance, isolating these institutions from their surroundings, further increasing the chances of their closure.

Latino Church: Language and Culture

We cannot understand or appreciate the Latino church and its importance without considering the role of religion and its cultural meaning within a community context. Community practice is not about simply moving in after a church closes and repurposing it as an act of intervention without grounding this action into a community's history and social fabric. This is as true for Latino churches as it is for Black churches. The two groups, although they have distinctly different backgrounds, often occupy the same neighborhoods and face many of the same social justice challenges (with the exception of immigration status). This opens opportunities to find common ground and undertake collaborative projects, as in the case of church closures and repurposing efforts. Of course, "lumping" all Latinos, regardless of country of origin, into one category is a serious mistake. Latinos from different countries can bring lifelong rivalries that interfere with generating group cohesion within a church. As with any ethnic or racial label, there can be significant differences within and between groups.

There is a call for the Catholic Church to reach out to Latinos more aggressively in this country through preaching ("creed"), influenced by an understanding of how life experiences shape how messages are received and acted upon by worshippers (Kueber, 2022). Words, after all, are critical in communicating within a religious context. Words can hurt, but they can also heal and give comfort.

Latino Catholics must not be ignored, taken for granted, or considered "pastoral afterthoughts" by the Catholic Church, as is often the case in the United States (Flores, 2018):

But promising demographic data can easily be interpreted in a way that overlooks the textured history of Latino Catholics in the United States. This history is not a romantic account of gradual awareness, acceptance and celebration by the larger U.S. Catholic Church. It has often been a painful past, one in which the very existence of Latino church communities has often come under threat.

The role of the Catholic Church in the "conquest" of the New World stands out and has left a tainted legacy that is impossible to erase and rightly has left lingering distrust of this institution!

An examination of the Catholic Church's interactions with Native Americans, too, highlights how this history has proven fertile grounds for distrust (Roberts, 2023, p. 95): "There is much bad feeling, both real and cultivated, circulating these days between peoples of European descent, and peoples of Native American (both North and South America) descent, especially with regard to recent discoveries of historical events which occurred at schools run by American and Canadian authorities, as well as by the Catholic Church."

Readers must remember that Latinos and Blacks share many similar beliefs, struggles, resources, and aspirations. They may live in the same geographical location. And they face unique challenges and opportunities. Their similarities far outpace their differences, making them natural allies in the search for social justice for their members. Church closings in these communities, and the structures that replace them, represent a social justice issue that can take its place alongside a multitude of other issues confronting them. This is particularly true for parishioners who are left "out in the cold" by a church closure and must find worship alternatives or simply stop attending services. This is well within the domain of community practice.

Viewing Latino and Black churches from a community stance helps us better predict, plan, and ground repurposing initiatives that can be more easily integrated into the sociocultural fabric of the community, expanding the field for both academics and practitioners. Of course, we can look at the broader national context for guidance, but we must do so with an understanding that repurposing initiatives cannot be viewed from a "cookie-cutter" standpoint. Contextually grounding churches is a critical element of community practice if what replaces them is to have merit and bring meaningful and long-lasting change. We must remember that just like communities, no two churches are similar.

The Latino church must be bilingual and bicultural, not just in terms of the language spoken and cultural beliefs, but also practices. Immigrants have seen their share of pain and suffering in their home country and in the United States. According to Robert Chao Romero (Christianity Today, 2022): To achieve an ethnically and racially diverse congregation, religious leaders must be able to "speak the language" of the worshippers—not just linguistically, but also in the sense of understanding their experiences, struggles, and concerns (Branson & Martinez, 2023). The Black community, of course, has also experienced great pain, opening the door for potential social justice collaborative efforts between these two groups when found in the same neighborhood. Such collaborative projects effectively increase the power and influence of these churches beyond their membership.

Latino Church Attendance and COVID-19

Like the Black church, the Latino church also suffered severe consequences from the COVID-19 pandemic. One-third of the members of Latino churches disappeared during the pandemic; more specifically, 70% of Millennials stopped attending in-person services, with online services becoming the new mode of worshipping (Christianity Today, 2022). COVID-19 was a major public health issue for religious groups, and that is why it was covered in the previous chapter and throughout this book. Regardless of community, the pandemic has taken a toll on churches that were economically vulnerable to begin with. Latino churches that had a considerable proportion of members who were undocumented immigrants were especially hard-hit.

Worshipping online, just like taking courses online, is a dramatically different experience. Due to the "digital divide," many Latinos were isolated from much-needed emotional and instrumental support during the pandemic (Hodges & Calvo, 2023).

Latino Church Attendance: Trends and Nuances

Latino church membership and attendance has increased over the past 23 years, an increase that has been attributed to upticks in immigration and evangelization. Continued community growth bodes well for the future of Latino churches. Special initiatives, too, are responsible for increases in Latino churches. In 2010, for example, the Southern Baptist Convention launched an ambitious initiative to expand in North America, planting 10,000 new churches, with 1,000 being Latino (Seidel, 2022).

Launching special initiatives means more than just having pastors who speak Spanish; the religious practices need to be culturally attuned to congregants' backgrounds and current circumstances. Social justice issues may be particularly relevant to the challenges they face in this country, which in many cases entails addressing immigration status.

Latinos and the Catholic Church

Latinos have widely been viewed as the future of the U.S. Catholic Church. Latinos currently represent over 40% of Catholics, with most of them under the age of 30 tracing their historical background to a Latin American country (Long-Garcia, 2022). For this trend to continue, the Catholic Church must invest in and re-emphasize its youth ministry and consider young people to be active parish members rather than just "junior members" with limited rights and responsibility.

Participatory democracy has a small role within the Catholic Church hierarchy. Thus, this viewpoint will be hard to put into play at a community level, where trust in the decision-making process is critical in order to accept outcomes such as church closures, for example. Church mergers are occurring with greater frequency and must be done strategically, ensuring that Latinos' needs are not overlooked in efforts to cut costs and deal with priest shortages. Parishioners' sentiments cannot be ignored, because a church ultimately rests on its membership.

Rates of disaffection with religion among Latino Catholics are almost exactly the same as those of White, non-Latino Catholics (Elie, 2023). Nevertheless, Latino Catholics are numerically increasing in select parts of the country; for instance, in Cincinnati, Ohio, there are an estimated 53,000 to 61,000 Latino members, and the number is growing (Curnutte, 2018). Twelve of the Cincinnati archdiocese's 19 counties saw Latino increases of more than 100% from 2000 to 2014. Nevertheless, numerical strength, as we argue throughout this book, does not equate to power in deciding whether churches remain open or close down.

The Catholic Latino (largely Guatemalan and Mexican) in Cincinnati's Price Hill neighborhood, which has that city's largest concentration, will bear the brunt of churches closures/mergers. Cincinnati's Catholic Church has sought to create centralized anchors for this community, while redeeming the notable Catholic architecture in this neighborhood. This is a challenge, needless to say. As part of a consolidation plan issued by the Archdiocese of Cincinnati, five existing Catholic parishes in the Price Hill neighborhood were reorganized into one family of parishes, with each containing rectories, schools, and offices on the respective properties. This initiative reimagined the Church to meet the needs of incoming Latino immigrants. This initiative will reduce costs, and all five parishes are expected to be neighborhood-based.

In 2014, there were 51 million Catholic adults in the country, with their share of the total Catholic population decreasing from 24% to 21%, singaling a trend (Masci & Smith, 2018). From 1999 to 2016, the number of Catholic parishioners decreased by 17%—from a peak of 547,000 to 453,000. If such a serious decrease occurred in a business, desperate measures would need to be taken if the business were to remain viable (Long-Garcia, 2022): "For every millennial that comes in, six leave. If a company was experiencing the same rate of loss, it would be a crisis.... They would completely revolutionize how they did business."

However, Latino membership in the U.S. Catholic Church has been significant and growing. Almost one-third of the nation's 70 million Catholics identify themselves as Latinos, up from 10% during the 1960s. Nevertheless, predictions are that Latinos are still the future of American Evangelicalism (Winter, 2021):

> Latinos are leaving the Catholic Church and converting to evangelical Protestantism in increased numbers, and evangelical organizations are putting more energy and resources toward reaching potential Latino congregants. Latinos are the fastest-growing group of evangelicals in the country, and Latino Protestants, in particular, have higher levels of religiosity—meaning they tend to go to church, pray, and read the Bible more often than both Anglo Protestants and Latino Catholics.

Latinos are a large source of potential converts for any denomination that hopes to grow. They are young, growing numerically, and often urban-centered, and represent a key source of current and future attendees to stem the tide of church closures.

The religious leaders of many Latino churches have assumed an instrumental role within their communities that transcends their official religious duties. They often fill the roles of "brokers" in order to fill critical voids, particularly if there are no Latino elected officials to represent their views. Increasing religious leaders' relevance in meeting parishioner instrumental and expressive needs, often filling an important void in their life, and making them indispensable in helping them navigate their social, economic, cultural, spiritual, and emotional circumstances (Lopez et al., 2022; Ramos et al., 2022).

Religious institutions play a key role in healing distress of various kinds, with the church a significant provider of social, educational, and spiritual resources for Latinos (Caplan, 2019). Where these churches close, regardless of religious affiliation, they are not easily replaced, causing a ripple effect throughout the community.

Latino Church Closures

Although the subject of Latino church closures has been integrated throughout this book, particularly in our discussions of the Catholic Church, it is important to pause and pay specific attention to them. A Latino presence brings distinctive social, cultural, and historical aspects when compared to their Black counterparts. The forces facing urban churches apply to this community, too.

For example, one of the Catholic churches in Tampa Bay, Florida, is closing, largely due to the departure of Latino Millennials and Gen Z members, paralleling the pattern found throughout the country (Chavez, 2023a) and among Blacks as well. The Catholic Church in St. Louis is undertaking a reorganization that will cause a substantial number of parish closures (Bernhard, 2023b). This reorganization has caused a negative reaction from marginalized parishioners. Priests will be assigned to multiple churches, making it difficult for priests to get to know their congregation and vice versa. This move runs counter to the Latino cultural propensity to set up relationships with individuals rather than institutions. Individuals are the bridge!

The goal of openness and an embrace of a participatory democracy stance is noble. However, in the case of Catholic parishioners, they can find themselves confronting a bureaucratic Church with a highly centralized power structure and a deliberative process fraught with political and financial considerations. This may even involve racism and classism because these communities having histories of being disenfranchised, which must not go unacknowledged. As we mentioned earlier, the historical legacy of the Catholic Church in Latino countries, too, must not be ignored.

Conclusion

Although Black and Latino churches are found almost next door to each other in many urban communities, their circumstances can put them on different trajectories concerning their future. Sharing geographical proximity brings the potential to join together to seek social justice in their community. Further, it opens the door for recruiting new members when one of these churches cannot keep its doors open. The handwriting is on the wall for all to see and we don't need a crytal ball to predict what churches will look like in the immediate future, and what actions are needed to shape this religious terrain. We have the requisite tools on hand but need new ones to help us repurpose closed churches to meet a variety of community needs. Latinos, like their Black counterparts, are increasingly urban-based, meaning that churches that are responsive to their spiritual and material needs will have the potential to serve these communities.

SECTION 3
IMPLICATIONS FOR RESEARCH, EDUCATION, AND PRACTICE

Readers have so far learned about many major organizations of diverse sizes and authorities at the national, state, and local levels speaking to the importance of repurposing. The knowledge and skill sets necessary to conduct church repurposing simply do not appear out of the heavens (pardon the pun). Well-coordinated and concerted efforts at the local, state, and national levels are needed to achieve the goals associated with repurposing projects. This section discusses a range of implications for research, education, and practice, three domains that are interrelated, with each bringing its own unique set of rewards, activities, techniques, and challenges.

SECTION 3

IMPLICATIONS FOR RESEARCH, EDUCATION, AND PRACTICE

7
Implications for Research, Education, and Practice

Introduction

Ideally, measures of successful repurposing should strive to incorporate or save "character-defining elements" of the original design, but churches bring added challenges to accomplish this goal (Barucco, 2023): "Historic religious properties, in addition to the physical manifestations of character, have what might be called experiential character-defining features related to the intangible sacred aspects of the building. Both physical and intangible characteristics of a historic church are often more complex and more challenging to preserve."

There is no question that urban community practice and church repurposing will necessitate dramatic changes in how we conduct research, how we practice, and how we educate future practitioners. All three aspects are required to bring a change in thinking when discussing church repurposing. The issues and recommendations raised in this final chapter represent but an initial start in this important transformative process.

Section A: Research

To increase the likelihood that a repurposing intervention involving an urban church will be successful, we must have a solid understanding of the reasons why it is being done. These outcomes are achieved through the systematic application of research in measuring them. We need to uncover important nuances that are often overlooked but are critical in shaping the outcomes. When focusing on urban neighborhoods, involving church repurposing or otherwise, researchers must also seek to enhance community capacities in the process and involve neighborhood residents as integral partners in these undertakings.

Research itself can be conceptualized as an intervention when the community that is the focus of this activity is decisively involved in crafting, implementing, interpreting, and celebrating the final results. Their capacities are enhanced, and this success can be transferred to other spheres in their lives, helping them and their community in the process of discovery. Street ethnography, for example, is one research approach that can be particularly relevant in engaging community members in documenting and interpreting research (Stevenson et al., 2019). Observational skills can accommodate various levels of depth and sophistication, making this approach useful in teams involving residents.

Research will be needed to help us better understand how demographic changes manifest themselves in church closures and what happens to these buildings over the short and long term. A search of historical research literature on church repurposing in Massachusetts, home to countless churches and universities, found a thesis by Kiley (2004) analyzing that state's efforts at addressing church closures. Over the next 10 to 20 years, however, we can expect to see a plethora of research as population shifts occur toward the Sunbelt and away from northern cities. These shifts will introduce regional pressures to contend with closed churches and their repurposing, as new groups occupy these abandoned houses of worship.

One of the wonderful qualities of a democratic form of government is that everyone, regardless of background, can be expected to engage in decision-making on their environment and living circumstances. That also applies to research in support of church repurposing projects. This field brings excitement associated with something "new" and worthy of increased attention and resources. This will also entail recording these discoveries for current and future generations.

Research involves many of the participatory elements and goals that community practice embraces. This participatory emphasis can be considered the signature element of this form of intervention. Practitioners will have no trouble finding the "right" participatory tools to get the job done, because the field is expanding every day, reflecting its importance in shaping the lives of "ordinary" members of society (Rolling Jr., 2013). From the array of available approaches, researchers can select that one that best meets local cultural traditions and circumstances.

One area of research stands out because it transcends the conventional approaches taken in this chapter, moving the church repurposing field forward. We need to gain a deeper understanding of the decision-making process on church closures versus mergers, for example. They both have long-term ramifications for communities, but these decisions have significant community input. Church mergers, as argued throughout this book, are increasing in frequency and represent a force to be reckoned with in the future in urban neighborhoods. Nagel (2011) initially raised this recommendation well over a decade ago and it still awaits meaningful actualization!

Preparing and supporting the current and next generation of urban community practitioners to address church repurposing is a challenge worth undertaking. Much can be learned and practiced with church closings; the same can also be said about their schools, bringing added community rewards and challenges. The repurposing field is here to stay if society is to be serious about ecology and the built environment, bringing church closings into a prominent movement with immediate and future consequences.

Section C in this chapter covers how community practice continues its evolution by embracing empowering guiding principles. These are essential in helping us to navigate the murky waters associated with any form of community intervention, particularly the brave new frontier associated with church repurposing. Readers, I am confident, will have much to contribute to the research arena and how current and new research tools can be applied to church repurposing.

Challenges in obtaining existing data

Any research undertaking often starts with obtaining available data, often quantitative, and then using this information as a basis for deciding on the best approach and the challenges that we must overcome to get the necessary information. Asking basic questions about church closures and repurposing will hopefully lead to developing research to answer them. This requires not only funding but also entities capable of seeking answers. A critical mass of institutions and researchers to carry out research in this arena is a basic requirement, following by the necessary funding.

Baseline data are not only inexpensive but also relatively easy to obtain, saving time and money. However, nowhere is this challenge more clear than when looking for statistical and quantitative data, which can be found in a wide variety of sources. These data, too, may involve different authorities, definitions, and parameters, making it difficult to obtain a clear picture on which to base decisions about how best to proceed.

Research comes in many forms

When we discuss "research" in the context of repurposed churches, we must expand this method beyond an "academic" frame to make it more practical and tailored for local situations. Research, particularly at a community everyday level, must look very different than when it is discussed in a classroom, because it must have practical dimensions and meaning for everyday life if the results are to be salient at the local level.

Research can encompass various documentation levels with real-life consequences, and this often requires the use of creativity, including residents having a major role in shaping the research questions. Pham (2017), for example, discusses the "Xhurches Project," which "began in 2010 as a self-published zine dedicated to charting the trend of adaptive reuse of religious spaces in Portland, Oregon," and "has since expanded to become a blog that profiles examples from around the world." Pham (2017) notes that repurposing churches has inherent challenges:

> Among the many instances of reuse of historical buildings, there is a unique thread of conversions that pertain specifically to the transformation of religious buildings. It is perhaps undeniable that all buildings hold some inventory of memories and significant history, but a house of worship operates under a complex set of conditions, contexts and values. In the case of churches, the values are manifold: aesthetic, historical, and cultural.

There is no denying that economic pressures and land values make it impossible to keep church buildings as "shell monuments" to their historical religious role in society.

Photovoice: Capturing an historical process

One theme emphasized throughout this book is the importance of the community having a prominent seat at a decision-making table (participatory democracy in action), and the need for community members to capture their history for their generation and those that follow. Photovoice, in which community members use photos, videos, and words to tell their stories, is a research method often grounded within a community context. It is powerful for a community and can be exciting for the community members involved in carrying it out.

Photovoice has attracted national and international attention due to its focus on community participation and its potential for emphasizing social justice themes throughout the endeavor (Holtman et al., 2022). It can play an instrumental role in capturing both (1) the church closure and (2) the rebirth of this institution in a different form. Photovoice places community members at the center of a project, capturing events from the residents' standpoint. In this case the two different points in the church's life cycle are equally important. The use of photovoice allows former parishioners to share in a collective moment of reflection that can be saved for posterity, as noted in the Hyde Square Task Force (HSTF) case example in Chapter 6. There is an abundance of scholarship guiding photovoice projects in terms of goals and demographic considerations, such as age (Delgado, 2015), for example.

This approach also lends itself to uncovering the intersection of religion and race, for example, two dimensions that wield tremendous influence on church participation (O'Leary et al., 2021), particularly in urban centers. A photovoice project that is undertaken by different demographic groups highlights how their vantage points are unique and part of a prism, and therefore must be reflected in this research undertaking (Eyres et al., 2019).

Capturing the closure of a church is incredibly significant for a community and church members. The church building may disappear, but the memories do not. Churches are associated with a wealth of positive experiences and memories for parishioners, thus influencing a community's identity. Talking to worshippers about their memories will uncover countless moving stories. With training and guidance, photovoice can represent an empowering collective project that will help future generations to better understand and appreciate their environment and their place in the institution's history.

Each church closure will have a collective set of stories that must not be lost. Providing a place where community members can share them is often overlooked in church closures. When Our Lady Queen of Angels (East Harlem, New York City) closed in 2007 as part of a Catholic parish reorganization initiative, a group of women parishioners formed a Sunday weekly protest and prayer group that met for over eight years; research stopped at that point, so it might have extended even longer (Oliva, 2015).I believe that having a group such as the East Harlem women undertake a photovoice project and then stage a public exhibition, along with local press coverage, would have helped immensely to capture the history of this protest in a way that is not only "therapeutic" but also political.

A photovoice project might not be embraced immediately; indeed, its novelty can be a hindrance. However, it can be surprisingly exciting if sponsored by the right organizations and individuals.

Capturing the birth rather than the death of an institution might be more palatable, and I can certainly appreciate that. Birth brings excitement and hope and will attract many who wish to be a part of this experience. Using photovoice, participants and communities can capture the various stages of the repurposing process. The results can inform future projects, as well as build competencies.

Taking photographs and capturing narratives can be seen as a gift from current generations to future ones, providing them with a ringside seat to the birth of a community institution, along with the hopes and excitement that it engendered. The photovoice project can be displayed at the opening ceremonies and stored at local libraries, with access to all. The local press can cover these events, providing another venue for sharing the exhibition.

These photovoice examples represent only a few of its possibilities (Dunlop, 2022; Plunkett et al., 2014; Williams, 2019). This research method is not limited by language, physical abilities, time, or resources. The projects can be expansive or limited in scope depending on local goals, budgets, and time frames, for example. This flexibility makes them responsive to local circumstances, thus increasing their relevance for improving the life of a community.

Community asset mapping

Community asset mapping has always held a near and dear spot in my heart because it forces us to think about a community's gifts. I must touch upon the virtues of community practitioners undertaking community asset assessments. Having a picture of these institutions can serve many different purposes in helping communities, including houses of worship. Having a profile of who they are and who they serve, for example, can lead to the development of initiatives large and small and can assist both houses of worship and other community institutions.

It is important to have a marker pointing out the space where a prominent church once stood, particularly when the structure no longer exists or when it has taken on a dramatically different form. A marker like this serves as a bridge between the past, present, and future and will be greatly appreciated by long-term residents. It honors the past while making room for "progress" that has taken its place.

K. D. Walker (2023) offers an historical summary of asset mapping in the United States and why this method has so much potential. Advances in technology have made mapping much more attractive. The initial data gathering requires feet on the ground and person-to-person interactions. This makes asset mapping labor intensive and costly. Generating new data is always an expensive undertaking, but also exciting!

Churches can provide spaces to hold community events. That has been my experience in Worcester, Massachusetts (located 40 miles west of Boston), the second largest city in the state. These churches are centrally located within a community and may have space available to hold meetings or provide a range of services. Depending upon the initiative, they can even publicly endorse these ventures. Nontraditional settings (Delgado, 1999) have a role in church repurposing ventures. When they are involved, the chances of these projects succeeding.

A charge to institutions of higher learning

Institutions of higher learning certainly have their share of challenges, the least of which is becoming financially accessible and better positioning graduates to take their place in a rapidly changing world. This is particularly the case for those seeking careers in human services, for example. Institutions of higher learning have a moral duty to prepare practitioners for the world as it exists by providing students with the opportunities and tools they need to go out into society and make communities more viable and just. This charge is formidable but, I would argue, essential if institutions are to remain relevant, particularly in relation to urban centers and people of color.

Institutions of higher learning must have their fingers on the pulse of the nation—the trends leading to church closures, for instance—and be responsive in meeting current and projected needs. I do not make this demand lightly. If these institutions are to ignore the phenomenon of church closures, for instance, that vacuum will be filled by other institutions, much more community-centered and located. The challenges that church repurposing presents have implications for the built environment, a movement far more consequential for the nation.

Research has a prominent place in community practice and the repurposing of churches, whether such research is undertaken at an institution of higher learning or in the community, with members shaping the research goals, questions, and methods. The problem of church closures is far too complex and important to take a simplistic view of this movement. Although data will be needed from throughout the world, the United States has a major role to play in helping to shape this movement, which has worldwide consequences.

Research techniques are a key part of the community practitioner's toolbox throughout the entire continuum of church repurposing—not just as an investigative tool, but also as an intervention. The knowledge gleamed through research will serve as a foundation for understanding the church repurposing movement and also identifying the approaches with the highest likelihood of achieving success.

Section B: Implications for Community Practice Education

Education is vital for practitioners in the field of church repurposing. This chapter is purposefully expansive in scope beyond institutions of higher learning because this activity must happen in an abundance of settings, formal and informal. The field of community practice education should not be conceptualized narrowly because this field is expanding, much like the universe. Although our society has conceptualized education as the almost exclusive domain of institutions of learning, more education actually happens outside of a classroom than in a classroom, particularly regarding community concerns. If we accept this basic premise, then community practice education and church repurposing can occur anywhere and at any time.

Practice education must occur at many distinct levels of the community's cross-section, because no one segment of the community can bear total responsibility for church repurposing interventions. This stance opens the door for the creative collaborative initiatives that are often needed. Education can take various forms, such as internships, community workshops, formal courses, certificates, and mentorships, to list only a few. This broad expanse allows for local circumstances to determine the type of education that is most appropriate. Overall participation that does not necessarily have to relate to houses of worship.

Community practice principles for guiding church repurposing

I am fond of identifying principles to guide urban community practice projects, and church repurposing is certainly no exception. All practitioners have guiding principles shaping their worldviews, bringing structure and direction to an intervention. Some of us have explicitly articulated them to help practice, dialogue, and mentorship; for others, they may be implicit but still significant. Readers are welcome to advance their own operating principles to guide how they conceptualize and implement interventions.

Wolfram, Borgström, and Farrelly (2019) identified four guiding principles that are particularly relevant to urban church repurposing: "(1) foster inclusion and empowerment as prerequisites, (2) close the intermediation gap and strengthen the role of local academia, (3) challenge and reinvent urban planning as a key arena, and (4) enhance reflexivity through novel self-assessment technique." These principles should resonate with many urban community practitioners. They are broad and flexible enough to accommodate a range of practitioners, including academics, who want to move this field forward.

Almost a quarter-century ago (Delgado, 2000) I identified six capacity enhancement principles, which I have amended in this chapter to be applicable to urban church repurposing. They are flexible enough to allow the local context to shape how they are manifested, considering analytical and interactional forces.

The first principle is to *create community participation, stressing relations between ethnic and racial groups*. Readers should not be surprised that this principle heads the list, because it explicitly or implicitly permeates this entire book. Urban church repurposing projects must never be "plopped" on a community. Community ownership of a project is highly dependent on the level of meaningful participation by different racial and ethnic groups. Fostering inter-group relationships will go a long way in communities and our society because it reflects the reality that this nation is increasingly becoming "of color" (and a key reason why the Christian nationalist movement exists).

This first principle also reminds us that urban communities are never homogeneous in composition, and many church closures reflect this reality. What may have started as a church serving one group is now confronting the reality of new groups entering a community, who may not share cultural or linguistic backgrounds with earlier generations of churchgoers. However, as in prior generations, the church represents a key institution in their lives, with the potential to bridge different segments of a community. Schools, too, can fulfill this goal. When churches have schools attached to them, their significance is geometrically increased within their communities.

It is essential to bring together the major ethnic and racial groups that form these communities, both long-term residents and newcomers, in order to create a sense that the community "owns" the new structures replacing closed churches. It also helps dispel stereotypes, which must be addressed if meaningful progress is to be achieved and maintained. Mind you, this noble goal will involve tensions and even conflicts that will make practitioners lose sleep at night. But these efforts, when successful, can serve as models for other projects with community-wide implications.

The second principle is to *adopt and build community spirit as a central goal*. This goal may seem self-evident but is rarely included in community-based projects. Anyone who has been part of a team will attest to the importance of feeling they are part of a unit of individuals with distinct qualities. The pursuit of "winning" quickly recedes into the background, with the relationships developed taking on more importance. These relationships can carry over outside of this activity into other spheres.

Esprit de corps is a term often associated with the military but, as any seasoned practitioner can attest, is indispensable with any "civilian" project. It cannot be taught but must be experienced. An attitude of "we're in this together" helps ensure that, when a repurposing project hits a speedbump, which it will surely do, there is a can-do attitude that no roadblock is insurmountable if we work together. Communicating to community members that you believe they can help solve the problem or challenge may be a new message for them. Community efficacy doesn't just happen; it needs to be identified as a goal and fostered whenever possible.

Team-building activities throughout a repurposing project represent time and funds well spent. These activities can be fun and can involve visionary exercises and problem-solving, for example. Sharing ourselves and our upbring is one activity that I have found extremely useful in breaking down stereotypes. Physical appearances can be quite deceiving; someone who looks privileged may actually have had a life full of adversity. Everyone takes part, including the exercise leader.

I have found periodic retreats to be particularly useful. They allow everyone to pause, reflect, and work together on solving problems. These retreats can also be a time to share and have fun. Providing child care during the retreats increases participation and reflects an inclusive philosophy.

The third principle is to *systematically build intergenerational activities into interventions*. Having a shared vision of an inclusive institution goes a long way toward creating community ownership of a repurposed church. Urban families, particularly those of color, are invariably intergenerational, and so are their communities. We live in a very age-segregated country, and this pattern is often reproduced in community projects. We must remember that churches are one of society's few institutions open to all age groups, and when they close, their closure is felt by all ages. Further, there is no ready substitute to take the place of a church, particularly in light of how the Black and Latino churches have historically shaped their respective communities, children, adults, older adults.

Ideally, repurposed churches will continue this tradition of bringing together all age groups; after all, "we are all God's children." Perhaps the new building can have activities that attract different generations—or even intergenerational activities, which will create an all-important chain across generations.

The fourth principle, which builds on the previous one (illustrating the close interconnectedness of these recommendations), is to *implement intergenerational (formal and informal) collaborative goals*. Readers, I am sure, are not surprised that I've included a recommendation regarding intergenerational collaboration. In fact, I cannot envision a church repurposing project that is totally driven by adults without trying to develop community collaboration between various age groups who have vested interests in the outcomes, and that includes the groups the repurposing efforts are meant to attract.

Intergenerational collaborative goals do not have to be restricted to formal organizations with prior congregational youth groups. Our vision must be one that includes all major groups, formal and informal. For example, youth do not have to be members of formal organizations to be included. In fact, youth who are not affiliated with the organization have much to contribute to any repurposing initiative. Engaging them may prove to be challenging and labor-intensive but is a worthwhile pursuit nonetheless.

The fifth principle is to *have community capacity as a central goal*. I have historically taken a personal and professional stance that all communities have assets, which they have gained from facing adversities in the past. I like to ask "What are a community's assets?" rather than "Are there community assets?" The difference is not just semantic. It reflects a fundamental belief that regardless of our plights in life—as individuals, groups, or communities—we have abilities that can be identified, tapped, and enhanced to benefit the community. Unfortunately, these assets are often overlooked when creating interventions intended to aid marginalized communities.

Uncovering assets is never easy because marginalized people and their communities have histories of being told that they have no assets. In reality, nothing could be further from the truth—being able to survive against incredible odds must never be minimized! Understanding how they have survived against incredible odds is a history lesson we can all enjoy learning about and sharing. Further, we live in a society that tends to focus only on funding, failing to take into consideration the local capital that is not financially based.

Also challenging is the fact that that informal assets are not universal. For instance, a grocery store in one community may be in a nontraditional setting where it is well integrated into the community and serves multiple needs beyond selling food and other products. Another community's grocery store may have a reputation for selling old food and at high prices. Consequently, taking a "cookie-cutter" approach to identify and engage these settings will simply not work.

The final principle is to *stress grassroots funding where viable*. This objective will not come as any great surprise to community practitioners, and it certainly takes on great significance in the case of repurposed churches. Funders that are external to the community will rarely have the same interests in the outcomes that an internally driven repurposing effort will entail. I have used the rule that any funding that amounts to more than one-third of a project's funding has undue influence over its outcome.

Grassroots fundraising efforts are most successful when they involve a large segment of the population. I can get a $100,000 grant from a foundation and write the entire proposal myself without any external participation, but if I can sell 100,000 raffle tickets at $1 each, I will have hundreds or even thousands of participants. Selling tickets, too, allows me to inform (community education) and assess the community's receptivity to a project. Yes, selling these tickets, as anyone who has done this will attest, is labor-intensive. However, there are no shortcuts to the potential benefits that can be arrived at through these efforts.

These six community practice principles illustrate the multifaceted considerations that need to be taken into account if a church repurposing project is going to be successful. Some of these principles will come naturally to readers and therefore will be easily embraced, while others need moments of deep reflection about what they actually mean—and that is to be expected. These principles function as a directional and moral compass that will come in handy when navigating unchartered and often turbulent waters.

Church repurposing and community service learning

Urban community practitioners must strive to create initiatives that enlist the participation of all community segments to increase ownership of the final product, plus important buy-ins along the way. The saying "Nothing about us without us" applies here. These segments include all age groups, with their unique needs and goals. Learning by doing is often the most important educational experience one can have.

Community service learning projects have historically been within the field of education and represent an avenue for engaging youth and other professions, as in the social work profession, for instance (Claes et al., 2022). Undertaking community service projects with local schools, for instance, can be a novel approach toward community engagement that increases the "ownership" of a repurposed building across a wide age range (Delgado, 2016). Not only youth participants but also their families and the schools sponsoring them own these projects. Such projects can inform the general public and create a window into a project that can have great potential in drawing the community together. Investments in youth translate into investment in the future of a community, and hence are worthy of our attention.

Service learning projects involving local college/university students aid not only the student participants but also communities (Gerstenblatt & Gilbert, 2014) and can break down social barriers between institutions of higher learning and where they are geographically found. Striving to better integrate institutions of higher learning into the local scene helps all sides by making these institutions part of the community.

Conferences and other gatherings of like-minded souls

Gatherings focused on church repurposing are rare, let alone institutes with this purpose in mind. However, gatherings of like-minded practitioners and other interested parties can play a significant role in advancing the church repurposing field and must be fostered whenever possible. Of course, I realize that the mere mention of a "conference" will elicit a wide range of responses from readers, negative to positive. Nevertheless, these meetings bring a wealth of potentially valuable information that can aid this movement and field of practice.

For instance, a conference held in Vienna, Austria, in 2023 was entitled *New Uses, Old Places: The Transformations of Religious Buildings in Contemporary Europe*. Its goals were as follows:

- Share, explore and develop methodologies and theories that can be used to analyze phenomena pertaining to the social and spatial transformation of religious architecture and heritage.
- Facilitate conversations across disciplines, research projects and countries, while trying to establish some degree of comparability.
- Lead to collaboration on a future application for international research funding.

Few practitioners have the resources to attend international conferences, but similar events can be held in the United States, at a local, regional, or national level. Regional and local events have a much higher likelihood of bearing fruit, including developing important relationships between attendees. The exchange of ideas, of course, is not limited to institutions of higher learning, although they can certainly host these types of gatherings.

These gatherings must not be narrowly conceptualized, as typified by the use of webinars and special issues of scholarly journals. One webinar, sponsored by the Southern New England Conference (2018, March 15), was entitled *Disruption: Repurposing the Church to Redeem the Community*:

> An increasingly diverse and cynical society will no longer find credible the mere explanation of theological truth apart from effective community engagement. Advancing the common good, then, and thus the very Gospel, itself, must involve more than mere words, and the building of large congregations filled with people of a similar race, class, or cultural background.

Blogs have particular appeal to a segment of the field. Main Street America, for example, had one entry entitled "Seeing the Glass as Half Full: Exploring the Reuse Opportunity for Houses of Worship on Main Street" (Reinhard, 2022a). Although blogs do not bring the synergy of an in-person contact and potential for action (this observation reflects my bias), they still provide a way to connect with others sharing similar interests and to facilitate the exchange of ideas.

Finally, the European Heritage Heads Forum (https://ehhf.eu/event/repurposing-churches/) has issued a call for papers on church repurposing, signifying the emergence of this topic on the scholarly scene:

> In addition to case studies and overviews, we are also looking for discussions of how the process of repurposing should be prepared and overseen: How can all those affected be involved in the process right from the start and in such a way that good solutions are found? Which urban-planning and sociological dimensions have to be borne in mind? Which general conditions might need adjustment? What should be the role of the state—besides overseeing the preservation of historical monuments—if even the non-Christian majority of society regards these buildings as landmarks? Also worthy of consideration as a source of ideas and inspiration would be the situation abroad.

One can expect more initiatives of this kind and other types to draw attention to church repurposing because of its national and international significance for the field and society. These efforts target specific audiences, in this case an academic one.

Community fellows cadre education

Creating a cadre of community fellows, with varying participation periods, such as summer, semester, and yearly, can provide local residents with knowledge and skill sets aiding these repurposing projects. It can also lead to a career track. These fellowships can take the form of paid internships, which are preferable; fellows might rotate through various aspects of a repurposing project. The fellowship can entail weekly seminars, skill-oriented workshops, mentoring, and other activities intended to increase their competencies, with the subject matter depending upon the fellow's needs and requests. Community fellowships can be sponsored by local foundations or businesses. These efforts represent one form of community investment because such fellowships will target upcoming leaders who will likely remain in the community and apply their newfound knowledge and skills on church repurposing.

Community fellows, it is important to point out, can cover a wide age range, with local elementary and secondary students taking part (and receiving academic credit). The programs can involve a wide range of topics and methods. Class projects using photovoice, for instance, can enhance community awareness of various facets of church repurposing undertakings.

Community technology education

Older generations face greater challenges using technology, but younger generations find it familiar and comfortable. Black youth can be tapped by Black churches to help make these institutions more technology-friendly (McCormack, 2022). Church repurposing is a subject that lends itself to using visual imagery to help communities realize what structure(s) will replace a closed church, but it's also important to obtain their input. Suggestions that are not possible from a structural point of view can be dealt with on the spot, taking the mystery of decision-making out of the final design.

The concept of "community" seems ubiquitous in any urban intervention on the built environment, and church repurposing is certainly no exception. Understanding how the built environment influences social interactions is important, and readers will find an increasing amount of popular and scholarly literature on this topic. When repurposing closed churches, the community's well-being must be part of the local decision-making process.

Community practice: church closures and collective history

I was an undergraduate history major and still have a soft spot for the subject matter. I could not discuss community practice without addressing the need for communities to have recorded histories they can turn to in order to educate future generations. Various methods can be used to document this history. Of course, strong oral history traditions exist, but it is no longer dangerous to keep and share this information, and advances in technology make it easier to do so.

Churches represent an integral part of the community's collective history, but these stories are rarely recorded in written form and are not readily accessible to residents (Plevoets & Van Cleempoel, 2019). When this history is lost, part of a community's identity is also lost in the process. One important dimension of community practice is helping residents to put together a collective history that is accessible to all segments of a community. Any church repurposing project must bear this in mind.

Repurposing churches into affordable housing is an attractive goal for many urban communities, particularly given the high cost of housing. Focusing on housing, however, limits the number of potential beneficiaries when compared to having an arts center, for example, because of the level of intensity assigned to this space. Houses of worship often own significant parcels of land. In Seattle, Washington, for example, churches own 300 acres out of a total of 53,163 acres; the city "is offering a density bonus to churches that develop affordable housing on their land" (Mian & Reinhard, 2023).

Capacity enhancement and community assets

I think it is fitting to end this part of the chapter by spotlighting community assets, although they have been covered in various forms earlier in this book and chapter. Marginalized groups face formidable barriers engaging in the decision-making process in urban development, but this hurdle can be surmounted by building their capacities/assets (Geekiyanage et al., 2020; Karmokar, 2019). We must be careful to distinguish between "building" and "enhancing" the community's capacity. The former involves introducing something that is missing; the latter emphasizes what is already there but just needs to be enhanced and supported. Enhancing a community's capacity requires enabling and strengthening community decision-making and action.

Harrison (2021, p. 1) calls on Black churches to reach out and embrace economic goals for their congregations and respective communities:

> Many inner-city black churches are located in thriving cities that have multi-billion-dollar budgets while simultaneously having some of the highest rates of income inequality in the world. Cities like Chicago, New York City, and Washington D.C. have thriving downtowns, while communities are plagued by record unemployment, poverty, gun violence,

dilapidated housing, rampant homelessness, and underfunded schools just blocks from downtown.

Church repurposing is a new and bold field of practice, awaiting new discoveries that will have implications for other structures as society embraces a green strategy and the built environment gains saliency within cities. The paradigm of focusing on a community's assets and enhancing its capacity will necessitate major initiatives that specifically stress cross-disciplinary collaboration. It is not a question of whether or not that will happen; rather, it is a question of when!

Education, much like research, whether undertaken at an institution of higher learning, a conference, an institute, a community agency, or a webinar, will take on importance in the field of church repurposing. Gatherings of similar-minded practitioners with varying experiences and knowledge bases would obviously be an ideal situation, but how likely is that to happen?

Community practice education must never be relegated to an institution of higher learning; it is too important to be narrowly viewed in such a fashion. Mind you, I am a fan of higher education and its potential role in transforming this nation to become inspired by social justice. However, education can happen in any and all settings, particularly at the community level.

This section of the chapter addressed various viewpoints that fit into an educational perspective. It also touched on outside-of-the-box views, which community practice education should always be open to. It's important to maximize community participation and to match local needs and resources. Readers will have to examine their local circumstances to see which of these viewpoints are most relevant.

Section C: Implications for Community Practice

This book so far has established a critical foundation for how community practice can unfold to achieve success in the church repurposing arena, regardless of geographical location. Because community practice is not a narrow field, bold methods and tools can emerge. This is an exciting development for academics, practitioners, and communities. Nevertheless, because the field can seem all-encompassing, practitioners can easily feel overwhelmed.

Duckworth (2010, p. iii), in addressing the repurposing of Catholic churches, came to a conclusion that sadly is still applicable today, almost 15 years later: "Currently, there is no general consensus on a set of best practices regarding the adaptive reuse of church buildings, and literature on the subject is limited." A lack of or incomplete information makes recommending practice strategies and techniques arduous, particularly when local circumstances, especially in marginalized communities, dictate the best approaches to what is a complex project under the best of circumstances.

This section of the chapter discusses concrete and promising strategies that deserve attention, and purposely "pushes the envelope" on approaches that have a high probability of achieving positive change in the church repurposing field. Both conventional and creative approaches will be needed to achieve successful church repurposing with a specific focus on this nation's urban centers and its most marginalized population groups, whether or not they are church members. Readers must bear in mind that just because a repurposing project is recommended, it does not automatically result in a new purpose from a former church. Unanticipated building faults may be encountered, resulting in a change in strategy and the possible demolition of a church.

As the repurposing field continues to evolve, including specialties such as houses of worship and more and more disciplines, a set of criteria based on multidisciplinary standpoints will need to be developed to help us navigate turbulent waters. Repurposing vacant or soon-to-be vacant churches, for example, can easily fall within the "highest and best use" classification system used to build and judge structural projects (Ribera et al., 2020). These standards, we need to emphasize, must not be applied without considering context, a key theme in this book (Fadhil & Al-Zaidi, 2023). This can only be done through wide participation at the local level to help ensure that the outcome is what is desired.

What urban community practice does *not* need is an army of similar-thinking practitioners and scholars. This field's future rests on a cadre of critical thinkers who think outside of the box in a search for local solutions to local problems (Kagan et al., 2019), including a willingness to draw upon a variety of fields to accomplish their goals. Church repurposing is a new universe for practice, which is an exciting challenge that the field should meet head on. The same can be said for the building construction and design industry. Many fields can enter this brave new world together, but because they may not share the same language, a Rosetta Stone is needed to facilitate communication.

One final point before covering key principles is the importance of practitioners individualizing their approach to communities and, as noted earlier, not relying on a cookie-cutter approach to community practice Thomas, 2022):

> Communities move, change and evolve all the time. A cookie-cutter approach to problem-solving will not work often, and a successful initiative in one community may not work in another. Approaching our work flexibly and being willing to change as needed is the first step to a positive outcome. Investing time to learn the intricate threads that connect the various pieces of a community is foundational to good connections and makes the work more organic.

We must never forget that no two houses of worship, communities, and repurposing projects are similar! That is frustrating from a practice standpoint, but it's reality.

Brokering gatherings of local faith organizations

Make no mistake about it, there is a major international crisis concerning religious practices, and decreased church memberships and the closing of churches are its physical manifestations. It touches all religious groups, although some are feeling the consequences more than others. Urban centers, which are my priority, must not be ignored in any open dialogue and concerted effort to address this problem.

Community practitioners assume many roles, but the role of working as a broker takes on key importance when there are major differences of opinion on the goal of a repurposing project, which is to be expected. In the following example, this role was taken on by a minister, although a community practitioner could easily have done so. When pastors of closing churches embrace a creative solution to the challenges facing their churches, one inspired by social justice motivations, it introduces options that can fulfill "the greater good" in the community, as in the case of a Santa Cruz, California, church (Smietana, 2022):

The decision to close down First Church of the Nazarene was worrying to Andy Lewis, pastor of Faith Community. The church had struggled to find a place to worship before renting space from the Nazarenes—and Lewis feared the church would have to leave the space. In this new arrangement, Faith Community—which is nondenominational—gets to stay as one of several community partners sharing the space. The idea is to use the space for the benefit not just of the church but the entire neighborhood, he said. During the COVID-19 pandemic, Faith Community has used the space to run a food ministry and to host mobile medical clinics and a vaccination site in the parking lot.

Broadening how church spaces can be used in service to community, and the faith community in general, helps ensure survivability. It's also important to reach out beyond a congregation to ground this institution in the basic social fabric of a community.

A crisis can be turned into an opportunity, or a "calling from God," if you wish. This type of initiative has been referred to as "kingdom-mindedness," capturing a broad view of a Christian ministry that extends far beyond a focus on a church's own self-interests. This stance embraces what many religious people would consider a holy mission to serve those in greatest need. Although the Santa Cruz example is very different from an urban community as conceptualized in this book, much can be learned from their experiences and adapted according to local conditions and circumstances.

Where churches have no choice but to close, their buildings stand as testimonies to a bygone era while bringing significant and multifaceted consequences for the neighborhoods where their structures remain. These structures stand on the crossroads of demolition or repurposing. If repurposed with the goal of helping the community, their glory will persist and honor their past. But if done to meet the narrow needs of a select group, such as real estate interests, they will send a message that the community is inconsequential and has no important legacy to leave future generations.

Holding open meetings/public forums is a practice tactic that has particular relevance for church repurposing initiatives (Thomas, 2021). Public meetings bringing together residents to discuss community matters have a long history in the United States. These meetings can be televised through public channels, for example, or conducted live online. The greater the opportunities for a community to obtain information on a pending church repurposing project and/or attend and give testimony, the greater the awareness and ultimate ownership of the final outcome ("community involved; community owned"). These meetings symbolize at the local level what democracy is supposed to be all about and represent a fitting method for planning the future of an institution that symbolically considers all members as equal and worthy!

Coalitions are another strategy common in community practice and the urban scene. Readers may have an automatic negative reaction against coalitions because of the potential competing interests at the table. However, bringing together faith organizations within a city or community to discuss church repurposing helps the exchange of ideas, concerns, and potential rewards of these actions. The collective political power of such a group, particularly when tapping their moral authority, makes it difficult to ignore in any decision-making process without political peril, centered on City Hall or otherwise.

Community practitioners, it is fair to say, may find allies in embracing a participatory approach to church repurposing. The church community has recognized the challenge that church closures present to their host sites. Partners for Sacred Spaces, for example, has a publication titled *Transitioning Older and Historic Sacred Places: Community-Minded Approaches for Congregations and Judicatories* to assist local communities that are approaching a project through a social justice lens:

> When religious buildings must be sold, our guide recommends a civic-minded process that brings congregations and communities together, encouraging new uses that maintain the public value of these sacred places, as well as steps to protect and preserve their character and cultural value.

The broker role can be assumed by various entities depending upon local circumstances, and enhanced when the broker and its sponsor enjoy wide acceptability (legitimacy). Municipalities may occupy these positions in one community but not others. Foundations and local nonprofits, too, can take on this role. There is no one entity that must be present, with the possible exception of municipal government, for example.

Born et al. (2021) chronicled how Seattle's historically Black churches are countering the forces of gentrification, which are pushing parishioners out of their community and leading to closure of their churches. Hope is wonderful, but it is not a plan. It takes initiatives such as those employed by the Nehemiah Initiative and Black churches to help fight these powerful forces, as well as helping more organizations fill this role, serving as a "lab" for lessons learned, and furthering the church repurposing field.

Brokering of transfer of church property

Facilitating the transfer of ownership of church property to a community organization represents another role that community practitioners can assume in facilitating repurposing projects. Houses of worship can be donated to their respective communities as a means of dealing with unwanted or unnecessary church properties.

For example, Salt Lake City's Latter Day Saints Church in Utah donated a building and 2.5 acres of land, with an assessed value of $1.3 million, to a nonprofit to develop affordable housing (Anderson, 2023). In 2019, these properties were valued at $453 million. The Church, however, kept the subterranean rights, which includes water and possible minerals, and also retained the right of first refusal to buy the property back if it went on the market. Readers, as I did, may find that clause unusual, but that may be more church- and site-specific.

Community practitioners and nonprofit institutions are in a propitious position to identify redundant church property that can be used to meet community needs. Their knowledge of the community, its needs, and key actors, for example, facilitates working with religious organizations that have excess property that might be better used in service to the community; this property, incidentally, does not have to be a church building.

The ability to form partnerships and collaborative undertakings

Everyone talks about the virtues of collaboration, but it's just another word for a team. Church repurposing is highly complex, and no one individual or organization will possess the requisite competencies to undertake it without partnerships, as we discussed in Chapter 6. Collaboration in the form of formal partnerships is central for increasing the chances of successfully achieving church repurposing outcomes, as noted by McBroom (2020):

> Whether you are building a brand-new facility or considering an adaptive reuse possibility, you will need to work with local government and the community related to development regulations as well as sharing the story of the positive impact your church desires to bring to the neighborhood. Depending on the adaptive reuse facility's nature and the community's vision for growth, you may find unexpected possibilities for local collaboration or support.

Urban community practitioners, regardless of goals, often occupy a central and defining role in a project or intervention strategy. Partnerships are helped when a practitioner has the foresight and skill set to accomplish them. These analytical-interactional competencies can be enhanced when practitioners have access to needed consultation.

Effective collaborations are difficult. They must be time-limited and extremely focused, and they must have clearly articulated guidelines. Our society stresses individuality. We learn to compete early on in our lives, which is often done through seemingly innocuous games such as Musical Chairs, for example. (Personally, I have always had trouble with a game that requires the "losers" to stand around until a winner is declared.) Our education system rewards individuality. We rarely work on student projects together, such as having three or four children draw a human body. For readers who have gone through the formal educational system to receive a doctorate, you were engaged in individual research; there is no such thing as a group dissertation.

The skill sets involved in cooperating will last a lifetime and will make it easier for us to collaborate with others as we enter adulthood and engage in professional practice. Bringing people together is a noble goal but is difficult to achieve! That makes it even more significant as an approach, and church repurposing guided by a social mission will surely be an asset.

Designation as historical property

Designating a property as historical to prevent it from being demolished or repurposed into luxury housing in desirable areas of a city, for example, is one role community practitioners can undertake. Helping preserve a church building through negotiating with bureaucracies and filling out necessary forms is an activist role and part of a community practice tradition—we must explore all options in our responsibility to communities. Negotiating with bureaucrats is not a task that everyone can do or will be willing to undertake, least of all community residents, and it can be considered a public service.

Municipalities can be very influential in helping a church receive an historical designation as a strategy to prevent it from being repurposed into luxury housing. Molina (2023) speculates on who the ultimate beneficiary will be if churches are repurposed into housing. Market rates effectively limit who can be housed, thus working against professed beliefs about helping the least fortunate.

In 2021, a group of residents of an historically Black community successfully undertook a four-year campaign to have the Los Angeles Cultural Heritage Commission designate the First Baptist Church of Venice, including its adjacent parking lots, as an historical cultural monument. This action prevented the publisher of *Rolling Stone* magazine from turning it into his private home. Some readers may think of this action as out of the ordinary because the church was being converted into a single home, but the principles are the same. The repurposing was not being undertaken in service to the community but rather to a private citizen.

Repurposing churches into nonprofit organizations: opportunities for local contributions

When a church is being repurposed into a nonprofit, local organizations and residents can contribute to this undertaking. We often conceptualize participation as being limited to residents, but broadening support for a repurposed church mission is what many advocates consider to be an ideal mission. Repurposing churches into nonprofit organizations to assume caregiving missions, for instance, opens the door for local businesses to contribute to these endeavors, increasing local ownership of these ventures and the likelihood of their success, as was the case in Peabody, Massachusetts (MassPlumbers, 2022):

> As Rebecca Bryan, minister of the First Religious Society Unitarian Universalist Church, explains, its congregation is hosting a large Afghan

family in Parish Hall, a building adjacent to the church. Typically used for Sunday school classes and social functions, the converted living space did not have a shower, nor a washer or dryer. Bryan, who serves as Newburyport's chair of Interfaith Coalition of Clergy, reached out to Kelleher, who had helped do plumbing work at the temporary housing provided by the city's Episcopalian church for another refugee family.

Creative efforts such as this can be replicated across the country, involving other local small businesses, broadening the caregiving system in highly innovative and community-centered ways and ensuring that local needs are met with community support across various segments. The success of these projects will be enhanced as a result.

Opening the door for innovation

Repurposing as a concept and strategy, of course, can extend far beyond church buildings. A great deal can be learned from other efforts, just as many lessons that can be shared from church repurposing. For example, churches that are closing often have to devote considerable time and energy to disposing of items that were instrumental in their function. Pews, organs, and chairs, to list but three, need to be discarded or repurposed. This decision-making process, including finding places to donate them to, requires time and energy and is emotionally draining for those making the decisions. The process requires deep discussions that can be uplifting but painful, too. The final distribution of resources will aid other institutions in carrying out their mission. Efforts to help this regenerative process take on greater significance in urban centers experiencing unprecedented numbers of church closures, making it even more difficult to donate items to other churches.

In one novel approach, Invested Faith (Albany, Georgia) developed an initiative and produced a mini-documentary series with the goal of inspiring closing churches to donate their assets to help local social entrepreneurs start projects in the communities they serve (Brumley, 2023). Invested Faith assumed the role of distributor of repurposed church items. This "centralized" function can be replicated in cities experiencing elevated levels of church closures. Although not specifically related to repurposing of buildings, this project helps with the disposition of items integral to a church's function that have monetary value or can find a "second life" in service to a community.

A website called usedpews.org, referred to as "Craigslist for Churches," will provide a reality check for those who are not worried about the "great dechurching" movement that is gaining momentum. This movement will have a major impact on the companies that have historically supplied churches, too, which is an economic dimension that has escaped scholarly attention.

Collaborative undertakings will benefit from "outside-the-box" thinking. Collaborative interventions for repurposing church property can involve schools of architecture, such as the University of Notre Dame School of Architecture's project in South Bend, Indiana (Grondelski, 2022). Urban-based architecture schools embracing the "new urbanism," for example, a movement that centers the human experience in shaping the environment, can help the church community, universities, and communities. These collaborations can have "win–win" outcomes for all participants, also serving as an impetus for other forms of collaboration.

Innovative efforts at aiding merging churches are also needed.[1] For instance, in Omaha, Nebraska, the Catholic Church brought together the members of churches facing mergers to seek input into the process (Johnson, 2023). This was a church-led effort, but these initiatives can be led by practitioners assuming broker roles.

Community practice and local talent

All communities, regardless of their history, economic wealth, and academic backgrounds, have talented residents—including highly marginalized communities. Local talent exists if we have open minds and a fundamental belief in the importance of identifying and supporting it. We should ask "Where is the talent and what does it consist of?" rather than "Is there talent?" The basic premise is different, with answers dictating the actions that we will need to take to enlist their support, with outcomes very much tailored to local needs.

---

[1] As we noted earlier in the book, mergers are a response to long-developing trends of fewer priests and declining church membership. Mergers allow easier deployment of existing resources.

For instance, residents with artistic talents can paint murals and take photos capturing the unfolding of a church repurposing project, which can also become part of the community's history (Feen-Calligan et al., 2022). One has only to spend a short amount of time in a community to witness artwork appearing in public spaces, be it murals, tagging, or sculptures, for example. This talent may be homegrown and lack formal training, but talent it is and it must not go to waste!

Communities came together to build and financially support church construction and communities kept them alive. It will take communities to repurpose them. For instance, what used to be St. Matthew's Episcopal Church in Hallowell, Maine, is now the Hallowell Multicultural Center, an organization providing multiple services to meet the needs of newcomers to this country (Adhikari & Page, 2022):

> "We see it as a wonderful space to bring cultures together, to learn from each other, to share stories with each other, to share food, break bread, and really build community," says Mr. Myers Asch. It's a place, he says, "where we can celebrate becoming America together, bringing the newest Americans into the fold."

Local needs dictate innovative approaches—never a cookie-cutter approach!

Merging local circumstances or needs and creativity can result in bold and highly creative projects. For instance, what used to be St. Liborius Church in St. Louis is now a skate park, Sk8Liborius (Chapman, 2023). Chapman (2023) makes the point regarding St. Louis that "no one is coming to repair America's forgotten cities except for the people who live in them. In St. Louis alone, there are about 25,000 abandoned buildings." Chapman explains how local marginalized communities can take on these repurposing projects:

> A few years ago, my friends and I pooled our resources to turn St. Liborius Church, a nationally registered historical site and the largest Gothic revival church west of the Mississippi, into a community space. Trying to develop a skate park inside a massive church was never a part of my five-, 10- or any-year plan. But I fell in love with the idea of giving a new generation of St. Louis kids a spectacular place where they would be welcome and where no one would ever shoo them away.

This repurposing opened the door for local community contributions, such as murals covering the walls. These murals, however, were not allowed to cover up walls adorned with original religious artworks. Tragically, a four-alarm fire destroyed the church and all of the work that had gone into this project. Efforts are currently under way to raise the funds to rebuild this structure.

Pictures and other items can be stored in repurposed buildings or local libraries, allowing current and future generations to develop a better understanding of their community. Connecting past, current, and future generations to their history creates a connectedness that is representative of a community's history, and often best typified by a house of worship. Current generations build upon the accomplishments of past generations, and set the foundation for future generations.

Sole community practitioner/activists and God's work

I commend those embracing the challenge of saving church buildings and their mission, or what I like to refer to someone as doing "God's work." This work certainly brings challenges, as Nickels (2022) describes in an article about Brody Hale, an attorney who "is known throughout the world as one of the foremost experts on how to save Catholic churches that have been closed by their respective Dioceses." I conceptualized this book as highlighting organizational efforts at undertaking church repurposing, but that does not have to be the case: Lasting social change starts at the bottom through collective, participatory action (Ledwith & Springett, 2022).

"Practitioners" can certainly be sole activists. However, we can compare their efforts to stopping a dam break with a bucket, and a small one at that! Nevertheless, they can help spark communities in their quest to save church structures by tapping the community's expertise, and there is no reason why organizational efforts cannot join forces with them. Expertise in this relatively new field is in short supply and will be in high demand.

A big-city municipal government will look dramatically different from one in a small town, not to mention the political pressures experienced in deliberating on what to do with an empty church. Large cities, however, will draw extra attention, financial resources, and expertise. They certainly have the media exposure to get the message out to the rest of the nation. With that comes a moral obligation to inform the nation, however.

Desperate times call for desperate measures?

I felt compelled to add this section near the end of this book. A crisis is an excellent point at which introduce changes in our lives and communities that we normally would not have considered. Institutions, too, face similar options, like churches facing the possibility that their doors will be closed forever. Keeping a church open by purposely bringing in "outside worshippers" may seem like a workable alternative to its closure, but this must be done carefully and in a planned manner.

Strategies to keep churches open must be localized to increase the likelihood of success. A model that is successful in one city may well need significant modification to be successful elsewhere. Coomans (2012, p. 222) addresses the potential community backlash when a different denomination takes over a church, which can worsen racial tensions where they exist:

> Perhaps the most controversial change of use is when a place of worship is taken over by another religion. This could be considered paradoxical because the places then remain sacred and, in a certain way, the buildings are not "reused" because they conserve a function related with worship. But it is well-known that the reuse of a church by a community of another religion is a particularly sensitive problem and is almost always considered a "defeat" by those who "desert" the place.

If there is a history of conflict between the two denominations, it brings added tensions. This conflict can spill over into the community, straining relationships even further. Involvement by political entities can aggravate the situation, with political ramifications.

Obtaining funding for repurposing and programming

The subject of money is always part of any discussion concerning community practice; we discussed the funding role of municipal government in Chapter 4. Writing proposals and undertaking grassroots fundraising necessitates special knowledge and skill sets. Funding for repurposing a structure will often entail different sources from those related to programming once a new structure has been erected.

Readers may ask, "Aren't capital grants for 'bricks and mortar' projects relatively easily available?" Yes, that is true to a certain extent. However, funding for the programming that goes on within these buildings is not. Operating grants tend to be short-lived and highly competitive. It reminds me of the dog that chases the mail truck: What happens once he catches it? It can be very easy to focus on repurposing a church, which is a long-term strategy. But deciding what happens within this new building will also prove challenging, particularly when looking at sustainability.

Community capacity enhancement as a strategy must embrace local fundraising whenever possible as a means of ensuring that the new structure and its programming reflects local priorities, and that certainly applies in church repurposing, as argued throughout this book. Further, these efforts must try to be intergenerational to help ensure that future generations are well positioned to continue programming.

No one individual, regardless of their knowledge base, can possibly fulfill all of the needs that arise across the repurposing of an old church and the programs that will happen within the new structure. This will need a team that will change as the needs change, although it is best to keep a core group in place that facilitates transitions across stages of intervention. Hopefully, municipalities will step forward and play an active role in helping across the continuum. The Boston case illustration in Chapter 3 highlights this very important point and the political nature of repurposing projects that need municipal consent to move forward.

Closing Reflections

Authoring a book always starts with great anticipation of new discoveries made along the journey. Although repurposing is the central thrust of this book, the choice to tear down a church and start over again is always a consideration. Tearing down makes room for a new structure that can offer a wealth of opportunities for a community. For instance, in Long Beach, California, a Lutheran church's school building will be torn down and replaced with affordable housing in a new taller building, with the church sharing parking with the new building. The sad occasion of closing their school led to an opportunity to broaden their mission.

There is no one answer! Readers seeking a simple solution will be quickly disappointed when they meet the maze that awaits them, and the time and energy that is needed. The subject matter is complex because of the significance of religion in society and how its structures assume symbolic significance locally and nationally. Further, no two church structures are ever similar or even found next to similar buildings, though they may appear as such until we take interiors into account, for example, in addition to their racial and ethnic composition.

The subject of writing a book on church closings did elicit a level of anxiety because I am not a deeply religious person and did not want to offend readers who are religious, as well as those who are not. It is no mistake that religion is considered a "third rail." Yet, to stay true to its mission, community practice must not avoid certain terrains for practice. The "resurrection" of churches as new entities brings high hopes and energy for communities when undertaken with them serving as a guiding light (pardon the pun) rather than "for" them! As the saying goes, "Nothing about us without us." If we want communities to own these institutions, then they must feel and believe they own them!

We must find a path that seeks to preserve historical buildings that no longer have their original function in a way that meets pressing current or projected future needs (Romanova, 2022), and finding a compromise through repurposing is a workable option. The original group that helped build the church will in all likelihood no longer be in the picture. Historically, public buildings did not lend themselves to patrons with mobility challenges; signage, too, has appeared, aiding visitors. Buildings do not have the "luxury" of ignoring changing times and needs; they must respond. Readers are aware of the challenge we face in answering this "simple" question, but answer it we must.

Community practitioners play multiple roles with church closures and repurposing, allowing for various degrees of interest, talent, commitment, and involvement in assessing their local circumstances. That is exciting because it introduces bold initiatives that can attract other professions into this field. However, just as importantly, communities ascend to prominence in this field and are an integral part of a partnership, with the promise of other bold forms of practices.

Readers have finally come to the end of the road! As promised in the introductory chapter, this travel took many different twists and turns. Urban community practice is about the journey. I am a big believer that cities are an important engine of innovation in a wide variety of domains, including a climate agenda. Churches are often the biggest buildings in communities and can therefore play an instrumental role in moving this agenda forward when they close and can reemerge as new entities responsive to current-day usage needs. In addition, they can achieve this goal while meeting local needs and a broader social climate agenda.

I hope that this book has advanced the debate on church closures and their repurposing. Critics will come forth and ask why I have taken a simplistic stance on such an important subject, or why the analysis and proposed solutions are inherently biased. Others will see merit in the arguments undergirding this book, leading to further research, action, and scholarship to move the field forward in urban America.

There is no "natural" ending to a book. Yes, there are deadlines, word limits, and so forth, but as a book unfolds, new and unplanned dimensions appear. There may be readers who love the thrill of discovery and thinking about a subject in a new or more nuanced light, and that is the case with church repurposing and community practice! The future is full of promise for those who embrace this mission!

Church closures and their repurposing represents a journey that straddles religious beliefs and earthly pursuits. Yes, welcome to the third rail. I hope readers take this challenge to heart and venture into the world of repurposing in general, church repurposing in particular. Welcome to this bold new world as it expands in the future, offering boundless opportunities for us to carry out a social justice mission!

References

Adhikari, T., & Page, E. (2022, January 26). Church buildings repurposed as community hubs. *Christian Science Monitor.* https://www.csmonitor.com/USA/Society/2022/0126/Sacred-spaces-Church-buildings-repurposed-as-community-hubs

Aigwi, I. E., Duberia, A., & Nwadike, A. N. (2023). Adaptive reuse of existing buildings as a sustainable tool for climate change mitigation within the built environment. *Sustainable Energy Technologies and Assessments, 56*, 102945.

Allen, S. E. (2019). Doing black Christianity: Reframing black church scholarship. *Sociology Compass, 13*(10), e12731.

Allen, S. E. (2023). Is the Black church dead? Religious resilience and the contemporary functions of Black Christianity. *Religions, 14*(4), 460. https://www.mdpi.com/2077-1444/14/4/460

Amayu, E. (2014). *New uses for old churches: An examination of the effects of planning regulations on the adaptive reuse of church buildings.* (Dissertation, Queen's University Kingston).

American Institute of Architects. (2020). *Buildings that last: Design for adaptability, deconstruction, and reuse.* Author.

Amezcua, M. (2021, June 24). How a little Mexican American church, soon to close, became a refuge from discrimination for 76 years. *Chicago Sun Times.* https://chicago.suntimes.com/2021/6/24/22548923/la-capilla-immaculate-heart-of-mary-back-yards-chicago-church-closings-mexican-americans

Anderson, J. (2014, Winter 12). *Millennials: The unreached in our midst. A practical theology of reaching millennials through organic church principles and repurposing the church.* Fire Scholars, Southeastern University. https://firescholars.seu.edu/cgi/viewcontent.cgi?article=1049&context=maml

Anderson, T. (2023, April 27). *Nonprofit focused on affordable housing acquires building for LDS.* Building Salt Lake City. https://buildingsaltlake.com/nonprofit-focused-on-affordable-housing-acquires-building-from-lds-church-in-central-city/

Anderton, F. (2021, December 16). *To build or not to build? Architects struggle with the future of their craft in a warming world.* Sierra Club. https://www.sierraclub.org/sierra/2021-6-winter/feature/build-or-not-build

Antal, J. (2023). *Climate church, climate world: How people of faith must work for change.* Rowman & Littlefield.

Anzani, A., & Capitani, G. (2022). Ethics of care and reuse of urban space. In *The city of care: Strategies to design healthier places* (pp. 19–27). Springer International Publishing.

Aranđelović, M., Videnović, A., Gadžić, N., & Tomanović, D. (2022). Repurposing and the impact of new facilities on the potential presentation of industrial heritage. *Sustainability, 14*(10), 5915.

Arboix-Alió, A., Pons-Poblet, J. M., Arboix, A., & Arboix-Alió, J. (2023). Relevance of Catholic parish churches in public space in Barcelona: Historical analysis and future perspectives. *Buildings, 13*(6), 1370.

Arfa, F. H., Zijlstra, H., Lubelli, B., & Quist, W. (2022). Adaptive reuse of heritage buildings: From a literature review to a model of practice. *The Historic Environment: Policy & Practice, 13*(2), 148–170.

Armstrong, G., Wilkinson, S., & Cilliers, E. J. (2023). A framework for sustainable adaptive reuse: Understanding vacancy and underuse in existing urban buildings. *Frontiers in Sustainable Cities*, 5(29), 1–14.

Asher, A. (2023, February 24). The city forced their church's expensive demolition. *The Austin Chronicle*. https://www.austinchronicle.com/news/2023-02-24/the-city-forced-their-churchs-expensive-demolition/

Assefa, G., & Ambler, C. (2017). To demolish or not to demolish: Life cycle consideration of repurposing buildings. *Sustainable Cities and Society*, 28, 146–153.

Associated Press. (2022, August 20). *Demolition of St. Laurentius Church in Fishtown begins after long battle*. WHYY. https://whyy.org/articles/philadelphia-fishtown-st-laurentius-church-demolition/

Audiq, T. (2023, December 18). One fourth of United Methodist churches in US have left in schism over LGBTQ ban. What happens now? *Fremont Tribune*. https://fremonttribune.com/life-entertainment/nation-world/faith-values/congregations-leaving-united-methodist-church-lgbtq-bans/article_79ad4484-0562-5c7b-9818-c6b7e5d11874.html

Australian Community Workers Association. (2017, January 25). *A new code of ethics for community workers*. http://www.acwa.org.au/_blog/Blog/post/a-new-code-of-ethics-for-community-workers/

Azzara, M. (2019). Grappling with the impermanence of place: A Black Baptist congregation in South Los Angeles. *City & Society*, 31(1), 77–93.

Bacon, C. M. (2022a, March 1). Where have all the churches gone? *Christian Chronicle*. https://christianchronicle.org/where-have-all-the-churches-gone/

Bacon, C. M. (2022b, March 30). Church closing trends before COVID-19. *Christian Chronicle*. https://christianchronicle.org/church-closing-trend-began-before-covid-19/

Ballinger, B. (2023). *Adaptive reuse surges as older buildings are rebirthed into new uses*. GLOBEST.Com. https://www.globest.com/2023/07/19/adaptive-reuse-surges-as-older-buildings-are-rebirthed-into-new-uses/?slreturn=20230629135337

Baltimore-Washington Conference. (2022, June 2). *Trustee report on church closings*. https://www.bwcumc.org/news-and-views/trustees-report-on-church-closings/

Bandlamudin, A. (2022, September 19). *California churches have space to create affordable housing, but there are hurdles*. NPR. https://www.npr.org/2022/09/19/1123926755/california-churches-have-space-to-create-affordable-housing-but-there-are-hurdle

Banks, S. (Ed.). (2010). *Ethical issues in youth work*, 2nd ed. Routledge.

Barba, L. (2022). Latina/o Pentecostalism. In K. Warren (Ed.), *The Oxford handbook of Latinx Christianities in the United States* (pp. 130–149). Oxford University Press.

Barnette, T. (2023). *Building an outreach ministry to your community: How to grow your church by ministering to people*. Tyndale House Publishers.

Barron, J. M., & Williams, R. H. (2017). *The urban church imagined: Religion, race, and authenticity in the city*. NYU Press.

Barucco, S. (2023, July 17). *Adaptive reuse of historic church buildings*. Partners for Sacred Spaces. https://sacredplaces.org/adaptive-reuse-of-historic-church-buildings/

Baruth, M., Wilcox, S., Saunders, R. P., Hooker, S. P., Hussey, J. R., & Blair, S. N. (2013). Perceived environmental church support and physical activity among Black church members. *Health Education & Behavior*, 40(6), 712–720.

Beech, C. (2022a, April 1). *One year later a structure rises on holy ground*. Spectrum News 1. https://spectrumnews1.com/ca/la-west/homelessness/2022/04/01/one-year-later--a-structure-rises-on-holy-ground-

Beech, C. (2022b, August 4). *Permanent supportive housing rises near church*. Spectrum News 1. https://spectrumnews1.com/ca/la-west/housing/2022/08/04/permanent-supportive-housing-rises-near-church-

Beer, A., Weller, S., Barnes, T., Onur, I., Ratcliffe, J., Bailey, D., & Sotarauta, M. (2019). The urban and regional impacts of plant closures: New methods and perspectives. *Regional Studies, Regional Science*, 6(1), 380–394.

Beers-Altman, J. (2023, January 12). *Bob Jaeger helps repurpose closed churches.* WPSU. https://radio.wpsu.org/2023-01-12/bob-jaeger-repurposing-churches-that-close-creative-reuse-featured-on-wpsu-tvs-keystone-stories-monday-at-9-p-m

Bell, M., & Lehto, H. M. (2019, August 14). *Megachurches, home churches, podcasts: American evangelicals are "not a monolith."* The World. https://theworld.org/stories/2019/08/14/evangelicals-america

Beltz, J. (2005, October 29). *A tidal wave of church closings.* World. https://wng.org/articles/a-tidal-wave-of-church-closings-1671586988

Bentzen, J. S. (2021). In crisis, we pray: Religiosity and the COVID-19 pandemic. *Journal of Economic Behavior & Organization, 192*, 541–583.

Beres, D. (2018, December 16). *What should we do with all of those empty churches?* Big Think. https://bigthink.com/high-culture/what-should-we-do-with-all-of-those-empty-churches/

Berg, R. (2023, July 2). *Church attendance declines locally, nationally.* The Free Press (Mankato, MN). https://www.yahoo.com/news/church-attendance-declines-locally-nationally-111800502.html

Berhó, D. L. (2020). An "echo in the soul": Worship music in Evangelical Spanish-language Latino churches of Oregon. *Ecclesial Practices, 7*(2), 203–225.

Bernhard, B. (2023a, February 13). *"Don't kick us out for being poor": Feedback from the faithful on St. Louis' Catholic parish reorganization.* St. Louis Post-Dispatch. https://www.stltoday.com/news/local/metro/don-t-kick-us-out-for-being-poor-feedback-from-the-faithful-on-st-louis/article_e0c63d38-be3d-59a4-a994-59dad4d4816e.html

Bernhard, B. (2023b, July 25). *Volunteer priests to serve at St. Louis Catholic parish after it is closed by church leaders.* St. Louis Post-Dispatch. https://www.stltoday.com/news/local/metro/volunteer-priests-to-serve-st-louis-catholic-parish-after-it-is-closed-by-church-leaders/article_a23465a8-2b1e-11ee-b5b0-3bc84d1ce297.html

Berrelleza, E. (2020). Exclusion in upscaling institutions: The reproduction of neighborhood segregation in an urban church. *City & Community, 19*(3), 747–770.

Berry, A., & Hutchins, R. (2023, January 22). *A historically Black church is now an event space. Who decides if it's gentrification?* The Daily Progress. https://dailyprogress.com/news/a-historically-black-church-is-now-an-event-space-who-decides-if-its-gentrification/article_9dc8bb10-983c-11ed-9ae7-cbb13ea44830.html

Bertholet, R. F. (2013). *These dead bones can rise again: Preventing church closures in North America.* (Dissertation, George Fox University).

Betz, J. (2022, December 22). *A tidal wave of church closings: Thousands of doors are being locked from the inside.* World. https://wng.org/articles/a-tidal-wave-of-church-closings-1671586988

Blackwell, D. L. (2022). *The role of the Black church as a transformational leader in economic stability and wealth creation for African American people through entrepreneurship.* (Doctoral dissertation, Alvernia University).

Blake, J. (2023, April 8). *Predictions about the decline of Christianity in America may be premature.* CNN. https://www.cnn.com/2023/04/08/us/christianity-decline-easter-blake-cec/index.html

Blokland, T. (2017). *Community as urban practice.* John Wiley & Sons.

Bolan, M. (2023, August). *Governments have faith church property can help property solve housing crisis.* Route Fifty. https://www.route-fifty.com/management/2023/08/governments-have-faith-church-property-can-help-solve-housing-crisis/389442/

Born, B., Berney, R., Baker, O., Jones, M. R., King, D., & Marcus, D. (2021). Pushing back on displacement: Community-based redevelopment through historically Black churches. *Societies, 11*(1), 10. https://www.mdpi.com/2075-4698/11/1/10

Bosman, J. (2022, December 17). *In Chicago a battle over a religious statue is about much more.* New York Times.

Boston's Jamaica Plain Section Hyde Square Task Force. (2020). *Blessed Sacrament Church.* https://www.hydesquare.org/wp-content/uploads/2020/10/RFP-Blessed-Sacrament-Church-JP.pdf

Brand, D. J. (2019). Barriers and facilitators of faith-based health programming within the African American church. *Journal of Cultural Diversity, 26*(1), 3–9.

Brandon, G. Q. (2022). *Preaching through desensitized emotions: Clergy burnout in the African American church.* (Doctoral dissertation, Virginia Union University).

Branson, M. L., & Martinez, J. F. (2023). *Churches, cultures, and leadership: A practical theology of congregations and ethnicities.* InterVarsity Press.

Brinig, M. F., & Garnett, N. S. (2019). *Lost classroom, lost community: Catholic schools' importance in urban America.* University of Chicago Press.

Brinklow, A. (2023, April 3). *SF churches have a hell of a time creating affordable housing.* The Frisc. https://thefrisc.com/sf-churches-have-a-hell-of-a-time-creating-affordable-housing-3d89401d71f9

Brown, E. (2023). *Church planting still essential for God's mission in UCC.* Northwest Adventists. https://nwadventists.com/feature/church-planting-still-essential-gods-mission-ucc

Brown, J. (2023, January 9). *Third of Americans have quit church as attendance fails to recover pre-pandemic numbers: Survey.* FoxNews. https://www.foxnews.com/us/third-americans-have-quit-church-attendance-fails-recover-pre-pandemic-numbers-survey

Brown, N. (2022, February 17). *Philadelphia's Black Catholics mourn closure of historic church.* CBS News. https://www.cbsnews.com/philadelphia/news/philadelphias-black-catholics-mourn-closure-of-historic-church/

Brown, N. L. (2018, September 30). The end of our journey: A historic Black church closes. *The Washington Post.* https://www.washingtonpost.com/local/the-end-of-our-journey-a-historic-black-church-closes-its-doors-in-a-changing-dc/2018/09/30/b2f3f222-c1c5-11e8-a1f0-a4051b6ad114_story.html

Brown, N. R., Alick, C. L., Heaston, A. G., Monestime, S., & Powe, N. (2022). The Black church and public health: A key partnership for theory-driven COVID-19 recovery efforts. *Journal of Primary Care & Community Health, 13.* https://www.ncbi.nlm.nih.gov/pmc/articles/PMC9150224/

Brown Jr., S. (2022, May 12). *COVID's impact on the Black church. St. Louis American.* https://www.stlamerican.com/religion/local_religion/covid-s-impact-on-the-black-church/article_ff8d387c-d063-11ec-8e0c-0b9f9b453256.html

Brubaker, D. (2023, March 13). *Life after death for congregations.* Congregational Consulting. https://www.congregationalconsulting.org/life-after-death-for-congregations/

Bruce, T. C. (2017). *Parish and place: Making room for diversity in the American Catholic Church.* Oxford University Press.

Bruce, T. C. (2023). Placemaking in a postsecular age: Sorting "sacred" from "profane" in the adaptive reuse of relegated US Catholic churches. *US Catholic Historian, 41*(1), 93–115.

Brumley, J. (2022, March 28). *Predominantly Black churches still have a future, Tisby asserts.* Baptist News. https://baptistnews.com/article/predominantly-black-churches-still-have-a-future-tisby-asserts/

Brumley, J. (2023, May 25). *New documentary series shows how churches that close can keep ministry open.* Baptist News. https://baptistnews.com/article/new-documentary-series-shows-how-churches-that-close-can-keep-ministry-open/

Brunson, S. (2023, March 3). *Church tax exemption: An explainer.* By Common Consent. https://bycommonconsent.com/2023/03/03/church-tax-exemption-an-explainer/

Budzyn, D. (2022, September 13). *Who owns more land: Bill Gates, McDonald's or the Catholic Church?* Yahoo. https://www.yahoo.com/video/owns-more-land-bill-gates-132113385.html?guccounter=1&guce_referrer=aHR0cHM6Ly93d3cuZ29vZ2xlLmNvbS8&guce_referrer_sig=AQAAADGLqKuHP5x7IbmsYsXBDF3SaTgs7ZffnAvWp7AiRN9ber-bH2MHAOVeeMT-MRXhBYJzKUXkBaOLrbPZHSVDOEclJ8ICqUE_lLGBlC_XuBCz3Eg-G3M2xmMrPY_2BYizq2jiu6ZgCd2e9uOkx6ztHLq57vOylj0lY2C4Y5ihk2-2

Bullen, P. A., & Love, P. E. (2009). Residential regeneration and adaptive reuse: Learning from the experiences of Los Angeles. *Structural Survey, 27*(5), 351–360.

Bullen, P. A., & Love, P. E. (2010). The rhetoric of adaptive reuse or reality of demolition: Views from the field. *Cities, 27*(4), 215–224.

Bullen, P. A., & Love, P. E. (2011a). A new future for the past: A model for adaptive reuse decision-making. *Built Environment Project and Asset, 1*(1), 32–44.

Bullen, P. A., & Love, P. E. (2011b). Adaptive reuse of heritage buildings. *Structural Survey, 29*(5), 411–421.

Bunn, C. (2021, September 9). *"It's been shattering": Headache and hope in America's Black churches.* NBC News. https://www.nbcnews.com/news/nbcblk/it-s-been-shattering-hearta che-hope-america-s-black-churches-n1252099

Burchell, R., & Listokin, D. (1981). *The adaptive reuse handbook.* Rutgers, The State University of New Jersey.

Burge, R. P. (2022, February 19). *Black Americans see the biggest shift away from faith.* Pew Research Center.

Burge, R. P. (2023). *The nones: Where they came from, who they are, and where they are going.* Fortress Press.

Buringh, E., Campbell, B. M., Rijpma, A., & van Zanden, J. L. (2020). Church building and the economy during Europe's "Age of the Cathedrals," 700–1500 CE. *Explorations in Economic History, 76,* 101316.

Burke, K. J., Juzwik, M., & Prins, E. (2023). White Christian nationalism: What is it, and why does it matter for educational research? *Educational Researcher, 52*(5). https://doi.org/10.3102/0013189X231163147

Burns, R. (2018, May 4). *Putting faith in housing: A primer for all partners.* The NHP Foundation. https://nhpfoundation.org/documents/NHPF_FaithBasedAffordableHou sing_Articl es.pdf

Butler, A. (2021, November 29). *Black Catholics have a right to be frustrated with a church that ignores racism.* MSNBC. https://www.msnbc.com/opinion/black-catholics-have-right-be-frustrated-church-ignores-racism-n1284598

Campbell, L. K., Svendsen, E., Johnson, M., & Landau, L. (2022). Activating urban environments as social infrastructure through civic stewardship. *Urban Geography, 43*(5), 713–734.

Camrass, K. (2022). Urban regenerative thinking and practice: A systematic literature review. *Building Research & Information, 50*(3), 339–350.

Capitol Hill Seattle. (2023, March 9). *With decisions spanning from North Broadway to Rome, Seattle Catholic churches plan consolidation amid a priest labor shortage and a drop in faith.* https://www.capitolhillseattle.com/2023/03/with-decisions-spanning-from-north-broad way-to-rome-seattle-catholic-churches-plan-consolidation-amid-a-priest-labor-short age-and-a-drop-in-faith/

Caplan, S. (2019). Intersection of cultural and religious beliefs about mental health: Latinos in the faith-based setting. *Hispanic Health Care International, 17*(1), 4–10.

Carlock, C. (2023, December 30). From boardrooms to bedrooms: These eight downtown Boston office buildings could soon become apartments. *The Boston Globe.* https://www.bost onglobe.com/2023/12/28/business/office-conversions-housing-crisis-downtown-boston/

Carter, J. (2022, January 29). *Don't blame the pandemic for low church attendance.* The Gospel Coalition. https://www.thegospelcoalition.org/article/church-attendance-pandemic/

Cataldi, S. (2023, July 30). Reinventing forgotten old buildings north of the city. *The New York Times,* p. 31.

Catholic World Report. (2023, June 29). *Fewer priests, closing parishes, dropping mass attendance.* The Catholic World Report. https://www.catholicworldreport.com/2023/06/29/less-priests-closing-parishes-dropping-mass-attendance/

CBS News. (2022, February 10). *Historic Harlem churches face declining membership, deteriorating landmarks.* CBS News. https://www.cbsnews.com/newyork/news/harlem-churches-declining-membership-landmarks/

Cep, C. (2020, January 27). *The fight to preserve African American history.* Christian Chronicle. https://christianchronicle.org/a-final-song-a-familiar-end/

Cguske. (2023, July 27). *The heathen's guide to going to church: Adaptive reuse of a bygone typology.* Inform Magazine. https://inform-magazine.com/adaptive-reuse-churches/

Challenger, J. K. (2016). *Infused: Millennials and the future of the black church.* (Doctoral dissertation, Duke University).

Chapman, R. (2023, August 17). We turned an abandoned church into a skatepark. Then tragedy struck. *The New York Times.* https://www.nytimes.com/2023/08/17/opinion/skatepark-community-stlouis-sk8-liborius.html

Chartres, R. (Undated). *Church buildings and the community.* Building Conservation. https://www.buildingconservation.com/articles/churchbuildings/churchbuildings.htm

Chavez, J. C. (2023a, May 6). Catholic Church is losing Hispanics in Tampa Bay and US. Why? *Tampa Bay Times.* https://www.tampabay.com/news/florida/2023/05/05/catholic-church-hispanic-worshippers-young-latinos-religion/

Chavez, J. C. (2023b, July 4). Florida's Latino evangelicals back DeSantis amid fear of new law. *Tampa Bay Times.* https://www.tampabay.com/news/florida/2023/07/04/floridas-latino-evangelicals-back-desantis-amid-fear-new-law/

Cheng, E., & Meng, S. (2023). The spatial distribution of religious organizations in the United States and their socioeconomic characteristics. *Applied Spatial Analysis and Policy, 16,* 789–812.

Chernick, K. (2017, June 29). *Saving South Philly's churches.* Curbed Philadelphia. https://philly.curbed.com/2017/6/29/15865362/philadelphia-historic-preservation-churches

Chicago Sun Times. (2023). *Chicago's 50 closed schools/buildings.* https://graphics.suntimes.com/education/2023/chicagos-50-closed-schools/buildings/

Christian, G. (2023, March 13). Trusted relationships with priests key to fostering vocations, study says. *The Boston Pilot.* https://www.thebostonpilot.com/article.php?ID=194418

Christianity Today. (2022, September 22). *How Latino churches transform communities.* Christianity Today. https://www.christianitytoday.com/ct/2022/september-web-only/transformational-role-of-latino-churches.html

Christman, J. (2021, November 15). *What should we do with closed churches?* US Catholics. https://uscatholic.org/articles/202111/what-should-we-do-with-closed-churches/

Cimaglio, C. (2011). *Sweet Home America: Imagining the small town in country music and American culture.* (Doctoral dissertation, Georgetown University).

Claes, E., Schrooten, M., McLaughlin, H., & Csoba, J. (2022). Community service learning in complex urban settings: Challenges and opportunities for social work education. *Social Work Education, 41*(6), 1272–1290.

Clark, B. E. (2023, May 3). *Repurposing smaller buildings.* On Common Ground. https://www.nar.realtor/on-common-ground/repurposing-smaller-buildings

Click On Detroit. (2019, November 14). *Church buys Detroit Land Bank Authority homes to help revitalize neighborhood.* Click On Detroit. https://www.clickondetroit.com/news/2019/11/14/church-buys-detroit-land-bank-authority-homes-to-help-revitalize-neighborhood/

Cloud, R. (2023, May 23). *Deconstructing a legacy.* Waupaca County News. https://waupacanow.com/2023/05/23/deconstructing-a-legacy/

Cnaan, R. A., Sinha, J. W., & McGrew, C.C. (2004). Congregations as social service providers: Services, capacity, culture, and organizational behavior. *Administration in Social Work, 28*(3/4), 47–68.

Colis, C. (2017, October 9). *MAP: Harlem's Black churches cash in on gentrification.* DNAinfo. https://www.dnainfo.com/new-york/20171009/central-harlem/gentrification-harlem-churches-selling-out-or-surviving/

Columbia University. (Undated). *"The most Catholic city."* https://ccnmtl.columbia.edu/projects/caseconsortium/casestudies/14/casestudy/www/layout/case_id_14_id_144.html

Conn, S. (2014). *Americans against the city: Anti-urbanism in the twentieth century*. Oxford University Press.

Conner, R. (2022). *The color of Christianity: How the Black church defines the African American experience and cultivates community relationships*. (Doctoral dissertation, Eastern University).

Conroy, J. D., & Cha, J. M. (2022). *Shrink the links: Analyzing the potential for repurposing golf courses in Los Angeles*. Occidental College. https://www.oxy.edu/sites/default/files/assets/UEP/Comps/2022/jack_denham_conroy_-_final_comps_paper_-_web_v.1.pdf

Contreras, R. (2023a, May 18). *American churches remain largely segregated—with one exception*. U.S. News. https://www.msn.com/en-us/news/us/american-churches-remain-largely-segregated-%E2%80%94-with-one-exception/ar-AA1bmDXb

Contreras, R. (2023b, May 18). *American churches remain largely segregated—with one exception*. Axios. https://www.foxnews.com/us/third-americans-have-quit-church-attendance-fails-recover-pre-pandemic-numbers-survey

Cook, D. T. (2022). Vernacular faith: Community, heritage, transition. *Contexts, 21*(1), 46–53.

Coomans, T. (2012). Reuse of sacred spaces: Perspectives for a long tradition. In T. Coomans, H. De Dijn, J. De Maeyer, R. Heynickx, & B. Verschaffel (Eds.), *Loci sacre: Understanding sacred places* (pp. 221–241). Leuven University Press.

Coontz, B. K. (2020, September 28). Repurposing or decommissioning houses of worship. *Forbes*. https://www.forbes.com/sites/bryanclontz/2020/09/28/repurposing-or-decommissioning-houses-of-worship/?sh=6256aaf5675a

Corrêa, V. S., Queiroz, M. M., Cruz, M. A., & Shigaki, H. B. (2022). Entrepreneurial orientation far beyond opportunity: The influence of the necessity for innovativeness, proactiveness and risk-taking. *International Journal of Entrepreneurial Behavior & Research, 4*, 952–979.

Costanza-Chock, S. (2020). *Design justice: Community-led practices to build the worlds we need*. MIT Press.

Costello, T. (2023, May 18). *Adaptive reuse: Where old meets new in Phoenix*. DTPHV. https://dtphx.org/2023/05/18/adaptive-reuse-where-old-meets-new-in-phoenix-warehouse-district/

COVID-Net. (2023, March 4). *Laboratory-confirmed COVID-19 associated hospitalizations*. https://gis.cdc.gov/grasp/COVIDNet/COVID19_3.html

Cox, H. (2013). *The secular city: Secularization and urbanization in theological perspective*. Princeton, NJ: Princeton University Press.

Crowley, H. (2021, August 20). The future of the Black church includes its ability to reckon with how it has treated its queer members. *The Washington Post*. https://www.washingtonpost.com/religion/2021/08/20/future-black-church-includes-its-ability-reckon-with-how-its-treated-its-queer-members/

Crumbley, D. H. (2012). *Saved and sanctified: The rise of a storefront church in great migration Philadelphia*. Oxford University Press.

Cudjoe-Wilkes, G. E. (2022). *Keeping it beta: Social innovation & the Black church: A case for strategy, design & social change*. (Doctoral dissertation, Duke University).

Cullen, B. (2023, August 16). *TIL that less than 1% of nuns in the US are under 40 and the average sister is 80 years old*. Reddit. https://www.reddit.com/r/todayilearned/comments/10fan7a/til_that_less_than_1_of_nuns_in_the_us_are_under/

Cunningham Stringer, E. (2023). Trauma technicians and wounded warriors: Using a Black feminist lens to understand how Black women clergy and lay leaders resist anti-Black state violence. *Sociological Focus, 56*(4), 1–19.

Cuperus, J. (2019). *The sacred lives of things: Revaluing church objects as heritage and commodities*. (Master's thesis, Utrecht University, Utrecht, Netherlands).

Curnutte, M. (2018, December 21). "This is our home": Old buildings cloud future for growing Latino Catholic church in Cincy. *Cincinnati Enquirer*. https://www.cincinnati.com/story/news/2018/12/12/old-buildings-uncertain-future-growing-latino-catholic-church-san-carlos-borromeo-cincinnati/1613238002/

Dallas, K. (2016, September 14). Economic impact of religion: New report say it is worth more than Google, Apple, and Amazon. *Deseret News.* https://www.deseret.com/2016/9/14/20596145/economic-impact-of-religion-new-report-says-it-s-worth-more-than-google-apple-and-amazon-combined#:~:text=Religion%2Drelated%20businesses%20and%20institutions,An%20Empirical%20Analysis%2C%22%20soon%20to

Dallas, K. (2023, September 13). What will American religion look like in 50 years? *Deseret News.* https://www.deseret.com/faith/2022/9/13/23349264/is-religion-dying-in-america

Daly, M. W. (2023). *God doesn't live here anymore: Decline and resilience in the Canadian church.* Wipf and Stock Publishers.

Dates, C. (2021, September 3). Why America needs the Black church for its own survival. *The Washington Post.* https://www.washingtonpost.com/religion/2021/09/03/black-church-future-education/

Davidson, J. (2017, April 18). The urban-rural divide matters more than red vs. blue state. *New York.* http://nymag.com/daily/intelligencer/2017/04/the-urban-rural-divide-matters-more-than-red-vs-blue-state.html

Davis, J., Graham, M., & Burge, R. P. (2023). *The Great Dechurching: Who's Leaving, Why Are They Going, and What Will It Take to Bring Them Back?.* Zondervan. Grand Rapids, MI.

DCG Strategies. (2015, May 22). *Saving grace: How a good story can protect your old church.* DCG Strategies. https://www.dcgstrategies.com/blog/faith-based/saving-an-old-church-with-the-power-of-a-good-story/DeGroot, D. A. (Undated). *Creating third spaces.* The Aspen Group. https://info.aspengroup.com/hs-fs/hub/288364/file-1210704834-pdf/Downloadable_Resources/Creating_Third_Spaces__Aspen_Group.pdf?hsCt aTracking=556b3c9b-23af-4a65-a2b8-d8792f2b9ec3%7C62f7e8cc-2047-4931-8b26-449a0836344f

Delargy, C., Cena, K., McFarlane, C., Dominguez, M., Waheed, J., & Murphy, A. (2022). *Urban Design Studio: Faith-based affordable housing.* http://hdl.handle.net/1853/70268

Delerme, S. (2023). *Latino Orlando: Suburban transformation and racial conflict.* (Dissertation, University of Florida).

Delgado, M. (1999). *Social work practice in nontraditional urban settings.* Oxford University Press.

Delgado, M. (2000). *Community social work practice in an urban context: The potential of a capacity enhancement perspective.* Oxford University Press.

Delgado, M. (2015). *Urban youth and photovoice: Visual ethnography in action.* Oxford University Press.

Delgado, M. (2016). *Community practice and urban youth: Social justice service-learning and civic engagement.* Routledge Ltd.

Delgado, M. (2023). *Urban gun violence: Empty lots, green spaces, and other ecologically focused interventions.* Rowman & Littlefield.

Delgado, M., & Staples, L. (2008). *Youth-led community organizing: Theory and action.* Oxford University Press.

Della Spina, L. (2020). Adaptive sustainable reuse for cultural heritage: A multiple criteria decision aiding approach supporting urban development processes. *Sustainability, 12*(4), 1363.

Denney, A. S., Torres, C. Denney, E., Oram, C., & Sutton, M. A. (2022). Crime at places of worship: A geospatial analysis. *Criminal Justice Studies, 35*(4), 347–363.

Dennis, Jr., R.C. (2022, April 13). Downtown Charleston church building to be repurposed as cycling studio. *The Post and Courier.* https://www.postandcourier.com/features/downtown-charleston-church-building-to-be-repurposed-as-cycling-studio/article_cb4be64c-1732-11ed-93cd-0f797460cd8d.html

DeRose, K. P., Cohen, D. A., Han, B., Arredondo, E. M., Perez, L. G., Larson, A., Loy, S., Mata, M. A., Castro, G., De Gutty, R., Rodríguez, C., Seelam, R., Whitley, M. D., & Perez, S. (2022). Linking churches and parks to promote physical activity among Latinos: Rationale and design of the Parishes & Parks cluster randomized trial. *Contemporary Clinical Trials, 123,* 106954.

De Sena, J., & Krase, J. (2015). Brooklyn revisited: An illustrated view from the street 1970 to the present. *Urbanities, 5,* 3–19.

DeSouza, F., Parker, C. B., Spearman-McCarthy, E. V., Duncan, G. N., & Black, R. M. M. (2021). Coping with racism: A perspective of COVID-19 church closures on the mental health of African Americans. *Journal of Racial and Ethnic Health Disparities, 8,* 7–11.

DeStazio, T. (2023, March 7). *Upward trend in deaths of despair linked to drop in religious participation economist finds.* Notre Dame News. https://news.nd.edu/news/upward-trend-in-deaths-of-despair-linked-to-drop-in-religious-participation-economist-finds/

de Urrutia Barroso, L., & Strug, D. (2016). Community-based social work in Cuba. In J. Coates, T. Hetherington, & M. J. Bird (Eds.), *Decolonizing social work* (pp. 107–127). Routledge.

Dewanjee, N. (2020). *Repurpose or rewrite.* RVCA Magazine. https://rvca.edu.in/wp-content/uploads/2022/09/5.-Repurpose-or-rewrite.pdf

DeYmaz, M. (2017). *Disruption: Repurposing the church to redeem the community.* Thomas Nelson.

DeYmaz, M. (2019). *The coming revolution in church economics: Why tithes and offerings are no longer enough, and what you can do about it.* Ada, MI: Baker Books.

DeYmaz, M. (2020). *Building a healthy multi-ethnic church: Mandate, commitments, and practices of a diverse congregation.* Fortress Press.

DeYmaz, M., & Michel, A. A. (2023, January 23). *The coming revolution in church economics: An in-depth interview with Mark DeYmaz.* Lewis Center for Church Leadership. https://www.churchleadership.com/leading-ideas/the-coming-revolution-in-church-economics-an-in-depth-interview-with-mark-deymaz/

Diamant, J., Mohamed, B., & Alvarado, J. (2022, March 15). *Black American Catholics.* Pew Research Center. https://www.pewresearch.org/religion/2022/03/15/black-catholics-in-america/

DiPaolo, J. (2022, June 24). *Major challenges facing the United Methodist Church.* Wesleyan Covenant. https://wesleyancovenant.org/2022/06/23/major-challenges-facing-the-united-methodist-church/

Dolloway, M. A. (2023). *The decline in attendance at local churches in Queens, New York: A biblically based strategic revitalization plan to bring local churches back to spiritual health.* (Dissertation, City University of New York).

Dougherty, K. D., Maier, J., & Lugt, B. V. (2008). When the final bell tolls: Patterns of church closings in two Protestant denominations. *Review of Religious Research, 50*(1), 49–73.

Dougherty, K. D., & Mulder, M. T. (2020). Worshipping local? Congregation proximity, attendance, and neighborhood commitment. *Review of Religious Research, 62*(1), 27–44.

Duan, Q., Wang, X., & Song, N. (2022). Reuse-oriented data publishing: How to make the shared research data friendlier for researchers. *Learned Publishing, 35*(1), 7–15. Duckworth, L. C. (2010). *Adaptive reuse of former Catholic churches as a community asset.* (Master's project, University of Massachusetts).

Dukelow, F., & Murphy, M. P. (2022). Building the future from the present: Imagining post-growth, post-productivist ecosocial policy. *Journal of Social Policy, 51*(3), 504–518.

Dunlop, S. (2022). Visual ethnography. In P. Ward & K. Tyeiereid (Eds.), *The Wiley Blackwell companion to theology and qualitative research* (pp. 415–424). John Wiley Publisher.

Dutra, D. (2021). *Closing costs: Reimagining church real estate for missional purposes.* Wipf and Stock Publishers.

Earls, A. (2021, January 4). *The economic fallout for churches from 2020.* Outreach Magazine. https://outreachmagazine.com/resources/research-and-trends/62628-the-economic-fallout-for-churches-from-2020.html

Earls, A. (2022, October 11). *Half of pastors say the economy is hurting their church.* Lifeway Research. https://research.lifeway.com/2022/10/11/half-of-pastors-say-the-economy-is-hurting-their-church/

Earls, A. (2023, January 25). *Survey: Hispanic Protestant churches are young, first gen, and growing.* Christianity Today. https://www.christianitytoday.com/news/2023/january/hispanic-protestant-landscape-survey-us-pastors-lifeway.html

Easum, B. (2018, January 22). *My predictions for 2050.* The Effective Church Group. https://effectivechurch.com/my-predictions-for-2050/

Edwards, K. L., & Kim, R. (2019). Estranged pioneers: The case of African American and Asian American multiracial church pastors. *Sociology of Religion, 80*(4), 456–477.

Edwards, K. L., & Oyakawa, M. (2022). *Smart suits, tattered boots: Black ministers mobilizing the Black Church in the twenty-first century.* NYU Press.

Eisenberg, J. (2023, January 23). *U.S. churches in steep decline: Studies disclose reported loss of Christian religion among nation's younger generations.* Newsbreak.com. https://original.newsbreak.com/@joel-eisenberg-561469/2900040703425-u-s-churches-in-steep-decline-studies-disclose-reported-loss-of-christian-religion-among-nation-s-younger-generations

Elie, P. (2023, May 29). More Latino Americans are losing their religion. *The New Yorker.* https://www.newyorker.com/news/daily-comment/more-latino-americans-are-losing-their-religion

Espinosa, G. (2023). Nones, no religious preference, no religion and the misclassification of Latino religious identity. *Religions, 14*(3), 420. https://www.mdpi.com/2077-1444/14/3/420

Estrada III, R. G. (2020, May 22). *"Free in Christ" to defy state closures? Latino churches offer insight.* Christianity Today. https://www.christianitytoday.com/ct/2020/may-web-only/covid-free-in-christ-to-defy-state-closures-latino-churches.html

Eyres, P., Bannigan, K., & Letherby, G. (2019). An understanding of religious doing: A photovoice study. *Religions, 10*(4), 269. https://researchonline.gcu.ac.uk/ws/portalfiles/portal/27166417/religions_10_00269.pdf

Fabris, P. (2023a, July 27). *Number of U.S. adaptive reuse projects jumps to 122,000 from 77,000.* Building Design & Construction. https://www.bdcnetwork.com/number-us-adaptive-reuse-projects-jumps-122000-77000

Fabris, P. (2023b, May 23). *One out of three office buildings in largest U.S. cities are suitable for residential conversion.* Building Design & Construction. https://www.bdcnetwork.com/one-out-three-office-buildings-largest-us-cities-are-suitable-residential-conversion

Fabris, P. (2023c, May 16). *Legislators aim to make office-to-housing conversions easier.* Building Design & Construction. https://www.bdcnetwork.com/legislators-aim-make-office-housing-conversions-easier

Fadhil, R. A., & Al-Zaidi, S. M. (2023, March). Community participation's role in the sustainability of adaptive reuse. In *AIP Conference Proceedings* (Vol. 2651, No. 1). AIP Publishing.

Falconer, J. (2023, March 27). Amherst pastor bringing church to a former bank location. *News & Advance.* https://newsadvance.com/community/new_era_progress/news/amherst-pastor-bringing-church-to-a-former-town-bank-location/article_d62f33bc-c9bf-11ed-bd12-3b39345dc6d4.html

Fannie Mae. (2020). *Eyesore to asset: Building housing affordability + sustainable communities: A guidebook for adaptive reuse of vacant property.* https://www.flhousing.org/wp-content/uploads/2020/05/Fannie-Mae-SCIC-Guidebook-04.2020-1.pdf

Farzan, S. (2019, August 24). *Houses of worship find new life after congregations downsize.* NPR. https://www.npr.org/2019/08/24/753256634/houses-of-worship-find-new-life-after-congregations-downsize

Fazio, M. (2019, June 28). From sacred to secular: What happens when a Catholic church shuts down? *The Chicago Tribune.* https://www.chicagotribune.com/news/ct-cb-catholic-churches-closure-how-20190628-k4t53a6nmnf5lltnn34doei5n4-story.html

Fedderly, E. (2019, September 9). A wealth of historic churches in New Orleans have been beautifully repurposed. *Architectural Digest.* https://www.architecturaldigest.com/story/historic-churches-new-orleans-repurposed

Feen-Calligan, H., Barton, E., Moreno, J., Buzzard, E., & Jackson, M. (2022). Murals and photography in community engagement and assessment. In E. Huss & E. Bos (Eds.), *Social work research using arts-based methods* (pp. 129–138). Policy Press.

Fenner, E. (2014, December 15). Catholics at the crossroad. *Chicago Magazine.* https://www.chicagomag.com/chicago-magazine/january-2015/catholics-at-a-crossroads/

Ferguson, R. (2023, February 5). *The Black church: A world within a world.* ACTON Institute. https://www.acton.org/religion-liberty/volume-33-number-1/black-church-world-within-world

Fernandez, L. (2012) *Brown in the Windy City: Mexicans and Puerto Ricans in postwar Chicago.* University of Chicago Press.

Filisko, G. M. (2023, May 3). *Show me the money for financing do-overs.* National Association of Realtors. On Common Ground. https://www.nar.realtor/on-common-ground/spring-2023-rethink-revitalize-rebuild

Fillinger, K. E. (2021, October 13). Noninstrumental Churches of Christ facing uncertain future. *Christian Standard.* https://christianstandard.com/2021/10/noninstrumental-churches-of-christ-facing-uncertain-future/

Finlay, J., Esposito, M., Kim, M. H., Gomez-Lopez, I., & Clarke, P. (2019). Closure of "third places"? Exploring potential consequences for collective health and wellbeing. *Health & Place, 60,* 102225.

Fisher-Gewirtzman, D. (2016). Adaptive reuse architecture documentation and analysis. *Journal of Architectural Engineering Technology, 5*(3), 1–8.

Fletcher, S. (2023, April 18). *Stained glass needs saving.* Christianity Today. https://www.christianitytoday.com/ct/2022/may-june/stained-glass-evangelical-restoration-history-crisis.html

Flores, N. M. (2018, December 13). *Why dioceses need to support struggling Latino churches.* America Magazine. https://www.americamagazine.org/faith/2018/12/13/why-dioceses-need-support-struggling-latino-churches

Fnais, A., Rezgui, Y., Petri, I., Beach, T., Yeung, J., Ghoroghi, A., & Kubicki, S. (2022). The application of life cycle assessment in buildings: Challenges, and directions for future research. *International Journal of Life Cycle Assessment, 27*(5), 627–654.

Foster-Frau, S., & Hatzipanagos, R. (2023, April 21). Latinos leaving Catholicism and organized religion, study says. *The Washington Post.* https://www.washingtonpost.com/nation/2023/04/21/latino-catholic-atheist/

Funch, J. (2023, January 19). *Growing crime and drug activity forces Redemption Church to move out of the neighborhood.* KREM2. https://www.krem.com/article/news/crime/growing-crime-drug-activity-redemption-church-spokane-move/293-b1034b90-cd9e-456b-82e0-598453d818fe

Gabbatt, A. (2023, January 22). Losing their religion: Why U.S. churches are on the decline. *The Guardian.* https://www.theguardian.com/us-news/2023/jan/22/us-churches-closing-religion-covid-christianity

Gambino, M. (2022). *Just and grave causes: Decline as religious change in Catholic Philadelphia.* (Dissertation, Princeton University).

Gambino, M. (2023a). "As we contemplate our future": Fiscal responsibility, archdiocesan authority, and race in Philadelphia's 1993 parish closures. *US Catholic Historian, 41*(1), 47–70.

Gambino, M. (2023b). Advancing "Catholic truth and American equality": Black self-determination in Philadelphia's first black parish and the American Catholic Church. *Journal of African American History, 108*(2), 163–188.

Gamble, V. N. (2010). "There wasn't a lot of comforts in those days": African Americans, public health, and the 1918 influenza epidemic. *Public Health Reports, 125*(3_suppl), 113–122.

García, I. (2019). Repurposing a historic school building as a teacher's village: Exploring the connection between school closures, housing affordability, and community goals in a gentrifying neighborhood. *Journal of Urbanism: International Research on Placemaking and Urban Sustainability, 2,* 153–169.

Gecewicz, C. (2020, August 7). *Amid pandemic, Black and Hispanic worshippers more concerned about safety of in-person religious services.* Pew Research. https://www.pewresearch.org/short-read/2020/08/07/amid-pandemic-black-and-hispanic-worshippers-more-concerned-about-safety-of-in-person-religious-services/

Gedeo, A. M. (2023). *The circle of building life: A rubbish revival.* (Doctoral dissertation, Virginia Tech).

Geekiyanage, D., Fernando, T., & Keraminiyage, K. (2020). Assessing the state of the art in community engagement for participatory decision-making in disaster risk-sensitive urban development. *International Journal of Disaster RiRk reduction, 51*, 101847.

Gerber, C. (2023, February 28). Saving the sacred: Indiana church closings cause real estate concerns. *The Herald Bulletin.* https://www.heraldbulletin.com/news/saving-the-sacred-indiana-church-closings-cause-real-estate-concerns/article_d23c6024-b464-11ed-a9ef-336c903dbf00.html

Gerber, J. (2023, February 8). *Repurposing church pews: How to weatherproof for long-term use.* Home Revamp. https://homerevamp.biz/repurposing-church-pews-how-to-weatherproof-for-long-term-use/

Gerber, N. (2022, September 8). *Harlem clergy took secret cash as they sold churches to developer.* Patch. https://patch.com/new-york/harlem/harlem-clergy-took-secret-cash-they-sold-churches-developer-ag

Gerstenblatt, P., & Gilbert, D. J. (2014). Framing service learning in social work: An interdisciplinary elective course embedded within a university–community partnership. *Social Work Education, 33*(8), 1037–1053.

Gibson, M. (2022, August 24). *Parishioners upset with Diocese of Corpus Christi's decision to demolish church in Concepcion.* 3 NEWS. https://www.kiiitv.com/article/news/local/parishioners-upset-with-diocese-of-corpus-christis-decision/503-a475ba07-78b9-4384-b9f6-d33b4d431c84

Gill, J. F. (2023, June 2). The Church of the Lady of Guadalupe, Manhattan's first church specifically created for a Latino congregation. *The New York Times.* https://www.nytimes.com/2023/06/02/realestate/lady-of-guadalupe-little-spain.html

Gilmore, C. (2022). *Architecture of agency: Fostering immigrant communities through participatory building.* (Doctoral dissertation, University of Cincinnati).

Glazer, N. (2014). Catholic school closures and the decline of urban neighborhoods: What is the cause, and what the effect? *Education Next, 14*(4), 81–83.

Gleason, B. C. (2023). *A study of replanting churches: Best practices for the Evangelical Free Church of America.* (Doctoral dissertation, Trinity International University).

Gola, M., Dell'Ovo, M., Scalone, S., & Capolongo, S. (2022). Adaptive reuse of social and healthcare structures: The case study as a research strategy. *Sustainability, 14*(8), 4712.

Good, R. M. (2022). Neighborhood schools and community development: Revealing the intersections through the Philadelphia school closure debate. *Journal of Planning Education and Research, 42*(4), 598–610.

Goodlow, L. (2023). *Transforming urban leadership with spiritual practice: C-walking to prayer walking alongside urban youth and young adults in south central Los Angeles.* (Doctoral dissertation, Azusa Pacific University).

Gourley, M., Starkweather, S., Roberson, K., Katz, C. L., Marin, D. B., Costello, Z., & DePierro, J. (2023). Supporting faith-based communities through and beyond the pandemic. *Journal of Community Health*, 1–7. https://www.ncbi.nlm.nih.gov/pmc/articles/PMC9929242/

Graham, J. (2023, September 6). America is experiencing a "great dechurching": What's happening to all the church buildings? *Deseret News.* https://www.deseret.com/faith/2023/9/6/23852594/great-dechurching-religious-nones-ryan-burge

Graham, R. (2023, December 18). With a deadline looming, the United Methodist Church breaks up. *The New York Times.* https://www.nytimes.com/2023/12/18/us/the-united-methodist-church-schism.html

Grant, A. M., O'Connor, S. A., & Studholme, I. (2019). Towards a positive psychology of buildings and workplace community: The positive built workplace environment. *International Journal of Applied Positive Psychology, 4*, 67–89.

Gray, R. (2020, October 11). *How many churches will close?* Baptist Courier. https://baptistcourier.com/2020/10/how-many-churches-will-close/

Grecchi, M. (2022). *Building renovation*. SpringerBriefs in Applied Sciences and Technology. Springer. https://doi.org/10.1007/978-3-030-89836-6_1

Green, T. L. (2017). "We felt they took the heart out of the community": Examining a community-based response to urban school closure. *Education Policy Analysis Archives/ Archivos Analíticos de Políticas Educativas, 25*, 1–30.

Grim, B. (2021, May 13). *The unseen economic-social impact of American faith*. Religious Freedom Foundation. https://www.deseret.com/faith/2021/5/12/22429166/the-unseen-economic-social-impact-of-american-faith-brian-grim-religious-freedom-business-foundation

Grinberg, E. (2013, December 9). *Old churches get remodeled*. CNN. https://www.cnn.com/2013/12/09/living/aj-irpt-remodeled-churches/index.html

Grondelski, J. (2022, November 6). *Catholic churches on the chopping block? Don't sell them— Do this instead*. National Catholic Register. https://www.ncregister.com/commentaries/catholic-parishes-on-the-chopping-block-don-t-sell-them-do-this-instead

Grose, J. (2023, June 21). The largest and fastest religious shift in America is well underway. *The New York Times*. https://www.nytimes.com/2023/08/23/opinion/christianity-america-religion-secular.html

Grusendorf, S., & Acevedo, Y. (2022). Investigating the nature of thriving Hispanic congregations within a U.S. Evangelical denomination. *Journal of Sociology and Christianity, 12*(1), 33–48.

Guhin, J., Holman, M., Coan, T., & Boussalis, C. (2023). When to preach about poverty: How location, race, and ideology shape White Evangelical sermons. *Journal for the Scientific Study of Religion, 62*(2), 312–335.

Guzman, L. (2023, 29). *Latinos shifting away from Catholicism, organized religion, report says*. MyRecordJournal. https://www.myrecordjournal.com/News/Meriden/Meriden-News/Religion-changing-among-U-S-Latinos-study-finds.html

Haas, P. (2013, November 10). *Huge economic benefits of churches*. PeterHaas.org. https://www.peterhaas.org/5-huge-economic-benefits-of-church/

Haertsch, E. (2023, March 22). *Perspective: Rural churches are economic powerhouses for their communities*. EDNC.org. https://www.ednc.org/perspective-rural-churches-are-economic-powerhouses-for-their-communities/

Haines, E. (2007, March 7). *Atlanta-area Black megachurch starts Hispanic outreach*. Statesboro Herald. https://www.statesboroherald.com/local/atlanta-area-black-megachurch-starts-hispanic-outreach/

Hall, T. N., & Park, J. J. (2022). "Plant my feet on higher ground": Understanding how Black megachurches create a college-going culture. *Journal of Diversity in Higher Education, 17*(1), 68–80. https://doi.org/10.1037/dhe0000390

Hamilton, B. (2022). *A case study of an urban church: Community development in action in the African American community*. (Doctoral dissertation, Creighton University).

Hardcastle, D. A., Powers, P. R., & Wenocur, S. (2011). *Community practice: Theories and skills for social workers*. Oxford University Press.

Hardy, E. (2023, May 23). *Hispanics abandoning the Catholic Church*. Unherd. https://unherd.com/2023/05/hispanics-are-abandoning-the-catholic-church/

Harper, N. (2005). *Urban churches: Vital signs: Beyond charity toward justice*. Wipf and Stock Publishers.

Harris, C. E. (2020). *The impact of Sunday school participation on spiritual formation in African American Baptist churches in North Carolina*. (Dissertation, Liberty University).

Harrison, A. (2022). *The Black church: The role of the church in the African American community*. (Doctoral dissertation, Eastern University).

Harrison, C. P. (2021). *A model for revitalizing urban churches that have experienced decline*. (Doctoral dissertation, Duke University).

Hartford Institute for Religion Research. (2021, December). *Congregational response to the pandemic: Extraordinary social outreach in a time of crisis*. Exploring the Pandemic Impact on Congregations. https://www.covidreligionresearch.org/research/national-survey-research/extraordinary-social-outreach-in-a-time-of-crisis/

Harvey, D., & Bogle, M. (2023, April 14). *How new investment in repurposed infrastructure can produce good jobs for residents of disinvested communities.* Urban Institute. https://www.urban.org/urban-wire/how-new-investment-repurposed-infrastructure-can-produce-good-jobs-residents-disinvested

Hasik, V., Escott, E., Bates, R., Carlisle, S., Faircloth, B., & Bilec, M. M. (2019). Comparative whole-building life cycle assessment of renovation and new construction. *Building and Environment, 161*, 106218.

Hassan, M. (2023). Adaptive reuse of historic buildings towards a resilient heritage. In K. Hmood (Ed.), *Conservation of urban and architectural heritage—past, present, and future.* https://www.intechopen.com/online-first/86828

Healy, K. (2017). Becoming a trustworthy profession: Doing better than doing good. *Australian Social Work, 70*(supp_1), 7–16.

Herbkersman, C. (2022). *Church attendance, social capital, and Iowa small towns from 1994 to 2014.* (Doctoral dissertation, Iowa State University).

Hibshman, G. (2023). Why the Jesus as mother tradition undermines the symbolic argument against women's ordination. *Religious Studies*, 1–13.

Hildebrandt, R. (2016, December 9). *Church demolition by the numbers: More questions than numbers.* Hidden Philadelphia. https://hiddencityphila.org/2016/12/church-demolition-by-the-numbers-more-questions-than-answers/

Hill, D. J., & Laredo, E. (2019). First and last and always: Streetwork as a methodology for radical community social work practice. *Critical and Radical Social Work, 7*(1), 25–39.

Hinojosa, F. (2021). *Apostles of change: Latino radical politics, church occupations, and the fight to save the barrio.* University of Texas Press.

Hodge, D. R. (2020). Religious congregations: An important vehicle for alleviating human suffering and fostering wellness. *Journal of Religion & Spirituality in Social Work: Social Thought, 39*(2), 119–137.

Hodges, J. C., & Calvo, R. (2023). Teleservices use among Latinx immigrant families during the Covid-19 pandemic. *Children and Youth Services Review, 145*, 106778.

Hoevelmann, J. (2019, April 17). *Fire attack: Old churches, big problems.* FireRescue1. https://www.firerescue1.com/church-fire/articles/fire-attack-old-churches-big-problems-30fFdhqMozC3xIyQ/

Holmes, B. A. (2017). *Joy unspeakable: Contemplative practices of the Black church.* Minneapolis, Minnesota: Fortress Press.

Holtmann, C., Robinson, E., & Williams, R. (2022). Interfaith photovoice: An example of Muslim-Christian engagement in Canada. *Visual Studies, 37*(1–2), 96–115.

Holznagel, H. (2021, March 11). *As MOLO opening nears, tenants "thank God" for Louisville pastor's vision.* United Church of Christ. https://www.ucc.org/as-molo-opening-nears-tenants-thank-god-for-louisville-pastors-vision/

Homan, C. P. (2022). *How competition, urban transformation, and race shape congregations: The case of Manhattan, 1939–1999.* (Doctoral dissertation, UC Berkeley).

Horowitz, T., & Povoledo, E. (2023, October 28). Vatican deems bigger church role for women "urgent," but postpones major issues. *The New York Times.* https://dnyuz.com/2023/10/28/vatican-deems-bigger-church-role-for-women-urgent-but-postpones-major-issues/

Housing and Urban Development. (2014, Winter). *Countywide land banks tackle vacancy and blight.* HUD. https://www.huduser.gov/portal/periodicals/em/winter14/highlight3.html

Hu, W., & Vilchis, R. (2023, December 3). In Queens, Little Caracas is taking root. *The New York Times*, 37.

Huckle, K. E. (2020). Latinos and American Catholicism: Examining service provision amidst demographic change. *Journal of Race, Ethnicity, and Politics, 5*(1), 166–195.

Hunter, C. (2022). The African American church house: A phenomenological inquiry of an Afrocentric sacred space. *Religions, 13*(3), 246–254.

Hyeon, Y. (2013). Succeeding or overcoming father: Two ideas on American cities in *Death of a Salesman* and *Fences*. *Trans-Humanities Journal*, 6(3), 23–54.ICMGLT. (2021, 2). Black Catholics have a right to be frustrated with a church that ignores racism. https://icmglt.org/black-catholics-have-a-right-to-be-frustrated-with-a-church-that-ignores-racism/

Inform Magazine. (2022, July 27). *The heathen's guide to going to church: Adaptive reuse of a bygone typology*. Inform Magazine. https://inform-magazine.com/adaptive-reuse-churches/

Inglehart, R. F. (2020). *Religion's sudden decline: What's causing it, and what comes next?* Oxford University Press.

Irwin, L. G. (2014). *Toward the better country: Church closure and resurrection*. Wipf and Stock Publishers.

ISA. (2023, January 26). *New Uses, Old Places: The Transformations of Religious Buildings in Contemporary Europe*. https://isa-rc22.org/new-uses-old-places-the-transformations-of-religious-buildings-in-contemporary-europe/#:~:text=Research%20Committee%2022-,New%20Uses%2C%20Old%20Places%3A%20The%20Transformations%20of,Religious%20Buildings%20in%20Contemporary%20Europe&text=The%20New%20Uses%2C%20Old%20Places,of%20religious%20architecture%20and%20heritage

Jackson, A. (2020, September 2). *A church-run business incubator grows its community's own solutions to poverty*. Episcopal News Service. https://www.episcopalnewsservice.org/2020/09/02/a-church-run-business-incubator-grows-its-communitys-own-solutions-to-poverty/

Joensuu, T., Edelman, H., & Saari, A. (2020). Circular economy practices in the built environment. *Journal of Cleaner Production*, 276, 124215.

Johanek, M. (2023). "If you want justice, organize for power!" Community organising, Catholicism and Chicago school reform. *Journal of Educational Administration and History*, 55(3), 307–322.

Johnson, R. (2023, June 3). *Holy Spirit at work in new families of parishes across Archdiocese of Omaha*. Catholic Voice of Omaha. https://catholicvoiceomaha.com/holy-spirit-at-work-in-new-families-of-parishes-across-archdiocese-of-omaha/

Johnson, S. D. (2019). The role of the black church in black civil rights movements. In S. D. Johnson & J. B. Tamney (Eds.), *The political role of religion in the United States* (pp. 307–324). Routledge.

Jones, J. M. (2021, March 29). *U.S. church membership falls below majority for first time*. Gallup. https://news.gallup.com/poll/341963/church-membership-falls-below-majority-first-time.aspx

Jones, K. J. (2023, March 3). *Decline in vocations to the priesthood is worse where priests serve larger flocks, report says*. Catholic News Agency. https://www.catholicnewsagency.com/news/253787/decline-in-vocations-to-the-priesthood-is-worse-in-dioceses-with-larger-flocks-report-says

Jones, M. D. (2020). *Youth decline in church growth and attendance*. Liberty University.

Jordan, K. (2023). Between the sacred and secular: Faith, space, and place in the twenty-first century. *Architecture and Culture*, 1–27.

Kagan, C., Burton, M., Duckett, P., Lawthom, R., & Siddiquee, A. (2019). *Critical community psychology: Critical action and social change*. Routledge.

Kagawa, R., Calnin, B., Smirniotis, C., Cerdá, M., Wintemute, G., & Rudolph, K. E. (2022). Effects of building demolitions on firearm violence in Detroit, Michigan. *Preventive Medicine*, 165, 107257.

Kahila, M. (2022, August 10). *Three types of community engagement in urban planning projects*. Maptionnaire. https://maptionnaire.com/blog-list/types-of-community-engagement-in-urban-planning

Kanter, D. E. (2021). Latino Catholics and parish boundaries: Notes from Chicagolandia. *American Catholic Studies*, 132(3), 14–18.

Karagkounis, V. (2021). Austerity, social work and the rediscovery of community work. *European Journal of Social Work*, 24(2), 278–289.

Karki, T. K. (2017). Should planners join politics? Would that help them make better cities? *Planning Theory, 16*(2), 186–202.

Karmokar, S. (2019). Community capacity building. *Journal of Ethnic and Cultural Studies, 6*(1), 162–173.

Kasselstrand, I., Zuckerman, P., & Cragun, R. T. (2023). *Beyond doubt: The secularization of society* (Vol. 7). NYU Press.

Keller, T. (2023, February 20). *Tim Keller on the decline and renewal of the American church.* The Gospel Coalition. https://www.thegospelcoalition.org/article/tim-keller-decline-renewal-american-church/

Kellner, M. J. (2023, January 24). Hispanic Protestant churches growing in face of overall Christian declines, survey reports. *The Washington Times.* https://www.washingtontimes.com/news/2023/jan/24/hispanic-protestant-churches-growing-face-overall-/

Kenney, A. (2018, May 10). Denver has a housing crisis. Guess who's got 5,000 acres and a moral mission? Denverite. https://denverite.com/2018/05/10/whos-got-whole-bunch-land-nothing-churches/

Kilde, J. H. (2013, June 26). *The afterlives of religious buildings: Some notes toward theorizing space and time.* Academia. https://www.academia.edu/41074840/The_Afterlives_of_Religious_Buildings_Some_Notes_toward_Theorizing_Space_and_Time_at_the_conference_on_Spatializing_Practices

Kilde, J. H. (2022). The impermanence of religious space. In J. H. Kilde (Ed.), *The Oxford handbook of religious space* (pp. 100–114). Oxford University Press.

Kiley, C. J. (2004). *Convert! The adaptive reuse of churches.* (Thesis, Massachusetts Institute of Technology).

Kim, G., Newman, G., & Jiang, B. (2020). Urban regeneration: Community engagement process for vacant land in declining cities. *Cities, 102*, 102730.

Kinney, J. (2018, April 5). *Using our biggest asset: Changing communities by repurposing buildings.* GNI News. https://www.gnjumc.org/news/using-our-biggest-asset-changing-communities-by-repurposing-buildings/

KNX. (2013, June 26). *L.A. Black heritage sites nominated for historic landmark designation.* https://www.audacy.com/knxnews/news/local/4-l-a-black-heritage-sites-nominated-for-landmark-status

Kostarelos, F. (1995). *Feeling the spirit: Faith and hope in an evangelical black storefront church.* University of South Carolina Press.

Krause, S. (2021, April 23). *As religious attendance in Michigan decreases, churches close.* Spartan Newsroom. https://news.jrn.msu.edu/2021/04/as-religious-attendance-in-michigan-decreases-churches-close/

Krejcir, R. J. (2007). *Statistics and reasons for church decline.* ChurchLeadership.org. http://www.churchleadership.org/apps/articles/default.asp?articleid=42346

Kresta, D. A. (2022, November). *Your church's soup kitchen doesn't create social change.* Sojourner. https://sojo.net/magazine/november-2022/soup-kitchen-social-change

Kresta, D. E. (2021). *Jesus on Main Street: Good news through community economic development.* Wipf and Stock Publishers.

Krishna, A., & Hall, E. (2019). Serendipitous conservation: Faith-to-faith conversion of historic churches in Buffalo. *Journal of Urbanism: International Research on Placemaking and Urban Sustainability, 12*(4), 496–521.

Kristof, N. (2023, August 23). America is losing religious faith. *The New York Times.* https://www.nytimes.com/2023/08/23/opinion/christianity-america-religion-secular.html

Krupp, L. (2023, February 24). *A church in North Thetford is getting new life as a community center for people of color.* Vermont Public. https://www.vermontpublic.org/local-news/2023-02-24/a-church-in-north-thetford-is-getting-new-life-as-a-community-center-for-people-of-color

Kueber, M. (2022). *Preaching to Latinos: Welcoming the Hispanic moment in the US church.* Catholic University Press.

K. S. (2023). Escape the 'Gods': All of Humanity Worships Ancient Cults The Rise of Religion, the Fall of Ethics, and the Cure: Christianity-Muslim-Islam-Buddhism-Judaism-Hinduism-Thuggee-Pedophilia-Cannibalism [Print Replica] Kindle Edition. https://www.amazon.com/Escape-Gods-Humanity-Worships-Christianity-Muslim-Islam-Buddhism-Judaism-Hinduism-Thuggee-Pedophilia-Cannibalism-ebook/dp/B0C4Z7LTCL

Kutty, A. (2020). Sanctuaries along streets: Security, social intimacy and identity in the space of the storefront church. *Journal of Interior Design, 45*(1), 53–66.

Kvit, A., Corrigan, A. E., Locke, D. H., Curriero, F. C., & Mmari, K. (2022). Can restoring vacant lots help reduce crime? An examination of a program in Baltimore, MD. *Urban Forestry & Urban Greening, 74*.

Lamb, A. (2022, August 7). Affordable housing plan for JP church: Plan calls for affordable housing, community center on ground floor. *Bay Street Banner*. https://www.baystatebanner.com/2022/08/17/affordable-housing-plan-for-jp-church/

Lami, I. M., Todella, E., & Prataviera, E. (2023). A replicable valorisation model for the adaptive reuse of rationalist architecture. *Land, 12*(4), 836.

Lampley, K. W. (2017). The ground has shifted: The future of the Black Church in postracial America. *Journal of the American Academy of Religion, 85*(3), 856–58.

Lawton, C. D. (2023). *A pilot study on the divine link: Considering the relationship between the church and economic outcomes in African Americans*. Preprints. https://www.preprints.org/manuscript/202305.0201/v1

Lechtchiner, F. (2023). *Sacred spaces, public goods: Affordable housing development in Boston's Catholic churches*. (Thesis, Brandeis University).

Ledwith, M., & Springett, J. (2022). *Participatory practice: Community-based action for transformative change*. Policy Press.

Lee, E. (2021). *Building for the future: Sacred space yesterday, today, and tomorrow*. (Dissertation, George Fox University).

Lefrak, M., & Meyer, T. (2023, February 23). *As Vermont churches close, debates flare up over building use*. Vermont Public. https://www.vermontpublic.org/show/vermont-edition/2023-02-27/as-vermont-churches-close-debates-flare-up-over-building-use

Levison, S. V., & Segall, E. J. (2020). *Forced closing of houses of worship during the coronavirus: Both legal and right*. American Constitution Society. https://www.acslaw.org/expertforum/forced-closing-of-houses-of-worship-during-the-coronavirus-both-legal-and-right/

Lifeway Research. (2023). *Hispanic American Church Study*. https://research.lifeway.com/wp-content/uploads/2023/01/Hispanic-American-Church-Study-Report.pdf

Lincoln, C. E. (2011). *Race, religion, and the continuing American dilemma*. Hill and Wang.

Lisi, C. (2023, September 4). *Attendance and giving rebound but churches still struggling from Covid-19*. Religion Unplugged. https://religionunplugged.com/news/2023/8/30/christianity-attendance-and-giving-rebounding-but-churches-still-struggling-from-covid-19

Livingston, J. N., Bell Hughes, K., Dawson, D., Williams, A., Mohabir, J. A., Eleanya, A., . . . & Brandon, D. (2017). Feeling no ways tired: A resurgence of activism in the African American community. *Journal of Black Studies, 48*(3), 279–304.

Llywelyn, D. (2022, April 30). *Global Christianity: The future of the Catholic Church*. USCDornsife. https://dornsife.usc.edu/iacs/2022/04/30/global-christianity/

Long-Garcia, J. D. (2022, June 28). *The future of the U.S. Catholic Church is Latino. Our youth ministry programs need to reflect that*. America Magazine. https://www.americamagazine.org/faith/2022/06/28/catholic-youth-ministry-latino-families-evangelization-bilingual-243241

Long-Garcia, J. D. (2023, June 29). *Latino Catholics are leaving the Church; can we welcome them back?* America Magazine. https://www.americamagazine.org/faith/2023/06/29/latino-catholics-protestant-church-245605

Longhi, A. (2022). Decommissioning and reuse of liturgical architectures. In J. H. Kilde (Ed.), *The Oxford handbook of religious space* (pp. 45–57). Oxford University Press.

Lopez, A., Galindo, R., Anguiano, R. P. V., Corkill, M., Jacob-Bellowe, J., & Weaver, Y. (2022). De la iglesia a servir el pueblo: The role of religious leaders in serving Latino immigrant families. *Advances in Social Work, 22*(1), 46–66.

Lopez-Villafana, A. (2020, July 26). Tensions grow between a San Diego church and the neighborhood around it. *San Diego Union-Tribune*. https://www.sandiegouniontribune.com/communities/san-diego/story/2020-07-26/tensions-grow-between-a-san-diego-church-st-anne-and-the-neighborhood-around-it

Luxmoor, J. (2023, May 16). *New report: Germany Catholic Church faces major decline in membership, revenue*. American Magazine. https://www.americamagazine.org/faith/2023/05/16/germany-catholic-church-major-decline-members-revenue-245306

Lynch, N. (2022). Remaking the obsolete: Critical geographies of contemporary adaptive reuse. *Geography Compass, 16*(1), e12605.

Magee, N. (2022, May 5). *Black churches are on the decline across America*. eurweb. https://eurweb.com/2022/black-churches-are-on-the-decline-across-america/

Major, D. (2022a, May 4). *Black churches are closing across the nation and public health officials should be worried*. Black Enterprise. https://www.blackenterprise.com/black-churches-are-closing-across-the-country-and-public-health-officials-should-be-worried/

Major, D. (2022b, April 19). *Black churches in Washington D.C. are losing their congregations due to gentrification*. Black Enterprise. https://www.blackenterprise.com/black-churches-in-washington-d-c-are-losing-their-congregations-due-to-gentrification/

Makridis, C. A. (2022). When houses of worship go empty: The effects of state restrictions on well-being among religious adherents. *European Economic Review, 149*, 104279.

Mankowski, M. (2016). *Catholic parishes in transition: Creating viable parishes through mergers, closures, and collaborations*. CreateSpace.

Manouchehrifar, B., & Forester, J. (2021). Rethinking religion and secularism in urban planning. *Planning Theory & Practice, 22*(2), 269–317.

Martyr, P. (2022). Worship choices and wellbeing of Australian churchgoing Catholics during COVID-19 church closures. *Mental Health, Religion & Culture, 25*(5), 531–542.

Masci, D., & Smith, G. A. (2018, September 19). *7 facts about American Catholics*. PEW Research Center.

Massingale, R. (2021, June 16). *Black Catholics are leaving the church. Why?* U.S. Catholics. https://uscatholic.org/articles/202106/black-catholics-are-leaving-the-church-why/

MassPlumbers. (2022, August 1). *Plumbers lend a hand to refugees*. https://massplumbers.com/2022/08/01/plumbers-lend-a-hand-to-refugees/

Mather, M. (2023, February 27). *Are Black churches, once civil rights vanguard, losing importance?* UVAToday. https://news.virginia.edu/content/are-black-churches-once-civil-rights-vanguard-losing-importance

Mathis, D. T. (2020, October 11). Why Black parishioners are leaving churches. *The Atlantic*. https://www.theatlantic.com/politics/archive/2020/10/why-black-parishioners-are-leaving-churches/616588/

Matt. (Undated). *9 lessons churches can learn from recession-proof businesses*. Churchtrac. https://www.churchtrac.com/articles/9-lessons-churches-can-learn-from-recession-proof-businesses

Mattis, J. S., Palmer, G. J., & Hope, M. O. (2019). Where our bright star is cast: Religiosity, spirituality, and positive Black development in urban and landscapes. *Religions, 10*(12), 654–677.

McBroom, E. (2020, September 29). *Could your new church facility be an old grocery store?* Aspen Group. https://www.aspengroup.com/blog/could-your-new-church-facility-be-an-old-grocery-store

McClung, K. (2019, June 29). *Why adaptive reuse matters: Repurposing historic gems*. Authentic. https://authenticff.com/insights/repurposing-historic-gems-why-adaptive-reuse-matters

McConnell, S. (2023, February 6). *How are church finances coming out of COVID and headed into a potential recession?* Church Leaders. https://churchleaders.com/voices/exchange/444285-church-finances-coming-out-of-covid.html

McCormack, M. B. (2022). Left to their own devices: Black youth, religion, and technologies of living. *The Black Scholar, 52*(3), 52–62.

McFadden, K. (2023). School-hosted urban development: The transformation of education facilities into residential real estate in Chicago. *Urban Geography, 44*(1), 128–148.

McGahey, R. (2023). *Unequal cities: Overcoming anti-urban bias to reduce inequality in the United States*. Columbia University Press.

McIntosh, K. W. (2021). *A gentrifying urban village: The role of church, money, and identity in a Philadelphia neighborhood*. (Dissertation, Temple University).

McIntosh, G. L. (2002). *One church, four generations: Understanding and reaching all ages in your church*. Ada, MI: Baker Books.

McKinney, S. (2023, February 7). *Role churches have played communities in Shenandoah Valley and beyond*. WHSV3. https://www.whsv.com/2023/02/07/journey-2023-role-churches-have-played-black-communities-shenandoah-valley-beyond/

McKnight Group. (2022). *Thinking outside the box store: Converting an old car dealership into a new church building*. McKnight Group. https://mcknightgroup.com/thinking-outside-the-box-store-converting-an-old-car-dealership-into-a-new-church-building/

McKnight, R., & Dodge, E. G. (2022, April 5). *LDS church has most valuable private real estate portfolio in the U.S., evidence suggests*. Truth and Transparency. https://www.truthandtransparency.org/news/2022/04/05/lds-church-has-most-valuable-private-real-estate-portfolio-in-the-us-evidence-suggests/index.html

McNichols, K. (2022). *Planting mangoes in the church: Economic development, social enterprise, and the global Christian church*. Westflow Press.

McRae, D. (2023). *Church closures and the loss of community capital*. PANL Perspectives. https://carleton.ca/panl/2023/church-closures-and-the-loss-of-community-social-capital-by-don-mcrae/

McRoberts, O. M. (2005). *Streets of glory: Church and community in a Black urban neighborhood*. University of Chicago Press.

Meller, P. (2023, July 19). From prayer to play: New ecclesiastic conversion trend. *The Brussels Times*. https://www.brusselstimes.com/607476/from-prayer-to-play-belgiums-new-ecclesiastic-conversion-trend

Melton, J. G. (2020). Toward a typology of the megachurch. In S. Hunt (Ed.), *Handbook of megachurches* (pp. 68–83). Brill Publisher.

Mendez, J. B., & Deeb-Sossa, N. (2020). Creating home, claiming place: Latina immigrant mothers and the production of belonging. *Latino Studies, 18*(2), 174–194.

Merlino, K. R. (2018). *Building reuse: Sustainability, preservation, and the value of design*. University of Washington Press.

Merritt, J. (2018, November 25). America's epidemic of empty churches. *The Atlantic*. https://www.theatlantic.com/ideas/archive/2018/11/what-should-america-do-its-empty-church-buildings/576592/

Mian, N. (2023, January 17). *Black churches become affordable housing developers*. Shelterforce. https://shelterforce.org/2023/01/17/black-churches-become-affordable-housing-developers/

Mian, M., & Reinhard, R.T. (2023, May 5). *Transforming empty churches into affordable housing takes more than a leap of faith*. American Planning Association. https://www.planning.org/planning/2023/spring/transforming-empty-churches-into-affordable-housing-takes-more-than-a-leap-of-faith/

Middleton, K. (2023). *Another way: Sustaining the health and longevity of Black urban churches through a co-vocational framework*. (Doctoral dissertation, Drew University).

Miller, A. F., Park, Y., Conway, P., Cownie, C. T., Reyes, J., Reynoso, M., & Smith, A. (2022). Examining the legacy of urban Catholic schooling in the US: A systematic literature review. *The Urban Review, 54*, 481–508.

Miller, M. (2023). *"Brought alight and alive": Community reuse of Church of Scotland churches*. (Dissertation, University of Edinburgh).

Milstein, H. (2023, January 30). 10 heavenly repurposed churches across the South. *Southern Living*. https://www.southernliving.com/repurposed-churches-7098790

Mirza-Avakyan, G. (2013). *Adaptive reuse of historic churches in New York City: The opportunities and challenges for community development*. (Thesis, Columbia University).

Miserandino, A. (2019). The funding and future of Catholic education in the United States. *British Journal of Religious Education, 41*(1), 105–114.

Mitchell, P. S. (2023). *No longer remaining silent: Defining, addressing, and exploring silence experienced among Black female clergy*. (Doctoral dissertation, Mercer University).

Modern Anthropology. (2023, July 23). *Faith leaders discuss closing churches as bestselling book criticizes organized religion*. Modern Anthropology. https://original.newsbreak.com/@modern-anthropology-1600418/3097173970814-faith-leaders-discuss-closing-churches-as-bestselling-book-criticizes-organized-religion

Mohamed, B., Cox, K., Diamant, J. & Gecewicz, C. (2021, February 16). *Faith among American Blacks*. Pew Research Center.

Mohr Carney, M., Adams, D., Mendenhall, A., & Ohmer, M. (2023). Civic engagement: An antidote to desperation? *Journal of Community Practice, 31*(2), 121–126.

Molina, A. (2021, July 26). *Rolling Stone's publisher planned to convert a black church into his home but residents fought back to preserve it*. Word&Way. https://wordandway.org/2021/07/26/rolling-stones-publisher-planned-to-convert-a-black-church-into-his-home-but-residents-fought-back-to-preserve-it/

Molina, A. (2023, May 17). *Latino faith leaders to gather for summit on Christian nationalism*. Church Leaders. https://churchleaders.com/news/451145-latino-faith-leaders-to-gather-for-summit-on-christian-nationalism-rns.html

Moon, W. J. (2020). When tithes and offerings are not enough. *Great Commission Research Journal, 12*(1), 19–42.

Moore, S. E., Jones-Eversley, S. D., Tolliver, W. F., Wilson, B. L., & Jones, C. A. (2022). Six feet apart or six feet under: The impact of COVID-19 on the Black community. *Death Studies, 46*(4), 891–901.

Morel, H., & Dorpalen, B. D. (2023). Adaptive thinking in cities: Urban continuity within built environments. *Climate, 11*(3), 54–67.

Morgan, T. (2023). *Understanding the 7 phases of a church's life cycle*. The Unstuck Group. https://theunstuckgroup.com/phases-church-life-cycle/

Moriarty, R. (2023, March 29). *How upcycling a 134-year-old church could help reshape a distressed corner of Syracuse*. Syracuse.com. https://www.syracuse.com/news/2023/03/how-upcycling-a-134-year-old-church-could-help-reshape-a-distressed-corner-of-syracuse.html

Moroni, S., De Franco, A., & Bellè, B. M. (2020). Vacant buildings. Distinguishing heterogeneous cases: Public items versus private items; empty properties versus abandoned properties. In I. M. Lami (Ed.), *Abandoned buildings in contemporary cities: Smart conditions for actions* (pp. 9–18). Springer.

Morris, C. (2023, September 11). *Catholic diocese of Cleveland issues official policy barring LGBTQ expression*. Ideastream Public Education. https://www.ideastream.org/education/2023-09-11/catholic-diocese-of-cleveland-issues-official-policy-barring-lgbtq-expression

Morton, C. (2019, February 19). *Churches are closing: These four models are thriving*. Missio Alliance. https://www.missioalliance.org/churches-are-closing-these-four-models-are-thriving/

Mulder, M. T., Ramos, A. I., & Martí, G. (2017). *Latino Protestants in America: Growing and diverse*. Rowman & Littlefield.

Munn, C. W. (2019). Finding a seat at the table: How race shapes access to social capital. *Sociology of Religion, 80*(4), 435–455.

Nabhan-Warren, K. (Ed.). (2022). *The Oxford handbook of Latinx Christianities in the United States*. Oxford University Press.

Nagel, R. M. (2011). *Renewed faith: A case for the preservation and adaptive reuse of urban neighborhood churches*. (Master's thesis, University of Cincinnati).

Naheed, S., & Shooshtarian, S. (2022). The role of cultural heritage in promoting urban sustainability: A brief review. *Land, 11*(9), 1508.

Namigadde, A. (2022, June 5). *Catholic Church closures spread in the Northeast and Midwest. Not all are upset.* NPR. https://www.npr.org/2022/06/05/1103172342/catholic-church-closures-spread-in-the-northeast-and-midwest-not-all-are-upset

National Trust for Historic Preservation. (2023, January 16). *Preserving Black churches: A project of the African American Cultural Heritage Action Fund.* https://savingplaces.org/black-churches

Neidig, B. (2023). *The built urban environment: Enduring impacts of historical and structural discrimination on health in urban communities.* (Doctoral dissertation, Temple University).

Neiss, K. I. (2019). *Social belonging and built space: Using contact, contention, and common conditions to create multicultural and multifaith shared-space in a repurposed Aurora, Colorado, church.* (Doctoral dissertation, University of Denver).

Netsch, S. (2019, April). Church buildings as a driver in the real estate development of cities. In *"Is this the real world?" Perfect smart cities vs. real emotional cities. Proceedings of REAL CORP 2019, 24th International Conference on Urban Development, Regional Planning and Information Society* (pp. 153–159). Competence Center of Urban and Regional Planning.

Netsch, S., & Gugerell, K. (2019). Reuse of churches in urban and rural Dutch landscapes. *Acta Horticulturae et Regiotecturae, 22*(1), 48–55.

Neuman, S. (2023a, May 17). *The faithful see both crisis and opportunity as churches close across the country.* NPR. https://www.npr.org/2023/05/17/1175452002/church-closings-religious-affiliation

Neuman, S. (2023b, July 14). *Megachurches are getting even bigger as churches close across the country.* OPB. https://www.opb.org/article/2023/07/14/megachurches-are-getting-even-bigger-as-churches-close-across-the-country/

Newcomb, T. (2014, November 5). *From stadium to . . . what? The seven best repurposed stadiums.* SI. https://www.si.com/extra-mustard/2014/11/05/stadium-what-7-best-repurposed-stadiums

Newman, M. (2018). *Desegregating Dixie: The Catholic Church in the South and desegregation, 1945–1992.* University Press of Mississippi.

Nguyen, A. W., Taylor, R. J., Chatters, L. M., & Hope, M. O. (2019). Church support networks of African Americans: The impact of gender and religious involvement. *Journal of Community Psychology, 47*(5), 1043–1063.

Nguyen, J. (2023, February 10). *How much money does the Catholic Church have?* Market Place. https://www.marketplace.org/2023/02/10/how-much-money-does-catholic-church-have/

Nickels, T. (2022, July 1). *Saving closed churches from the wrecking ball.* Broad & Liberty. https://broadandliberty.com/2022/07/01/saving-closed-churches-from-the-wrecking-ball/

Nierenberg, A. (2020, October 25). New spirits rise in old repurposed churches. *The New York Times.* https://www.nytimes.com/2020/10/25/us/abandoned-churches-covid.html

Nieuwhof, C. (2023). *10 predictions about the future church and shifting attendance patterns.* https://careynieuwhof.com/10-predictions-about-the-future-church-and-shifting-attendance-patterns/

Niewhof, C. (2023). *Future church: 8 church trends to watch in 2023.* https://careynieuwhof.com/future-church-trends/

Nuamah, S. A. (2021). "Every year they ignore us": Public school closures and public trust. *Politics, Groups, and Identities, 9*(2), 239–257.

Oldenburg, R. (1989). *The great good place: Cafés, coffee shops, community centers, beauty parlors, general stores, bars, hangouts, and how they get you through the day.* Paragon House Publishers.

O'Leary, T. K., Stowell, E., Hoffman, J. A., Paasche-Orlow, M., Bickmore, T., & Parker, A. G. (2021, May). Examining the intersections of race, religion & community technologies: A photovoice study. In *Proceedings of the 2021 CHI Conference on Human Factors in Computing Systems* (pp. 1–19).

Oliva, A. (2015). *The death and resurrection of a church: Group formation and shifting identity after parish closure*. (Doctoral dissertation, Columbia University).

Omezzine, F., Oruganti, V., & Bodas Freitas, I. M. (2022). Learning from crisis: Repurposing to address grand challenges. *Innovation and Development, 12*(1), 59–69.

Otterman, S. (2014, November 3). Heartache for New York's Catholics as church closings are announced. *The New York Times*. https://www.nytimes.com/2014/11/03/nyregion/new-york-catholics-are-set-to-learn-fate-of-their-parishes.html

Owens, M., McKnight, J., Tiner, M., & Dunlap, M. R. (2020). Black church and liberal arts institutions: Forming reciprocal relationships for thriving urban communities and churches. *Metropolitan Universities, 31*(3), 181–196.

Park, J. J., Dizon, J. P. M., & Malcolm, M. (2020). Spiritual capital in communities of color: Religion and spirituality as sources of community cultural wealth. *The Urban Review, 52*, 127–150.

Parker, J. S., Purvis, L., & Williams, B. (2023). Religious/spiritual struggles and mental health among Black adolescents and emerging adults: A meta-synthesis. *Journal of Black Psychology, 49*(2), 153–199.

Partners for Sacred Spaces. (2021, November 16). Transitioning Older and Historic Sacred Places: Community-Minded Approaches for Congregations and Judicatories. https://sacredplaces.org/info/publications/transitioning-older-and-historic-sacred-places/

Peacock, R. (2023, February 15). *The poorer the area the quicker the churches are closing*. Religion Media Centre. https://religionmediacentre.org.uk/news/the-poorer-the-area-the-quicker-the-churches-are-closing/

Pearson, E. (2022, May 19). *Congregational shift over worship roils some Catholic congregations*. Frederick News Post. https://www.fredericknewspost.com/news/lifestyle/generational-shift-over-worship-roils-some-catholic-congregations/article_8566794d-73ab-5640-9991-e69386fc57e5.html

Pearson, E. (2023, May 23). *Evangelizing in the street: Something every Catholic can do*. Church Militant. https://www.churchmilitant.com/news/article/CM-evangelizing-in-the-street

Penn State Extension Service. (Undated). *Importance of incorporating local culture into community development*. https://extension.psu.edu/importance-of-incorporating-local-culture-into-community-development

Perks, M. (2020). *Rescuing rural churches*. Homestead. https://www.homestead.org/homesteading-construction/rescuing-rural-churches/

Peteet, B., Watts, V., Tucker, E., Brown, P., Hanna, M., Saddlemire, A., . . . & Simmons, K. (2022). Faith, fear, and facts: A COVID-19 vaccination hesitancy intervention for Black church congregations. *Vaccines, 10*(7), 1039.

Petersen, K. (2022, March 20). *The fastest-growing Episcopal churches*. The Living Church. https://livingchurch.org/2020/03/11/the-fastest-growing-episcopal-churches/

Pew Research Center. (2023a). *Religious landscape study*. https://www.pewresearch.org/religion/religious-landscape-study/racial-and-ethnic-composition/latino/

Pew Research Center. (2023b, December 14). *Race & ethnicity*. https://www.pewresearch.org/topic/race-ethnicity/

Pfeiffer, R. (2022, May 25). *After 2,000 U.K. church buildings close, new church plants get creative*. Christianity Today. https://www.christianitytoday.com/news/2022/may/uk-england-church-close-anglican-buildings-restore-new.html

Pham, V. (2017, July 28). *Disused churches: Documenting the adaptive reuse of religious buildings*. LSE. https://blogs.lse.ac.uk/religionglobalsociety/2017/07/disused-churches-documenting-the-adaptive-reuse-of-religious-buildings/

Phillips, G. C. (2017, September 5). Losing my religion: Church condo conversions and neighborhood change. In *Evidence and Innovation in housing law and policy* (pp. 132–150). Cambridge University Press. https://www.cambridge.org/core/books/evidence-and-innovation-in-housing-law-and-policy/losing-my-religion-church-condo-conversions-and-neighborhood-change/881C65747E01CE15A359264C04821898

Plante, T. G. (2023). Principles for managing burnout among Catholic Church professionals. *Pastoral Psychology, 72*(1), 23–31.

Plekon, M. (2021). *Community as church, church as community*. Wipf and Stock Publishers.

Plenty, S., & Jonsson, J. O. (2017). Social exclusion among peers: The role of immigrant status and classroom immigrant density. *Journal of Youth and Adolescence, 46*, 1275–1288.

Plevoets, B., & Van Cleempoel, K. (2019). *Adaptive reuse of the built heritage: Concepts and cases of an emerging discipline*. Routledge.

Plunkett, R., Leipert, B., Olson, J. K., & Ray, S. L. (2014). Understanding women's health promotion and the rural church. *Qualitative Health Research, 24*(12), 1721–1731.

Pockras, N. (2020). *The RP church and the 1918 pandemic: Over a century later, congregations are being affected in similar ways*. Liberty University. https://digitalcommons.liberty.edu/cgi/viewcontent.cgi?article=1230&context=lib_fac_pubs

Polson, E., & Scales, T. L. (2020). Good Neighbor House: Reimagining settlement houses for 21st-century communities. *Social Work & Christianity, 47*(3),100–122.

Porter, L. C., De Biasi, A., Mitchell, S., Curtis, A., & Jefferis, E. (2019). Understanding the criminogenic properties of vacant housing: A mixed methods approach. *Journal of Research in Crime and Delinquency, 56*(3), 378–411.

Posner, G. (2015). *God's bankers: A history of money and power at the Vatican*. Simon and Schuster.

Preservation Chicago. (2019, March 4). Roman Catholic churches of Chicago—2019 most endangered. https://www.preservationchicago.org/roman-catholic-churches-of-chicago/

Preston, C. E. (2023, June 13). *Repurposing—rebranding and restoring empty churches in Virginia*. NEWSBREAK.Com. https://original.newsbreak.com/@cheryl-e-preston-1594046/3055950031251-repurposing-rebranding-and-restoring-empty-churches-in-virginia.

Priuses, I. (2023). What is the place for megachurches? A comparison of 22 American cities based on the causes of effects approach. *Sociological Forum, 38*(4), 169–191.

Propmodo Research. (2021, February). *Building portfolio value by repurposing underperforming assets*. https://www.propmodo.com/wp-content/uploads/2021/02/Repurposing-obsolete-spaces.pdf

Purcell, S., & Tweedie, F. (2023). *Church on the margins: Is the Church losing faith in low-income communities in Greater Manchester?* Church Action on Poverty. https://savetheparish.com/wp-content/uploads/2023/03/Is-the-Church-losing-faith-in-low-income-communities.pdf

Putscher, L. A. (1980). *The preservation and reuse of urban churches as a contribution to the urban landscape*. (Doctoral dissertation, Massachusetts Institute of Technology).

Rainer, T. (2020). *Anatomy of a revived church: Seven findings of how congregations avoided death*. Rainer Publishing.

Rainer, T. S. (2022, November 28). *The new very large church*. Church Answers. https://churchanswers.com/blog/the-new-very-large-church/

Ramos, A. I., Martí, G., & Mulder, M. T. (2018). The growth and diversity of Latino Protestants in America. *Religion Compass, 12*(7), e12268.

Ramos, A. I., Martí, G., & Mulder, M. T. (2022). Latino/a Protestantisms. In K. Nabhan-Warren (Ed.), *The Oxford handbook of Latinx Christianities in the United States* (pp. 109–128). Oxford University Press.

Rana, A., & Kumar, A. (2022). Epistemological study of urban voids. *ECS Transactions, 107*(1), 14791.

Ransome, Y., Song, I., Pham, L. & Busette, C. (2022, May 3). *Churches are closing in predominantly Black communities: Why public health officials should be concerned*. The Brookings Institute.

Rasmussen, J. H. (2020). *The marketization of religion*. Routledge.

Reinhard, R. (2021a, April 13). *Churches are closings: It's a challenge for local governments*. Governing. https://www.governing.com/community/churches-are-closing-its-a-challenge-for-local-governments.html

Reinhard, R. (2021b). Surplus sacred space: Reflections on the impending glut of US church property. *Journal of Urban Regeneration & Renewal, 14*(3), 247–254.

Reinhard, R. (2021c, April 1). Redeveloping houses of worship. *Heritage, 41*, 166–177.

Reinhard, R. (2022a, May 20). *Seeing the glass as half full: Exploring the reuse opportunity for houses of worship on Main Street*. Strong Towns. https://www.strongtowns.org/journal/2022/5/20/seeing-the-glass-as-half-full-exploring-the-reuse-opportunity-for-houses-of-worship-on-main-street

Reinhard, R. (2022b). *Converting and reusing declining houses of worship for community benefit*. National Civic League. https://www.nationalcivicleague.org/ncr-article/converting-and-reusing-declining-houses-of-worship-for-community-benefit/

Reinhard, R. (2023, April 14). *What would Jane Jacobs do? Toward a new model for houses of worship*. Arch Daily. https://www.archdaily.com/999494/what-would-jane-jacobs-do-toward-a-new-model-for-houses-of-worship

Reinhard, R., & Elisara, C. (2022, June 7). *A call to rethink dying houses of worship*. Public Square. https://www.cnu.org/publicsquare/2022/06/07/call-rethink-dying-houses-worship

Reisman, N. (2023, April 16). *Lawmaker wants churchgoers to have voice in mergers/closures*. Spectrum News. https://spectrumlocalnews.com/nys/central-ny/ny-state-of-politics/2023/04/06/lawmaker-wants-churchgoers-to-have-voice-in-mergers--closures

Renn, A. M. (2022, July 31). *Why cities are important to the church's mission*. TGC. https://www.thegospelcoalition.org/article/cities-mission/

Reynolds, S. B. (2023a). "I will surely have you deported:" Undocumenting clergy sexual abuse in an immigrant community. *Religion and American Culture, 33*(1), 1–34.

Reynolds, S. B. (2023b). "This is not nostalgia": Contesting the politics of sentimentality in Boston's 2004 parish closure protests. *US Catholic Historian, 41*(1), 71–92.

Rhea, L. J. (2019). *Community members' perceptions concerning community empowerment and church-led coalitions*. (Doctoral dissertation, Capella University).

Ribera, F., Nesticò, A., Cucco, P., & Maselli, G. (2020). A multicriteria approach to identify the highest and best use for historical buildings. *Journal of Cultural Heritage, 41*, 166–177.

Ricourt, M., & Danta, R. (2003). *Hispanas de Queens: Latino panethnicity in a New York City neighborhood*. Cornell University Press.

Riebemesabi, A. (2019, February 4). *Old church demolition saddens, improves Catholic community*. AP News. https://apnews.com/article/369c7f07ffcd4322a04945df782b1fb5

Roach, D. (2023, September 25). *100,000 reuses for the church to find*. Christianity Today. https://www.christianitytoday.com/news/2023/september/church-buildings-size-sale-development-multiuse-empty.html

Roberts, B. G. (2023). Reparations for truth: Native Americans and the Catholic Church. *Catholic Social Science Review, 28*, 95–119.

Rockwood, K. (2017, March 1). Born again: Church closings spark development projects. *PM Network, 31*(3), 12–13. https://www.pmi.org/learning/library/born-again-church-closings-spark-redevelopment-projects-10648#

Roewe, B. (2023, January 10). *How Catholic institutions are building sustainability into aging infrastructure*. Earthbeat. https://www.ncronline.org/earthbeat/faith/how-catholic-institutions-are-building-sustainability-aging-infrastructure

Rogers, R. C. (2022). *The stressors Black pastors experience: A counseling perspective*. (Dissertation, Montclair State University).

Rolling, Jr., J. H. (2013). *Art-based research*. Peter Lang Primer.

Romanova, B. Y. (2022). *Preservation of religious heritage in the Netherlands by transforming its functional purpose*. (Thesis, Masaryk University).

Romero, R. C. (2020). *Brown church: Five centuries of Latina/o social justice, theology, and identity*. InterVarsity Press.

Rose, L. (2020, January 3). *Some churches get creative with downsizing issues.* Florida-Times Union. https://www.jacksonville.com/story/news/2020/01/03/some-churches-get-creative-with-downsizing-issues/112139008/

Rucker, F. (2023, June 23). *Houses of worship and religious architecture: Identity, place, end Effects of repurposing.* Canopy Forum. https://canopyforum.org/2023/06/22/houses-of-worship-and-religious-architecture-identity-place-and-effects-of-repurposing/

Russell, T. B. (2017, January 30). *Can health and human service ministries prove key to local churches' survival?* Vital Signs & Statistics. https://carducc.wordpress.com/2017/01/30/can-health-and-human-service-ministries/

Russell, T. B. (2019, October 21). *Repurpose-relocate-relinquish-rethinking church buildings.* Vital Signs & Statistics. https://carducc.wordpress.com/2019/10/21/repurpose-relocate-relinquish-rethinking-church-buildings/

Sader, C., & Maldonado-Estrada, A. (2021, October 21). *How Roman Catholics conquered Massachusetts: The inside story.* GBH. https://www.wgbh.org/news/local/2015-04-10/how-roman-catholics-conquered-massachusetts-the-inside-story

Sanchez, P. (2022). The Latino church. In G. Hiestand & J. Lawrence (Eds.), *Confronting racial injustice: Theory and praxis for the church* ( ). Cascade Books.

Santana, M. & Blanco, O. (2014, November 13). *Financial pain leads to NY churches' closures.* CNN Business. https://money.cnn.com/2014/11/13/news/economy/catholic-church-closures/index.html

Sarason, S. B. (1974). *The psychological sense of community.* Jossey-Bass.

Sathyamurthi, K. (2017). Community social work: An evolutionary concept. *International Journal of Research in Economics and Social Sciences, 7,* 110–118.

Schuster, T. (2017, October 18). *Mapping one of the world's largest landowners.* Curbed. https://archive.curbed.com/2017/10/18/16483194/catholic-church-gis-goodlands-esri-molly-burhans

Seidel, L. G. (2022, October 28). *More than 1 in 10 New Southern Baptist churches are Hispanic.* Christianity Today. https://www.christianitytoday.com/ct/2022/october-web-only/send-network-espanol-felix-cabrera-hispanic-church-planting.html

Seitz, J. C. (2011). *No closure: Catholic practice and Boston's parish shutdowns.* Harvard University Press.

Senator Scott Wiener. (2023, February). *Senate Bill 4: Affordable Housing on Faith Lands Act.* https://cayimby.org/wp-content/uploads/2023/02/Fact-Sheet-SB-4-Affordable-Housing-on-Faith-Lands-Act.pdf

Serlin, C. (2023, July 6). *Former LA church site to become mixed-use development.* Design & Development. https://www.multifamilyexecutive.com/design-development/former-la-church-site-to-become-mixed-use-development_o

Shapiro, N. (2022, July 24). Spiritual refugees feel the loss of closed Catholic churches in Seattle. Some are appealing to the Vatican. *Seattle Times.* https://www.seattletimes.com/seattle-news/spiritual-refugees-feel-the-loss-of-closed-catholic-churches-in-seattle-some-are-appealing-to-the-vatican/

Sharp, E. (2021). A voice for immigrants: Latino activism, testimonial practices, and public Catholicism in Indianapolis. *US Latina & Latino Oral History Journal, 5*(1), 66–93.

Shaw, R. (2023a, June 29). *Fewer priests, closing parishes, dropping Mass attendance.* Catholic World Report. https://www.catholicworldreport.com/2023/06/29/less-priests-closing-parishes-dropping-mass-attendance/

Shaw, R. (2023b, June 27). *Welcome to our changing church.* National Catholic Register. https://www.ncregister.com/blog/welcome-to-our-changing-church

Shellnut, K. (2018, February 2). *Puerto Rico: 3,000 churches damaged, fewer Christians left behind.* Christianity Today. https://www.christianitytoday.com/news/2018/february/puerto-rico-hurricane-maria-churches-migration-nhclc-nalec.html

Sheridan, S. (2023, September 21). *Oakpark's vacant churches can be converted without adding parking*. OAKPARK. https://www.oakpark.com/2023/09/21/oak-parks-vacant-churches-can-be-converted-without-adding-parking/

Shimron, Y. (2018, December 12). *As one historically Black church closes others face strong headwinds*. Episcopal News Service. https://www.episcopalnewsservice.org/2018/12/12/as-one-historically-black-episcopal-church-closes-others-face-strong-headwinds/

Shimron, Y. (2021, May 27). *Study: More Protestant churches closing than opening in recent years*. The Roys Report. https://julieroys.com/more-churches-closing-opening/

Shipman, C., & Siemiatycki, M. (2024). Building in common: (re) integrating social services and community space in church redevelopment projects. *Journal of Urbanism: International Research on Placemaking and Urban Sustainability, 17*(1), 69–88.

Simons, R., & Choi, E. (2010). Adaptive reuse of religious buildings and schools in the US—determinants of project outcomes. *International Real Estate Review, 31*(1), 79–108.

Simons, S., DeWine, G., & Ledebur, L. (2017). *Retired, rehabbed, reborn: The adaptive reuse of America's derelict religious buildings and schools*. Kent State University Press.

Smeengee, M. (2023). *Repurposing sublime religious heritage: Preserving experiential value during transformation*. Delft University of Technology.

Smietana, B. (2022, March 15). *Thousands of churches close every year: What will happen to their buildings?* Religion News. https://religionnews.com/2022/03/15/thousands-of-churches-close-every-year-what-will-happen-to-their-buildings/

Smietana, B. (2023, September 6). *Nationwide study shows giving is up at churches, people are back and clergy are still thinking about quitting*. ENS. https://www.episcopalnewsservice.org/2023/09/06/nationwide-study-shows-giving-is-up-at-churches-people-are-back-and-clergy-are-still-thinking-about-quitting/

Smith, P. J. (2022, April 19). *New life in old buildings: Catholic's repurpose church property for today's needs*. National Catholic Registry. https://www.ncregister.com/news/new-life-in-old-buildings-catholics-repurpose-church-property-for-today-s-needs

Solis, G. (2017). *MAP: Harlem's Black Churches Cash in on Gentrification*. https://www.dnainfo.com/new-york/20171009/central-harlem/gentrification-harlem-churches-selling-out-or-surviving/

Soul Thursdays. (2023, March 16). *The future of the Black church in the Black community*. Southerndays.com. https://www.southernsoulthursdays.com/the-future-of-the-black-church-in-the-black-community/

Spencer, W. F. (2022). *The Black church: A place of rogue, a place of prayer*. (Thesis, John Carroll University, University Heights, OH).

Statista.com (2023, July 21). *Share of the Spanish population who consider themselves Catholic from 2011 to 2022*. https://www.statista.com/statistics/992681/share-of-catholics-in-spain/

St. Clare, J. (2022, December 29). *Why a woman is not called to be a priest*. Catholic Stand. https://catholicstand.com/why-a-woman-is-not-called-to-be-a-priest/

Stephens, D. P. (2023, March 27). *Crisis of faith: How Black churches are contending with shrinking congregations*. Cardinal News. https://cardinalnews.org/2023/03/27/crisis-of-faith-how-black-churches-are-contending-with-shrinking-congregations/

Stevenson, A., Oldfield, J., & Ortiz, E. (2019). Image and word on the street: A reflexive, phased approach to combining participatory visual methods and qualitative interviews to explore resilience with street connected young people in Guatemala City. *Qualitative Research in Psychology, 12*(1), 176–203.

Stiffman, E. (2023, May 10). *Churches build affordable housing*. AP News. https://apnews.com/article/churches-build-affordable-housing-0d8033cbe1259aeabd3d110bf8434bb4

St. Louis American Staff. (2023, January 23). *$20M Lilly donation to help preserve historic Black churches*. St. Louis American. https://www.stlamerican.com/religion/local_religion/20m-lilly-donation-to-help-preserve-historic-black-churches/article_04885022-7c41-11ec-9de4-975d91c1a617.html

Stone, S. (2019). *UnDoing buildings: Adaptive reuse and cultural memory*. Routledge.

Strott, S. (2022, April 17). *In Vegas' historically Black Westside, churches are "heart" of both civic and spiritual life*. The Nevada Independent. https://thenevadaindependent.com/article/in-vegas-historically-black-westside-churches-are-heart-of-both-civic-and-spiritual-life

Su, M., Yan, W., & Harvey, N. (2022). Pecking order theory and church debt financing: Evidence from the United Methodist church. *Nonprofit Management and Leadership, 33*(1), 179–201.

Subramanian, A. (2023, April 18). *The Black church in the African diaspora: An examination of the role of the Black church*. Fun Times Magazine. https://www.funtimesmagazine.com/2023/04/18/432045/the-black-church-in-the-african-diaspora-an-examination-of-the-role-of-the-black-church-

Subsplash. (2022, July 14). *Some experts predict a recession. Here's how to prepare your church*. https://www.subsplash.com/blog/recession-preparation

Sugrue, T. J. (2014). *The origins of the urban crisis: Race and inequality in postwar detroit* (updated edition). Princeton University Press.

Swarns, R. L. (2016). 272 slaves were sold to save Georgetown. What does it owe their descendants? *The New York Times*, p. 16.

Sweas, M. (2016, April 6). *African-American church embraced Hispanic neighbors*. Baptist Press. https://www.baptistpress.com/resource-library/news/african-american-church-embraces-hispanic-neighbors/

Syeed, E. (2019). "It just doesn't add up": Disrupting official arguments for urban school closures with counterframes. *Education Policy Analysis Archives, 27*, 110–110.

Szopińska-Mularz, M. (2022). *Adaptive reuse for urban food provision*. Springer Publisher.

Tavernise, S., & Mervosh, S. (2020, April 20). City dwellers weigh saying goodbye to all that. *The New York Times*, pp. A1, A10.

The Editors. (2018, May 18). *Closing parishes is painful—but there's a better way to do it*. America: The Jesuit Review. https://www.americamagazine.org/faith/2018/05/18/closing-parishes-painful-theres-better-way-do-it

The New York Times. (2023, February 3). *582,462 and counting*. https://www.nytimes.com/2023/02/03/business/economy/us-homeless-population-count.html

The Pillar. (2022, November 29). *Chicago protestors arrested in bid to stop church sale*. https://www.pillarcatholic.com/p/chicago-protestors-arrested-in-bid-to-stop-church-sale

Thielen, L. (2023, April 2). *Churches need to work on bringing people back*. SC Times. https://www.sctimes.com/story/opinion/2023/04/02/churches-need-to-work-on-bringing-people-back/70064575007/

Thomas, A. (2022). Foundations for community development practice: Lessons from the field. In *Community development practice: From Canadian and global perspectives* (Chapter 12). https://ecampusontario.pressbooks.pub/communitydevelopmentpractice/chapter/foundations-for-community-development-practice-lessons-from-the-field/

Thomas, D. N. (2021). *Organising for social change: A study in the theory and practice of community work*. Routledge.

Thomson, M., & Pojani, D. (2019). *Emerging trends of modern churches and spatial planning implications*. UQ|UP Research Paper no. 1. University of Queensland, Australia.

Thorpe Jr., E. Y. (2023). *Leadership in mission: A Protestant pastor's implementation of an afterschool program*. (Doctoral dissertation, Fordham University).

Tieken, M. C., & Auldridge-Reveles, T. R. (2019). Rethinking the school closure research: School closure as spatial injustice. *Review of Educational Research, 89*(6), 917–953.

Todd, S., & Drolet, J. L. (Eds.). (2020). *Community practice and social development in social work*. Springer.

Tomberlin, J., & Bird, W. (2020). *Better together: Making church mergers work* (expanded and updated). Fortress Press.Tulsa World. (2023, October 2). *Repurposing of Hitler's birthplace sparks concern*. https://tulsaworld.com/news/nation-world/repurposing-of-hitlers-birthplace-sparks-concern/video_1bbb0d81-b445-5fb2-b1d3-0bd7cbd15f24.html

Turner, N. M. (2022, February 11). *Changing faces of 21st-century Black churches and politics*. Black Perspective. https://www.aaihs.org/changing-faces-of-21st-century-black-churches-and-politics/

Tyler, N. (2000). *Historic preservation: An introduction to its history, principles, and practice*. W.W. Norton and Company.

Úcar, X., Soler-Masó, P., & Planas-llad, A. (Eds.). (2020). *Working with young people: A social pedagogy perspective from Europe and Latin America*. Oxford University Press.

Van Buren III, H. J., Syed, J., & Mir, R. (2020). Religion as a macro social force affecting business: Concepts, questions, and future research. *Business & Society, 59*(5), 799–822.

van de Kamp, L. (2022). Churches and urban regeneration in postindustrial Amsterdam. *Space and Culture, 26*(2). https://journals.sagepub.com/doi/10.1177/12063312221130240?icid=int.sj-abstract.citing-articles.11

Van Tessle, R. (2022, October 31). *Surplus church property into affordable housing guide*. Catholic Charities USA. https://www.catholiccharitiesusa.org/wp-content/uploads/2023/10/Converting-Surplus-Church-Property-1st-edition.pdf

van Zantvliet, M. (2023). *Sacred care: The societal role of vacant churches in the elderly housing crisis*. TU Delft, Netherlands.

Vermeulen, B., Regnerus, M., & Cranney, S. (2023). The ongoing conservative turn in the American Catholic priesthood. *Sociological Spectrum, 43*(2–3), 72–88.

Vinayaraj, V. K. (2022). Repurposing public library spaces: The Indian Public Library Movement (IPLM) way. *Journal of Indian Library Association, 57*(1), 1–14.

Viola, S., & Diano, D. (2019). Repurposing the built environment: Emerging challenges and key entry points for future research. *Sustainability, 11*(17), 4669.

Vogl, C. (2016). *The art of community: Seven principles for belonging*. Berrett-Koehler Publishers.

Wachter, D. (2023, May 21). *Church closing brings back worshippers, memories*. New Castle News. https://www.ncnewsonline.com/news/local_news/churchs-closing-brings-back-worshippers-memories/article_7bc26fc4-ff35-11ed-b78b-d726510a0e6e.html

Wagner, D. (2023, June 28). *"Yes, in God's backyard": Why L.A. churches want to build housing*. The Weekender. https://laist.com/brief/news/housing-homelessness/los-angeles-churches-housing-sb4-religious-properties-yigby-whittier-compton-ikar

Walker, A. (2022, February 15). *Top 5 reasons Black millennials are leaving the church*. Defender Network. https://defendernetwork.com/news/opinion/top-5-reasons-black-millennials-are-leaving-the-church/

Walker, A. (2023). *Why is Western Christianity living in a fantasy land about its own future?* https://medium.com/backyard-theology/why-is-western-christianity-living-in-fantasy-land-about-its-own-future-496f7e2fe1ab

Walker, K. D. (2023). Asset mapping. In J. M. Okoko, K. D. Tunison, & K. D. Walker (Eds.), *Varieties of qualitative research methods: Selected contextual perspectives* (pp. 47–51). Springer International Publishing.

Walker, G., Devine-Wright, P., Hunter, S., High, H., & Evans, B. (2010). Trust and community: Exploring the meanings, contexts and dynamics of community renewable energy. *Energy Policy, 38*(6), 2655–2663.

Walsh, M., & Marshall, C. (2023, May 25). *Columbus Catholic diocese to close 15 churches over upcoming years*. NBC4. https://www.nbc4i.com/news/local-news/columbus/catholic-diocese-of-columbus-to-close-15-churches-merge-others-in-massive-overhaul/

Wang, H. L. (2015, September 14). *It is all about church closings in Northeast and Northwest*. WBUR. https://www.wbur.org/npr/436938871/-it-s-all-about-church-closings-catholic-parishes-shrink-in-northeast

Wang, W. (2022). *The decline in church attendance in COVID America*. Institute for Family Studies. https://ifstudies.org/blog/number-2-in-2022-the-decline-in-church-attendance-in-covid-america#:~:text=Black%20Americans%20are%20also%20more,5%20to%206%20Opercentage%20points

Weber, J., & Lee, M. (2021, February 16). *The Black church, explained by Pew's biggest survey of African-Americans*. Christianity Today. https://www.christianitytoday.com/news/2021/february/black-church-african-american-christians-pew-survey.html

Weins, G. (2018, May 10). *A season for everything—Life cycle of a church*. HGC. https://healthygrowingchurches.com/a-season-for-everything-life-cycle-of-a-church/

Welch, B. J. (2012). A dual nature: the archdiocesan community development corporation. *Community Development, 43*(4), 451–463. Heritage, *41*, 166–177.

Wellman Jr., J., Corcoran, K., & Stockly, K. (2020). *High on God: How megachurches won the heart of America*. Oxford University Press.

White, A. (2023, April 26). *From decline to renewal*. North West Adventists https://nwadventists.com/feature/decline-renewal

White, J. K. (2022, August 9). *The Catholic Church is at a crossroads: Will it choose renewal or decline?* The Hill. https://thehill.com/opinion/international/3592111-the-catholic-church-is-at-a-crossroads-will-it-choose-renewal-or-decline/

Wiens, G., & Turner, D. (2018). *Dying to restart: Churches choosing a strategic death for a multiplying life*. https://static1.squarespace.com/static/57f80092b3db2b529d354654/t/638fb57aa67ee167250c0d6f/1670362492721/Dying-to-Restart-ojamxi.pdf

Williams, J., Jackson, M. S., Barnett, T., Pressley, T., & Thomas, M. (2019). Black megachurches and the provision of social services: An examination of regional differences in America. *Journal of Religion & Spirituality in Social Work: Social Thought, 38*(2), 161–179.

Williams, R. R. (2019). Engaging and researching congregations visually: Photovoice in a mid-sized church. *Ecclesial Practices, 6*(1), 5–27.

Wilson, W. D. (2017). *Economic ethics and the Black church*. Springer.

Winter, M. (2021, July 26). Latinos will determine the future of American Evangelicalism. *The Atlantic*. https://www.theatlantic.com/culture/archive/2021/07/latinos-will-determine-future-american-evangelicalism/619551/

Wisniewski, M. (2023, August 9). *No sanctuary: Are historic churches the lost souls of a city?* Design New City. https://design.newcity.com/2023/08/09/no-sanctuary-are-historic-churches-the-lost-souls-of-a-city/

Wodon, Q. (2019). Measuring the contribution of faith-based schools to human capital wealth: Estimates for the Catholic Church. *The Review of Faith & International Affairs, 17*(4), 94–102.

Wodon, Q. (2022). Decline in student enrollment, parental willingness to consider Catholic schools, and sources of comparative advantage in the United States. *Journal of Global Catholicism, 6*(2), 94–115.

Wolfram, M., Borgström, S., & Farrelly, M. (2019). Urban transformative capacity: From concept to practice. *Ambio, 48*, 437–448.

Wood, M. L., Soelberg, G., & Rugh, J. S. (2023). Making space behind the veil: Black agency within a predominantly White religion. *Journal for the Scientific Study of Religion, 62*(S1), 105–123.

Woodard, T. (2022, September 4). JP's Blessed Sacrament may see new life as affordable housing, performance space. *The Boston Globe*. https://www.bostonglobe.com/2022/09/04/metro/jps-blessed-sacrament-may-see-new-life-affordable-housing-performance-space/

WTOL11. (2020, October 21). *Land bank OKs gift of St. Antony Church land*. https://www.wtol.com/article/news/land-bank-oks-gift-of-st-anthony-church-land/512-b30d97c7-5d89-4e0c-a080-26d85e0fb1a6

Yahoo News. (2023, July 21). *St. Mary's of Manchester to merge with St. John's of Vernon*. https://news.yahoo.com/st-marysof-manchester-merge-st-150200486.html

Yarr, K. (2023, June 4). *How a church destroyed by Fiona could bring affordable housing to Charlottetown*. CBC News. https://www.cbc.ca/news/canada/prince-edward-island/pei-calvary-church-residential-development-1.6863743

Yazdani Mehr, S. (2019). Analysis of 19th-and 20th-century conservation key theories in relation to contemporary adaptive reuse of heritage buildings. *Heritage, 2*(1), 920–937.

Yosso, T. J. (2005). Whose culture has capital? A critical race theory discussion of community cultural wealth. *Race Ethnicity and Education, 8*(1), 69–91.

Youngman, M. (2022). *ReStory your church*. (Dissertation, George Fox University).

Zaniewski, A. (2017, December 30). Final Mass, All Saints Church, Southwest Detroit. *The Detroit Free Press*. https://www.freep.com/story/news/local/michigan/detroit/2017/12/30/final-mass-all-saints-church-southwest-detroit/946910001/

Zeng, X., Yu, Y., Yang, S., Lv, Y., & Sarker, M. N. I. (2022). Urban resilience for urban sustainability: Concepts, dimensions, and perspectives. *Sustainability, 14*(5), 2481.

Zhang, P., & Park, S. (2023). VLAS: Vacant Land Assessment System for urban renewal and greenspace planning in legacy cities. *Sustainability, 15*(12), 9525.

Zheng, X., Heath, T., & Guo, S. (2022). From Maslow to architectural spaces: The assessment of reusing old industrial buildings. *Buildings, 12*(11), 2033.

Zijlstra, H. (2022). Spatial building typology: Function follows form. *European Journal of Architecture and Urban Planning, 1*(5), 1–17.

Zouves, N. (2023, September 24). *The great dechurching hitting cities across America*. News Nation. https://www.newsnationnow.com/religion/the-great-dechurching-hitting-cities-across-america/

Index

For the benefit of digital users, indexed terms that span two pages (e.g., 52–53) may, on occasion, appear on only one of those pages.

Figures are indicated by an italic *f* following the page number.

adaptive reuse, definition of, 36
Adhihari, T., community practice
Adventist Church, declines in membership, 98
afterschool programs, 54
age, church attendance and, 99–100, 207–8
All Saints Neighborhood Church, Detroit, Michigan, 62
Amayu, E., repurposing of churches, 117, 150
Americans Against the City (Conn), 55
Anderson, J., reaching Millennials, 99–100
apartments, from repurposed office buildings, 10–11
Archdiocese of Chicago, history and significance of, 138–41
architecture and design
    Italian Renaissance Revival churches, 82, 83*f*
    saving "character-defining elements," 217
Arfa, F. H., repurposing heritage buildings, 38
Atlanta, Georgia, Faith-based Development Initiative, 23
Australian Community Workers Association, 52

Bacon, C. M., church closings nationally, 145
Banks, S., 51
Barucco, S., character-defining elements of buildings, 217
Beltz, J., wave of church closings, 28
Berrelleza, E., research on urban life and churches, 102
Berry, A., church presence in the community, 121
Betz, J., wave of church closings, 144
Black churches
    burnout among clergy, 188
    closings in Harlem, 176
    closings nationwide, 183–84
    combining mission and structure of, 188
    COVID-19 and church closings, 181–82
    defining "the Black Church," 172–77
    demographic shifts, 174
    economic importance of, 132–33
    economic pressures for, 174, 177
    effects of COVID-19 pandemic on, 123–26
    exodus of Millennials from, 188–92
    faith traditions today, 173
    future of, 170–71
    historical and current-day significance, 167–72, 186–87, 189, 195–96
    individual character of, 177
    initiatives to save, 193–95
    inward and outward missions of, 187
    as living institutions, 186–88
    loss of Sunday School facilities, 191
    and managing aging real estate, 190
    outreach initiatives, 184–86
    philanthropic interest in saving, 194–95
    and preaching on social justice issues, 169–70, 173
    recording histories of, 176–77
    regional perspective on, 174
    religiosity and church attendance, 177–78
    repurposing as housing, 192–93
    role in Black communities, 169, 172, 186
    similarities with Latino churches, 209
    social justice agenda, generational importance of, 178–81
    storefront and smaller churches, 171
    as training grounds for social activism, 188
    urban *versus* rural settings, 173
    in U.S. religious landscape and history, 167
    working beyond ministerial duties, 181
    worship style in, 175
Blessed Sacrament Church, Boston, Massachusetts
    architecture and design, 82, 83*f*
    closing of, 82–88
    demographic profile of city, 81
    development expertise, need for, 87
    efforts by Hyde Square Task Force, 85–86
    historical overview, 79–81

Blessed Sacrament Church, Boston, Massachusetts (*cont.*)
  interior, 84*f*, 85*f*
  lessons learned for urban community practice, 88–93
  outdoor space, 82, 83*f*
  and real estate context, 85
  religious beliefs, church attendance and, 81–82
  stipulations for property, 84–85
  subsequent property owners, 84
blogs, and community practice education, 230–31
Borgström, S., guiding principles for church repurposing, 225
Boston, Massachusetts, Blessed Sacrament Church
  architecture and design, 82, 83*f*
  closing of, 82–88
  demographic profile of city, 81
  development expertise, need for, 87
  efforts by Hyde Square Task Force, 85–86
  historical overview, 79–81
  interior, 84*f*, 85*f*
  lessons learned for urban community practice, 88–93
  outdoor space, 82, 83*f*
  and real estate context, 85
  religious beliefs, church attendance and, 81–82
  stipulations for property, 84–85
  subsequent property owners, 84
Boston, Massachusetts, Catholic population of, 139
Braman, Sandra, 49
Brinig, M. F., 148
Brooklyn, New York, St. Vincent de Paul Church, 38
Brown in the Windy City (Fernandez), 139
Brown Jr., S., effects of COVID-19 pandemic on Black churches, 125
Brubaker, D., stages of grief in church closings, 121–22
Brunson, S., tax status of churches, 141
built environment
  and challenges for church repurposing, 36
  and shaping public spaces, 35–36
Bullen, P. A., criteria for repurposing, 9
Burchell, R., definition of adaptive reuse, 36
Burge, R. P., 191
Burke, K. J., Christian nationalism, 95

California
  First Church of the Nazarene, Santa Cruz, 236–37
  Long Beach, Lutheran school and church in, 247
  Los Angeles, Catholic population of, 139
  Los Angeles, unhoused populations in, 32–33
  St. Stephen Missionary Baptist Church, La Puente, 185
  state legislature and church repurposing, 156
Canada, church closings in, 29–30
carbon emissions, and building repurposing, 17
case illustrations and studies, advantages of, 78–79
Catholic Charities of the Archdiocese of Chicago Housing Services, 136–37
Catholic Church
  Black Catholics and social justice, 169–70
  Black congregations and worship attendance, 42–43
  church closings in Pittsburgh and Chicago, 108
  Church of the Lady of Guadalupe, New York, 108
  course-correction efforts, 110–13
  departure of Latinos from, 204
  expansion internationally, 110
  history of parishes in Boston, Massachusetts, 79–81
  landownership by, 113–16
  and Latinos, 211–13
  LGBTQ-related policies, 112–13
  national declines in membership, 81–82
  Native Americans, interactions with, 209
  and outreach to Latino churches, 208–9
  reductions in numbers of clergy, 108–10
  role in enslavement, 6–7
  sexual abuse claims and legal verdicts, 26, 80–81
  and U.S. demographic changes, 198
  in U. S. population centers, 139
  See also Blessed Sacrament Church, Boston, Massachusetts
Catholic Parishes in Transition (Mankowski), 66
Catholic schools, and repurposing movement, 147–49
Chicago, Illinois
  church closings in, 108, 138–42
  Pilsen neighborhood, 138–39, 140–41
  school closings in, 37
  St. Adalbert Church, 140–41
Christian nationalism, rise of, 95–96
Christman, J.
  appropriate activities for repurposed churches, 13–14

INDEX 283

church attendance
   Adventist Church, 98, 99
   age and, 99–100
   Catholic Church and Black congregations, 42–43
   demographic changes, 97–102
   and donations, 175
   and predicting church closing, 123
   and religiosity, 177–78
   religious beliefs and, 81–82, 98
   responses to declines in, 104–7
   United Methodist Church, 98, 99
church-closing trends
   and Abraham Maslow's hierarchy of needs, 103–4
   Catholic schools and repurposing movement, 147–49
   and changes in religious practice, 104–10
   in Chicago, Illinois, 138–42
   and Christian nationalism, 95–96
   church-closing challenges, 142–45
   and church landownership, 113–16
   church repurposing from life-cycle view, 146–47, 171
   and Churches of Christ, 145–46
   course-correction efforts in Catholic Church, 110–13
   and COVID-19 pandemic, 123–26
   demography and, 97–102
   economics of church closings, 127–36
   land banks, church properties and, 160–61
   language used in closings and repurposing, 127
   and megachurches, 157–59
   municipal governments, potential role of, 150–55
   new models for deploying clergy, 162–63
   and nuances of repurposing, 159–60, 163
   organizational efforts to repurpose churches, 136–38
   predicting church closings, 119–23
   religious organizations as real estate developers, 161–62
   social forces shaping, 94–96
   state legislatures, role in repurposing, 155–56
   statistics, 96–97, 100
   and the urban church, 102–3
   vacant churches and the urban landscape, 116–18, 129
church closings
   approaching "wave" of, 144
   challenges of, 142–45
   in Chicago, Illinois, 138–42
   and church leadership, 100
   and community practice, 29
   community protests against, 139–40
   cost to marginalized groups, 108
   extent nationally, 145
   and individual character of churches, 176
   language used in, 127
   Latino churches, 213–14
   opportunities for financial wrongdoing, 192
   predicting, 119–23
   ripple effects of, 40, 120
   stages of, 122
   of storefront and other smaller churches, 175–76
   and urban economic development, 22, 27–28
   worldwide, 30–31
church closings, economics of, 127–36
   alternative sources of funding, 134–36
   Black churches, economic importance of, 132–33
   church size, 133–34
   and community services, 131
   consequences of closings, 128–29
   donations, national economy and, 131–32
   economic viability of churches, 133
   entrepreneurial orientation of clergy, 133
   and gun violence, 129
   local crime rates, 128–29
   nonprofit sector and, 128
   religion, economic contributions of, 129–31
   role of churches in creating social change, 132
   underutilized church property, 132
   vacant churches, 129
church membership, ethnicity and, 101, 104–7, 202
church missions, community practice and, 53–54
Church of the Lady of Guadalupe, New York, 108
church pews, repurposing, 17–18
church plantings, importance of, 122–23
church property, transfer of, 239
church repurposing
   advantages of faith-based organizations, 137
   advantages of stable communities, 137–38
   appropriate activities for former churches, 13–14, 20, 47, 63
   based on the past, 90
   capacity enhancement principles, 225–29
   and Catholic schools, 147–49
   challenges of, 142–45, 247–49
   challenges of sacred spaces and history, 220

284 INDEX

church repurposing (cont.)
  and church pews, 17–18
  and churches as sacred structures, 18–21
  collective leadership for, 195
  community-centered outcomes, 64–65
  and community economic benefits, 26–27
  community practice roles, 74–77
  and community service learning, 229
  criteria for, 136
  development expertise, need for, 87
  emotions and, 15–16
  examples of, 10, 20–21, 23
  financial capital needed, 43
  funding for, 246–47
  and government entities, 65–66
  green spaces and, 62
  history of, 23
  versus industrial sites, 145
  language used in, 127
  from life-cycle view, 146–47, 171
  limits of, 19–20, 21
  memories and, 15–16
  municipal governments, potential role of, 150–55
  nuances of, 159–60
  objections to, 49–50
  organizational efforts, 136–38
  principles for guiding, 225–29
  religious objects and, 18
  and rural community practice, 7
  and saving "character-defining elements," 217
  time as enemy of, 90–91
  trends in, 23
  and urban youth and people of color, 7–8
  use by other religious orders, 38
  worldwide, 27, 30–31
  See also Blessed Sacrament Church, Boston, Massachusetts
church repurposing, as urban concept and strategy, 8–17
  appropriate activities for repurposed churches, 13–14, 20, 47, 63
  complications presented by, 10
  criteria for examining, 9
  deconstruction *versus* demolition, 16–17
  emotional reactions, 15–16, 27
  examples of repurposing, 10, 20–21, 23
  and housing strategies, 10–11, 12–13, 23
  memories and repurposing buildings, 15–16
  and neighborhood appreciation of churches, 11–12
  site-specific approaches, 12
  and sustainability, 9, 10
  varieties of repurposing, 10
  zoning regulations, 12
churches
  buildings as community assets, 61–65
  as communities, 59–60
  and community connections, 34, 186
  as community landmarks, 23–24, 121
  and community life, 40
  declining membership, 26, 30–31
  economic viability of, 133
  fires in vacant buildings, 118
  landownership, 113–16
  maintenance of buildings, 24–25
  neighborhood appreciation of, 11–12, 194
  place in society, 38–39
  role in creating social change, 132
  role in neighborhoods, 5, 34, 45, 145
  role in socio-cultural-political life, 35, 48, 187
  as sacred structures, 18–21
  and social agency, 39
  storefront churches, 134
  tax status of, 141–42
  and their public spaces, 31–32
  as "third places" between home and work, 39–40
  toxic climates within, 179
  See also religious spaces
Churches of Christ, 145–46
Cimaglio, C., anti-urban sentiments and praise of rural lifestyle, 55
Cincinnati, Ohio, Price Hill neighborhood in, 211–12
cities
  and anti-urban sentiments, 54–57
  response to demographic changes, 4
clergy
  and Black church as living institution, 187
  burnout among clergy in Black churches, 188
  and course-correction efforts in Catholic Church, 111–12
  effects of COVID-19 pandemic, 126
  entrepreneurial orientation of, 133
  ministerial duties, envisioning work beyond, 181
  and multiracial church pastors, 107
  new models for deployment, 162–63
  and preaching in Black churches, 169–70
  reduction in numbers of, 108–10
  and trusted pastoral leadership in Latino churches, 199
Cleveland, Ohio, church closings in, 40–42
climate change, and building demolition *versus* deconstruction, 17

INDEX 285

coalitions, and community practice, 238
collaborations, and community practice, 239–40
collective history, church closings and, 232–33
Coming Revolution in Church Economics, The (DeYmaz), 133
community assets, mapping, 222–23, 227–28
community connections, role of churches in supporting, 34, 186
community decision-making, 68
community economic development, cultural wealth and, 33, 34
community engagement, importance of, 33–34
community identity, role of churches in, 43
community landmarks, churches as, 23–24, 121
community life, churches and, 40
community participation, importance of, 225–26
community practice
   and engagement, 33–34
   impact of church closings for, 29
   and repurposing churches, 5, 7–8
   and research practices, 218
   and role of municipal governments, 155
community practice, implications for, 234–47
   capacity enhancement, 247
   church property, transfer of, 239
   coalitions, 238
   faith organizations, brokering gatherings of local, 236–39
   funding for repurposing and programming, 246–47
   historic buildings, 240–41
   innovation, opening the door for, 242–43
   local talent, utilizing, 243–45
   nonprofit sector and local contributions, 241–42
   open meetings and public forums, 237–38
   partnerships and collaborations, 239–40
   sharing space with outside worshippers, 246
   sole community practitioners, 245
community practice, key competencies, 66–69
   community decision-making, 68
   enhancing community competencies, 66–67
   incorporating local culture, 67–68
   interactive skills, 68–69
community practice, lessons learned for, 88–93
   ambitious projects, needs of, 88–89
   closed churches, repurposing challenges with, 89
   essential municipal support, 91
   inclusive viewpoints, 91–92
   negotiation with varied interest groups, 89–90
   repurposing based on the past, 90
   seeking expertise when needed, 92–93
   time as enemy of repurposing, 90–91
community practice, within an urban context, 47, 49–50
   and anti-urban sentiments, 54–57
   appropriate activities for former churches, 13–14, 20, 47, 63
   breadth of practice, 52, 53–54
   church buildings as community assets, 61–65
   and churches as communities, 59–60
   community practitioners, characteristics of successful, 69–73
   components of, 48
   contextual grounding, 3–4
   and defining communities, 57, 59–60
   definitional parameters, 50–54
   expansion of, 51–52
   history of community practice, 52–53
   immigration, and anti-urban cultural sentiment, 55–56
   international terminology, 51–52
   objections to church repurposing, 49–50
   participatory democracy in projects, 73
   perspectives on, 51
   potential roles for church repurposing, 74–77
   role of churches in socio-cultural-political life, 35, 48
   social activism, churches as targets and vehicles for, 60–61
   trust and community practice, 57–59
community practice education, implications for, 224–34
   capacity enhancement and community assets, 233–34
   church repurposing and community service learning, 229
   collective history, church closings and, 232–33
   community fellows, 231–32
   community technology education, 232
   conferences and other gatherings, 229–31
   principles for guiding church repurposing, 225–29
   regional and local gatherings, 230
community practitioners, characteristics of successful, 69–73
   affection for people, 71–72
   enthusiasm, 72
   lifelong learning, 71, 72
   optimism, 71
   resiliency, 72–73
   self regard, 70

community spirit, importance of building, 226–27
competencies, community practice and, 66–69
　community decision-making, 68
　enhancing community competencies, 66–67
　interactive skills, 68–69
conferences, implications for community practice education, 229–31
congregations
　declining membership, 26
　ethnic groups and, 41–42, 202
　formation of, 21
　mergers of, 41–42, 82, 107–8, 218–19
Conn, Stephen, 55
connectedness, and urban community practice, 58
Conner, R., significance of Black churches, 170
Cook, D. T., churches and community connections, 34
Coomans, T., sharing space with outside worshippers, 246
Costanza-Chock, S., 49
course-correction efforts, in Catholic Church, 110–13
COVID-19 pandemic
　and closings of Black and Latino churches, 123–26
　and closings of Black churches, 181–82
　and Latino church attendance, 210
　staff layoffs and reduced salaries, 133
Cox, Harvey, 101
crime rates, and church closings, 128–29
cultural life
　incorporating local culture into initiatives, 67–68
　role of churches in, 35, 48
cultural wealth, and community economic development, 33, 34
culture and language, in Latino churches, 208–10

Danta, R., churches and community social fabric, 201
data, challenges in obtaining, 219
Dates, C., Black churches and community social relations, 167–68
Davidson, J., anti-urban cultural sentiments, 56
DCG Strategies, churches as communities, 59–60
Death and Life of Great American Cities, The (Jacobs), 31
deconstruction, *versus* demolition, 16–17
　and churches as sacred structures, 18–21

houses of worship in Philadelphia, 25
and repurposing, 25–26
DeGroot, D. A., churches as "third places," 39
Delgado, M.
　anti-urban cultural sentiments, 55–56
　capacity enhancement principles, 225–29
demographic changes
　in Black churches, 174
　and church-closing trends, 97–102
　cities' response to, 4
　expansion of Roman Catholic Church internationally, 110
　Latino churches and, 203–7
　and multiracial church pastors, 107
　researching, 218
　and responses to declines in church membership, 104–7
demolition, *versus* deconstuction, 16–17
　and churches as sacred structures, 18–21
　houses of worship in Philadelphia, 25
demolition, *versus* repurposing, 25–26
Desegregating Dixie (Newman), 26
Design Justice (Costanza-Chock), 49
Detroit, Michigan, All Saints Neighborhood Church, 62
Dewanjee, N.
　architecture and memory, 15
DeYmaz, M., church economic viability, 133, 134–35
Diano, D. challenges for church repurposing, 36
donations to churches, national economy and, 131–32
Dukelow, F., participatory democracy in projects, 73
Durkheim, Emile, church as single moral community, 38–39

ecological trends
　and appropriate activities for repurposed churches, 13–14
　cities' response to, 4–5
economics of church closings, 127–36
　alternative sources of funding, 134–36
　Black churches, economic importance of, 132–33
　church size, 133–34
　and community services, 131
　consequences of closings, 128–29
　donations, national economy and, 131–32
　economic viability of churches, 133
　entrepreneurial orientation of clergy, 133
　gun violence and, 129

local crime rates, 128–29
nonprofit sector and, 128
religion, economic contributions of, 129–31
role of churches in creating social change, 132
underutilized church property, 132
vacant churches, 129
education. *See* schools
Elie, P., socially progressive Latino viewpoints, 204–5
Elisara, C.
 urban churches, 31, 114
 zoning barriers, 142
enslavement
 role of Catholic Church in, 6–7
enthusiasm, and successful community practice, 72
Escape the "Gods" (K. S.), 105
ethnic groups, and congregational membership, 41–42, 101, 187
 costs of closing to marginalized groups, 108
 in Latino churches, 202
 multiracial church pastors, 107
European Heritage Heads Forum, 231
expertise, seeking necessary, 92–93
Eyesore to Asset (Fannie Mae), 65

Faith-based Development Initiative, Atlanta, Georgia, 23
faith organizations, brokering gatherings of local, 236–39
Farrelly, M., guiding principles for church repurposing, 225
Feeling the Spirit (Kostarelos), 175
Fenner, E., Catholic immigration to Chicago, 139
Ferguson, R., Black churches, 168
Fernandez, L., 139
Filisko, G. M., 153
fires, and vacant church buildings, 118
First Church of the Nazarene, Santa Cruz, California, 236–37
Flores, N. M., Latino Catholics, 208–9
Florida, effects of displaced migrants in, 201–2
funding
 obtaining for repurposing and programming, 246–47
 stressing grassroots, 228–29

Garnett, N. S., 148
generational differences, and social justice agenda, 178–81
gentrification

and Black churches in Washington, DC, 182
and closings of Black churches nationwide, 183–84
and religiously affiliated groups, 153
and repurposing of heritage buildings, 38, 43
geographic displacement, effects in Latino communities, 201–2
Gerber, Jerry
 repurposing church pews, 17–18
Glazer, N., Catholic-school closings, 148
golf courses, repurposing of, 20–21
government entities, church repurposing and, 65–66
Graham, R., LGBTQ-related policies in U. S. Methodist Church, 113
grassroots funding, stressing, 228–29
"The Great Dechurching" (Davis & Graham), 98
green spaces, and repurposing churches, 62
grief, stages of, 121–22
gun violence, effects on church attendance, 129
Guo, S., psychology and repurposed structures, 103–4
Guzman, L., role of the church in Latino communities, 200

Hallowell Multicultural Center, 244
Harrison, C. P.
 capacity enhancement and community assets, 233–34
 external mission of Black churches, 187
health and human service ministries, 54
healthcare facilities, repurposing of, 20, 21
Healy, K., trust and community practice, 57–58
Heath, T., psychology and repurposed structures, 103–4
heritage
 repurposing as a way to honor, 9, 13
heritage buildings
 framework for repurposing, 38
 and neighborhood gentrification, 38, 43
Hildebrandt, R., church demolitions, 25
Hispanas de Queens (Ricourt & Danta), 201
historic buildings
 churches as community landmarks, 23–24
 and community practice, 240–41
 plaques commemorating, 177
 repurposing as a way to honor, 9
history of church repurposing, 23
Hoevelmann, J., fires in vacant churches, 118
Horowitz, T., LGBTQ-related policies in Catholic Church, 112

housing
  Catholic Charities of the Archdiocese of Chicago Housing Services, 136–37
  as example of church repurposing, 23, 32–33, 86
  key elements of converting churches into, 12–13
  National Housing Preservation Foundation, 137
  repurposed office buildings and, 10–11
  repurposing Black churches as, 192–93
  and substandard surroundings, 36, 38
human services, finding alternate locations for, 75
Hutchins, R., church presence in the community, 121
Hyde Square Task Force, Boston, Massachusetts, 79, 85–86

immigration
  and anti-urban cultural sentiment, 55–56
  and Catholic parishes in Chicago, Illinois, 138–39
  churches as social centers for immigrants, 187
individuality, societal stresses on, 240
influenza epidemic of 1918, 124–25
Inglehart, R. F., 105
innovation, opening the door for, 242–43
institutional responses, to COVID-19 pandemic and other crises, 126
intergenerational activities and goals, incorporating, 227
internships, and seeking expertise, 92–93
Irwin, L. G., 146–47

Jacobs, Jane, 31
Jesus on Main Street (Kresta), 133
Jiang, B., role of municipal governments in repurposing, 152–53
job creation, church repurposing and, 62
Juzwik, M., Christian nationalism, 95

Kahila, M., community decision-making, 68
Keller, T., decline in church membership, 119–20
Kilde, J. H.
  study of religious spaces, 5
Kim, G., role of municipal governments in repurposing, 152–53
Kinney, J., churches as community landmarks, 24
Kostarelos, Frances, 175

Kresta, D. E., church economic viability, 133
Kristof, N., Black churches and social well-being, 178
Kübler-Ross, Elizabeth, 121–22
Kutty, A., Black churches, 175

Lami, I. M.
  site-specific approaches to repurposing, 12
land banks, church properties and, 160–61
landownership, by churches, 113–16
language
  and culture in Latino churches, 208–10
  used in church closings and repurposing, 127
Latino churches
  and age demographics, 207–8
  bicultural and bilingual characteristics, 210
  closings, 213–14
  community diversity and complexity, 204, 206
  COVID-19 pandemic and church attendance, 210
  demographic distribution and projections, 203–7
  effects of COVID-19 pandemic on, 123–26
  and effects of geographic displacement, 201–2
  factors in church growth, 199
  growth of, 203
  language and culture, 208–10
  leadership roles in, 205
  and outreach from Catholic Church, 208–9
  pastoral leadership in, 199
  present and future significance, 197–200, 214
  Price Hill neighborhood, Cincinnati, Ohio, 211–12
  religious beliefs and practices, 202–3
  role in Latino communities, 200–2, 206–7
  similarities with Black churches, 209
  trends and nuances in church attendance, 210–11
Lefrak, M., church closings in Vermont, 36–37
libraries, closings of, 144
life-cycle view, church repurposing from, 146–47, 171
Lincoln, C. E., Black churches and Black communities, 168–69
Lincoln Congressional Temple United Church of Christ, closing of, 182–83
Listokin, D., definition of adaptive reuse, 36
Long Beach, California, Lutheran school and church in, 247
Longhi, A.
  churches as sacred structures, 19

Los Angeles, California
  Catholic population of, 139
  unhoused populations in, 32–33
Lost Classroom, Lost Community (Brinig & Garnett), 148
Louisville, Kentucky, MOLO Village in, 181
Love, P. E.
  criteria for repurposing, 9
Lubelli, B., repurposing heritage buildings, 38

maintenance, of church buildings, 24–25
Mankowski, M., 66
Maslow, Abraham, 103–4
Massachusettts. *See* Boston, Massachusetts, Blessed Sacrament Church
Massingale, R., Black Catholics, 169–70
Mathis, D. T., social justice agendas, 180
McBroom, E., local collaboration opportunities, 239–40
McIntosh, Gary L., 99
McRae, D., church closings in Canada, 29–30
megachurches, in national landscape, 157–59
Melton, J. G., megachurches, 157–58
memory, and repurposing buildings, 15–16
mergers, of congregations, 41–42, 82, 107–8
  research implications, 218–19
Methodist Church
  declines in membership, 98
  LGBTQ-related policies, 113
Meyer, T., church closings in Vermont, 36–37
Miami, Florida, Catholic population of, 139
Mian, N., repurposing Black churches as housing, 193
Michel, A. A., church economic viability, 134–35
ministerial duties, envisioning work beyond, 181
Miserandino, A., Catholic school system, 149
MOLO Village, Louisville, Kentucky, 181
Morgan, T., life-cycle view and proactive action plans, 147
Mormon Church, landownership by, 114–16
municipal governments, potential repurposing role, 150–55
  and community practice, 155
  coordinating with stakeholders, 151–53
  facilitation, 154–55
  and planning regulations, 150
  resident stability, and thriving communities, 154
  strategic plans, 151
Murphy, M. P., participatory democracy in projects, 73

National Association of Realtors, 184
National Housing Preservation Foundation, 137
Native Americans, Catholic Church's interactions with, 209
Nehemiah Initiative, 193–94, 195, 238–39
neighborhoods
  heritage buildings and gentrification, 38, 43
  and libraries, 144
  role of churches in, 5, 34, 138, 145
Neuman, S.
  megachurches, 158
  ripple effects of church closings, 120
New Birth Missionary Baptist Church, 185
"New Spirits Rise in Old, Repurposed Churches" (Nierenberg), 63
New York
  Catholic population of, 139
  Church of the Lady of Guadalupe, 108
  closings of Black churches in Harlem, 176, 183
  Our Lady Queen of Angels, Harlem, 221
  St. Vincent de Paul Church, 38
  state legislature and church repurposing, 156
Newman, G., role of municipal governments in repurposing, 152–53
Newman, M., 26
Nguyen, J., church landownership, 115
Nierenberg, A., 63
Nieuwhof, C., megachurches, 157
"Nones, The" (Burge), 191
nonprofit sector
  and economics of church closings, 128
  and repurposed churches, 241–42

One Church, Four Generations (McIntosh), 99
optimism, and successful community practice, 71
Our Lady Queen of Angels, Harlem, New York, 221
outreach initiatives, Black churches and, 184–86

Page, E., community practice, 244
Partners for Sacred Spaces, 238
partnerships, and community practice, 239–40
Pearson, E., Catholic clergy, 111
Pennrose real estate development company, 86
people of color
  and church repurposing, 7–8
pews, repurposing of, 17–18
Pham, V.
  churches as sacred structures, 19, 220

Philadelphia, Pennsylvania
  Catholic population of, 139
  church closings in, 42–43
  church demolitions in, 25
philanthropic interest, in saving Black churches, 194–95
photovoice, capturing an historical process, 220–22
Pittsburgh, Pennsylvania
  Catholic population of, 139
Pittsburgh, Pennsylvania, church closings in, 108
planning regulations, and role of municipal governments, 150
Plante, T. G., managing burnout among clergy, 112
Pojani, D.
  churches as community assets, 61
  sustainability and church repurposing, 9
political life, role of churches in, 35
Povoledo, E., LGBTQ-related policies in Catholic Church, 112
"Principles for Managing Burnout Among Catholic Church Professionals" (Plante), 112
Prins, E., Christian nationalism, 95
prosperity, church literature and, 22
protests, against church closings, 139–40
psychology, and repurposed structures, 103–4
public spaces, churches and their, 31–32
Puerto Rico, displaced populations from, 201
Putscher, L. A.
  role of churches in neighborhoods, 5

Quist, W., repurposing heritage buildings, 38

racial groups, and congregational membership, 42–43
Rainier, T. S., closings and church leadership, 100
Ramos, A. I., Latino religious beliefs and practices, 202–3
real estate
  closed churches as, 35, 85
  managing aging, 190
  religious organizations as developers, 161–62
Reinhard, R.
  consequences of church closing, 27–28
  role of municipal governments in repurposing, 151–52, 154–55
  urban churches, 31, 114
  zoning barriers, 142

religion, and affiliated institutions, 21–40
  built environment, and shaping public spaces, 35–36
  church closings, impact of, 22, 27
  churches, role in socio-cultural-political life, 35, 48
  community connections, role of churches in supporting, 34
  community economic development, cultural wealth and, 33, 34
  community engagement, importance of, 33–34
  community landmarks, churches as, 23–24
  congregations, formation of, 21
  consequences of church closing, 27–28, 128–29
  crises as opportunity, 22, 192, 237
  declining membership, 26
  demolition, *versus* repurposing, 25–26
  history of church repurposing, 23
  and housing strategies, 23
  maintenance of church buildings, 24–25
  neighborhoods, role of churches in, 5, 34, 138
  prosperity, church literature and, 22
  public spaces, churches and their, 31–32
  real estate, closed churches as, 35
  religiosity, definition of, 22
  repurposing and and local history, 31
  repurposing worldwide, 27, 30–31
  secularization and, 21–22
  sexual abuse claims and legal verdicts, 26
  and societal priorities, 21
  trends in church repurposing, 23
  unhoused populations, church repurposing and, 32–33
  urban churches, 31
religion, economic contributions of, 129–31
Religion's Sudden Decline (Inglehart), 105
religiosity
  definition of, 22
  as measured by attendance, 177–78
religious beliefs, church attendance and, 81–82
religious education, and closing of church schools, 96
religious objects, repurposing of, 18
religious practice
  cities' response to changes in, 4
  functions of, 6
  Latino churches and, 202–3
  responses to declines in, 104–7
religious spaces
  approaches to study of, 5
  place in society, 38–39

INDEX   291

sharing with outside worshippers, 246
tax status of, 141–42
and traumatic experiences, 44
urban planning and, 63
repurposing
    advantages of faith-based organizations, 137
    advantages of stable communities, 137–38
    based on the past, 90
    challenges and opportunities, 247–49
    churches *versus* industrial sites, 145
    community-centered outcomes, 64–65
    complications presented by, 10
    deconstruction *versus* demolition, 16–17
    emotional reactions, 15–16, 27
    examples of, 10, 20–21, 23
    funding for, 246–47
    and government entities, 65–66
    green spaces and, 62
    and housing strategies, 10–11, 12–13, 23
    limits of, 19–20, 21
    and local history, 31
    nuances of, 159–60
    psychology and repurposed structures, 103–4
    and rural community practice, 7
    and saving "character-defining elements," 217
    site-specific approaches, 12
    and sustainability, 9, 10
    time as enemy of, 90–91
    types of interventions for, 27
    and urban youth and people of color, 7–8
    varieties of, 10
    zoning regulations and, 12
Repurposing Smaller Buildings (National Association of Realtors), 184
research, implications for, 217–24
    community assets, mapping, 222–23
    community practice and research practices, 218
    data, challenges in obtaining, 219
    demographic changes, understanding, 218
    forms of research, 220
    in higher education, 223–24
    photovoice, capturing an historical process, 220–22
    research as an intervention, 218
resident stability, and thriving communities, 154
resiliency, and successful community practice, 72–73
resource library, and church repurposing, 74
Rhode Island, Catholic population of, 139
Ricourt, M., churches and community social fabric, 201

Roach, D.
    churches as sacred structures, 19–20
Rockwood, K., church buildings as community assets, 64
Roman Catholic Church
    Black congregations and worship attendance, 42–43
    church closings in Pittsburgh and Chicago, 108
    Church of the Lady of Guadalupe, New York, 108
    course-correction efforts, 110–13
    departure of Latinos from, 204
    expansion internationally, 110
    history of parishes in Boston, Massachusetts, 79–81
    landownership by, 113–16
    and Latinos, 211–13
    LGBTQ-related policies, 112–13
    national declines in membership, 81–82
    Native Americans, interactions with, 209
    and outreach to Latino churches, 208–9
    reductions in numbers of clergy, 108–10
    role in enslavement, 6–7
    sexual abuse claims and legal verdicts, 26, 80–81
    in U. S. population centers, 139
    See also Blessed Sacrament Church, Boston, Massachusetts
Rose, L., challenges for large urban churches, 159–60
Rucker, F., church repurposing from a life-cycle view, 146
rural community practice
    and church repurposing, 7
rural lifestyle, praise of, 55
Russell, T. B., religiosity, 22

Santa Cruz, California, First Church of the Nazarene, 236–37
Sathyamurthi, K., literature review by, 52
schools
    Catholic schools and repurposing movement, 147–49
    closing and repurposing, 37–38
    functions of, 6
    social forces closing, 96
    See also education
Seattle, Washington, Nehemiah Initiative, 193–94, 195, 238–39
Secular City, The (Cox), 101
secularization
    and declines in church membership, 101–2
    and religiously affiliated institutions, 21–22

Sheridan, S.
  appropriate activies for repurposed churches, 20
Shipman, C., spatial analysis of church real estate activity, 36
"Show Me the Money for Financing Do-Overs" (Filisko), 153
Siemiatycki, M., spatial analysis of church real estate activity, 36
Smeengee, M.
  repurposing religious objects, 18
Smietana, B., work of local faith organizations, 236–37
social activism
  Black churches as training grounds for, 188
  churches as targets and vehicles for, 60–61, 179
social agency, churches and, 39
social change, role of churches in creating, 132
social forces, and church-closing trends, 94–96
  and Abraham Maslow's hierarchy of needs, 103–4
  Catholic schools and repurposing movement, 147–49
  in Chicago, Illinois, 138–42
  Christian nationalism, 95–96
  church-closing challenges, 142–45
  church landownership, 113–16
  church repurposing from life-cycle view, 146–47
  and Churches of Christ, 145–46
  course-correction efforts in Catholic Church, 110–13
  COVID-19 pandemic, 123–26
  demographic changes, 97–102
  economics of church closings, 127–36
  land banks, church properties and, 160–61
  language used in closings and repurposing, 127
  and megachurches, 157–59
  municipal governments, potential role of, 150–55
  new models for deploying clergy, 162–63
  and nuances of repurposing, 159–60, 163
  organizational efforts to repurpose churches, 136–38
  predicting church closings, 119–23
  religious organizations as real estate developers, 161–62
  state legislatures, role in repurposing, 155–56
  and statistics on church closings, 96–97, 100
  trends in religious practice, 104–10
  and the urban church, 102–3

vacant churches and the urban landscape, 116–18, 129
social justice agenda, generational importance of, 178–81
social justice issues, preaching on, 169–70, 173
social life, role of churches in, 35, 48
social services, and churches in wider community, 142
social work, and religious communities, 63
spatial justice, school closings and, 38
Spencer, W. F., urban *versus* rural Black churches, 173
spirituality, as cultural wealth, 33, 34
St. Adalbert Church, Chicago, Illinois, 140–41
St. Katharine Drexel parish, Roxbury, Massachusetts, 88
St. Liborius Church, St. Louis, Missouri, 244
St. Peter Claver church, Philadelphia, Pennsylvania, 42–43
St. Stephen Missionary Baptist Church, La Puente, California, 185
St. Vincent de Paul Church, Brooklyn, New York, 38
state legislatures, role in repurposing, 155–56
Stephens, D. P., role of the Black Church in social activism, 179
Stiffman, E., religious organizations as real estate developers, 161
storefront churches, 134, 171
  closings of, 175–76
  structure of, 177
stories, preserving and sharing, 59–60
Strott, S., significance of Black churches, 187
Subramanian, A., history and significance of the Black church, 168
suburbanization, Catholic schools and, 148–49
Sunday School, loss of facilities in Black churches, 191
sustainability
  and building demolition *versus* deconstruction, 17
  and building repurposing, 10
  and church repurposing, 9

tax status, and houses of worship, 141–42
taxes, creating strategies for, 74
team-building activities, 226
Thielen, L., closed churches as real estate, 35
Thomas, A., individualizing approaches to communities, 236
Thomson, M.
  churches as community assets, 61
  sustainability and church repurposing, 9
Thorp, E. Y. Jr., church missions, 53–54

Toward the Better Country (Irwin), 146–47
Transitioning Older and Historic Sacred Places, 238
trauma, religious spaces and, 44
trust, and community practice, 57–59
Turner, D., importance of church plantings, 122–23

unhoused populations, church repurposing and, 32–33
United Methodist Church
   declines in membership, 98
   LGBTQ-related policies, 113
urban areas
   and anti-urban sentiments, 54–57
   church landownership in, 113–16
   and church repurposing, 7–8
   fires, and vacant church buildings, 118
   impact of church closings in, 27–28
   vacant church buildings in, 116–18, 129
urban churches, and social trends shaping
   church closings, 102–3
   church landownership, 113–16
urban community practice, 49–50
   and anti-urban sentiments, 54–57
   breadth of practice, 52, 53–54
   church buildings as community assets, 61–65
   and churches as communities, 59–60
   community practitioners, characteristics of successful, 69–73
   components of, 48
   contextual grounding, 3–4
   and defining communities, 57, 59–60
   definitional parameters, 50–54
   expansion of, 51–52
   immigration, and anti-urban cultural sentiment, 55–56
   international terminology, 51–52
   objections to church repurposing, 49–50
   participatory democracy in projects, 73
   perspectives on, 51
   potential roles for church repurposing, 74–77
   principles of, 47
   and repurposing churches, 5, 7–8
   role of churches in socio-cultural-political life, 35, 48
   social activism, churches as targets and vehicles for, 60–61
   trust and community practice, 57–59
urban community practice, key competencies, 66–69
   community decision-making, 68
   enhancing community competencies, 66–67
   incorporating local culture, 67–68
   interactive skills, 68–69
urban community practice, lessons learned for, 88–93
   ambitious projects, needs of, 88–89
   closed churches, repurposing challenges with, 89
   essential municipal support, 91
   inclusive viewpoints, 91–92
   negotiation with varied interest groups, 89–90
   repurposing based on the past, 90
   seeking expertise when needed, 92–93
   time as enemy of repurposing, 90–91
Urban Gun Violence (Delgado), 62
urban planning
   religious communities and, 63
urban planning, and demolition *versus* repurposing, 43–44
urban renewal
   and crisis as opportunity, 22, 192, 237
   exempting churches from, 143–44
   and religiously affiliated groups, 153

Viola, S., challenges for church repurposing, 36

Walker, A., declines in religious practice, 104
Washington, DC
   effect of city gentrification on Black churches, 182
   Lincoln Congressional Temple United Church of Christ, closing of, 182–83
White, A., Adventist Church membership, 98
Wiens, G., importance of church plantings, 122–23
Winter, M., Latino churches, 212
Wisniewski, M.
   emotions and church repurposing, 15–16
   history of St. Adalbert Church, Chicago, Illinois, 140–41
Wolfram, M., guiding principles for church repurposing, 225
Woodard, T., pace of decision-making, 87

youth of color
   church repurposing and, 7–8

Zheng, X., psychology and repurposed structures, 103–4
Zijlstra, H.
   and repurposing urban churches, 15
Zijlstra, H. repurposing heritage buildings, 38
zoning regulations
   creating strategies for, 74
   and repurposing efforts, 12, 142